Trade Liberalisation and Poverty

This book uses Alan Winters's analytical framework to investigate the effects of trade liberalisation on economic growth and poverty in Vietnam. In the mid-1980s, the country launched a programme of economic and trade reforms known as Doi Moi, which placed the economy on a transitional path from central planning to a market economy. Since then, Vietnam has attained a number of remarkable achievements in terms of economic growth and poverty reduction. Although some formidable problems (such as inequality and inflation) remain, it is apparent that trade liberalisation has been associated with a big reduction in poverty.

The analysis in the book focuses on the microeconomic (household) level, and there is an emphasis on tracing the effects of trade liberalisation through the four separate channels identified by Winters. Such in-depth and microlevel analyses yield new insights that support important policy lessons and recommendations for Vietnam in particular and, more generally, for similar developing countries.

Minh Son Le, PhD (Griffith University), is a lecturer at the International Economics Faculty, Banking University Ho Chi Minh City, Vietnam. His current teaching areas are econometrics, macroeconomics, and economics of development. His primary research interests include trade liberalisation and poverty, institutional economics, and private sector development.

Tarlok Singh, PhD (University of New South Wales), is a senior lecturer at Griffith University, Brisbane, Australia. He teaches applied econometrics, international economics, financial economics, macroeconomics, and monetary economics at both undergraduate and postgraduate levels. His main research interests are applied econometrics, economic growth, monetary economics, and open economy macroeconomics.

Duc-Tho Nguyen, PhD (Australian National University), is an adjunct professor at Griffith University, Brisbane, Australia, where he previously held senior positions, including Dean of Commerce and Administration, and Head of the School of Economics. His main research interests are economic growth and development, macroeconomic issues in Asia-Pacific economies, financial economics, and applied economics.

Trade Liberalisation and Poverty

Vietnam now and beyond

Minh Son Le, Tarlok Singh, and Duc-Tho Nguyen

Routledge
Taylor & Francis Group

LONDON AND NEW YORK

First published 2016
by Routledge

2 Park Square, Milton Park, Abingdon, Oxfordshire OX14 4RN
711 Third Avenue, New York, NY 10017

Routledge is an imprint of the Taylor & Francis Group, an informa business

First issued in paperback 2018

British Library Cataloguing in Publication Data
A catalogue record for this book is available from the British
Library

Library of Congress Cataloging-in-Publication Data
Le, Minh Son.
    Trade liberalisation and poverty : Vietnam now and beyond /
Minh Son Le, Tarlok Singh and Duc-Tho Nguyen.—1 Edition.
        pages cm
    1. Vietnam—Commercial policy.   2. Vietnam—Economic policy,
3. Free trade—Vietnam.   4. Poverty—Vietnam.   5. Economic
development—Vietnam.   I. Title.
    HF1594.5.L415 2015
    382'.309597—dc23
    2015009220

ISBN: 978-1-138-88674-2 (hbk)
ISBN: 978-1-138-31700-0 (pbk)

Typeset in Galliard
by Apex CoVantage, LLC

Contents

Figures

Tables

Preface

Trade liberalisation is frequently advocated as a major potential contributor to economic growth and development. Yet the empirical literature on the relationship between trade liberalisation and poverty is far from settled: critics have argued that the literature suffers from inadequate methodology and inconclusive evidence (Rodriguez and Rodrik, 2001; Wacziarg and Welch, 2008; Pacheco-Lopez and Thirlwall, 2009; Singh, 2010). The persistence of poverty amongst a considerable proportion of the population in developing economies that have pursued trade liberalisation also raises questions about the strength and robustness of any desired effects. Some authors have come to view the trade–poverty relationship largely as a case- and country-specific issue (McCulloch *et al.*, 2001; Berg and Krueger, 2003; Pacheco-Lopez and Thirlwall, 2009; Rodrik, 2010). In recent years the focus of empirical research on the trade–poverty nexus has shifted to examining the relationship at a microeconomic level. Winters (2002) and Winters *et al.* (2004) suggest four channels through which trade liberalisation reaches households and contributes to the reduction in poverty: economic growth, market distribution, employment, and government revenue.

This study employs a microeconomic approach and the Winters framework to investigate the effects of trade liberalisation on economic growth and poverty in Vietnam. Since the country launched a programme of economic and trade liberalisation known as Doi Moi in the mid-1980s, it has been on a transitional path from the central planning model to the market system, and has attained a number of remarkable achievements in terms of both economic growth and poverty reduction. The average annual rate of economic growth was 8 per cent during the 1990s and 7 per cent in the 2000s. The poverty headcount ratio declined from 58.17 per cent in 1993 to 37.4 per cent in 1993, and to 15.9 per cent in 2006.

To our knowledge, this is the first study to apply the entire Winters framework to Vietnam – our objective is to provide a comprehensive analysis of all four above-mentioned channels of the trade–poverty nexus. This study contributes to the literature in several respects. It systematically reviews the process of trade liberalisation and reduction in poverty and assesses the impacts of trade liberalisation on welfare and poverty in Vietnam. A common drawback of the existing studies regarding the linkage to Vietnam is that these studies simply examine the impacts of trade liberalisation on welfare and poverty, ignoring the context of the development of the economy. The analysis of the history of trade liberalisation and poverty will help to better understand the trade–poverty nexus. Those studies that focus on one or two impacts of trade liberalisation seem inadequate. This study thoroughly analyses the trade liberalisation effects on poverty, following the four channels outlined in Winters (2002) and Winters *et al.* (2004). The investigation of many pathways through which trade liberalisation affects poverty provides a more adequate picture of the relationship in Vietnam. To dig deeper into this relationship, the study conducts a primary field survey of trade policy in agriculture that sheds more light on the market effects of trade liberalisation on farm households. This survey aims at farm households and agricultural production because most of the poor in Vietnam engage in farming activities. The current studies dealing with the link to Vietnam, using macroeconomic data or general household survey data, are unlikely to capture farm households' perception of trade policy, which is important for understanding the flaws of trade policy in agriculture. In particular, such studies have yet to provide insight into the inadequate marketing system in agricultural production and trade that may impoverish farm households. The results provided by this survey are expected to be a reference for policymakers who are devising strategies for reducing poverty. This study also takes the effects of institutional reforms into account. Institutions constitute an important dimension of poverty and relate closely to trade policy reforms. Institutions are seen to underpin the channels through which trade liberalisation affects households and poverty. The inclusion of the effects of institutional reforms makes the trade–poverty relationship more comprehensive. This study provides evidence for supporting the argument that local or domestic trade is as important for poverty reduction as international trade. Most of the poor live in rural or remote areas, where the effects of external trade are unlikely to reach. The development of trade in local regions therefore greatly benefits the poor. The problems with trade policies in agriculture that probably impoverish farm households in Vietnam lie mainly in the domestic market distribution of agricultural products, not in the international market. An attempt is made to answer the question as to why most farm households remain poor while Vietnam is one of the influential rice export countries in the world.

This book will be of interest not only to researchers and scholars of Asian studies – especially studies of Vietnam and its economic transition and development – but also to policymakers, analysts, and advisers who are concerned with the benefits and costs of globalisation, in terms of socioeconomic development and well-being.

Acronyms and abbreviations

AC	Agricultural Census Data
ADB	Asian Development Bank
AFTA	ASEAN Free Trade Area
AGO	Agricultural Output
ASEAN	Association of Southeast Asian Nations
bn	Billion
BOT	Build Operation Transfer
CA	Capability Approach
CEPT	Common Effective Preferential Tariff
CGE	Computable General Equilibrium
CIS	Commonwealth of Independent States
CIT	Corporate Income Tax
CMEA	Council for Mutual Economic Assistance
CPE	Centrally Planned Economy
CPI	Consumer Price Index
CR	Consumption Ratio
DCs	Developed Countries
DDA	Doha Development Agenda
EEGs	Employment Elasticities of Growth
EPAs	Economic Partnership Agreements
EPZ	Export Processing Zone
ERP	Effective Rate of Protection
EU	European Union
FDI	Foreign Direct Investment
FGT	Foster–Greer–Thorbecke
GATT	General Agreement on Tariffs and Trade
GDP	Gross Domestic Product
GEP	Growth Elasticity of Poverty
GMM	Generalised Method of Moments
GNP	Gross National Product
GRIPS	Graduate Institute for Policy Studies
GSEP	Growth Semi-Elasticity of Poverty
GSO	General Statistics Office

HCMC	Ho Chi Minh City
HEPR	Hunger Elimination and Poverty Reduction Programme
HS	Harmonised System of Tariff Nomenclature
IIA	Independence from Irrelevant Alternatives
IMF	International Monetary Funds
IPSARD	Institute of Policy and Strategy for Agriculture and Rural Development
IVs	Instrumental Variables
LM	Lagrange Multiplier
LSDV	Least Square Dummy Varibale
LSMS	Living Standards Measurement Study
M	Import
m	Million
MARS	Multivariate Adaptive Regression Splines
MDGs	Millennium Development Goals
MFC	Marginal Cost of Funds
MNL	Multinomial Logit Model
MPI	Multidimensional Poverty Index
NBR	Net Benefit Ratio
OECD	Organisation for Economic Co-operation and Development
OLS	Ordinary Least Squares
PA	Participatory Approaches
PCI	Provincial Competitiveness Index
PGI	Pro-Poor Growth Index
PHC	Population and Housing Census Data
PME	The Brazilian Monthly Employment Surveys
PPP	Purchasing Power Parity
PR	Production Ratio
PT	Provincial Trade
QR	Quantity Restriction
R&D	Research & Development
RPCE	Real Per Capita Expenditure
RPCT	Real Per Capita Trade
RRR	Relative Risk Ratios
SAM	Social Accounting Matrix
SE	Social Inclusion
SMART	Specific Measurable Attainable Relevant Time Bound
SOEs	State-Owned Enterprises
TEP	Trade Elasticity of Poverty
TFP	Total Factor Productivity
TPP	Trans-Pacific Partnership
UNCTAD	United Nations Conference on Trade and Development
UNDP	United Nations Development Programme
US$	US Dollar
USDA	United States Department of Agriculture

VARHS	Vietnam Access to Resources Household Survey
VASS	Vietnam Academy of Social Science
VAT	Value Added Tax
VCCI	Vietnam Chamber of Commerce and Industry
VHLSSs	Vietnam Household Living Standards Surveys
Vietnam–US BTA	Vietnam–US Bilateral Trade Agreement
VIF	Variance Inflation Factor
VLC	Vietnam Law on Competition
VLSSs	Vietnam Living Standards Surveys
VNCI	Vietnam Competitiveness Initiative
VND	Vietnam Dong or Dong (Vietnamese currency)
WB	World Bank
WTO	World Trade Organization
X	Export
..	In tables means "not available"
-	In tables means "not applicable"

1   Introduction

The effects of trade liberalisation on the acceleration of growth and reduction in poverty remain on the central stope of both academic research and policy forums. A sizeable body of literature suggests that the open or outward-oriented economies perform better than the autarchic or inward-oriented economies. In the 1980s and 1990s, several developing countries adopted development strategies initiated by the Washington Consensus, which centred on the adoption of privatisation, liberalisation, and macroeconomic stabilisation strategies. Despite the enormous potential benefits of trade liberalisation, some developing countries and transitional economies – especially Latin American countries that followed the reform package prescribed by the Washington Consensus – have achieved little success. One of the possible reasons for such inefficacies has been that the reform package ignores the country's specific economic and political conditions. In contrast, several East Asian countries have been successful with their export promotion strategy. The judgement of these development strategies, as such, continues to be highly disputed (Rodrik, 2010). Acemoglu and Robinson (2012) conflate experiences of the development of nations and conclude that a country's own institutions determine its success or failure. Trade policy reforms are akin to institutional reforms, and therefore a country's own trade policy is crucial to its economic development (Rodrik, 2010; Le, 2014). However, even a country that succeeds in trade liberalisation cannot ensure that every individual in the country benefits from trade and growth, although most are likely to be better off, on average. Its success in economic development depends on how trade liberalisation affects household welfare and poverty in the country.

The well-documented benefits of trade to economic development have motivated many studies that analyse the relationship between trade liberalisation, growth, and poverty. The role of trade liberalisation in developing countries is often highlighted in reports by the World Bank and the International Monetary Fund (IMF) (see, for example, World Bank, 1987, 2005, 2011; Berg and Krueger, 2003). Several synonymous terms have been used in the literature on international trade to describe the integration of an economy with the rest of the world, such as trade openness (measured in terms of export plus import as a percentage of GDP) and trade liberalisation (measured in terms of the ease or eradication of tariff and nontariff barriers to trade). The literature on the trade–poverty relationship has been criticised for its inadequate methodology and inconclusiveness (Rodriguez and Rodrik, 2001; Wacziarg and Welch, 2008; Pacheco-Lopez and Thirlwall, 2009; Singh, 2010).

1.1   Trade–poverty nexus: an overview of the transmission channels

Trade and poverty are both multidimensional concepts; empirical research finds difficulty in establishing an ambiguous link between the two. Winters (2002) and Winters *et al.* (2004) suggest a framework where the effects of trade liberalisation reach households via four channels: economic growth, market, employment, and government spending. These channels cover the microeconomic and macroeconomic dimensions of the relationship, as well as the main stakeholders of the economy: households, enterprises, and government.

Economic Growth Channel: For the growth channel, Bhagwati and Srinivasan (2002) divide the impact of economic growth on poverty into two stages: trade promotes economic growth, and this growth, in turn, reduces poverty through the trickle-down effect that provides the poor with many opportunities for employment. The former hypothesis has been the focus of many studies. Some have supported the positive role of trade in stimulating growth (Sachs and Warner, 1995; Frankel and Romer, 1999; Greenaway *et al.*, 2002; Wacziarg and Welch, 2008), whereas others have cast a sceptical note on the significant effects of trade on economic growth (see, for instance, Rodriguez and Rodrik, 2001; Rigobon and Rodrik, 2004; Rodrik *et al.*, 2004; Rodríguez, 2006; Pacheco-Lopez and Thirlwall, 2009; Singh, 2010). The second stage, where economic growth contributes to the reduction in poverty, is also as challenging and controversial as the first. Dollar (2005) documents that in the last 20 years, the developing countries which have most rapidly integrated into the world economy have tended to grow, reducing their poverty faster. The studies estimating the elasticity of poverty with regard to economic growth also find a roughly one-to-one relationship between economic growth and poverty reduction (Ram, 2006, 2011; Kalwij and Verschoor, 2007). In addition to the two-stage effects, some studies that attempt to relate trade directly to poverty find little systematic evidence (see, for example, Dollar and Kraay, 2004) or cast doubt on the presumption of the positive impact of trade openness on poverty (see, for instance, Ravallion, 2006). The effects of trade-led growth on poverty, therefore, continue to be highly contentious and inconclusive.

Market Channel: For the market channel, trade liberalisation can affect households and alleviate poverty via its effects on the prices of tradable goods (Minot and Goletti, 1998; Seshan, 2005; Justino *et al.*, 2008; Marchand, 2012). Price changes greatly matter to the poor. One of the most important conditions for an outward-oriented strategy to be successful is to maintain the macroeconomic stability or, more specifically, to contain inflation, which is indirectly beneficial for the poor (Bhagwati and Srinivasan, 2002). In this linkage, trade policy can cause price distortions that result from trade monopoly, the marketing system, and transaction costs. The complicated market distribution can drive a considerable wedge between firm-gate prices and consumer prices. Inadequate trade regulations can increase transaction costs, constituting higher prices of goods. The poor are therefore unlikely to benefit from trade liberalisation, due primarily to the ineffective transmission of prices from markets to households as a consequence of inadequate trade policies (Winters *et al.*, 2004).

Employment Channel: Creating or detracting jobs is one of the most visible effects of trade liberalisation. High level of trade activities and/or production will boost the demand for labour. Studies show that the effect of trade liberalisation is largely positive for employment, the key source of income for the poor (Krueger, 1983; World Bank, 2001; Niimi *et al.*, 2007; Justino *et al.*, 2008). If properly developed, trade expansion can establish backward and forward linkages that can help to sustain employment and growth in the long run. The poor can also benefit from employment created through regional production networks in manufacturing, such as textile and shoe processing (Athukorala, 2010a). Trade-induced employment is therefore crucial to poor households.

Government Revenue Channel: Trade policy reforms in the government revenue channel may shrink the government budget, thereby potentially restricting governmental spending for social security and poverty alleviation programmes (Heo and Nguyen, 2009; Baunsgaard and Keen, 2010). For reasons of social stability, governments usually assign top priority to public expenditure (Winters *et al.*, 2004). Trade reforms may also result in increases in government revenue, due to the efficient rearrangement of trade barriers. Baunsgaard and Keen (2010) conclude that middle-income countries have succeeded in offsetting reductions in trade tax revenues by increasing their domestic tax revenues, whilst many low-income countries have not. The revenue effect of trade liberalisation on poverty, which can be positive or negative, depends mainly on the effectiveness of trade reforms and policies on poverty reduction.

Institutional Channel: Institutions underpin the important channels through which trade liberalisation affects poverty, although this is not stated explicitly in the Winters framework. Trade policy reforms, which accompany institutional reforms (Rodrik, 2002), help the poor to reduce social costs relating to institutional barriers (World Bank, 2001). Institutions are the rules that shape the interaction between citizens, firms, and the state (World Bank, 2010). The impacts of institutions on poverty are pervasive (Deolalikar *et al.*, 2002; Le, 2014), and are seen to be the main determinants of the differences in prosperity across countries (World Bank, 1997; Acemoglu and Robinson, 2008).

Amongst economic policies that most likely affect poverty reduction, for policymakers trade policies stand out as most practical, for two main reasons. First, poverty is a multidimensional concept, including material deprivation, poor health, and education. The approach to poverty reduction stresses three important intrinsic values for the poor: promoting opportunity, facilitating empowerment, and enhancing security (World Bank, 2001). Trade development can provide the poor with many opportunities for employment and income. Trade can also create positive externalities that are pro-poor, such as the promotion of knowledge exchange. As a result of a higher level of income, the poor can improve their status, empowerment, and security in society. Second, trade liberalisation may be the most feasible option for policymakers, as trade policy reforms involve virtually no additional cost to governments (Hertel and Winters, 2005).

The effectiveness and impacts of trade policy reforms on welfare and poverty depend primarily on the context of economic development and institutions in a country, as the trade–poverty relationship is arguably a case- and country-specific issue (McCulloch *et al.*, 2001; Berg and Krueger, 2003; Pacheco-Lopez and Thirlwall, 2009). The focus of the recent research on this relationship has shifted towards examining the impacts at the microeconomic level (see, for example, Seshan, 2005; Ravallion, 2006; Justino *et al.*, 2008; Marchand, 2012; Le, 2014). Trade policies in developing countries such as Vietnam are usually a complex combination of trade protection and export promotion. In the 1990s, Vietnam achieved remarkable economic outcomes in terms of the acceleration of economic growth and a reduction in poverty, after transforming its economic system from a centrally planned economy (CPE) to a market economy. The miracle of Vietnamese economic development has attracted a number of studies examining the effects of trade on economic growth and poverty (see, for instance, Minot and Goletti, 1998; Glewwe *et al.*, 2004; Dollar, 2004; Seshan, 2005; World Bank, 2005; Nguyen and Tran, 2006; Justino *et al.*, 2008; Heo and Nguyen, 2009; Le, 2014). However, not much attention has been devoted to unveiling the reasons that have made Vietnam unsuccessful in its development model so far. One key reason is that Vietnam has not yet completely abandoned its old economic system. This has resulted in numerous inconsistencies in its reform process. Trade policy reforms in a country like Vietnam may involve substantial adjustment costs, although the poor may initially suffer more from these. Unlike many other developing countries, Vietnam is struggling to reform the underdeveloped institutional framework inherited from the CPE. The analysis that follows provides an overview of the Vietnamese economy and puts in perspective the key issues that are given in-depth analysis in the book.

1.2   Trade liberalisation and poverty in Vietnam

Vietnam is amongst the countries that witnessed a remarkable reduction in poverty, associated with high economic growth and rapid integration into the world economy (World Bank, 2005). In 1986, Vietnam launched a programme of renovation, known as Doi Moi, to transform its centrally planned and inward-oriented economy into a market-driven and outward-oriented economy.[1] Trade reforms constitute the bulk of economic reforms in the transitional process. Before these reforms, exports and imports were conducted, through state-owned enterprises (SOEs), within the Council for Mutual Economic Assistance (CMEA) area, the Comecon. Trading prices were based on agreements between the Comecon governments, not on the market. The Vietnamese government monopoly was imposed upon both domestic and international trade. From the late

1980s, trade liberalisation was carried out by a series of reforms. The Law on Foreign Investment in 1987 for the first time invited foreign enterprises to invest in Vietnam, opening the economy to the world market. The government gradually abolished its monopoly on trade, loosened the controls over the prices of most goods, and let the market determine prices. Only about a dozen prices remained controlled after the 1989 price reforms (Leipziger, 1992). Households were given the right to own land, to manage agricultural production, and to conduct trade transactions across provinces. The relaxation of control on foreign exchange and the abolition of most quotas for imports and exports have paved the way for enterprises to expand their production and penetrate international markets.

The 1990s witnessed a series of trade reforms, such as the introduction of the Enterprise Law 1990, the establishment of export processing zones (1991), the application of the harmonised system (HS) of tariff nomenclature (1992), the announcement of the first list of goods (1996) complying with the Common Effective Preferential Tariff (CEPT) of the ASEAN Free Trade Area (AFTA), and the termination of trade licenses (1999) to allow all legally established domestic enterprises to export and import goods specified in the business registration certificate. In this decade, Vietnam also made a remarkable effort to integrate into the regional and world economy, such as its participation in the free trade area of the Association of Southeast Asian Nations (ASEAN), the AFTA, and its application for membership in the World Trade Organization (WTO). In the early 2000s, Vietnam signed a bilateral trade agreement with the United States of America (the Vietnam–US BTA), and thereafter made an action plan to implement the commitments to this trade agreement. The Vietnam–US BTA has been crucial to the process of trade liberalisation, because the United States of America is the most desired, but most difficult, market for enterprises in Vietnam. The attainment of WTO membership in 2007 marked an important milestone in the process of trade liberalisation, bringing many potential opportunities to catch up with other countries in the region. The rest of the 2000s dealt with the reforms to implement commitments to the WTO, the Vietnam–US BTA, and the AFTA. Although the process of trade and economic reforms on the whole may not be adequate and efficient, it has helped Vietnam to achieve remarkable outcomes in terms of the pace of its economic development.

Before reforms, Vietnam was one of the poorest countries in the world, with over 70 per cent of its population living in poverty. The transition to the market economy resulted in boosted economic growth and exports, steadily increasing GDP per capita, and declining poverty throughout the 1990s and the 2000s. The average annual economic growth was nearly 8 per cent in the 1990s and 7 per cent in the 2000s. The poverty rate declined remarkably, from 58.1 per cent to 37.4 per cent over the period spanning 1993 to 1998. This trend appears to have continued until 2008. Vietnam thus obtained one of the first millennium development goals (MGDs)[2] in 2008 by reducing its poverty rate to below 15 per cent. By the end of 2010, Vietnam had become a lower-middle-income country, with per capita income of about US$1,130. It has also achieved, and in some circumstances surpassed, many of the MDGs (Government of Vietnam, 2010; World Bank, 2012). This economic development is arguably the result of economic reforms and openness to trade and investment.

Vietnam initiated its poverty reduction programmes in 1998 and, through continual effort and substantial resources, has reduced poverty remarkably. Tremendous challenges to the reduction of poverty, however, are still ahead, as the strategy for poverty alleviation is unsustainable. In fact, poverty appears to have increased in the late 2000s, following the slowdown in the economy. The World Bank (2012) reports that remote poverty and ethnic inequality are the emerging challenges in Vietnam. More than 90 per cent of the poor still largely live in rural areas, especially in upland regions. Many are farmers (65 per cent of the poor), with livelihoods dependent on agriculture. The rise in ethnic inequality worsens the effort to reduce the incidence of poverty. Groups of ethnic minorities account for nearly half of the total poor. The report suggests that poverty has shown discernible increases when assessed using the new methods of poverty measurement. Other reports have also observed that economic inequality has emerged as a new dimension of poverty and has become increasingly acute (Vietnam Academy of Social Sciences, 2007, 2011). Overall, the successful reduction of poverty, over the two decades of development, has resulted from economic growth, trade liberalisation, and government efforts.

Vietnam provides a good example of the effects of trade liberalisation on poverty alleviation. Trade liberalisation has a pervasive impact on the economy, in light of boosting foreign direct investment and exports, lowering prices, and improving the quality of goods, services, and institutions (World Bank, 2011). Trade liberalisation has been seen to be by far the most effective way of reducing poverty, in both the short and the long run. As trade policy reforms are the main pillar of the reform package (Berg and Krueger, 2003), effective trade policies can create positive effects on other policies, such as fiscal policy, employment, and especially institutions. The assessment of the impacts of trade liberalisation on poverty needs to be based on as many dimensions as possible.

1.3   Previous studies on the trade–growth–poverty nexus

Influential studies acknowledge a major challenge in establishing the relationship between trade liberalisation and poverty. A growing body of empirical literature is based on a variety of methods that are different in terms of the usage of data, the partial or general equilibrium analysis, and the reliance on single or combined data sets or methods. The empirics on the trade–growth–poverty linkage can be grouped into four major categories: cross-country studies, partial equilibrium studies, computable general equilibrium studies, and macro/meso/micro studies (Goldberg and Pavcnik, 2004; Hertel and Reimer, 2005; Aisbett, 2007; Bandara, 2011).

Cross-country studies

Cross-country studies use aggregate data from countries to estimate the impacts of trade openness on economic growth, and then of economic growth on poverty. Solow's extended neoclassical economic growth model is commonly used for this purpose.[3] Dollar and Kraay (2004) find a strong positive effect of trade on economic growth. Their study also reveals that the increase in trade-expanded growth is in proportion to increases in incomes of the poor. The study shows that globalisation leads to faster growth and poverty reduction in poor countries. This approach is, nevertheless, subject to several criticisms, primarily relating to the measures and definitions of globalisation, poverty, and trade policy instruments. The research focus since the 2000s has apparently shifted to the microeconomic country-specific approach (McCulloch *et al.*, 2001; Berg and Krueger, 2003; Ravallion, 2004; Nissanke and Thorbecke, 2007; Bandara *et al.*, 2011).

Partial equilibrium studies

Partial equilibrium studies use a country's survey data to examine the relationship based on various channels through which trade liberalisation affects poverty. These studies usually construct a set of trade-related variables, such as price, employment, agricultural production, infrastructure, location, trade transaction, and institutions. The studies then estimate the impacts of these trade-related variables on welfare, productivity, or a poverty measure. The static poverty regressions have become a standard tool in poverty analysis (Ravallion, 1998; Haughton and Khandker, 2009). The regression method of poverty analysis is based on an income equation that postulates real consumption or income as a function of a number of observed household characteristics. Based on this approach, two common types of models are used to analyse poverty: the levels regression model and the binary regressand model. The trade-related variables are included in a poverty regression model to estimate the effects of trade liberalisation on welfare and poverty. Many studies follow this partial equilibrium approach (e.g. Glewwe *et al.*, 2000; Niimi *et al.*, 2007; Topalova, 2007; Justino *et al.*, 2008; Topalova, 2010; Marchand, 2012). The estimated impacts, based on this approach, remain indirect, because the trade-related variables are just the proxies for trade liberalisation. Despite this disadvantage, it continues to be a promising microeconomic-based method used to investigate the trade–poverty linkage.

Many studies on Vietnam use household survey data and income equation or poverty models. Vietnam has conducted a national household survey series, the VHLSSs, embarked on in 1992. These surveys have high-quality data and are based on random sampling. These surveys contain a wealth of data on households, especially expenditure and income. Many studies have used data taken from these surveys to analyse the trade–poverty relationship. These studies construct some trade-related variables taken from household traits, and examine their effects on welfare or poverty (e.g. Minot and Goletti, 1998; Seshan, 2005; Niimi *et al.*, 2007; Justino *et al.*, 2008; Coello *et al.*, 2010). The studies by

Niimi *et al.* (2007) and Justino *et al.* (2008) use similar methods, finding that trade liberalisation has a positive impact on rural welfare and has helped to reduce poverty substantially over the period 1993 to 1998. Although this approach has the advantage of directly analysing the effects of trade on household welfare and poverty, the data used to analyse are nationwide, not trade-focused, and the impacts of trade liberalisation on poverty are thus indirect.

Computable general equilibrium studies

A growing amount of empirical literature shows developing interest in general equilibrium analysis using computable general equilibrium (CGE) models. These models are computer-based simulations of the possible effects of a specific set of policy changes, including trade policy. The CGE models allow the capture of economy-wide effects of trade policy, and the changes in one sector to give feedback on other sectors (Corbishley *et al.*, 2006). Nguyen and Heo (2009) reveal that the distributional effects of overall welfare gain could lead to increasing inequality in Vietnam. Critiques of the CGE models centre on their questionable assumptions (Bandara, 2011), ex-ante analysis (Greenaway *et al.*, 2002), their focus on tariff and subsidies (Abbott *et al.*, 2009), and, as pointed out by Harrison et al. (2003), the combination of CGE models and household data.

Many studies on the trade–poverty linkage for Vietnam are grounded on CGE models – for instance, Centre for International Economics (2002b), Nguyen (2002), Pham (2003), Jensen and Tarp (2005), Abbott *et al.* (2006, 2011), Nguyen and Tran (2006), Harris *et al.* (2007), Boumellassa and Valin (2008), and Nguyen and Heo (2009). The simulation results of the CGE studies vary, but the general finding is that the impacts of trade liberalisation on poverty are modest. A critical review by Abbott *et al.* (2006) shows that not only do these studies demonstrate little impact of trade liberalisation on poverty, but they also face many problems, similar to those studies for other countries.

Macro/meso/micro studies

Slightly deviating from the above approaches are the macro/meso/micro studies, which establish the relationship between globalisation and poverty by investigating the impacts of the world value chain on poverty. Jenkins (2005) attempts to link the macroeconomic impacts of globalisation on employment to poverty in the cases of Bangladesh, Kenya, South Africa, and Vietnam. The link is analysed through the impact analysis of the effects of specific value chains in horticulture, textiles, and garments on employment and poverty. The study finds that the growth of labour-intensive manufacturing and agricultural exports does create employment.

In addition to the studies using these four approaches, some studies on the trade-poverty relationship of Vietnam attempt to capture the impacts of trade liberalisation on poverty using analytical reviews and descriptive analysis. By analytically reviewing facts and analysing data, they provide evidence on this trade–poverty linkage. For instance, Heo and Nguyen (2009) provide evidence on the relationship between trade liberalisation and poverty reduction through economic growth, market, enterprise, and government revenue. Several reports on sectors such as agriculture, textile, and garment also provide different aspects of the relationship. The United Nations Environment Programme (2005) finds that the trade reform process leads to significant changes in rice production and to exports that discernibly affect poverty reduction. Nadvi *et al.* (2004) provide evidence of the impacts on textile and garment labourers of the integration of Vietnamese garment and textile firms into the global garment and textile value chains. These studies provide a wealth of information on different aspects of trade liberalisation impacts that serves a better understanding of the relationship.

1.4   Key research gaps

Several gaps in the literature on the trade–poverty linkage remain unexplored. First, both poverty and trade liberalisation impacts are multidimensional concepts. The measures of poverty and trade openness remain challenged and controversial. Second, most empirical studies of the relationship are claimed to be indirect. The review of the literature has shown that few studies provide direct and compelling evidence on the link between trade and poverty. Third, trade liberalisation comprises both policy and outcomes. Studies in this vein are commonly based on the outcome-based approach. Some of them attempt to measure trade policy, to evaluate just its impacts on growth, not poverty, but are subject to several limitations. Fourth, trade liberalisation covers both international trade and internal (or domestic) trade. Nonetheless, little attention has been paid to the impacts of domestic trade on poverty. The poor probably benefit more from local trade development than from exports, which mainly depend on the world market. These two areas of trade are in fact closely related. Fifth, the studies of the relationship appear to ignore the impacts of trade liberalisation on urban poverty. The issue of urban poverty is increasingly important in developing countries, because it tends to increase as a consequence of rural-to-urban migration. To some extent, urban poverty affects rural poverty, in the sense that urban unemployment influences rural unemployment. Sixth, the studies following the outcome-based methods tend to ignore the institutional effects of trade liberalisation, which are very case specific and important to understand the differences in the effects of trade liberalisation on poverty amongst developing countries. Seventh, these studies appear to focus on one or two channels through which trade liberalisation affects poverty. The investigation of many facets of the trade liberalisation effect on poverty would provide a more rigorous evaluation of the linkage.

To sum up, the literature on the trade–poverty nexus remains contentious in several respects. Studies of the effects of trade liberalisation that are based on cross-country analysis and/or CGE models are discernibly subject to some critical shortcomings. Apart from the likely problems with methodology, they apparently overlook a country's characteristics of trade policy and institutions. The examination of the relationship using the case- or country-specific approach may dispense a more particular picture of the relationship. By and large, the judgement about the impacts of trade liberalisation on poverty for a country should be comprehensive, as merely focusing on one or two aspects/pathways may be flawed. The literature on trade liberalisation and poverty suggests that the trade–poverty relationship is largely country specific in nature. Similar studies of the relationship for Vietnam generally provide a partial analysis.

1.5   Research objectives

The study examines the effects of trade liberalisation on household welfare and poverty in Vietnam in order to assess comprehensively the benefits of trade liberalisation on households and the poor. The aim is to examine two general research questions. The first is whether trade liberalisation impacts poverty in Vietnam. In particular, it seeks to:

1. Conduct a survey of the literature on the relationship between trade liberalisation and poverty so as to examine the issue in a broader global setting.
2. Review the process of trade liberalisation and poverty reduction in Vietnam over three decades of economic development, comparing the periods before and after the opening of the economy in 1986.
3. Use Winters's framework to analyse the impacts of trade liberalisation on poverty in Vietnam through the four channels – economic growth, market, employment, and government revenue – in order to evaluate the trade–poverty nexus comprehensively and at the microeconomic level.
4. Provide evidence of the effects of trade-led growth on poverty over two decades of development in order to support the important role of economic growth in the reduction of poverty.
5. Find evidence of the impact of employment on household welfare and poverty to support the crucial role of employment in addressing poverty.
6. Review the process of trade reforms in relation to government revenue and public expenditure to find the link between trade liberalisation and poverty via government revenue.

The literature on the trade–poverty relationship for Vietnam appears to have ignored or have yet to capture the inadequacy of the market system in agriculture, which presumably impoverishes farm households. The second general research question, therefore, is whether the poor experience such an inadequate trade policy. Although trade liberalisation is believed to have an overall positive impact on poverty, poor farm households are hypothesised to experience inadequate trade policy. This question is better answered by farm households, the primary victims of agricultural trade policy. The study seeks to:

7. Examine the effect of agricultural production on welfare to value the market effect on poverty.
8. Conduct a comprehensive primary field survey of trade policy perception on farm households to assess the effects of the market in agriculture in reality from their point of view.

The examination of these two general questions will reveal the relationship between trade liberalisation and poverty, and will simultaneously provide an adequate assessment of the impacts of trade liberalisation on household welfare and poverty in Vietnam. By virtue of Winters's approach, this study focuses on its four channels to conduct the analysis. Analysing the trade liberalisation effect based on this framework requires a combination of methods.

1.6 Methodology and data

Cross-country studies use various methods to measure trade openness, such as the level of tariff and nontariff barriers to trade, as well as the ratios of exports to GDP and of trade volume (exports plus imports) to GDP. These measures of trade openness, however, may not link up with welfare and poverty at the household level. This study examines the relationship primarily at the micro-economic level, and mainly uses the household survey data. The study, therefore, does not utilise the direct indicators of trade liberalisation, such as tariffs, effective exchange rates, and openness indexes, to analyse the trade–poverty nexus. To evaluate the impacts of trade openness on household welfare, some specific household characteristics can be linked to trade reforms (Justino *et al.*, 2008). These linkages can be based on the Winters pathways. Agricultural production and employment are important trade-induced factors in the framework. The study focuses on setting the trade-related variables, the key to investigating the impacts of trade liberalisation on household welfare and poverty.

The comparative analysis, analytical review, case study, and econometric models are integrated with Winters's channels to achieve the study's objectives. The study begins with the analytical review and evaluation of the effects of trade liberalisation on economic growth, household welfare, and poverty through economic growth, market, employment, and government spending over the last three decades of development (1980–2010), using descriptive statistics and comparative methods. The historical and comparative analyses provide a more comprehensive picture of the relationship before examining its effects in the channels. The growth elasticity of poverty is estimated over two decades of development, the 1990s and the 2000s, to measure the responsiveness of poverty to trade-led growth. This analysis also extends to explain the effects of both growth and local trade openness on poverty in a poverty model, using a panel data set constructed from the Vietnam household living standards surveys (VHLSSs). It should be noted that this elasticity approach can be estimated using the direct indexes of trade liberalisation, as discussed above. However, this analysis examines the relationship at the household and provincial levels, where the data on tariffs, effective exchange rates, and openness indexes are unavailable. Provincial trade transactions and growth of household welfare are therefore utilised instead in this analysis.

The market effects, primarily agricultural production and trade, are also partly revealed in the analysis of the model of microdeterminants of growth. In addition to the model-based analysis, the study also conducts a case study based on a comprehensive primary field survey of agricultural production and distribution on farm households. The case study makes this research different from other similar studies, as it focuses on farm household perception of trade policy in agriculture. This survey was conducted in 2011 in three different provinces in Vietnam, covering more than 300 farm households. The primary survey data are expected to provide insight into the real facts of trade policies in agriculture. The employment effect is examined by employing a model of microdeterminants of growth, using household panel data sets constructed from the VHLSSs. These effects are investigated using both continuous and discrete approaches. The continuous approach employs a model of microdeterminants of growth, fixed effects, and random effects models. The discrete approach uses a multinomial logit model to analyse the transition of poverty.

The revenue effects of trade liberalisation are examined through an analytical review. The literature suggests that governments usually give top priority to expenditure on social security and poverty reduction programmes. The Vietnamese government has, in fact, made a great effort to reduce poverty, regardless of the situation of the economy. The study assumes that government revenue that is related to trade reforms has a minor impact on poverty. This effect is intensively analysed through descriptive statistics. Institutions are regarded as underpinning the trade–poverty relationship in Winters's framework. In an attempt to provide a more adequate picture of that relationship, the analysis is undertaken to examine the effects of institutional reforms on rural household welfare and poverty. This investigation is carried out by using the Vietnam Provincial Competitiveness Index (PCI) as a proxy for institutional reforms, in combination with the VHLSS data.

1.7 Chapter scheme

The rest of the book is organized as follows:

Chapter 2: This chapter provides a comprehensive survey of the literature and discusses the trade–growth–poverty nexus in a global setting. It first discusses the concepts and measurements of poverty and trade liberalisation, as these are important but mostly contentious. The chapter thereafter discusses the trade–poverty linkage, based on the pathways outlined in Winters's framework. This conceptual framework postulates that trade liberalisation affects households and poverty through economic growth, market, employment, and government revenue. The survey of the literature has revealed some research gaps: the questionable cross-country studies, the difficulty of establishing the direct links to poverty, an inadequate market distribution system in agriculture, and the difficulty of examining institutional reform effects.

Chapter 3: This chapter analytically reviews the background of Vietnam's economy, the process of trade liberalisation and poverty reduction, and the impacts of trade liberalisation on poverty. This chapter is important because it lays the historical foundation for better understanding of the subsequent chapters in the book. The specific impacts of trade liberalisation on poverty should be perceived in the specific context of Vietnam's economy: its transition to a market economy from a CPE. The development of the economy from 1980 is divided into three stages, corresponding to three decades of development. These economic reforms were embarked on from the late 1980s. After reviewing the process of reforms and development, the chapter follows Winters's pathways to examine the effects of trade liberalisation on poverty by descriptive statistics. Particularly, it compares and judges the impacts of economic growth, market, employment, and government revenue on poverty before and after economic reforms. The analysis suggests that trade liberalisation has contributed in terms of all four channels that affect poverty: economic growth, market, employment, and government spending. These contributions of trade liberalisation appeared to be most significant in the 1990s. Although inequality in Vietnam is low compared with neighbour countries, as discussed in the literature, the analysis recognises the notable increase in income inequality in recent years, which could dampen the benefits of economic growth to the poor.

Chapter 4: This chapter examines the growth effect of trade liberalisation on poverty by estimating the growth elasticity of poverty, using alternative methods and both national accounts data and the VHLSSs. This is a direct route to link growth to poverty. Use of a panel data set constructed from the VHLSSs and a poverty model extends this chapter to estimate the effects of trade openness and growth of welfare on poverty at the provincial level in order to shed more light on the effects of growth and trade. Trade openness in this analysis is internal or local trade, which is as important as external or international trade, as discussed earlier. This chapter thus attempts to link growth and trade directly with poverty. The results suggest that growth of welfare and internal trade are typically pro-poor in Vietnam. The effect of welfare growth was particularly significant in rural areas. The results also raise some concerns about the insignificant role of agriculture in the reduction of poverty, and about the obsession of inflation, which can largely offset the benefits of growth to the poor.

Chapter 5: This chapter provides insight into the market effects of trade liberalisation on poverty. It differs from other similar studies in that it analyses trade policies in agriculture from the farm household point of view. As farmers experience trade policies on agricultural production and trade, they can perceive and describe the inadequacy of the marketing system in farming business. The analysis in this chapter is based on a primary field survey of production and market distribution of rice and coffee in three different provinces: An Giang, Dong Nai, and Dak Lak. An Giang is one of the leading rice production provinces, while Dak Lak is one of the leading coffee production provinces. Dong Nai was chosen because the study seeks to discover the characteristics of the poor in an industrial area, which is different from the other provinces. This case study thus captures farm households' perception of agricultural production and trade in different regions of Vietnam. This chapter explains why farm households remain poor in a globally influential, rice export country. It also identifies the relationship between welfare and farm household awareness of trade policy. Overall, the production and distribution of rice and coffee were found to be liberalised to a large extent, but mismanaged. The farmers faced several risks in relation to crop distribution, inflation, capital shortage, unstable supply of fertiliser and fuel, and rice export delays. They also lacked support from the multiagency cooperation proposed by the government that was meant to be the farmers' primary source of support.

Chapter 6: This chapter investigates the employment effect of trade liberalisation on the welfare of rural households through a model of microdeterminants of growth. This study uses two approaches to explain the determinants of welfare and poverty: continuous and discrete. Each method has its own strengths and weaknesses. The continuous approach uses the model of microdeterminants of growth, in combination with fixed effects and random effects models. The discrete approach employs a multinomial logit model to analyse the dynamics of poverty; that is, household escape from or fall into poverty under the impacts of trade liberalisation. This chapter thus examines the effects of trade-induced employment on poverty in alternative approaches. The analysis, using a household panel data set for the period 2002–2006 and combined methods, including fixed and random effects models, as well as the multinomial logit model, suggests that the employment effects of trade liberalisation have significantly contributed to the improvement of rural household welfare and thereby to the reduction of poverty.

Chapter 7: This chapter examines the effects of employment on urban poverty. Studies in the field appear to have ignored the impacts of trade liberalisation on urban poverty, assuming that urban poverty is inconsequential. This chapter indicates that urban poverty is increasingly important for developing countries, given the rise in rural-to-urban migration. Urban poverty is somewhat different from rural poverty in a country, but is closely related to it. The chapter provides an overview of urban poverty and characteristics of the urban poor in Vietnam, with special attention to the cases of Ho Chi Minh City (HCMC) and Hanoi, the two largest cities in Vietnam. Amongst the impacts of trade liberalisation, employment is the most crucial to urban households. After providing the big picture, the chapter examines the effects of employment on urban welfare in Vietnam, using fixed and random effects models and a panel data set established from the VHLSSs. Employment is significant for both urban welfare and the reduction of urban poverty. The analysis suggests that local trade and employment in the import-competing sectors improved urban welfare. Local trade per capita has a consistent impact on household welfare in urban areas. These effects on urban household welfare are presumably transmitted to the urban poor, as a considerable proportion of the urban population migrate from the countryside areas.

Chapter 8: Although not explicitly outlined in Winters's framework, institutions are the important determinant of household welfare and poverty.

Institutional reforms of law systems help enterprises to develop and farm households to cultivate and market their crops. Existing studies of the relationship have yet to capture the effects of institutional reforms on welfare and poverty. This chapter, Chapter 8, uses the PCI as a proxy for institutional reforms, in combination with the VHLSS data in the model of microdeterminants of growth, to examine the effects of institutional reforms on household welfare. The inclusion of institutional reforms in this study therefore makes it different from other similar studies, and contributes to the adequacy of the picture of the trade–poverty relationship for Vietnam in this study. It provides evidence that local trade and institutional reforms improved rural welfare and thereby contributed to poverty reduction in Vietnam; this finding is striking, given that most rural households are poor.

Chapter 9: This chapter synthesises the key findings of the research and provides a policy perspective. Trade liberalisation in Vietnam has been found to contribute considerably to welfare through economic growth, market, employment, and government revenue. The sustainment of high economic growth, market system, labour market, and exports, with the underpinning of a sound institutional framework, would be the ultimate amongst economic reforms for Vietnam, now and beyond. The study draws important policy lessons for the developing economies in general and for Vietnam in particular. Vietnam needs to accelerate its economic reforms, particularly the reforms in agricultural trade, and strengthen its institutions towards a sustainable economic growth and a reduced level of poverty.

1.8   Novelty of the book

This study employs both a country-specific approach, using Vietnam as a case study, and a holistic approach, using Winters's pathways to analyse and evaluate the impacts of trade liberalisation on poverty. Virtually no study has intensively investigated many effects of trade liberalisation on poverty in Vietnam. Unlike several studies on trade liberalisation at the macroeconomic level that use 'trade openness' as a core concept, this study uses 'trade liberalisation' as a core concept, and examines the microeconomic effects of trade liberalisation. Thus trade liberalisation has a broad spectrum, in that it includes both trade policy and its outcomes, as well as both international and internal trade.

This study contributes to the literature in the following ways. First, it systematically reviews the process of trade liberalisation and reduction in poverty and assesses the impacts of trade liberalisation on welfare and poverty in Vietnam. A common drawback of the existing studies on the linkage for Vietnam is that these studies simply examine the impacts of trade liberalisation on welfare and poverty, ignoring the context of the development of the economy. The analysis of the history of trade liberalisation and poverty will help to better understand the trade–poverty nexus. Second, those studies that focus on one or two impacts of trade liberalisation seem inadequate. This study thoroughly analyses the trade liberalisation effect on poverty following the four channels outlined in Winters

(2002) and Winters *et al.* (2004). The investigation of many pathways through which trade liberalisation affects poverty provides a more adequate picture of the relationship in Vietnam. Third, the study conducts a primary field survey of trade policy in agriculture that sheds more light on the market effects of trade liberalisation on farm households. This survey aims at farm households and agricultural production because most of the poor in Vietnam engage in farming activities. The current studies on the link for Vietnam using macroeconomic data or general household survey data are unlikely to capture farm households' perception of trade policy, which is important for understanding the flaws of trade policy in agriculture. In particular, such studies have yet to provide insight into the inadequate marketing system in agricultural production and trade that may impoverish farm households. The results provided by this survey are expected to be a reference for policymakers who are devising strategies for reducing poverty. Fourth, this study also takes the effects of institutional reforms into account. Institutions constitute an important dimension of poverty and relate closely to trade policy reforms. Institutions are seen to underpin the channels through which trade liberalisation affects households and poverty. The inclusion of the effects of institutional reforms makes the trade–poverty relationship more comprehensive. Fifth, this study provides evidence for supporting the argument that local or domestic trade is as important for poverty reduction as international trade. Most of the poor live in rural or remote areas, where the effects of external trade are unlikely to reach. The development of trade in local regions therefore greatly benefits the poor. The problems with trade policies in agriculture that probably impoverish farm households in Vietnam lie mainly in the domestic market distribution of agricultural products, not in the international market. An attempt is made to answer the question as to why most farm households remain poor while Vietnam is one of the influential rice export countries in the world.

The analysis is confined to investigating the impacts of trade liberalisation on poverty, primarily at the microeconomic level. The book intends to thoroughly examine neither the process of trade policy reforms nor the effects of trade policy reforms on the economy as a whole. It also does not examine openness in general, including international trade, foreign direct investment (FDI), and international finance. In this study, farm households are chosen as the units of analysis, assuming that they are mostly poor in Vietnam. By producing, selling, and consuming rice and paddy, farm households are presumably very involved in agricultural trade and experience the effects of trade policy reforms in agriculture. This assumption may also be a likely shortcoming of the study. It probably ignores other groups of households that may also be affected by trade policy manipulation. The second limitation is that the study focuses on investigating the trade–poverty channels without measuring trade liberalisation. Finally, by using Winters's channels, evidence of the relationship provided in the book is virtually indirect. Even with these shortcomings, the research provides a relatively comprehensive picture and substantial evidence of the relationship between trade liberalisation and poverty in Vietnam.

Notes

1 The economy of Vietnam is officially called the socialist-oriented market economy. It basically pursues a market economy, yet the Vietnamese government likes to retain the socialist form. Vietnam's economy is commonly described as a market-driven or market-led economy.
2 The first goal of the MGDs, between 1990 and 2015, is to halve the proportion of people whose income is less than US$1 a day (United Nations, 2010).
3 For details of this model, see Solow (1956, 2007), Mankiw *et al.* (1992), and Sachs and Larrain (1993).

References

Abbott, P., Bentzen, J., Pham, T.L.H., and Tarp, F. (2006). *A Critical Review of Studies on the Social and Economic Impacts of Vietnam's International Economic Integration*. Central Institute for Economic Management (CIEM), Vietnam, Discussion Working Papers (No. PRG2.06.01).

Abbott, P., Bentzen, J., and Tarp, F. (2009). Trade and Development: Lessons from Vietnam's Past Trade Agreements. *World Development, 37*(2), 341–353.

Abbott, P., Wu, C., and Tarp, F. (2011). *Transmission of World Prices to the Domestic Market in Vietnam*. Paper presented at the 8th Midwest International Economic Development Conference, Wisconsin.

Acemoglu, D., and Robinson, J. (2008). *The Role of Institutions in Growth and Development*. Commission on Growth and Development, Working Paper (No. 10), 44.

Acemoglu, D., and Robinson, J.A. (2012). *Why Nations Fail: The Origins of Power, Prosperity, and Poverty* (1st ed.). New York: Crown Publishers.

Aisbett, E. (2007). Why Are the Critics So Convinced that Globalization is Bad for the Poor? In A. Harrison (ed) *Globalization and Poverty* (pp. 33–85). Chicago: University of Chicago Press.

Athukorala, P. (2010a). *Production Networks and Trade Patterns in East Asia: Regionalization or Globalization?*. ADB, Working Paper Series on Regional Economic Integration (No. 56), 76.

Bandara, J.S. (2011). Trade and Poverty – Theory, Evidence and Policy Issues. In J.S. Bandara, P. Athukorala, and S. Kelegama (eds) *Trade Liberalisation and Poverty in South Asia* (p. 224). London: Routledge.

Bandara, J.S., Athukorala, P., and Kelegama, S. (eds). (2011). *Trade Liberalisation and Poverty in South Asia*. London: Routledge.

Baunsgaard, T., and Keen, M. (2010). Tax Revenue and (or?) Trade Liberalization. *Journal of Public Economics, 94*(9–10), 563–577. DOI: http://dx.doi.org/10.1016/j.jpubeco.2009.11.007

Berg, A., and Krueger, A. (2003). *Trade, Growth, and Poverty: A Selective Survey*. IMF, Working Paper (WP/03/30).

Bhagwati, J.N., and Srinivasan, T.N. (2002). Trade and Poverty in the Poor Countries. *American Economic Review, 92*(2), 180–183. DOI: 10.1257/000282802320189212

Boumellassa, H., and Valin, H. (2008). *Vietnam's Accession to the WTO: Ex-post Evaluation in a Dynamic Perspective*. CEPII, Working Paper (No 2008–31), 55.

Centre for International Economics (CIE) (2002). *Vietnam Poverty Analysis*. Canberra.

Coello, B., Fall, M., and Suwa-Eisenmann, A. (2010). *Trade Liberalization and Poverty Dynamics in Vietnam 2002–2006*. Paris School of Economics, Working Paper (No. 11), 43.

Corbishley, J., Garrett, D., and Stoeckel, A. (2006). *Trade Liberalisation and Structural Change* (p. 90). Canberra: RIRDC–CIE.

Deolalikar, A.B., Brillantes, J.A.B., Gaiha, R., Pernia, E.M., and Racelis, M. (2002). *Poverty Reduction and the Role of Institutions in Developing Asia*. ERD, Working Paper Series (No. 10).

Dollar, D. (2004). Reform, Growth, and Poverty. In P. Glewwe, N. Agrawal, and D. Dollar (eds) *Economic Growth, Poverty, and Household Welfare in Vietnam* (pp. 29–51). Washington, DC: World Bank.

Dollar, D. (2005). Globalization, Poverty, and Inequality since 1980. *The World Bank Research Observer, 20*(2), 145–175. DOI: 10.1093/wbro/lki008

Dollar, D., and Kraay, A. (2004). Trade, Growth, and Poverty. *The Economic Journal, 114*(493), F22–F49. DOI: 10.1111/j.0013–0133.2004.00186.x

Frankel, J.A., and Romer, D. (1999). Does Trade Cause Growth?. *The American Economic Review, 89*(3), 379–399.

Glewwe, P., Agrawal, N., and Dollar, D. (eds) (2004). *Economic Growth, Poverty, and Household Welfare in Vietnam*. Washington, DC: World Bank.

Glewwe, P., Gragnolati, M., and Zaman, H. (2000). *Who Gained from Vietnam's Boom in the 1990s: An Analysis of Poverty and Inequality Trends*. World Bank, Policy Research Working Paper (No. 2275), 64.

Goldberg, P.K., and Pavcnik, N. (2004). *Trade, Inequality, and Poverty: What Do We Know? Evidence from Recent Trade Liberalization Episodes in Developing Countries*. NBER, Working Paper Series (No. 10593), 52.

Government of Vietnam (2010). *Millennium Development Goals 2010 National Report: Vietnam 2/3 of the Way Achieving the Millennium Development Goals and Towards 2015* (p. 135). Hanoi.

Greenaway, D., Morgan, W., and Wright, P. (2002). Trade Liberalisation and Growth in Developing Countries. *Journal of Development Economics, 67*(1), 229–244.

Harris, R.G., Robertson, P.E., and Wong, M. (2007). *Analysing Economy Wide Effects of Trade Liberalisation on Vietnam Using a Dynamic Computable General Equilibrium Model*. UNSW School of Economics, Discussion Paper (No. 24), 56.

Harrison, G., Rutherford, T.F., and Tarr, D.G. (2003). *Quantifying the Impact of Trade Reform on Poverty*. Available at GU Proquest, World Bank.

Haughton, J., and Khandker, S.R. (2009). *Handbook on Poverty and Inequality*. Washington, DC: World Bank.

Heo, Y., and Nguyen, K.D. (2009). Trade Liberalisation and Poverty Reduction in Vietnam. *The World Economy, 32*(6), 934.

Hertel, T.W., and Reimer, J.J. (2005). Predict the Poverty Impacts of Trade Reform. *Journal of International Trade and Economic Development, 14*(4), 377–405.

Hertel, T.W., and Winters, L.A. (2005). Estimate the Poverty Impacts of a Prospective Doha Development Agenda. *The World Economy, 28*(8), 1057–1071.

Jenkins, R. (2005). *Globalization, Production and Poverty*. WIDER, Research Paper (No. 2005/40), 25.

Jensen, H.T., and Tarp, F. (2005). Trade Liberalization and Spatial Inequality: a Methodological Innovation in a Vietnamese Perspective. *Review of Development Economics, 9*(1), 69–86. DOI: 10.1111/j.1467–9361.2005.00264.x

Justino, P., Litchfield, J., and Pham, H.T. (2008). Poverty Dynamics during Trade Reform: Evidence from Rural Vietnam. *Review of Income and Wealth, 54*(2), 166–192. DOI: 10.1111/j.1475–4991.2008.00269.x

Kalwij, A.S., and Verschoor, A. (2007). Not by Growth Alone: The Role of the Distribution of Income in Regional Diversity in Poverty Reduction. *European Economic Review, 51*(4), 805–829. DOI: http://dx.doi.org/10.1016/j.euroecorev.2006.06.003

Krueger, A.O. (1983). *Trade and Employment in Less Developed Countries: Synthesis and Conclusion* (vol. 3). Chicago: University of Chicago Press.

Le, M.S. (2014). Trade Openness and Household Welfare within a Country: A Microeconomic Analysis of Vietnamese Households. *Journal of Asian Economics, 33*, 56–70.

Leipziger, D.M. (1992). *Awakening the Market: Viet Nam's Economic Transition.* World Bank, Discussion Papers (No. 0157), 52.

Mankiw, N.G., Romer, D., and Weil, D.N. (1992). A Contribution to the Empirics of Economic Growth. *The Quarterly Journal of Economics, 107*(2), 407–437. DOI: 10.2307/2118477

Marchand, B.U. (2012). Tariff Pass-Through and the Distributional Effects of Trade Liberalization. *Journal of Development Economics, 99*, 265–281.

McCulloch, N., Winters, L.A., and Cirera, X. (2001). *Trade Liberalization and Poverty: A Handbook.* London: Centre for Economic Policy Research.

Minot, N., and Goletti, F. (1998). Export Liberalization and Household Welfare: The Case of Rice in Vietnam. *American Journal of Agricultural Economics, 80*(4), 738–749.

Nadvi, K., Bui, T.T., Nguyen, T.T.H., Nguyen, T.H., Dao, H.L., and Armas, E.B.D. (2004). Vietnam in the Global Garment and Textile Value Chain: Impacts on Firms and Workers. *Journal of International Development, 16*(1), 111–123.

Nguyen, C., and Tran, K.D. (2006). *The Impact of Trade Liberalization on Household Welfare in Vietnam.* MPIA, Working Paper (No. 2), 27.

Nguyen, K.D., and Heo, Y. (2009). Impacts of Trade Liberalisation Commitments on the Vietnamese Economy: A CGE Approach. *The World Economy, 32*(4), 606–628.

Nguyen, T.D. (2002). Trade Reforms in Vietnam: A Computable General Equilibrium Analysis. *Forum of International Development Studies, 21*, 189–216.

Niimi, Y., Vasudeva-Dutta, P., and Winters, L.A. (2007). Trade Liberalization and Poverty Dynamics in Vietnam. *Journal of Economic Integration, 22*(4), 819–851.

Nissanke, M., and Thorbecke, E. (eds) (2007). *The Impact of Globalization on the World's Poor: Transmission Mechanisms.* Basingstoke: Palgrave Macmillan.

Pacheco-Lopez, P., and Thirlwall, A.P. (2009). *Has Trade Liberalisation in Poor Countries Delivered the Promises Expected?* Department of Economics, University of Kent, Discussion Paper (No. KDPE 0911).

Pham, T.L.H. (2003). *The Impacts of Vietnam's Accession to the WTO on Income Distribution Using a General Equilibrium Framework.* Asia Pacific School of Economics and Government, Australian National University, Working Paper, 3(7), 1–20.

Ram, R. (2006). Growth Elasticity of Poverty: Alternative Estimates and a Note of Caution. *KYKLOS, 59*(4), 10.

Ram, R. (2011). Growth Elasticity of Poverty: Direct Estimates from Recent Data. *Applied Economics, 43*(19), 2433–2440.

Ravallion, M. (1998). Poor Areas. In A. Ullah and D.E.A. Giles (eds) *Handbook of Applied Economic Statistics* (pp. 63–91). New York: Marcel Dekker.

Ravallion, M. (2004). *Competing Concepts of Inequality in the Globalization Debate.* World Bank, Policy Research Working Paper (No. 3243).

Ravallion, M. (2006). Looking Beyond Averages in the Trade and Poverty Debate. *World Development, 34*(8), 1374–1392. DOI: http://dx.doi.org/10.1016/j.worlddev.2005.10.015

Rigobon, R., and Rodrik, D. (2004). *Rule of Law, Democracy, Openness, and Income: Estimating the Interrelationships.* NBER, Working Paper Series (No. 10750), 30.

Rodríguez, F. (2006). *Openness and Growth: What Have We Learned?.* Wesleyan Economics, Working Papers (No. 011), 39.

Rodriguez, F., and Rodrik, D. (2001). *Trade Policy and Economic Growth: A Skeptic's Guide to Cross-National Evidence.* NBER, Working Paper Series (No. 7081), 82.

Rodrik, D. (2002). Trade Policy Reform as Institutional Reform. In B. Hoekman, A. Mattoo, and P. English (eds) *Development, Trade, and the WTO: A Handbook* (pp. 3–10). Washington, DC: World Bank.

Rodrik, D. (2010). Diagnostics before Prescription. *Journal of Economic Perspectives, 24*(3), 33–44.

Rodrik, D., Subramanian, A., and Trebbi, F. (2004). Institutions Rule: The Primacy of Institutions over Geography and Integration in Economic Development. *Journal of Economic Growth, 9*(2), 131–165.

Sachs, J. D., and Larrain, B. (1993). *Macroeconomics in the Global Economy* (1st ed.). New Jersey: Prentice Hall.

Sachs, J. D., and Warner, A. (1995). Economic Reform and the Process of Global Integration. *Brookings Papers on Economic Activity, 1995*(1), 1–118.

Seshan, G. (2005). *The Impact of Trade Liberalization on Household Welfare in Vietnam.* World Bank, Policy Research Working Paper (No. 3541).

Singh, T. (2010). Does International Trade Cause Economic Growth? A Survey. *The World Economy, 33*(11), 1517–1564. DOI: 10.1111/j.1467–9701.2010.01243.x

Solow, R. M. (1956). A Contribution to the Theory of Economic Growth. *The Quarterly Journal of Economics, 70*(1), 31.

Solow, R. M. (2007). The Last 50 Years in Growth Theory and the Next 10. *Oxford Review of Economic Policy, 23*(1), 12.

Topalova, P. (2007). Trade Liberalization, Poverty and Inequality: Evidence from Indian Districts. In A. Harrison (ed) *Globalization and Poverty* (p. 47). Chicago: University of Chicago Press.

Topalova, P. (2010). Factor Immobility and Regional Impacts of Trade Liberalization: Evidence on Poverty from India. *American Economic Journal: Applied Economics, 2*(4), 1–41. DOI: 10.1257/app.2.4.1

United Nations (UN) (2010). *The Millennium Development Goals Report 2010.* New York.

United Nations Environment Programme (UNEP) (2005). *Integrated Assessment of the Impact of Trade Liberalization: A Country Study on the Viet Nam Rice Sector.* Geneva.

Vietnam Academy of Social Sciences (VASS) (2007). *Vietnam Poverty Update Report 2006: Poverty and Poverty Reduction in Vietnam 1993–2004* (p. 60). Hanoi.

Vietnam Academy of Social Sciences (VASS) (2011). *Poverty Reduction in Vietnam: Achievements and Challenges.* Hanoi.

Wacziarg, R., and Welch, K.H. (2008). Trade Liberalization and Growth: New Evidence. *The World Bank Economic Review, 22*(2), 45.

Winters, L.A. (2002). Trade Liberalisation and Poverty: What are the Links? *The World Economy, 25*(9), 1339–1367. DOI: 10.1111/1467–9701.00495

Winters, L.A., McCulloch, N., and McKay, A. (2004). Trade Liberalization and Poverty: The Evidence So Far. *Journal of Economic Literature, XLII*(1), 72–115.

World Bank (1987). *World Development Report 1987: Barriers to Adjustment and Growth in the World Economy, Industrialization and Foreign Trade, and World Development Indicators* (p. 299). Washington, DC.

World Bank (1997). *World Development Report: The State in a Changing World* (p. 278). Washington, DC.

World Bank (2001). *World Development Report 2000/01: Attacking Poverty* (p. 356). Washington, DC.

World Bank (2005). *Pro-poor Growth in the 1990s: Lessons and Insights from 14 Countries* (p. 116). Washington, DC.

World Bank (2010). *Vietnam Development Report 2010: Modern Institutions* (p. 227). Hanoi.

World Bank (2011). *Vietnam Development Report 2012: Market Economy for a Middle-Income Vietnam* (p. 90). Hanoi.

World Bank (2012). *Well Begun, Not Yet Done: Vietnam's Remarkable Progress on Poverty Reduction and the Emerging Challenges* (p. 190). Hanoi.

2 Trade liberalisation, economic growth, and poverty in a global setting

2.1 Introduction

The recent miracle of economic growth and development in the 1980s and 1990s in some Asian countries, such as China, Hong Kong, Singapore, South Korea, and Taiwan, supports the significant role of trade liberalisation in economic growth. After transforming a centrally planned economy into a market economy in 1986, Vietnam attained remarkable achievements in economic growth and reduction in poverty. Although several other open economies also attained high economic growth and reduced poverty considerably, the empirical literature on the relationship between trade liberalisation, economic growth, and poverty is not devoid of concerns, particularly with respect to the strength of empirical evidence (see Rodriguez and Rodrik, 2001; Wacziarg and Welch, 2008; Pacheco-Lopez and Thirlwall, 2009; Singh, 2010). The persistence of poverty amongst a considerable proportion of the population in transitional or liberalised developing economies also casts a dubious light on the impacts of trade liberalisation on poverty. The literature on trade and poverty acknowledges the difficulties in establishing the relationship between these two, primarily because both the concepts, trade and poverty, are multidimensional and therefore hard to measure (Winters *et al.*, 2004). Many pathways through which trade affects households and poverty have been identified in the literature on the trade–poverty nexus. As noted, a strand of studies suggests that the trade–poverty relationship is largely case and country specific (McCulloch *et al.*, 2001; Berg and Krueger, 2003; Pacheco-Lopez and Thirlwall, 2009). The impacts of trade liberalisation could be enormous and pervasive, but are to a large extent difficult to verify empirically. Some studies have shown that trade development can generate positive externalities that are pro-poor; for instance, trade development spurs knowledge exchange and thereby benefits the poor. Trade policy reforms also accompany institutional reforms (Rodrik, 2002) that reduce social costs associated with institutional discrimination and thus help the poor (World Bank, 2001). Bannister and Thugge (2001) point out that trade liberalisation can impinge on the vulnerability to negative external shocks that could affect the poor. Abrupt changes in terms of trade can directly affect agricultural production or informal production, the main activities of the poor. McCulloch *et al.* (2001, however, contend that, although trade liberalisation is believed to have an enormous potential impact on welfare and poverty, the direct effects on poverty are negligible for many dimensions of trade liberalisation.

The focus of research on the trade–growth–poverty relationship has recently shifted towards examining the impacts at the grass-roots, microeconomic level. Winters (2002a) and Winters *et al.* (2004) suggest four main pathways through which trade liberalisation reaches households and thereby affects poverty: economic growth, employment, market distribution, and government revenue. These channels sufficiently cover the main stakeholders in the market economy, and can be empirically verified. Several studies have examined these channels both theoretically and empirically (e.g. McCulloch *et al.*, 2001; Winters, 2002a; Berg and Krueger, 2003; Winters *et al.*, 2004; Harrison, 2007; Nissanke and Thorbecke, 2007a; Athukorala, 2010; Bandara *et al.*, 2011). The empirical literature, as classified in terms of the Winters transmission channels, suggests that trade liberalisation affects households, and thereby poverty, via its effects on (1) long-run economic growth (Dollar and Kraay, 2002, 2004; Ravallion, 2006; Singh, 2010; Kang and Imai, 2012), (2) price and/or market distribution of tradable goods (Minot and Goletti, 1998; Seshan, 2005; Justino *et al.*, 2008, (3) employment/ enterprise (Krueger, 1983; Niimi *et al.*, 2007; Justino *et al.*, 2008), and (4) government revenue (Baunsgaard and Keen, 2005, 2010; Heo and Nguyen, 2009).

In Winters's first channel, trade development can benefit the poor through the contribution to economic growth. Bhagwati and Srinivasan (2002) divide the process into two stages: trade stimulates growth through accumulation and innovation and growth, in turn, reduces poverty by providing the poor with more employment. One effect of economic growth on poverty is the trickle-down effect generated that benefits people in general, including the poor (Winters, *et al.*, 2004). This trickle-down effect is, in fact, the employment effect of economic growth. In the second channel, trade liberalisation affects households and alleviates poverty via the prices and/or market distribution of tradable goods. Price changes and/or the characteristics of market distribution greatly affect the poor. One of the most important conditions for the outward-oriented strategy to be successful is to maintain macroeconomic stability, which is indirectly beneficial for the poor (Bhagwati and Srinivasan, 2002). In this linkage, trade policy can cause price distortions, resulting from trade monopoly, the marketing system, and transaction costs. The poor are unlikely to benefit from trade liberalisation due primarily to the ineffective transmission of prices to households as a consequence of inadequate trade policies (Winters *et al.*, 2004). In the third channel, the creation of jobs is an important contribution of trade liberalisation. The high levels of trade activities and/or production are considered to boost the demand for labour. If properly developed, trade expansion can generate backward and forward linkages which sustain employment and growth in the long run, due to their effects in terms of raising the demand for labour and reducing the industrial output costs in primary export countries (Todaro and Smith, 2009). In terms of government revenue, trade policy reforms may shrink the government budget, thereby potentially restricting governmental spending for social security and poverty alleviation programmes (Heo and Nguyen, 2009; Baunsgaard and Keen, 2010). For reasons of social stability, governments usually give top priority to public expenditure (Winters *et al.*, 2004). Trade reforms may also contribute to the increases in government revenue. The revenue effects of trade liberalisation on poverty, which can be positive or negative, depend mainly on the effectiveness of trade reforms and policies towards reducing poverty. Not only is Winters's framework useful for examining the relationship at both microeconomic and macroeconomic levels, it covers the main stakeholders in a market economy as well.

This chapter undertakes an analytical review of the trade–growth–poverty nexus in a global setting. Since the issue of poverty remains inherent to developing economies, major attention is devoted to these countries. The findings of the major empirical studies conducted to date are synthesised in terms of Winters's four transmission channels to give a coherent comprehension of the key dimensions of the relationship. The rest of this chapter is planned as follows. Section 2.2 presents the concepts and measurements of poverty and economic inequality, the characteristics of the poor, the causes of poverty, and the approaches to poverty reduction. Section 2.3 discusses the concepts and measurements of trade liberalisation, the benefits of trade to the economy and the poor, and the practice of trade policy in developing countries. Section 2.4 explains the effects of trade liberalisation on poverty in the Winters setting. Section 2.5 provides a review of the studies that have examined this relationship in Vietnam. Section 2.6 recapitulates the analysis and summarises the research on the trade–growth–poverty nexus. Section 2.7 concludes the chapter.

2.2   Poverty and economic inequality

The reduction in poverty should command a high priority for the governments of developing countries. A thorough understanding of poverty is a prerequisite for any poverty reduction strategy. Various approaches have been developed to measure poverty as a multidimensional concept. The comprehension of the characteristics of the poor, as well as of the causes of poverty, is essential for the policies towards poverty reduction. The multidimensional characteristics of poverty change the approaches for addressing poverty. Inequality is seen to become an important dimension of poverty.

Measurement of poverty

One of the most important and difficult tasks for empirical studies on poverty is the definition and measurement of poverty. Poverty or affluence is the degree of constraint on economic choice behaviour; poverty is a property of an individual's plight, rather than a characteristic of the individual, or of his pattern of behaviour (Watts, 1968). The concept of poverty is historically derived from thoughts of subsistence, basic needs, and relative deprivation. People are poor when their incomes are insufficient to get the minimum necessities for physical needs. Basic needs include the minimum consumption needs of a family, such as food, shelter, and clothing, and essential public services, such as safe water, sanitation, public transport, health care, and education. Relative deprivation occurs in income and in material and social conditions. The concept of poverty has been developed from its initial, exclusive focus on income and consumption to a focus on multidimensional deprivation (UNDP, 2005). According to Sen's conceptual framework, poverty covers functionings and capabilities. Some basic functionings are life expectancy, infant mortality, and adult literacy. More complex functionings include achieving self-respect, participating in social and/or political life, or being happy in one's work. Capabilities are a set of real opportunities, such as the ability to read and write, to live long, to avoid mortality during infancy and childhood, and to have human rights (Sen, 1993, 2005). Although advanced in the understanding of poverty, Sen's approach is not easy to use as a measure (McCulloch *et al.*, 2001).

In a bid to address poverty, the World Bank (1990) defines it as the inability to attain a minimal standard of living. The inclusion of other dimensions of poverty, such as nutrition, life expectancy, under-five mortality, and school enrolment rates, in the consumption-based measure of minimal standards of living suggests that poverty is multidimensional. The World Bank (2001) acknowledges poverty as a multidimensional concept, encompassing material deprivation (e.g. starvation, lack of shelter and clothing, illness), low levels of education and health care, institutional discrimination, impediments from social barriers and norms, and vulnerability. These dimensions of poverty can be categorised as lack of opportunity, or vulnerability, or powerlessness, or their combination. All this deprivation be referred to as capability deprivation (Sen, 1989; UN, 2005). The measurement of poverty is, thus, a problem of finding a logical synthesis of many dimensions (McCulloch *et al.*, 2001). Some common measures of poverty are summarised in Table 2.1.

The dichotomy between these different concepts of poverty leads to alternative approaches to measuring poverty: monetary, capability (CA), social exclusion (SE), and participatory approaches (PA). The monetary approach defines poverty as a shortfall in income or consumption from a benchmark, commonly the poverty line. The social exclusion approach centres on the process and dynamics of deprivation. The participatory approach gets people involved in decisions about what it means to be poor and the magnitude of poverty. Poverty rates will empirically vary according to the approach selected (UNDP, 2005). Ravallion and Chen (2009) classify these approaches as either welfarist or nonwelfarist. The former is, in fact, the monetary approach. The capability, social exclusion, and participatory approaches are seen to have evolved from the monetary approach.

The benchmark, the basic tool to define and measure poverty, is the poverty line benchmark. The level of income or consumption used to classify households as being poor or not poor is defined as a poverty line. Poverty is commonly measured by the poverty head count index (the incidence of poverty): the share of households whose income or consumption is below a certain level of income or expenditure in a country or region. In addition to the poverty head count index,

Table 2.1 Some common measures of poverty

Poverty measure	Method of measurement	Author/Institution
Head count	HCR = H/N where HCR is head count rate of poverty (incidence of poverty), H is the number of poor individuals, N is the total population	World Bank (1990), United Nations (2005)
Poverty gap	Total Poverty Gap : $TPG = \sum_{i=1}^{H}(z - y_i)$ Average Poverty Gap: $\qquad$ APG = TPG/N Normalised Poverty Gap: $\qquad$ NPG = APG/z Average Income Shortfall: $\quad$ AIS=TPG/H Normalised Income Shortfall: NIS=AIS/z where z is a poverty line, y_i is the individual income	United Nations (2005), Foster *et al.* (2010)
Squared poverty gap	$$P\alpha = \frac{1}{N}\sum_{i=1}^{H}\left(\frac{z - y_i}{z}\right)^{\alpha}$$ P_α: Foster–Greer–Thorbecke (FGT) indexes $\alpha = 0$: P_o is the HCR or the incidence of poverty $\alpha = 1$: P_1 is the poverty gap or the depth of poverty $\alpha = 2$: P_2 is the squared poverty gap or the severity of poverty	Foster *et al.* (1984, 2010)
Watts index	$$W = \frac{1}{N}\sum_{i=1}^{H}\left[\ln(z) - \ln(y_i)\right]$$	Watts (1968), United Nations (2005)
MPI	Multidimensional Poverty Index (MPI)	UNDP (2010), Alkire and Santos (2010, 2011, 2013), Alkire and Foster (2011)

Multidimensional Poverty Index (MPI)

Health		Education		Standards of living						
Child mortality	*Nutrition*	*Years of schooling*	*Child enrolment*	*Electricity*	*Drinking water*	*Sanitation*	*Flooring*	*Cooking fuel*	*Assets*	

poverty is also often measured by the poverty gap index (the depth of poverty) or the squared poverty gap index (the severity of poverty). The former adds up the distance to which poor households fall below the poverty line. The latter, which is the sum of the squared poverty gap, aims to take into consideration inequality amongst the poor. These measures of poverty are based on the approach developed by Foster *et al.* (1984) (Table 2.1).

A desirable measure of poverty and inequality has four criteria: anonymity, population independence, monotonicity, and distributional sensitivity. The principles of anonymity and population independence mean that the measure of poverty should be irrespective of who are the poor and of what is the size of the country's population. The monotonicity principle states that the country's poverty line does not change if some income is added to someone living below the poverty line, provided that all other incomes remain unchanged. According to the distributional sensitivity principle, *ceteris paribus*, if some income is transferred from a poor to a rich person, the economy as a whole will be poorer or more inequitable, and vice versa. These principles have been discussed at length in several studies: for instance, Sen (1976), Foster *et al.* (1984), the United Nations (2005), and Todaro and Smith (2009). These studies also lay the foundation for many measures of poverty and inequality.

The World Bank follows the monetary approach and defines a consumption-based poverty line as the expenditure necessary to buy a minimum standard of nutrition and other basic necessities, plus the extra cost of participating in the everyday life of society. Consequently, the international poverty line is estimated to be US$1 per person per day (lower poverty line) and US$2 (upper poverty line)[1] (World Bank, 1990, 2001). As assembled by Ravallion *et al.* (2008) and Chen and Ravallion (2010), the latest version of the dollar-a-day international poverty line is US$1.25 per person per day at 2005 prices, and the other lines are also in use. Deaton (2010), however, argues that the confusion of the purchasing power parity (PPP) exchange rates causes measures of global poverty to be sensitive. These contradictions in poverty statistics result in difficulty in identifying the trends in world poverty (Deaton, 2001, 2002). Extreme poverty in the world has declined substantially over the past three decades (Figure 2.1).

For convenience, each nation has had its own set of poverty lines, called country-specific poverty lines, that reflect a minimal level of consumption or income or, in particular, a minimal basket of goods and services that people within the country can afford. One advantage may be that national poverty lines are not affected by international comparisons. The use of poverty lines, whether international or national, is generally subject to several constraints. However, they are useful, allowing poverty policymakers to count the poor, target resources, and monitor poverty progress against a clear benchmark (UN, 2005). By virtue of its simplicity, the poverty line has been used widely, especially in the common measures of poverty.

One of the most notable poverty indexes is the MPI (Table 2.1). This index is primarily based on the capability approach, with a combination of the conventional and new approaches. It measures poverty by using three dimensions: living standards, health, and education. These dimensions are reflected in 10 indicators, each with equal weight within its dimensions. A household is poor by the MPI if it is poor in at least two to six indicators (UNDP, 2010). Vietnam's MPI

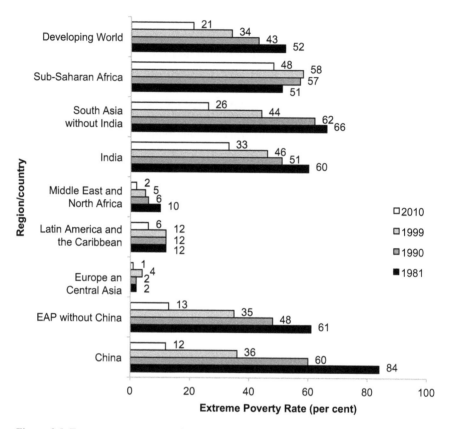

Figure 2.1 Extreme poverty rates by region (per cent), 1981–2010
Source: Based on Olinto *et al.* (2013)

has been 0.075 over the period 2000–2008, compared with the other East Asian countries (Table 2.2).

Characteristics of the Poor

The World Bank (1990) has documented several characteristics of the poor, some of which are still valid today. First, poverty has regional features. The poor mainly live in rural areas and engage in agricultural and associated activities (Olinto *et al.*, 2013).[2] Poverty is thus more severe in rural areas. The urban poor have a higher level of income, visibility, and vocality than their rural counterparts. Amongst the poor, poverty can vary substantially according to level of income, family size, age, and sex. There is generally a lower level of education. The poor also have few assets, as well as low incomes: land is usually their most valuable asset. They

Table 2.2 Poverty indicators in some selected East Asian countries, 2000–2008

Country	MPI	Head count (per cent)	PPP US$1.25 a day (per cent)	National poverty line (per cent)
Cambodia	0.263	53.90	25.80	30.10
Indonesia	0.095	20.80	29.40	16.70
Lao People's Democratic Republic	0.267	47.30	44.00	33.50
Malaysia	..	..	< 2	..
Myanmar	0.088	14.20	..	32.00
Philippines	0.067	12.60	22.60	..
Thailand	0.006	7.10	< 2	..
Vietnam	0.075	14.30	21.50	28.90

Source: UNDP (2010)

typically use land unproductively, owing to their lack of knowledge, capital, and access to credit. Their inherently difficult access to land impinges upon income opportunities, and thereby aggravates poverty. Generally, most poor households have few assets and receive small and sporadic incomes.[3]

The poor are also believed to have several informal sources of income, mainly from agricultural activities, in which they can be self-employed or wage labourers. As noted by the United Nations (2005), in developing countries and transitional economies household sources of income vary more than types of consumption. They can be from farm and nonfarm employment, informal sector jobs, and transfers or remittances.[4] These activities are typically unstable and vulnerable because of unanticipated events. More significantly, family incomes and savings vary substantially by season. In most periods, their incomes from agriculture are lower than their consumption, so the poor often resort to other sources of income, such as borrowing, even though their access to formal credit from financial institutions is very limited. The poor spend almost all their yearly income primarily on food. As a result, their welfare is very sensitive to the relative prices of food staples. For these characteristics, poor households could easily and repeatedly fall into poverty or escape poverty by income shocks. Poverty is, therefore, usually believed to be transient rather than chronic.[5]

In addition to income sources, consumption within a poor household is commonly decided primarily by males or income-earning adults. The reason is very straightforward: most poor households are headed by men. As a result, women and children are most likely to suffer from deprivation, although women generally devote most of their incomes to their family. Income disparity between households headed by men and women is largely attributed to the difference in wages between male and female labourers. In reality, female employment has tended to increase in recent years in some countries. In Vietnam, women account for 77 per cent of the labour force (World Bank, 2012b). The income or consumption measures of poverty and inequality find it difficult to explain the income distribution within households. There is evidence that a strong discrimination against females exists in areas such as nutrition, medical care, education, and inheritance (Todaro and Smith, 2009).

Socially, the poor on the whole have a lower position than do other groups in society. Being in the low class prevents them from having full access to public services. They usually have low access to social services due to the barriers of knowledge, culture, and ethnicity. Therefore, although public services are made available to the poor, they are unable to use them fully. A thorough understanding of vulnerability of the poor will help to demystify the causes of poverty, in order to be able to devise policies towards addressing poverty.

Causes of poverty

The World Bank (2001) divides the causes of poverty into three groups. In the first group, poverty results from a lack of the income and assets that enable acquisition of basic needs: food, shelter, clothing, and acceptable levels of health and education. In the second group, the poor are voiceless and powerless in the institutions of state and society. They are normally discriminated against by state and social institutions that prevent them from obtaining new economic opportunities, social power, and security. The third group of reasons for poverty covers the poor's vulnerability to the shocks of income, natural disaster, and illness. Besides these three general groups, poverty can result from inequality associated with gender, ethnicity, and racism.

Beyond the World Bank's framework, the persistence of poverty could be ascribed to social and cultural factors, possession of low-productivity assets, and a lack of crucial knowledge, skills, and collective education. Technological change may also render poor individuals' employment unstable, as improving technology will exclude less well-trained and educated people, who mostly constitute the poor (UN, 2005). Poverty is a combined effect of some economic, social, and political processes that act on and reinforce each other (World Bank, 2001). More broadly, as Rodrik (2000) puts it, 'poverty is naturally associated with market imperfections and incompleteness . . . An exclusive focus on consumption or income levels constitutes too narrow an approach to development.'

Alleviation of poverty

As generalised by the World Bank (1990), the poor's access to opportunities for earnings and their capability to respond are two important determinants of poverty. The World Bank's general policy framework for poverty reduction is, on the one hand, to increase the incomes of the poor by pursuing a labour-intensive growth strategy that requires a full combination of a policy package. On the other hand, the World Bank calls for investment in human capital for the poor, by providing them with basic education and health to improve their productivity and capability, so that they can take advantage of earning opportunities. Economic growth is seen to be an underpinning for the World Bank framework. Perkins *et al.* (2006), however, note that the focus on growth as a central solution for poverty needs to be justified in the case of 'immiserising growth', where the poor's average income declines despite high growth in the economy. This is one of the paradoxes in the literature on trade distortions (Bhagwati, 1958, 1968; Bhagwati *et al.*, 1978).

The World Bank (2001) develops a more general framework for action that emphasises three important, intrinsic values for the poor: promoting opportunity, facilitating empowerment, and enhancing security. This new approach needs action on all three fronts, through combination of many social agents: government, civil society, the private sector, and the poor themselves. More importantly, the new framework highlights the crucial role of institutions in economic development and poverty reduction. This framework therefore aims to provide the poor with economic and social opportunities, provided that the economy maintains high growth and employment. The poor can benefit from growth only as long as they take part in and contribute to the growth. Thus far, a sustained reduction in poverty may only be coupled with sustained growth (World Bank, 1990).

Trade development is crucial to the development of a country, since trade strategies are closely related to development strategies (Krueger, 1998). Among the policies potentially capable of addressing poverty, trade policy is believed to be by far the most effective way of promoting human capital and labour-intensive growth. Trade liberalisation is regarded as a crucial part of the policy package for wealth, growth, and poverty reduction (McCulloch *et al.*, 2001). Hertel and Winters (2005) also argue that amongst poverty reduction policies, trade reform is relatively cheap, because it does not require additional government expenditure. Besides the relatively persuasive effect of trade on growth, trade liberalisation can affect many dimensions of poverty which transcend the economic domain. Berg and Krueger (2003) consider that the growth driven by trade liberalisation may be different from normal growth, because this kind of growth can be particularly anti- or pro-poor.

In reality, apart from providing the poor with many opportunities for income and employment, trade can create positive externalities that are pro-poor. The increase in income helps the poor to achieve higher status, empowerment, and security in society. More importantly, as argued by Rodrik (2002), trade reforms accompany institutional reforms: the more open a country, the more effective its institutions. The effectiveness of institutions will help the poor to reduce their vulnerability to the risks of economic shocks, natural disasters, and illness (World Bank, 2001). Trade liberalisation can thereby address poverty in several dimensions. Although underpinning the solutions to poverty reduction, trade liberalisation is certainly not a panacea (Rodrik, 2010). It should be combined and accorded with other policies to form a policy package in which trade policy should be the key.

Inequality

Inequality and poverty are different but closely related cousins. The difference between poverty and inequality has raised some concerns in the literature. Conventionally, poverty concentrates on those whose absolute standards of living fall below some threshold level such as a poverty line – that is, the poor – whereas inequality reflects the variations in relative living standards throughout the whole society (World Bank, 1990; McCulloch *et al.*, 2001; McKay, 2002). Simply, inequality refers to the gap between the rich and the poor within a nation or between nations in terms of income, consumption, wealth or assets, and opportunity. One of the consequences of inequality is that unequal economic opportunities lead to unequal outcomes and reinforce unequal political power (World Bank, 2006). McCulloch *et al.* (2001) claim that inequality can influence poverty via its effect on growth, because growth is a pathway through which trade affects poverty. For Perkins *et al.* (2006), inequality is an important determinant of poverty in the sense that inequality affects the quantity of poverty generated by a given level of income. There is evidence that inequality can increase in defiance of an overall reduction in poverty occurring at the bottom end of the income distribution (World Bank, 2001). According to Todaro and Smith (2009), inequality is a crucial factor for understanding how the depths of poverty, the impacts of market, and policy changes affect the poor. In short, the level of income, combined with the extent of inequality, determines the magnitude of absolute poverty. Inequality can be considered as a dimension of poverty.

Todaro and Smith (2009) suggest two main approaches to measuring income distribution: the personal or size distribution of income and the functional or distributive factor share distribution of income. The first measure concentrates on individuals or households and the total income they receive. Several methods are grounded on this approach. A common method is to partition the population into fifths (quintiles) or tenths (deciles) according to their ascended income levels and to calculate the percentage of total national income each income group receives. Another common measure is the Kuznets ratio, measured by the proportion of the income received by the top 20 per cent to the income earned by the bottom 40 per cent of the population. The Lorenz curve, a well-known measure of inequality, calculates the percentage of total income that a particular percentage of income recipients actually acquire. On the grounds of the Lorenz curve, the Gini coefficient, an aggregate measure of inequality, is built up. It is the ratio of the area between the diagonal and the Lorenz curve to half the total square area in the Lorenz chart. The Gini coefficient is often used along with the Lorenz curve to study income and wealth distribution. The second measure of income distribution is based on the theory of functional distribution of income, which defines the total national income that each of the factors of production (labour, capital, and land) receives. Income is distributed in accordance with the function or contribution of factors of production: for instance, wages for labour, rents for owners of land, profits for capitalists. This theory, however, has yet to take into account the case of the imperfect competitive market. The two approaches suggested by these authors lay the foundation for the measurement of inequality in countries. Note that the measurements of poverty using the FGT indexes, such as P_1 or P_2 (Table 2.1), are also the measurements of inequality.

With respect to world inequality, Milanovic (2006) suggests three concepts to measure global income inequality. Concept one is the inequality among countries' mean incomes. Concept two is the inequality among countries' mean incomes weighted by countries' populations. Concept three is the inequality between world individuals or global inequality. The classification of these concepts is based on the kinds of data used to calculate inequality. In contrast to many orthodox views and indicators of inequality, such as the Kuznets curve that shows the relationship between per capita income and inequality, the trickle-down effect hypothesis, and the Gini coefficient, which only depict the average picture of the income and wealth distribution, Piketty (2014) has recently conducted a painstaking analysis which indicates that inequality has been rising at the top (wealthiest) 1 per cent of society in recent decades. This sharp rise in inequality is mostly due to the wage inequality between the top one-percentage income share and the rest of society. This steady surge in inequality is contrary to what the well-known Kuznets inverse-U pattern predicts. This increasing inequality would be particularly harmful to growth and poverty reduction: if the very rich, who accumulate a huge fortune, save more and invest less, the trickle-down effect would not hold true. Despite some likely disadvantages, the traditional indicators of inequality are still useful for analysis. Compared with other countries in the regions, the level of income inequality in Vietnam was comparatively low in the 2000s (Table 2.3). This suggests that the inequality situation in this country is at least contemporarily not among the most concerned issues, although the pace of income inequality in Vietnam is considered to be rising, which is likely to have a strong impact on poor households. The income inequality is shown to be higher in the countries with higher income levels, such as Malaysia or Thailand. This issue would matter much more once Vietnam becomes a middle- or high-income country.

Table 2.3 Income inequality in some selected countries, 2003–2012

Country	Quintile ratio	Palma ratio	Gini coefficient
Cambodia	5.6	1.5	36.0
Indonesia	6.3	1.7	38.1
Lao People's Democratic Republic	5.9	1.6	36.7
Malaysia	11.3	2.6	46.2
Myanmar	..	..	..
Philippines	8.3	2.2	43.0
Thailand	6.9	1.8	39.4
Vietnam	5.9	1.5	35.6

Source: UNDP (2014)

By and large, the multidimensional attributes of poverty make the measurement of poverty difficult. How can one measure capture all of the dimensions of poverty? Such a measure is, according to the World Bank's terms, a comprehensive, multidimensional frame. Practically, the methods that satisfy the desired criteria are, to some extent, the best choices. The measurement of poverty and inequality is a prerequisite for the foundation of poverty reduction policies. Addressing poverty requires a multidimensional framework for action, which is usually a burden on governments in poor countries and which is sometimes beyond their capability. Poor countries often have recourse to external aid to cope with poverty. They are, however, very capable of promoting trade to stimulate growth. Growth and trade development can ultimately create a natural and effective mechanism to help countries reduce poverty. Nevertheless, trade policies in developing countries are not always pro-poor. In some cases, they can be harmful to the poor.

2.3   Trade liberalisation and trade policy in developing countries

The positive effects of trade liberalisation have led to the adoption of trade liberalisation as the underpinning for the economic development strategy in many developing countries. Amongst these countries, some previously closed economies have liberalised trade and become transitional economies, moving towards open and market systems. The process of liberalisation or transition is not always even. Some developing economies are not successful with their trade liberalisation strategy for a variety of reasons, deriving from internal or external constraints. One of the main reasons has been inadequate trade policy reforms that preclude a country from the benefits of trade liberalisation and that impoverish its citizens. This section reviews the issues of trade liberalisation to provide the foundation for the analysis of its impacts on poverty in developing countries.

Measurement of trade liberalisation and openness

The concept of trade liberalisation, with its related terms such as trade openness and trade reform, is diverse and ambiguous. Trade liberalisation can comprise tariff liberalisation, relative price neutrality, and tariff quota substitution or the second-best liberalisation. The conception of trade liberalisation is ambiguous at both the conceptual and empirical levels (Greenaway *et al.*, 2002). Trade reforms are the reforms of trade policy towards trade liberalisation. Trade openness usually refers to the outcomes of trade reforms. The concept of trade reform is relevant to a process of trade policies, and trade openness is commonly the outcome of the process. Trade liberalisation and trade openness are closely related and imply both trade policies and outcomes. According to the World Bank (1987) and Thomas and Nash (1991), trade liberalisation means a neutral trade regime: zero rates of protection or no discrimination between the exportables and exportables. In particular, trade liberalisation includes not only the reduction in average levels of protection and the average dispersion of rates of protection, but also the changing form of protection from quantitative restrictions to tariffs. Note that the levy of an equal rate of protection on imports and exports can also result in the neutrality of a trade regime. Trade policy reforms do not necessarily induce trade liberalisation per se (Shafaeddin, 2005). Harrison (1996) points out that neutrality also means that incentives are neutral between saving a unit of foreign exchange via import and earning a unit of foreign exchange via export. More broadly, Berg and Krueger (2003) define the openness of an economy to be the degree to which a country and its foreign trade counterparts can transact without incurring the artificial costs of government interventions, delays, or uncertainties which are not imposed on domestic transactions. These arguments suggest that trade liberalisation or trade openness reflects a country's movement towards neutrality and indiscrimination of trade policy.

The divergence in the concept of trade liberalisation has led to many attempts to measure openness and to the diversification of such measures of openness. McCulloch *et al.* (2001) outline two different approaches to measuring openness: in practice and in policy. The former emphasises the importance of trade in a country's economic activities and the existence of actual price distortion, which governments cannot control. The latter stresses the existence and extent of policy measures designed to manipulate trade that government can control. Baldwin (1989) suggests that measures of openness can be based on outcome or incidence (see Table 2.4). Outcome-based measures, comprising price-based measures or trade flow–based measures, evaluate the deviation of the observed outcome from the outcome without trade barriers. Incidence-based measures quantify the frequency of occurrence of various types of nontariff barriers. Both incidence and outcome measures are flawed, however (Pritchett, 1996).

These two approaches to the measurement of openness both attempt to link the outcomes with policy elements of trade liberalisation. Although strongly insisting that trade is an important determinant of growth, the International Monetary Fund (2006) admits that none of the measures of openness are altogether satisfactory in the studies of the trade–growth nexus. The measurements of trade openness are commonly used to classify countries' orientation and to analyse the relationship between, for instance, trade openness and economic growth. The data used for these aims are primarily cross-country data and/or macroeconomic data. Almost none of these measures were developed for the purpose of relating trade openness to poverty, partly because poverty itself is a multidimensional concept that is not solely determined by trade liberalisation.

Gains from trade

At the macroeconomic level, neoclassical economics accounts for poverty through economic growth by the change in demand for labour and the trickle-down effect (Aghion and Bolton, 1997). In the neoclassical theory of international trade, trade liberalisation affects economic growth through the gains from exchange, resource allocation, and economies of scale. As trade barriers are lowered, consumers benefit from these gains from trade as a result of lower import prices. In addition, when trade barriers are lower, firms reallocate resources and specialise

Table 2.4 Measurement of trade openness: a summary

Author/Institution	Openness measure	Method
1. Outcome-based measures		
World Bank (1987), Berg and Krueger (2003), Leamer (1988), Pritchett (1996), Frankel and Romer (1999), Spilimbergo *et al.* (1999), Alesina *et al.* (2003), Alcalá and Ciccone (2004), Squalli and Wilson (2011)	Trade ratios	M/GDP, X/GDP, (X + M)/GDP; where X = export, M = import, GDP = gross domestic products
Leamer (1988), Maggi and Rodriguez-Clare (1998), OECD (2010)	Import penetration ratios	Dividing imports of a given commodity by the total domestic supply of that commodity. Total domestic supply is defined as imports plus gross output of the domestic producers minus exports of that commodity.
Alcalá and Ciccone (2004), Esqueda and Assefa (2011)	Real openness	Imports plus exports divided by purchasing power parity GDP. This is a constant price equivalent of the simple trade ratio measures, or the total trade as a percentage of GDP measured in constant prices.
Leamer (1988), Frankel and Romer (1999), Edwards (1992), Dollar (1992), Hiscox and Kastner (2002)	Adjusted trade flows	Deviations of actual trade flows from predicted free trade flows (the counterfactual) to form measures of trade policy. Hecksher–Ohlin factor model and gravity model are based on this approach.
Linnemann (1966), Aitken (1973), Frankel *et al.* (1995), Guttmann and Richards (2006)	Gravity model	Trade between two nations is an increasing function of the incomes of those nations and a decreasing function of the distance between them; although other variables, including whether the countries share a common border and/or a common language, are often added to the model.
Dollar (1992), Rogoff (1996), Edwards (1997)	Price-based	Seeking price distortions in either goods markets (through comparison across international prices) or foreign exchange markets (generally through the black market premium).

2. Incidence-based measures

World Bank (1987), Anderson (2003), Love and Lattimore (2009)	Tariffs	Simple tariff averages, trade-weighted tariff averages, revenue from duties as a percentage of total trade (a shortcut method for estimating the import weighted average tariff), and the effective rate of protection (ERP).
World Bank (1987), Bhagwati (1989), Edwards (1992), Deardorff and Stern (1997), Staiger (2012), UNCTAD (2013)	Nontariff barriers	Content provisions, restrictions on services trade, trade-related investment measures, administrative classification, export subsidies.
World Bank (1987), Greenaway and Nam (1988), Leamer (1988), Alam (1991), Anderson and Neary (1994, 2003), Sachs and Warner (1995), Nash and Andriamananjara (1999), Wacziarg (2001), Baldwin (2003)	Composite indexes	Measures based on subjective evaluations of trade barriers, structural characteristics, and institutional arrangements. One of them is the World Bank's outward orientation index.

in sectors or industries that have comparative advantage. Finally, reduced trade protection encourages firms to expand production and output in order to obtain lower average total costs and to gain production efficiency. The gains from trade can be static in the short term or dynamic in the long term.

Feenstra (1995) identifies six channels through which trade policy affects welfare. First, trade protection causes a dead-weight loss from distorting consumption and production decisions. Second, trade provides possible gains from improving terms of trade. However, the decline in terms of trade can offset the gains from trade, leading to immiserising growth, making a country worse off (Bhagwati, 1958; Thirlwall, 2000). Third, trade creates a gain or loss due to changes in the scale of firms. Fourth, trade leads to a gain or loss from shifting profits between countries. Fifth, trade renders changes in wages that affect individuals directly. Sixth, trade gives a variety of products and satisfies people's demand. Apart from the above channels, trade liberalisation also conditions entrepreneurial spirit to thrive, comparative advantages to be disclosed and taken advantage of, and resources to be efficiently allocated. It thereby reduces the economic costs of growth. In addition, access to cheap, better-quality imports at the right exchange rate increases the competitiveness of domestic production (Krueger, 1998; Rodrik, 2002).

Neoclassical economics provides the foundation for some orthodox arguments, such as that trade is good for growth, and growth is good for the poor; or that globalisation will make everyone better off in the long run;[6] or that poor countries can benefit from globalisation since they have comparative advantage in terms of labour-intensive products that require unskilled labourers, who are primarily poor (Krueger, 1998; Berg and Krueger, 2003; Dollar and Kraay, 2004; Perkins *et al.*, 2006). Some studies oppose the above arguments: they claim that the mainstream theories are unable to deal adequately with the real problems that globalisation is causing, in terms of its impacts on intellectual property, trade, global financial markets, natural resources, and the environment, or that the gains from trade are highly unequal, and the poor do not always benefit from globalisation (see, for instance, Harrison and McMillan, 2007; Stiglitz, 2008). While advocating the role of international trade in spurring economic growth, neoclassical international economics does not define the relationship between trade liberalisation or trade policy and economic growth (Pacheco-Lopez and Thirlwall, 2009). However, Brown and Srinivasan (2007) observe that the poor countries whose economies have transfers are better off in the free trade world equilibrium than those without transfers. These observations suggest that the theory of trickle-down mechanism and the gains from trade should be justified to explain the impacts of trade liber-alisation on economic growth and poverty.

The WTO, trade, and the poor in developing countries

Poor countries do not always have easy access to industrial countries' markets, notwithstanding the large potential benefits of international trade. Industrial countries erect trade barriers that can be nontariff barriers or tariff escalation, imposed mainly on agricultural products and even on manufacturing products, and that aim to protect their domestic producers by impeding exports from developing countries (World Bank, 1990; McCulloch *et al.*, 2001). Trade barriers cost developing countries and developed countries approximately 1.37 per cent and 0.37 per cent of their annual GDP, respectively. They cost, in some areas, the equivalent of up to 2 per cent of GDP (Patrick and Ralph, 2009). Exports from developing countries are primarily labour-intensive, less value added, belonging to some main industries such as food processing, textiles, and clothing, which provide employment as one of the main income sources of the poor. Poor countries are believed to gain considerably from trade liberalisation in industrial economies. The poor in middle-income countries may receive most benefits, due to their higher capability to respond to the export market. How much the gains are depends on the degree of value added of exporters' products: the higher the value added level of products, the higher the profits from exports of the products (World Bank, 1990). There is evidence, however, that trade protection by indus-trial countries increases with the level of processing and, while the WTO's rules exclude most formal trade barriers, many implicit trade barriers have tended to increase (Todaro and Smith, 2009).

In addition, as predicted by the Prebisch–Singer hypothesis of the declining terms of trade for primary products,[7] developing countries that chiefly rely on pri-mary exports will have difficulty with economic development and poverty reduc-tion, unless they reform their trade system effectively. As a likely result of trade liberalisation, the poor in countries importing food probably suffer from higher prices of food staples. This may also be one of the predicted effects of the Doha Development Agenda (DDA) (Hertel and Winters, 2005). These viewpoints are also reflected in the trade pessimist arguments.[8] The other side of the coin is that higher agricultural prices benefit agricultural exporters. Developing countries' share of world agricultural GDP rose from 54 per cent in 1980 to 65 per cent in 2004. They achieved much faster growth in agriculture (2.6 per cent a year) than that of industrial countries (0.9 per cent a year) (World Bank, 2007).

Recent world trade agreements have increasingly concentrated on the benefits to developing countries. Two agreements may have great potential benefits for developing countries and the poor. The Uruguay Round Agreement on agriculture in the 1990s was described as a significant achievement. Anderson and Morris (2000) consider this to be the first time that a comprehensive set of disciplines was imposed on the trade distortion measures that have impinged upon agricultural products. Further achievements in agricultural trade in favour of the poor would not be easy to obtain in the Doha round (DDA). The DDA stressed three pillars of agricultural distortion: market access, export subsidy, and domestic support. If successful, the ongoing DDA is expected to provide developing countries with immense opportunities for penetrating markets of developed countries, thereby helping them to reduce poverty. Conversely, the scenarios provided by Hertel and Winters (2005) and Anderson and Martin (2005) demonstrate that the DDA could have only a relatively small effect on reducing poverty. They conclude that the amount that the poor in developing countries will be able to take advantage of market opportunities provided by the DDA will depend on the complementary domestic reforms in these developing countries. The most recent ongoing trade agreement is the Trans-Pacific Partnership (TPP), which aims to bring 12 countries in the Pacific region, including Vietnam, into the largest free trade area in the world. Some sceptics, however, argue that the TPP would not benefit the poor, because its priority is to support international corporations in the regions, and the trickle-down effect is not always observable.

Trade policy in developing countries

The issues of trade policy and trade reforms in developing countries and transitional economies remain contentious. Developing countries typically have complicated and ambiguous trade policies. Although widely believed to damage economic development, trade restrictions are frequently in use in many countries, especially in developing countries (Rodrik, 2013). While McKinnon (1979) suggests that the main reason that they are so common in practice is the poor performance of capital markets, Rodrik (2013) argues for the existence of the interest groups in the economy. In terms of the motivation for openness of the economy, some developing countries open up their economies after unsuccessfully experiencing the import substitution strategy. Some countries that have to transition to an open market economy from autarchies usually face an incomplete transition with dichotomous trade policies. Hence, trade policy reforms in developing countries virtually induce substantial adjustment costs.

Conceptually, trade policy can be outward-oriented or inward-oriented. The outward-oriented strategy, also referred to as an export promotion strategy, has no discrimination in favour of export promotion or against import substitution. Outward-oriented trade policies prefer tariffs to quantitative restrictions. For these trade policies, the exchange rate is maintained at a level that provides equal incentives to produce exports, as well as import substitutes. The overall protection is generally low, and the variance between the extreme rates of protection is narrow. The inward-oriented strategy, also referred to as an import substitution strategy, by contrast, is biased in favour of domestic production and against foreign trade. It favours quantitative restrictions over tariffs. Governments pursuing these policies often overvalue the exchange rate and regulate industrial incentives using a detailed and expensive bureaucracy. In reality, a country's trade policies have elements of both strategies (World Bank, 1987).

The classification of a country as outward or inward oriented is rather intricate. Most developing countries tend to open their economies and pursue the outward-oriented strategy to various degrees. Before reforming, their trade policies usually have some common characteristics. First, their trade policies are complicated and dichotomous. They serve conflicting objectives, which governments are unable to control. Second, trade policies in developing countries normally contain more nontariff than tariff instruments. The nontariff instruments, which are diverse and change unexpectedly, consist of import licenses, voluntary export restraints, exemptions, quotas, official reference prices, foreign exchange allocations, tariff quotas, and protection-equivalent tariffs. These instruments lessen the transparency of a country's structure of protection and the certainty of the import system. Nontariff barriers are thus more difficult to administer and more subject to delay, inefficiency, and rent-seeking activities. As a consequence, the link between domestic and international prices is extremely uneven (Thomas and Nash, 1991; Todaro and Smith, 2009). Third, these policies are likely to harbour interest groups that may have power to manipulate policymaking for rent-seeking activities. Fourth, tariff rates and their variances are generally high. Tariff reduction is thereby usually a key content of a trade reform package. Fifth, trade policies cover a long list of exemptions and prohibitions. Sixth, they are implemented with a cumbersome and expensive bureaucracy. Due to these common characteristics, not many developing countries pursuing an outward-oriented strategy develop successfully.

Efficient trade policies in open economies allow developing countries to expand trade, and thereby to grow faster, as well as to reduce poverty. Those countries that have unilaterally reduced their trade barriers have grown faster (Stoeckel *et al.*, 2007). Though the potential gains from trade are enormous, developing countries are not likely to take advantage of international trade due primarily to their ineffective trade policies. Harrison *et al.* (2003a, 2003b) assert that trade policy reforms generally cause some households to win and some to lose. Trade policy reforms in developing countries are not always successful, and more often than not cause damage, especially to the poor. As the poor have too little power to prevent the transfers from being captured by other groups, McCulloch *et al.* (2001) argue that specific interventions in international trade (e.g. export subsidies, antidumping duties, and local content requirements) would seldom benefit them. Trade reforms are, in fact, institutional reforms (Rodrik, 2001, 2002). Institutions are the rules that shape the interaction between citizens, firms, and the state (World Bank, 2010). Institutions in developing countries are usually not effective for facilitating the reform process or for reducing poverty. Theoretically, the impacts of trade policies on developing economies themselves are difficult to observe. Research on the relationship between trade and poverty finds it difficult to trace a country's economic development in general, and its poverty in particular, to trade policy reforms (Rodrik, 2010), primarily because of the thorny issue of measurement of both trade policy reforms and poverty.

2.4   The pace of trade liberalisation and poverty

Countries have, in general, different levels of openness and speeds of poverty reduction. The level and speed of openness in Southeast Asian countries was higher than that of the South Asian region over two points in time (Table 2.5).

Table 2.5 Openness and poverty in some countries and regions, 1990 and 2010

Country	1990		2010	
	Poverty US$2.5 a day, PPP (% population)	*Openness [(Export + Import)/GDP]*	*Poverty US$2.5 a day, PPP (% population)*	*Openness [(Export + Import)/GDP]*
Southeast Asia				
Cambodia	84.4	14.8	64.5	106.1
Indonesia	91.4	37.8	60.4	41.4
Lao PDR	..	30.5	78.1	56.5
Malaysia	18.3	123.4	6.2	147.2
Myanmar	..	11.5	..	31.8
Philippines	66.4	43.1	53.3	55.1
Thailand	50.1	63.5	9.6	110.3
Vietnam	91.3	79.6	58.2	147.6
South Asia				
Bangladesh	95.0	18.8	86.2	47.2
Bhutan	..	54.2	..	94.4
India	90.8	12.7	81.1	34.4
Sri Lanka	66.4	56.1	38.2	44.7
Pakistan	93.3	27.2	76.4	34.1
Nepal	..	23.2	71.8	36.7
Maldives	..	85.1	..	62.1

Source: UNESCAP database, World Bank (2014)

The pace of poverty reduction in this region has therefore been shown to be faster than in the South Asian countries. Among the Southeast Asian countries, Thailand dramatically reduced poverty, while doubling the level of openness between 1990 and 2010. Vietnam also almost doubled the level of openness, but its reduction in poverty was not as significant as Thailand. Cambodia had the highest level of openness amongst these countries in this period.

The relationship between trade liberalisation and poverty in the South Asian region is somewhat inconsistent. The level of openness was shown to decline in Sri Lanka and Maldives, despite the reduction of poverty in Sri Lanka. India tripled the level of openness, but poverty in this country reduced just to 81.1 per cent in 2010 from 90.8 in 1990. An inverse relationship between trade liberalisation and poverty is found in the majority of countries, especially the Southeast Asian countries. However, the comparison of the pace of trade liberalisation and poverty reduction using the macroeconomic indicators is inadequate, given that the openness indices themselves have drawbacks. This link should be explored further at the microeconomic level.

2.5   Trade liberalisation and poverty: the Winters framework

The literature on trade and poverty acknowledges the difficulties in establishing the relationship between trade liberalisation and poverty, as noted previously. The main reason is that both trade policy and poverty are difficult to measure (Winters *et al.*, 2004). The neoclassical theories and studies on the openness–growth relationship have few implications for poverty. The cross-country literature ignores welfare effects at the microeconomic level (Justino *et al.*, 2008). Many significant attempts have been made to link trade openness and/or trade policy with poverty. Some studies directly link trade openness to poverty. Ravallion (2006) regresses poverty on growth and casts doubt on the presumption that trade openness reduces poverty. At the microeconomic level, a common way is to establish trade-related variables that can affect households and poverty via some theoretical pathways.

Several channels through which trade liberalisation affects households and poverty have been recognised in the literature on the trade–poverty nexus. Many studies have conducted theoretical and empirical surveys on these channels: for instance, Bannister and Thugge (2001), McCulloch *et al.* (2001), Berg and Krueger (2003), Winters (2002), Winters *et al.* (2004), Goldberg and Pavcnik (2004), Nissanke and Thorbecke (2007a), Harrison (2007), Bandara *et al.* (2011), and Santos-Paulino (2012). As discussed earlier, the channels outlined by Winters are the most plausible for investigating the linkage between trade and poverty. Trade liberalisation affects households and alleviates poverty via long-run economic growth, market distribution or prices of tradable goods, employment, and governmental spending (Figure 2.2). This section undertakes a channel-by-channel account of theory and empirical evidence on the relationship between trade liberalisation, economic growth, and poverty.

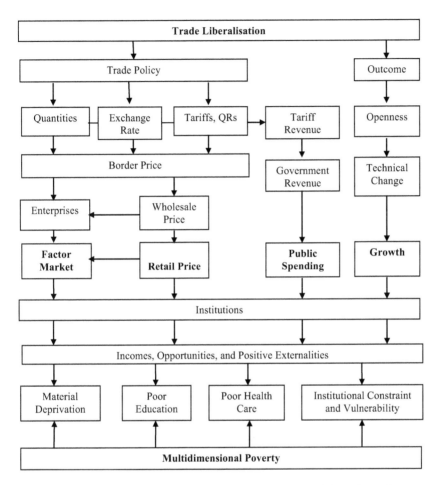

Figure 2.2 Trade liberalisation and poverty: Winters's transmission channels
Source: Adapted from Winters (2002)

Economic growth channel

Trade development benefits the poor through its contribution to economic growth. Bhagwati and Srinivasan (2002) divide the process into two stages: trade stimulates growth through accumulation and innovation, and growth reduces poverty by providing the poor with more opportunities for employment. This process is also one of the principal lessons drawn by McCulloch *et al.* (2001): openness to trade is good for growth, and growth benefits the poor. The mainstream of the literature on the relationship between trade and growth is the neoclassical growth model and its extensions. The empirical studies on the trade–growth linkage appear to be mixed. For the pathway from growth to poverty, the relationship is based on the assumption of the trickle-down effect, which postulates that growth benefits the poor through benefiting the rich. In practice, the empirical studies of the growth–poverty relationship commonly estimate the response of poverty to growth directly. The discussion of the growth effect of trade liberalisation on poverty begins with the impact of trade on growth, and then considers the impacts of growth on poverty.

Trade–Growth Causality. Many attempts have been made to relate trade openness to economic growth. Trade can explain growth through three strands of theory: the neoclassical growth model, the endogenous or new growth models, and the institutional approach. In Solow's extended classical growth model[9] (Solow, 1956), growth can be explained by capital accumulation, growth of labour force, and technical change. The starting point for the model is the aggregate production function that demonstrates the dependence of output (Y) on capital accumulation (K), labour (L), and the technological state (T) of the economy:

$$Y = Y(K, L, T) \tag{2.1}$$

The growth form of the model,

$$g_Y = (s_K \times g_K) + (s_L \times g_L) + g_T \tag{2.2}$$

suggests that the growth rate of output (g_Y) in (2.2) is the sum of the growth rate of the capital input multiplied by its share (s_k) in total output, the labour input multiplied by its share (s_L) in total output, and the technological progress (g_T).[10] While the Solow framework provides a standard method for accounting growth, it is limited to explaining long-run growth and the difference in growth patterns between countries. The model is based on the assumptions of constant returns to scale, a positive but diminished marginal product of factors, and static technology. Rate of return on investment diminishes and eventually becomes zero. Capital accumulation can maintain a higher average level of output, but is unable to sustain output growth in the long run. The model predicts that each economy will reach a steady state, poor countries will grow faster than rich counterparts, and income and growth will converge amongst economies. Evidence of such convergence appears to be inconclusive (Barro and Sala-i-Martin, 1990; Fukuda and Toya, 1995; Holmes, 2005).[11] Technology, assumed to be exogenously determined, is defined as the residual difference between the growth of output and growth of factor inputs, since it cannot be directly calculated, and is often followed from (2.2):

$$g_T = g_Y - (s_K \times g_K + s_L \times g_L) \tag{2.3}$$

The growth of Solow residual, g_T, is a part of growth that cannot be explained by capital or labour. This is a factor that captures all of the changes in technology, as well as other production factors raising productivity. Trade is widely believed to be one of the few variables in an economy that could provide a powerful explanation for the change in total productivity. This might be one of the main reasons why many studies attempt to explain growth by trade openness.

Most of the empirical studies on the openness–growth relationship are based on cross-country data and pooled regression analyses. Notable studies in this field are Balassa (1978), Krueger (1978a), Tyler (1981), Ram (1985, 1987), Sachs and Warner (1995), Frankel and Romer (1999), Hallaert (2006), Foster (2008), and Singh (2011). These studies use various measures of openness. Many reach similar conclusions: openness to trade is one of the most crucial factors in explaining the growth of GDP or GDP per capita (see a summary in Table 2.7). Although trade is arguably the main driver of economic growth and development, studies on the openness–growth linkage for Vietnam appear to be unfruitful. They largely use the Solow accounting growth model or the Social Accounting Matrix (SAM) to estimate the contribution of factors to GDP, in which trade factors have yet to be in focus. Dollar (2004), applying the results of the two similar studies (e.g. Dollar and Kraay, 2002, 2004) to the changes in policies in Vietnam, reveals that trade liberalisation is estimated to account for an increase of 0.1 per cent in the growth rate.

These attempts to link trade to growth, however, have been subject to criticism. Harrison and Hanson (1999), Rodriguez and Rodrik (2001), Berg and Krueger (2003), Winters *et al.* (2004), Foster (2008), and Singh (2010) point out several drawbacks undermining the cross-country studies. First, considerable attempts have been made to measure openness or trade policy, but none are perfect. Second, some influential studies have data problems. Third, the causality of the relationship has, to a large extent, not yet been adequately established. Openness appears endogenous and depends on growth. Fourth, trade policy is often highly correlated with other policies in the reform package (Singh, 2010). Some studies argue that scrutinised case studies of policy regimes of individual countries can provide more compelling evidence. Nevertheless, the critical shortcomings appear not to undermine the positive belief in trade liberalisation (Krueger, 1997; Srinivasan and Bhagwati, 2001).

In contrast to the neoclassical growth model, the new growth theories endogenise the technological progress. The foundation of the endogenous growth models is the accumulation of knowledge, combined with the extension of the conventional production function. Strikingly, the capital concept is extended to cover human capital: broadly, technological knowledge that generates a positive externality. By virtue of that, return on capital can be increased under the impacts of savings and investment. It is thus not necessary for the economy to reach the steady state, and the convergence of income is unlikely to occur. The new growth theories provide a more powerful explanation of different growth patterns in developing countries. Technological knowledge is arguably accumulated through the process of the spillover effect, learning by doing, and research and development (R&D), which are called dynamic economies of scale (Grossman and Helpman, 1991; Hansson, 1993).

With respect to the role of trade, Grossman and Helpman (1991) point out that the accumulation of knowledge capital depends on the cumulative volume of trade. Trade policy reforms cope with four dynamic distortions. First, they streamline the link between foreign businessmen and markets, thereby creating benefits of spill-over for the local economy. Second, trade policy reforms enhance incentives for local R&D to create the positive externality. Third, lowering the tariff as a result of trade liberalisation alleviates the static consumption distortion resulting from trade protection. Fourth, trade policy reforms reduce the static distortion arising from the noncompetitive pricing of intermediate goods. For these reasons, Grossman and Helpman conclude that trade reforms will raise the welfare of the economy. Furthermore, trade policies for trade expansion promote contacts between local and foreign residents, and thus accelerate the rate of knowledge accumulation and growth, and vice versa. Trade reforms are seen to play a more critical role in the new growth theories, compared with the classical growth model, because trade in the latter is associated with technology and greater investment (Perkins *et al.*, 2006; Mankiw, 2012), especially investment in human capital and technology that helps to sustain long-run growth. Several attempts have investigated the Grossman and Helpman hypothesis (see, for example, Young, 1991; Ederington and Minier, 2008; Anwar and Nguyen, 2011). Young (1991) uses an endogenous growth model to examine the dynamic effects of international trade and finds that, under free trade, developing countries experience rates of technical progress and GDP growth less than or equal to those under closed economies, and that free trade may improve the welfare of consumers in developing countries. More recently, Anwar and Nguyen (2011) demonstrate that, through horizontal and forward linkages, the presence of foreign firms in Vietnam significantly impacts the decision of domestic firms to export, as well as affects their export share.

Apart from the neoclassical growth model and the new growth models, insti-tutional theories provide an indispensable supplement. Berg and Krueger (2003) contend that, in the presence of other distortions, free trade might not be good for growth. Institutions, according to North, are the humanly devised constraints that shape political, economic, and social interaction. They include informal con-straints (sanctions, taboos, customs, traditions, and code of conduct) and formal rules, such as constitutions, laws, and property rights (North, 1989, 1991). In the institutional perspective, the market economy performs well only under effective institutions. The degree to which trade influences growth depends on the effectiveness of institutions. A reasonable structure and strong institutions in an economy can be helpful in minimising transaction costs due to asymmetric information, managing copyright, and abolishing barriers to new entries (North, 1981). Institutions are considered to be the main determinants of differences in prosperity across countries (Acemoglu and Robinson, 2008), and their impact on poverty is pervasive (Deolalikar *et al.*, 2002).

Trade policy reforms are not enough for an open market economy. It is neces-sary to establish institutions to facilitate markets, such as copyright protection, law systems, and institutions for macroeconomic stabilisation, social security, and conflict settlement (Rodrik, 2002): in short, institutional innovations (Perkins *et al.*, 2006). Sachs and Warner (1995) posit that the inherited structure of the economy will determine the very short-term growth of a trade reform. The reason is that the rules and principles of market guide the economy to allocate resources, but its structure and institutions ensure that market mechanisms perform well to achieve efficient resource allocation. Consequently, the institutional framework in a country is regarded as an underpinning for the trade–growth nexus. In summary, endogenous growth models suggest several channels through which trade openness spurs growth, including embodied technology, availability of inputs, associated technical assistance and learning, and reduction in networking costs (McCulloch *et al.*, 2001). Wacziarg (2001) identifies six theoretical channels that link trade policy with economic growth, grouped into three broad categories: government policy (macroeconomic policies, the size of government), allocation and distribution (price distortion, factor accumulation), and technological transmissions (importation of technological goods, foreign direct investment). These channels are considered to be covered in the above approaches. Harrison and Tang (2004) firmly conclude that, notwithstanding the debate over the trade–growth relationship, trade protection is harmful to growth, and trade openness itself is not sufficient for growth. Given high trade-induced growth, the poor in developing countries are unlikely to benefit from trade; worse, growth may widen the gap between the rich and the poor.

Growth–Poverty Causality. Economic growth is widely believed to play the central role in the reduction of poverty in the long run. As countries become wealthier, not only does the incidence of income poverty decline, but other well-being indexes, such as education and health, also tend to be improved on average (World Bank, 2001). Winters *et al.* (2004) argue that economic growth raises incomes and creates trickle-down effects. The question arises whether growth benefits the poor. Bhagwati and Srinivasan (2002) consider that the effect of growth on poverty depends on the labour market. If the growing areas accompany an inelastic supply of labour, growth will provide more jobs and reduce poverty. Growth will not affect poverty if the poor are not in the growing areas. In most cases, growth benefits the poor in the same way growth benefits the others in society. Average income within each quintile is usually found to increase if GDP grows faster than population (Berg and Krueger, 2003; Perkins *et al.*, 2006). Nonetheless, in the case of 'immiserising growth', the poor's average income declines, regardless of high growth in the economy (Bhagwati, 1958; Thirlwall, 2000; Perkins *et al.*, 2006). The World Bank (2001) observes that, if economic growth boosts the income share of the poorest, the poor population's income will grow faster than the average income, and vice versa. Many studies also support the viewpoint that economic growth is associated with poverty reduction (Roemer and Gugerty, 1997; Dollar and Kraay, 2002, 2004; Goldberg and Pavcnik, 2004; Perkins *et al.*, 2006). Generally, while many studies support the positive correlation between trade-induced growth and poverty, some doubt the presumption that greater trade openness reduces poverty (e.g. Ravallion, 2006; Pacheco-Lopez and Thirlwall, 2009).

Compared to the growth–poverty nexus, the relationship between growth and inequality is somewhat different. Although a vast literature argues for some relationship between inequality and growth, a comprehensive evaluation of the empirical literature suggests that empirical evidence on this link is inconclusive (Bruno *et al.*, 1998; Banerjee and Duflo, 2003; Bourguignon, 2004; World Bank, 2006, 2012a; Ravallion, 2007), and questions whether growth reduces inequality depending on the characteristics of economic growth (World Bank, 2001; Berg and Krueger, 2003; Todaro and Smith, 2009). The early strands of thinking assert that high inequality is good for growth: as the rich gain more and invest more, the poor benefit from the trickle-down effect of economic growth. Empirical views later point out that lower inequality can increase efficiency and economic growth through a variety of channels. This point of view is critical, according to McCulloch *et al.* (2001).

More recently, Berg and Ostry (2011) find that longer periods of growth are associated with more equality in income distribution. Berg *et al.* (2012) provide evidence that growth duration is positively related to the degree of equality of income distribution, democratic institutions, export orientation, and macroeconomic stability. Kang and Imai (2012) reveal that the effect of economic growth on poverty in Vietnam is estimated to be higher if inequality remains unchanged. Balakrishnan *et al.* (2013) find that, although poverty rates have fallen through the Asian region, increasing inequality has been dampening the impact of growth on poverty reduction. One of the findings by Ostry *et al.* (2014) is that lower net inequality is associated with faster and more durable growth, for a given level of redistribution. Olinto *et al.* (2014) also indicate that, as poverty declines, policies for reducing poverty are more important than policies for promoting economic growth. The World Bank (2001) and Perkins *et al.* (2006) posit that the characteristics of inequality determine the effect of growth on poverty, in the sense that high initial inequality or distributional changes undermine the impact of growth and are also harmful to the poor through lowered overall economic growth. All in all, though high economic growth is considered to benefit the poor in the long run, with a higher level of average income and the trickle-down effect, it does not ensure equality in income distribution and opportunities. In reality, inequality also leads to several social consequences, such as reduced life expectancy, poor mental health, and high levels of crime.

Similar to the growth–inequality relationship, the link between trade liberalisation and inequality is far from confirmed. In neoclassical theory, the effect of trade on income distribution within a country is based on the effect of international trade on relative factor prices and income in that country. International trade causes the real income of labour to rise and the real income of owners of capital to fall in a country with cheap labour and expensive capital, which is typical of developing countries (Salvatore, 1998). Trade openness in this theory leads to redistribution in favour of the poor within a poor country. In the world as a whole, Milanovic (2010) and Mankiw (2012) consider that geographical difference, which is trade relevant, plays a vital role in explaining income differences. The United Nations (2005) maintains that, as trade openness provides the poor with many opportunities, it helps to increase income mobility, which decreases income inequality in the long run. Conversely, Myrdal (1956) claims that international trade generates unequal returns to factors of production.[12] Todaro and Smith (2009) add that, with the development of multinational corporations, most benefits from trade may accrue to foreign residents. The World Bank (1990) also observes that middle-income groups in a country may benefit more from trade policy reforms. The conclusions of the openness–inequality link appear mixed in the empirical literature on trade and inequality (Anderson, 2005). Dollar and Kraay (2004) point out that no systematic correlation between changes in inequality and changes in trade volumes has been confirmed. For Vietnam, Gallup (2004) demonstrates that wage inequality fell slightly as a whole in the 1990s, but rose in HCMC and Hanoi over the same period.[13] In this decade, Vietnam also achieved remarkable things, as a result of its economy transitioning into an open market economy, embarked on in the late 1980s. Phan and Coxhead (2010) also find a robust, inequality-reducing impact of migration for the migration flows into the provinces in Vietnam where most trade-oriented industrial investments are located.

Some studies attempt to link growth with poverty directly, by estimating the growth elasticity of poverty to measure the response of poverty to growth. The World Bank conceptualises growth elasticity of poverty as the degree of effective transmission of benefits from economic growth into poverty reduction, and defines the total growth elasticity of poverty as the percentage change in poverty with respect to a one-percentage change in per capita GDP, mean income, or expenditure per capita.

$$\varepsilon = -\left(\frac{\partial P}{\partial \Upsilon}\right) \times \left(\frac{\Upsilon}{P}\right) \tag{2.4}$$

where P is any of the Foster–Greer–Thorbecke poverty measures, and Υ is per capita GDP, or income, or expenditure. This indicator of elasticity should be interpreted with caution, because the total growth elasticity of poverty reflects many data issues and different factors, such as the initial level of GDP per capita and the growth rate (World Bank, 2005). Pernia (2003) contends that a change in growth-induced poverty can be divided into a pure growth effect and an inequality effect, and the growth elasticity of poverty comprises both these effects.

The growth elasticity of poverty lays the foundation for the studies of pro-poor growth. This concept is broadly defined as growth that leads to significant reductions in poverty or that benefits the poor (UN, 2000; OECD, 2001; World Bank, 2005; Son, 2007b). Pernia (2003) argues that it obviously originates from the concept of the trickle-down effect, where economic growth benefits the rich first, and the poor second, indirectly via the spending of the rich. Thus, pro-poor growth is a type of growth that drives the poor to be actively involved in economic activities and to benefit from the rise in overall income relatively more, compared to the nonpoor. A key to its definition is to take the income distribution into account. The World Bank differentiates between two strands of the definition of pro-poor growth, also known as the Kakwani–Ravallion debate. The Kakwani approach takes into consideration both the magnitude of growth and the proportion of growth benefits being distributed to the poor and the nonpoor. In this approach, growth is pro-poor if the poor benefit proportionally more than the nonpoor, so that there is a reduction in inequality (Kakwani and Pernia, 2000;

White and Anderson, 2001; Kakwani *et al.*, 2004, Kakwani and Son, 2008). The Ravallion approach highlights the rate of poverty reduction as a result of the acceleration of the rate of income growth (Ravallion and Datt, 2002). In this approach, any growth in mean income that reduces poverty is termed pro-poor growth, regardless of how much benefit the poor receive from growth, compared with the nonpoor. This definition of pro-poor growth is consistent with the first goal of the MDGs, which targeted reducing by half the proportion of people in the world living on less than US$1 a day between 1990 and 2015 (World Bank, 2005; UN, 2010). Nevertheless, this approach has been criticised by a number of scholars, who argue that the simple reduction of poverty is an insufficient condition for growth to be pro-poor (Grinspun, 2009; Osmani, 2009). Although there is as yet no consensus regarding the definition and measurement of growth elasticity of poverty and pro-poor growth (Son, 2007a, 2007b), there is little dispute that economic growth is one of the main determinants of poverty reduction.

Growth and poverty are the two important indicators of the development of a nation. Many studies have measured the growth elasticity of poverty and provided different results (Table 2.6). Studies in the late 1990s provide somewhat high

Table 2.6 Some selected studies and estimates of growth elasticity of poverty

Study	Growth elasticity of poverty	Sample coverage and period
Ravallion and Chen (1997)	–3.12	Cross countries, 1981–1994
Bruno *et al.* (1998)	–2.12	Cross countries, 1980s
McCulloch and Baulch (2000)	–2.00	India
Ravallion (2001)	–2.50	Cross countries, 1990s
World Bank (2001)	–2.00	Cross countries
Collier and Dollar (2001)	–2.00	Cross countries
Collier and Dollar (2002)	–2.00	Cross countries
Bourguignon (2003)	–1.65 to –7.87	Cross countries
UNDP (2003)	–2.00	Cross countries
Adams (2004)	–1.73 to –5.02	Cross countries
World Bank (2005)	–1.7	14 countries, 1990s
Ram (2006)	–1.00	Cross countries
Kalwij and Verschoor (2007)	–1.31	Mid-1990s
Lenagala and Ram (2010)	–1.42[1/]	Cross countries, 1981–2005
Ram (2011)	–0.84	Cross countries, 1990s and 2000s
Tahir *et al.* (2014)	–1.9	Pakistan, 1980–2012

Source: Adapted from Ram (2006, 2011)

Note: 1/ The growth elasticity of poverty is for the period 1999–2005, based on the US$1.25 poverty line.

estimates, while the estimates from the late 2000s are relatively lower. The studies by Ravallion (2001) and Ravallion and Chen (1997) provide relatively high estimates, from 2.5 to –3.12. Many of the studies estimate the elasticity of around –2: the World Bank (2001) and the UNDP (2003) acknowledge that the elasticity of –2 is a typical estimate. However, Ram (2006, 2011) contends that estimates reported in many influential studies are inflated, and suggests that a more realistic and useful number is around –1. Similarly, Kalwij and Verschoor (2007) find that the income elasticity of poverty in the mid-1990s was –1.31 on average, ranging from –0.71 for Sub-Saharan Africa to –2.27 for the Middle East and North Africa.

Despite the difference in numerical estimates, the studies share the view that growth is negatively correlated with poverty. This means that, holding other things constant, growth helps to reduce poverty. The concept of pro-poor growth should be placed in a broader context: that growth is pro-poor only if it is supported by other factors. GRIPS Development Forum (2003) suggests three critically important channels to sustain growth and poverty reduction: direct channel, market channel, and policy channel. The direct channel impacts the poor directly through the programmes for basic health, sanitation, education, and rural roads. In the market channel, growth helps the poor through economic linkages, such as inter-sector/region labour migration, increased demand, and reinvestment. The policy channel guides the development process towards improving equality, through subsidies, fiscal transfer, and proper design of trade policy. In that context, the estimate of growth elasticity and the evaluation of whether a country's growth is pro-poor or not are very useful for setting the economic development strategy, since poverty reduction is one of the leading development targets, especially in developing countries.

Market distribution channel

Trade liberalisation also affects households and poverty through altering the prices of tradable goods and market distribution. Prices greatly affect some measures of poverty and the poverty line (Deaton, 2008). Price changes and/or the characteristics of market distribution greatly matter to the poor. One of the most important conditions for the outward-oriented strategy in an economy to be successful is to maintain macroeconomic stability, which is indirectly beneficial for the poor (Bhagwati and Srinivasan, 2002). In this linkage, trade policy can cause price distortion, resulting from trade monopoly, market distributional channels, transaction costs, and other institutional costs. The poor are unlikely to benefit from trade liberalisation, due primarily to the ineffectiveness of price transmission to households as a consequence of inadequate trade policies. Many studies provide evidence for the impacts of prices and market distribution on the welfare and income distribution (e.g. Deaton, 1989; Minot and Goletti, 1998; Porto, 2004; Winters *et al.*, 2004; Seshan, 2005; Isik-Dikmelik, 2006; Justino *et al.*, 2008; Nicita, 2009; Marchand, 2012).

Deaton (1989), studying the case of Thailand, concludes that higher prices for rice are likely to benefit rural households at all levels of living. Ravallion (1990) investigates the dynamics of wage formation in Bangladesh and suggests that the rural rich are likely to gain while the rural poor lose from a rise in the relative price of food staples. Minot and Goletti (1998) use the multimarket spatial-equilibrium model to stimulate the effect of export liberalisation on paddy and rice prices and find that the liberalisation in rice exports raised food prices, consequently increasing average real income and reducing the incidence of poverty in Vietnam in the 1990s. Using the decomposition technique and the framework for the net benefit ratio (NBR) suggested by Deaton (1997), Isik-Dikmelik (2006) finds that growth in Vietnam is pro-poor on the whole, and the poorer and net buyer households benefit more from growth than other groups do. Also in the case of Vietnam, Seshan (2005) uses a multi-output production function to examine the trade–poverty relationship, indicating that trade liberalisation explains about half of the reduction in the incidence of poverty.

In the case of Ethiopia, Dercon (2006) uses price changes as the proxy for trade reforms and discloses that the main factors driving consumption changes are relative price changes. In Latin America, Porto (2006b) estimates the impacts of trade on the prices of the tradable and nontradable, and on wages. The study finds that the average poor and middle-income families in Argentina benefit from trade agreements. Porto (2004) also studies the impacts of export procedures on poverty in Moldova and predicts that halving informal export barriers would reduce poverty from 48.3 per cent to between 43.3 and 45.5 per cent. Additionally, examining responses to trade reforms from Mexican households, Porto (2006a) reveals that the evaluation of prices or trade reforms is sensitive to the inclusion of the responses of consumption and income. Also in Mexico, Prina (2007) indicates that trade liberalisation increases the level of earning of poor farmers relative to that of rich farmers in the central region of Mexico, which has good land quality and low transportation costs to the border, compared with other regions. Nicita (2009) discloses that households residing near the border with the United States of America benefit more from the effects of tariff liberalisation than those living in southernmost states. In the case of India, Marchand (2012) uses non-parametric local linear regressions, finding that Indian households experience gains as a result of trade liberalisation, and that the average price effect is generally pro-poor, varying significantly across the per capita expenditure scope. Although the effect of price and/or market distribution is one of the most visible impacts of trade liberalisation on poverty, studies on the trade–poverty link apparently ignore the effect of the market distribution system. In fact, market distribution in developing countries is discernibly the main cause of ineffective price transmission.

Employment channel

Creating or detracting jobs is also one of the most visible effects of trade liberalisation. Krueger (1978a) posits that the aim to create more jobs will be strongly consistent with the change in trade strategies towards a greater export orientation. In addition to the effect on the creation of employment, trade policy also affects wage inequality by changing the relative demand for skilled workers

(Goldberg and Pavcnik, 2007). On the whole, the effects of trade liberalisation are largely positive for employment and wages, one of the main sources of income for the poor (Krueger *et al.*, 1981; Krueger, 1982, 1983; World Bank, 1990; Niimi *et al.*, 2007; Justino *et al.*, 2008). For developed countries, the OECD reports that more open markets can make positive contributions to income, employment, and productivity growth. Openness to trade can also reduce unemployment in crisis economies in the short run (OECD, 2011). In contrast, Ghose (2000) analyses the changing pattern of trade and shows that the employment and labour market effects of trade liberalisation fall in industrialised economies, but rise in developing countries, and that growth of trade has a significantly positive effect on manufacturing employment and wages.

Topalova (2010) measures the impacts of trade liberalisation in India and reveals that these are most pronounced in the areas with the lowest level of geographical mobility of labour, inflexible labour laws, and the lowest level of income distribution. Also in the case of India, Das (2008) indicates that trade liberalisation has a positive impact on labour market indicators, whether it be employment, real wage, or labour productivity in the labour-intensive sectors, such as cotton textile, textile products, leather, and leather products. Taking Brazil as a case study, Pavcnik *et al.* (2004) suggest that industrial affiliation is an important component of labour earnings. Adding to this, Ferreira *et al.* (2007) find that trade liberalisation seems to contribute significantly towards reducing wage inequality in Brazil. Also in Latin America, Feliciano (2001) reveals that industries with greater reductions in trade protection levels have a larger share of low-skilled workers, and that reductions in tariffs in Mexico between 1986 and 1990 had no statistically significant effect on relative wages or relative employment. This study also suggests that trade reforms increase wage inequality. In Europe, Christev *et al.* (2005), using industrial panel data in Ukraine, observe that trade openness did affect job movements in the Ukraine over the period 1993 to 2000, and that, while trade with the Commonwealth of Independent States (CIS) reduced job destruction, trade with the European Union (EU) increased excess reallocation, mainly through job creation. Although trade liberalisation has a positive impact on employment and wages, especially in developing countries, its effects on wage inequality appear to be mixed.

Government revenue channel

Trade liberalisation also affects welfare and poverty through changes in government revenue and public spending. Public expenditure might be curtailed as a result of trade policy reforms. The investigation of these impacts has two strands: the effect of trade liberalisation on government revenue and the effect of the decreasing tariff revenue on the poor (Winters *et al.*, 2004). The International Monetary Fund (2005) documents that trade tax revenue typically accounts for between one-quarter and one-third of the total tax revenue in low- and middle-income countries. Over the last 20 years, trade liberalisation has been associated with a marked decline in trade tax revenue relative to GDP, in both developing

Table 2.7 Selected empirical studies of the trade–growth–poverty nexus: a summary

Author (year)	*Main variables*	*Methodology*	*Main findings/Conclusions*
I. Economic growth channel			
I.1 Trade–growth causality			
Little *et al.* (1970)	Effects of trade policies on economic growth	A sample of seven developing countries: Argentina, Brazil, India, Mexico, Pakistan, the Philippines, and Taiwan. No formal models and tests have been made.	Growth generated through import substitution is intrinsically limited. Manufacturing employment in high tariff countries has risen far less than manufactured output. Agriculture is discouraged and so is its employment. Import substitution has worsened the distribution of income within developing countries by creating a privileged but small class of industrialists and modern industrial workers. By raising the domestic price of manufactured goods, protection also increases artificially the share of manufacturing in a domestic price-weighted measure of total output. This is a cause of the 'immiserising growth'.
Michaely (1977)	Mean annual growth of per capita GNP and mean annual increase in the share of exports in GNP	Pooled data for 41 developing countries (1950–1973). Simple correlation is used.	The Spearman rank correlation coefficient between two variables is 0.38. Exports help only when countries achieve some minimum level of development.
Krueger (1978b)	GNP growth and export growth	Pooled data for 10 countries (1954–1971). Simple log linear regression is used.	An increase in the export's rate of growth of 1 per cent will increase the GNP's rate of growth by just over 0.1 per cent.
Balassa (1978)	Export growth and GNP growth	Pooled data for 11 countries (1960–1973). Using both correlation and regression.	Considerable positive effects of export growth on economic growth.

Tyler (1981)	Export growth and GDP growth	Pooled data for 55 middle-income, developing countries (1960–1977). Both correlation and regression analysis are employed.	A 1 per cent increase in the rate of growth of total exports is associated with an increase of 0.057 per cent in GDP growth. Additional empirical evidence demonstrates a strong cross-country association between export performance and GNP growth.
Ram (1985)	Real GDP growth and export growth	Pooled data for 73 developing countries (1960–1977). Assumptions: (1) output is a linear function of labour, capital, and technological change, and (2) technological change is a linear function of export. Linear regression is used.	Export variable (X) has large and statistically significant coefficients.
Sachs and Warner (1995)	Growth and openness	The study sets five criteria to determine whether a country's trade policy is closed or open. It establishes three criteria to classify political conditions of countries. It uses three criteria to define a severe macroeconomic crisis. It employs pooled data for 111 countries, divided into many subgroups. Several linear regressions are estimated for specific tests.	Strong reformers seem to outperform weak reformers. Open economies grow, on average, by 2.45 per cent more than closed economies. Strong evidence of unconditional convergence for open countries; no evidence of unconditional convergence for closed countries. Closed countries systematically grow more slowly than do open countries. Poor trade policies seem to affect growth directly, controlling for other factors, and impact the rate of accumulation of physical capital. Open economies tend to adjust more rapidly from being primary intensive to manufacturing-intensive exporters. Economic growth is indeed higher after trade liberalisation.
Frankel and Romer (1999)	Per capita income and trade volumes	Cross-country regressions of the log level of per capita income on trade volumes.	A 1 per cent increase in share of trade in GDP leads to an increase of 2.04 per cent in labour productivity.

(*Continued*)

Table 2.7 (Continued)

Author (year)	Main variables	Methodology	Main findings/Conclusions
Singh (2002)	Real export, real import, and real income	Indian data (1951–1996). It uses both the Engle–Granger two-step procedure and the Johansen maximum likelihood systems estimator.	It supports the presence of a short-run dynamic relationship with unidirectional Granger causality flowing from imports to exports and from exports to income.
Singh (2003)	Exports and output per capita and the total factor productivity	It uses 10 industries in the manufacturing sector in India. It uses an extended version of the model developed by Mankiw et al. (1992).	Evidence for the effects of exports on the level of output per capita and TFP in the manufacturing sector. No evidence for export-induced convergence among the manufacturing industries.
Foster (2008)	Trade liberalisation and growth	A sample of 75 liberalising countries. It uses quantile regression model.	Countries with lowest rates of growth benefit most from liberalisation in the long run. Countries are most likely to suffer from short-run negative effects of trade liberalisation.
Singh (2011)	Effects of trade (export and import) and investment on output	The country study is Australia. The study tests the null hypothesis of the Granger noncausality between trade and economic growth.	It provides consistent evidence of the positive and significant long-run effects of exports and investment on output. Effects of imports are largely negative. Evidence supporting the positive and significant long-run effects overwhelms the evidence providing a mixed and weak support for the effects of trade and investment on output.
I.2 Growth–poverty–inequality causality			
Roemer and Gugerty (1997)	Economic growth and poverty	A sample of 26 developing countries. Elasticity approach is employed.	Annual GDP growth of 10 per cent is associated with the income growth of 10 per cent for the poorest 40 per cent of the population. Annual GDP growth of 10 per cent is associated with the income growth of 9.21 per cent for the poorest 20 per cent. Stabilisation of the economy is crucial to the reduction in poverty.

Dollar and Kraay (2002)	Growth and poverty	Impact of growth-enhancing policies on the income distribution, after controlling for their impact on mean income, in a panel covering 80 countries and four decades. Definition of the poor as those in the bottom 20 per cent of the income distribution.	A one-to-one relationship between the growth rate of income of the poorest and the growth rate of per capita income. Share of income that accrues to the poorest fifth of society is not systematically associated with the growth rate and average incomes.
Dollar and Kraay (2004)	Average annual growth and average annual change in trade volumes	Decade over decade changes in the volume of trade are used as an imperfect proxy for changes in trade policy. Pooled data of 100 developed and developing countries. Analysis of within country variations.	A 100 per cent increase in trade share would have the cumulative effect of raising incomes by 25 per cent over a decade. A strong positive correlation between changes in trade and changes in growth. Strong relationship between growth of average incomes and growth of incomes of the poorest. No significant (systematic) correlation between changes in inequality and changes in trade volumes.
Dollar (2004)	Reform, growth, and poverty in Vietnam	A simulation using Vietnam's data, based on the results of author's cross-country studies. It uses descriptive analysis.	Trade liberalisation is estimated to account for an increase in the growth rate of 1.3 percentage points. Total effect of a reform package increases the growth rate by 7.2 percentage points. Reforms in Vietnam have led to a dramatic increase in income of the poor. There is a tendency for the initial high growth rate in a low-income country to slow down as it develops.
Kalwij and Verschoor (2007)	Income growth, distribution, and poverty	Study uses panel data of 58 developing countries for the period 1980–1998. It employs the elasticity approach.	Income elasticity of poverty in the mid-1990s is −1.31 on average, and ranges from −0.71 for Sub-Saharan Africa to −2.27 for the Middle East and North Africa. Gini elasticity is 0.80 on average, and ranges from 0.01 in South Asia to 1.73 in Latin America.

(Continued)

Table 2.7 (Continued)

Author (year)	Main variables	Methodology	Main findings/Conclusions
Kakwani and Son (2008)	Growth and poverty	It proposes the poverty equivalent growth rate (PEGR). PEGR is tested on the National Household Survey (PNAD) in Brazil (1995–2005)	Magnitude of PEGR determines the pattern of growth: whether growth is pro-poor in relative or absolute sense or is 'poverty-reducing' pro-poor.
Berg and Ostry (2011), Berg et al. (2012)	Economic growth and inequality	Cross-country data are used. These studies use structural breaks in economic growth to define growth spell periods of high growth, beginning with an up-break and ending with a down-break.	African and Latin American countries apparently have shorter growth spells than those of other countries. Longer growth spells are robustly associated with more equality in income distribution. Growth duration is positively related to the degree of equality of income distribution, democratic institutions, export orientation, and macroeconomic stability.
Ram (2011)	Economic growth and poverty	It is the cross-country study for developing countries over the 1990s and the 2000s. It examines the growth elasticity of poverty.	Global estimate of the growth elasticity of poverty is -0.84. Growth elasticity of poverty for the South Asia region and India are estimated to be -0.22 and -0.13, respectively.
Kang and Imai (2012)	Growth, poverty, and inequality	It uses data from the Vietnam Household Living Standards Surveys (VHLSSs) from 2002 to 2006. Elasticity approach, regression, and decomposition technique are utilised.	Disparity in standards of living is increasing. Effect of economic growth on poverty is estimated to be higher if inequality remains unchanged.

1.3 Trade–poverty–inequality causality

Author (year)	Main variables	Methodology	Main findings/Conclusions
Gallup (2004)	Wage inequality	Data from the Vietnam Living Standards Surveys (VLSSs). Descriptive analysis and the OLS regression model of the determinants of wages.	Wage inequality falls slightly in Vietnam as a whole in the time of rapid reforms towards trade liberalisation (the 1990s), but rises in Hanoi and Ho Chi Minh City over the same period. Income from agriculture helps to reduce overall income inequality.

Study	Focus	Method	Findings
Ravallion (2006)	Poverty and trade openness	Both micro and macro, empirical approaches, using cross-country data, household-level data, and case studies of China and Morocco.	Study doubts some stylised facts from both sides of the globalisation debate. Micro approach indicates considerable heterogeneity in the welfare impacts of trade reforms. It identifies a number of individual gains. Results suggest the importance of combining trade reforms with other well-designed social protection policies.
Shahbaz Akmal *et al.* (2007)	Trade openness and poverty head count ratio	The country studied is Pakistan. It applies the Johansen cointegration techniques and error correction method.	The findings suggest that trade liberalisation has a cumulative effect on poverty reduction in the long run but not in the short run. Low poverty is associated with low taxation and high foreign direct investment, not with trade openness.
Phan and Coxhead (2010)	Interprovincial migration and inequality	It uses the 1989 and 1999 population and housing censuses data in Vietnam. It employs the gravity equation.	It suggests the existence of poverty-related labour mobility at the provincial level. It finds a robust inequality impact of migration for migration flows into the provinces in Vietnam where most of trade-oriented industrial investments are located.
Haughton and Phong (2010)	Urban/rural gap and location-specific characteristic	Study uses the VLSS data of Vietnam. It employs the multilevel model. It applies the method of small area estimates at commune levels.	Hanoi, HCMC, and Ba Ria Vung Tau display the highest location-specific random contributions to the urban–rural gap.
Le (2014)	Rural poverty, trade liberalisation, and institutional reforms	It combines VHLSS data of 2006 and 2010 with the Vietnam Provincial Competitiveness Index (PCI), a proxy for institutional reforms. It employs OLS regression model.	Welfare of rural households improved. Institutional reforms in Vietnam appeared to be sluggish in the late 2000s in the provinces with high institutional reforms and trade openness. Both access to land and lower informal charges were the important determinants of welfare improvement over time.

(*Continued*)

Table 2.7 (Continued)

Author (year)	Main variables	Methodology	Main findings/Conclusions
II. Market channel			
Minot and Goletti (1998)	Welfare impact of price changes on different household groups in Vietnam	Multimarket spatial-equilibrium model is used to stimulate the effect of export liberalisation on paddy and rice price in seven regions of the country. It applies a framework by Deaton (1997): Net Benefit Ratio (NBR) = Production Ratio (PR) – Consumption Ratio (CR). Combined data are used.	One-third of Vietnamese households have net sales of rice. Higher rice prices associated with export liberalisation exacerbate the inequality among regions and within urban and rural areas. As average income of the poor rises, the incidence of poverty declines slightly. Eliminating rice export quota would increase prices and hurt many Vietnamese households. The poor gain more than the nonpoor.
Glewwe et al. (2000)	Determinants of poverty in Vietnam in the 1990s	Both descriptive and regression analysis are employed, using a panel data of more than 4,300 households drawn from the VLSSs. Dummy variables are largely used. Multinomial logit model is used to examine characteristics enabling households to escape poverty.	Education, location formal (white-collar) occupation, and productivity of rice were the factors that mostly affected a household's probability of escaping poverty during the 1990s.
Minot (2000)	Analysis of poverty in Vietnam	Disaggregated poverty maps for Vietnam are generated. VLSS data and agricultural census data (AC) are used.	Rural poverty in Vietnam is strongly associated with the distance from cities and the coast.
Minot (2003)	Income diversification and poverty reduction in Vietnam	Descriptive analysis using the panel data drawn from the VLSSs. Decomposition of sources of income.	Rural incomes and nonfarm incomes have increased substantially over the observed period. Crop diversification has made a non-negligible contribution to rising living standards in the north uplands. Crop income growth among the poor households is largely based on yield increases.

Study	Topic	Methodology	Findings
Niimi et al. (2004)	Poverty and rice market liberalisation in Vietnam	Multinomial logit model is used with a panel data of 4,302 households drawn from the 1992–1993 VLSS. Probability of a household staying or escaping poverty is analysed in relation to trade liberalisation. Some trade-related variables are employed: fertiliser and ratio of household members working in leading export industries. Two-stage least square (2SLS) regression and instrumental variables (IVs) are used.	Positive effects of trade-related variables: production of rice and coffee and the proportion of workers initially holding jobs in export industries. A one-standard deviation increase in rice output raises the probability of escaping poverty by 50 per cent. Rice sector contributed significantly to poverty reduction over the 1990s. Reforms have significant effects on the prices of rice and fertilisers and on the rice quantity produced, used, and sold.
Haughton and Le (2005)	Determinants of consumption at two different points in time	Directed acyclic graphs are applied. Multivariate adaptive regression splines (MARS) is employed.	Education, household composition, and community infrastructure are strongly associated with consumption changes.
Seshan (2005)	Trade liberalisation, through price changes and household welfare in Vietnam	A multi-output production function is used. Household panel data drawn from the VLSSs are used. Marginal revenue product or shadow wage of family labour is generated. IVs are used.	Trade liberalisation explains about half the reduction in poverty incidence among farm households and does not enlarge the income gap. Rural poor benefit from trade liberalisation at the expense of their urban counterparts.
Minot and Baulch (2005)	Geographic (spatial) distribution of poverty	Small area estimation method is applied. A household survey data and population and housing census data (PHC) are employed.	Incidence of poverty in Vietnam is highest in the northern uplands and lowest in cities and the southeast. Density of poverty is highest where the incidence of poverty is lowest, or most poor people live in less poor areas.
Isik-Dikmelik (2006)	Trade reforms and welfare in Vietnam	Study uses VLSS data. It examines the market effect of trade reforms on welfare in Vietnam. It uses the concept of net benefit ratio (NBR) by Deaton (1997) to define net seller and buyers. It uses a model of the microeconomic determinants of household welfare using fixed effects model. It also employs the decomposition technique.	Growth is pro-poor. Poorer households benefit more from growth than rich households. Net buyer households benefit more from growth than their net seller counterparts. Direct effects of trade liberalisation are more significant than the indirect effects on rural welfare.

(*Continued*)

Table 2.7 (Continued)

Author (year)	Main variables	Methodology	Main findings/Conclusions
Niimi et al. (2007)	Poverty and trade liberalisation in Vietnam	Winters's conceptual framework is applied. Multinomial logit model is used with a panel data of 4,302 households drawn from the VLSSs. Probability of a household staying or escaping poverty is analysed in relation to trade liberalisation.	Production of rice and coffee is strongly significant in explaining the escape from poverty. An increase of 11 per cent in the chance of escaping poverty is resulted from a one–standard deviation increase in the proportion of export workers. Trade reforms in the 1990s helped to reduce poverty.
Dercon (2006)	Economic reform, growth, and poverty	Study uses a panel data set from Ethiopia (1989–1995). It uses income equation and decomposition of growth in incomes.	Relative price changes are the main factor driving consumption changes. The poor with relatively good land and location are better off than those poor with even lesser endowments.
Nguyen et al. (2007)	Inequality in welfare, measured by real per capita household consumption expenditure (RPCE) between urban and rural areas in Vietnam	Quantile regression decomposition is used. Urban–rural log of real per capita expenditure (RPCE) gap across the distribution is decomposed into two components: covariate effects and return effects. It uses VLSS data.	Both effects are larger at the top of the log RPCE than at the bottom. Return effects increase dramatically between 1993 and 1998, especially for education. Difference between the urban and rural household characteristics makes the poor worse off.
Justino et al. (2008)	Welfare, price, and employment	Study uses the VLSS data. Multinomial logit model is used.	Trade liberalisation has a material and positive effect on rural household welfare. Labour market is the main channel for the effects of trade liberalisation on poverty.
Figuié and Moustier (2009)	Supermarkets and poor consumers	Study is based on surveys of food purchasing practices conducted in Hanoi, Vietnam from 2004 to 2006. It is based on descriptive analysis.	Poor consumers rely on a diversified network of formal and informal outlets to ensure food access, credit opportunities, and low prices. They buy little from supermarkets.

III. Employment/enterprise channel

Krueger *et al.* (1981), Krueger (1982, 1983)	Trade policy and employment	The case studies of developing countries, including Argentina, Brazil, Chile, Colombia, Hong Kong, India, Indonesia, Ivory Coast, Kenya, Pakistan, South Korea, Taiwan, Thailand, Tunisia, Uruguay.	Shifting to an outward-oriented trade strategy leads to resource allocation and employment that bring gains from trade. Manufacturing exports in developing countries are more labour intensive and less skill intensive than import substitutes. Eradication of distortions in factor market will contribute to the more rapid growth of exports. Trade liberalisation will consequently foster employment and income distribution.
Ghose (2000)	Trade liberalisation and manufacturing employment	Study uses data on manufacturing sectors in 13 developing countries. It descriptively analyses the manufacturing sector in 13 countries in relation to industrial countries.	Growth of trade is seemingly associated with declining wage inequality in the manufacturing sector in the United States, but unchanging wage inequality in Japan. Expansion of trade is associated with growing wage inequality in several developing countries. Trade does not have any necessary adverse effect on the employment of skilled workers.
Feliciano (2001)	Workers and trade liberalisation	Study uses microlevel data in Mexico from 1986 to 1990. It uses a two-stage estimation framework, based on wage model.	Industries with greater reductions in protection levels have a larger share of low-skilled workers. Decline in import license coverage appears to reduce relative wages of workers in reformed industries by 2 per cent. Reductions in tariffs have no statistically significant effects on relative wages or relative employment.
Pavcnik *et al.* (2004)	Trade liberalisation and industry wage structure	Country study is Brazil, using the labour market data from the Brazilian monthly employment survey (PME) for 1987–1998. It uses a two-stage estimation framework, based on wage model.	Industry affiliation is an important component of worker earnings. Trade liberalisation does not increase wage inequality between skilled and unskilled workers.

(*Continued*)

Table 2.7 (Continued)

Author (year)	Main variables	Methodology	Main findings/Conclusions
Christev et al. (2005)	Trade liberalisation and employment	Study employs disaggregated panel data on manufacturing industries and customs data on trade flows in Ukraine over the period 1993–2000. It uses GMM analysis.	Three-digit sector job flows are largely driven by idiosyncratic factors within industries. Trade openness indeed affects job flows in Ukrainian manufacturing. Trade with CIS decreases job destruction, trade with the EU increases excess reallocation mainly through job creation.
Nguyen et al. (2005)	Trade liberalisation and labour market	It uses a CGE model.	There are differences in the impacts of trade liberalisation across the segmented labour markets.
Ferreira et al. (2007)	Trade liberalisation, employment flows, and wage inequality	Study uses nationally representative, economy-wide data in Brazil during 1988–1995. It uses a two-stage estimation framework, based on wage model.	Trade liberalisation appears to significantly contribute to the reduction in wage inequality. Effects of trade liberalisation come from trade-induced changes in employment levels across sectors, industries, and formality categories (formal, informal, self-employed, employer).
Das (2008)	Trade liberalisation, employment, labour productivity, and real wages	Study uses a panel data set of selected industries in India over four phases of trade liberalisation: 1980–1985, 1986–1990, 1991–1995, and 1996–2000. Trade liberalisation is quantified by customs tariff and nontariff measures. It uses descriptive analysis.	Tariff reductions help to increase employment growth, while nontariff barriers decrease employment growth. In labour-intensive sectors, such as cotton textile, textile products, leather, and leather products, trade liberalisation has a positive impact on the indicators of labour market, whether it be employment, real wage, or labour productivity.
Topalova (2010)	Labour mobility, geography, trade liberalisation, and poverty	Country of study is India in 1991. It uses difference-in-difference approach.	Rural areas with concentrated production sectors more exposed to trade liberalisation have the slower reduction in poverty and slower growth in consumption. Impacts of trade liberalisation are most pronounced in the areas with the lowest level of geographical mobility of labour, inflexible labour laws, and at the bottom of the income distribution.

IV. Government revenue channel

Baunsgaard and Keen (2005)	Trade tax revenue and trade liberalisation	It is a cross-country study, based on a panel data for 111 countries over 25 years. It uses combined methods: fixed effects and random effects models, and GMM.	For high-income countries, the recovery is complete. For middle-income countries, there are strong signs that from 45 to 60 cents of additional domestic tax are compensated for each US dollar of lost trade tax revenue. Revenue recovery is both weak and incomplete in low-income countries, with the compensation less than 30 cents.
Anderson (1996)	Trade reform and government budget	Study develops a general framework for the analysis of trade reform when the government cuts public good supply or alternative tax increases. It combines marginal cost of funds (MFC) of trade taxes with CGE models. It uses data from Korea in 1963.	Study doubts the desirability of trade reform for convex competitive economies with active government budget constraints. Cuts in tariffs, matched by the rise in revenue-neutral indirect taxes, would lower Korean welfare.
Zafar (2005)	Trade liberalisation and revenue and fiscal impact	The case study of Niger. It uses a static, partial equilibrium SMART model, developed by UNCTAD and the World Bank to conduct simulations for Niger.	It predicts some welfare gains for consumers and importers from lower import tariffs and the possibility of trade creation. It foresees that further trade liberalisation in Niger will have significant fiscal costs.
Combes and Saadi-Sedik (2006)	Trade openness and budget deficits	It is a cross-country study, based on 66 developing countries during 1974–1998. It uses GMM system estimator.	Trade openness increases a country's exposure to external shocks. Trade openness affects budget balances through several other channels: corruption and income inequality. Natural openness worsens budget balances, whereas trade policy-induced openness improves them.

(Continued)

Table 2.7 (Continued)

Author (year)	Main variables	Methodology	Main findings/Conclusions
Heo and Nguyen (2009)	Trade liberalisation and poverty reduction	It employs economic data from Vietnam. It uses descriptive analysis for the trade–poverty relationship through four channels: economic growth, enterprise, market, and government spending.	Growth elasticity of poverty has relatively increased over time. Incomes of the poor increase as a result of an increase in real wage growth. Households producing commodities for exports, such as coffee and rice, have a substantially better chance of lifting themselves out of poverty. There is an increase in government revenue from export earnings.
Baunsgaard and Keen (2010)	Trade tax revenue and trade liberalisation	It is a cross-country study, based on a panel data for 117 countries over 32 years. It uses combined methods: fixed effects model, 2SLS, and GMM.	For high-income countries, there is evidence of full compensation. For middle-income countries, there is robust evidence that, from 35 to 50 cents (in the short run) or dollar-for-dollar (in the long run) of additional domestic tax is compensated for each US dollar of trade tax revenue lost. Revenue recovery is both weak and incomplete in low-income countries.
Bilal *et al.* (2012)	Trade liberalisation and fiscal adjustment	The case of economic partnership agreements (EPAs) in Africa. It uses combined methods.	It ranks countries according to their expected impacts from the EPAs. It identifies the groups of countries with high, modest, and low estimated fiscal impact. It recognises a general tendency to overestimate the direct fiscal losses resulted from the EPAs.

and developed countries. A contrary view suggests that trade liberalisation does not necessarily lead to a reduction in revenue from trade taxes. McCulloch *et al.* (2001) argue that, in certain conditions, trade liberalisation which results in reorganising tariffs, reducing tariff rates, and converting nontariff barriers into tariffs tends to increase revenue. The proportion of trade taxes in the total government revenue apparently falls as the country is thriving. Heo and Nguyen (2009) also provide evidence supporting this argument. They argue that the increase in export earnings in Vietnam has an indirect benefit that is channelled into poverty-reducing activities. Adding to this, Combes and Saadi-Sedik (2006) provide evidence that, while natural openness worsens budget balances, trade policy–induced openness improves these in developing countries.

Another concern is whether countries have compensated for the reductions in trade tax revenue by using domestic taxation. Using a panel of 117 countries over 32 years, Baunsgaard and Keen (2010) find that, for low-income countries with a loss of trade tax revenue due to trade liberalisation, the recovery from the loss is not sustained and complete. They further pinpoint that many developing countries face an intense need for sustainable finance for poverty alleviation and development, which leads them to resort to other sources of finance, such as corporate tax revenue. Additionally, some poorer countries tend to be unable or unwilling to recover lost trade tax revenue through strengthening domestic taxation (IMF, 2005). The second strand is whether trade liberalisation leads to pruning government budget areas that can affect public spending, especially poverty reduction programmes. According to Winters *et al.* (2004), no direct evidence on the link between trade liberalisation and reductions in social expenditure has been found. In reality, for the reason of social stability, governments usually give top priority to poverty reduction programmes.

Other frameworks similar to Winters's outline are also worth noting. Nissanke and Thorbecke (2006, 2008) argue that trade liberalisation influences poverty through growth and inequality, and the mechanism through which globalisation affects poverty is the openness–growth–inequality–poverty pathway, where the interaction between openness-induced growth and inequality affects poverty. This framework, however, highlights globalisation rather than trade liberalisation, which may complicate empirical work. Adding to the literature discussed above are some other views on the trade–poverty relationship that are worth considering. Practically, trade liberalisation benefits the poor by providing them with cheap food. In so doing, trade policy reforms should remove all distortions of food prices and somehow increase rice productivity in a country (Nash and Mitchell, 2005). In addition, sustaining agricultural production helps the country to contain inflation and to secure food staples for people.

Although Winters's framework is plausible for examining the trade–poverty relationship, evidence provided by studies covered in this framework is almost all indirect. Virtually no direct evidence on the relationship between trade liberalisation and poverty has been found, as acknowledged by Winters *et al.* (2004) and Goldberg and Pavcnik (2004). McCulloch *et al.* (2001) contend that the direct effects on poverty for many dimensions of trade liberalisation are negligible, since they are, in fact, difficult to verify. Amongst the four channels, the effects of price and employment stand out as relatively direct and verifiable, and draw the attention of many studies. Since rural households mostly engage in agricultural production, the practical way to link trade liberalisation with poverty at the microeconomic level is to establish a set of trade-related variables drawn from household characteristics relevant to agricultural production and market, employment, and location, and subsequently to examine their impacts on household welfare and poverty. Litchfield *et al.* (2003) also add that the primary difficulty facing their research on the trade–poverty linkage is how to isolate the effects of trade liberalisation from the effects of other policies and factors. Their study thereby relies on the outcomes, the observed prices and quantities. For these reasons, our study confines its attention to the pathways generalised in Winters's framework to investigate the relationship for Vietnam.

2.6   Trade–poverty linkages in Vietnam

The remarkable development of the Vietnamese transitional economy in the 1990s has drawn much research attention to analysing the effects of trade liberalisation on growth and poverty. As Vietnam was engaged in the Vietnam War before 1975, the studies of the development of the economy and trade liberalisation have really been fruitful since the 1980s, when the centrally planned system was mired in its severe recession since the war. The shift from the old economic system into an open market economy in the late 1980s helped Vietnam to obtain dramatic economic achievements in the 1990s. The studies of the effects of trade liberalisation on poverty can be divided into three groups. The first group consists of studies using descriptive and/or documenting analysis. They provide useful information on the process of trade liberalisation and poverty, and on a comparison of economic development between periods. The second group investigates the partial impacts of trade liberalisation on poverty, such as through the impacts on growth, market, employment, or the combination. The third group covers studies using computable general equilibrium (CGE) models to analyse the economy-wide effects of trade policy. The CGE studies are not the focus of our study, as they are based on the simulation analysis of scenarios, and not used for evaluating outcomes.

For the first group, several studies provide a review of the impacts of trade liberalisation on poverty in Vietnam. According to the World Bank (2011), Vietnam is a clear story of success amongst the transitional economies, and trade liberalisation has a significant impact on the economy. Vietnam is also amongst the countries that have a strong link between overall economic growth and the speed of poverty reduction (World Bank, 2005). The United Nations Environment Programme (2005) finds that the trade reform process, including trade liberalisation, has led to significant changes in rice production and exports, which affect the reduction of poverty. Heo and Nguyen (2009) provide evidence for the relationship between trade liberalisation and poverty reduction through the four channels: economic growth, market, enterprise, and government revenue. In the summary of the results of three multi-country research projects financed by the Globalisation and Poverty Research Programme of the UK Department for International Development, Thoburn (2004) draws some important conclusions on the process of globalisation and poverty in Vietnam. First, the poor in Vietnam benefit from globalisation less than other higher income groups, which is likely to increase inequality. Second, economic reforms result in increasing rice production, and the poor have better chances of escaping poverty as a consequence of higher rice prices. Third, however, the poor gain almost nothing from employment in the high wage and most competitive field of the industry, due to labour shedding during the restructuring of the economy. The International Monetary Fund (2004) also adds that the transformation of the economic and ownership structure in the state sector has led to labour redundancy.

For the second group, most of the studies of the partial effects of trade liberalisation can be covered in the Winters framework. These studies primarily examine the effects of market and employment on households and poverty, as these are the most visible and direct in the Winters channels. Dollar (2004) uses the parameter estimates from a cross-country panel growth regression estimated by Dollar and Kraay (2002) to apply them to the changes in policies in Vietnam between the late 1980s and the late 1990s. The study finds that trade liberalisation is estimated to explain an increase of 0.1 per cent in growth rate, 1.9 per cent in disinflation, 1.0 per cent in financial deepening, and 1.6 per cent in property rights reform. These results are, however, very similar to simulations.

Regarding the effects of price and market distribution, Figuié and Moustier (2009) show that poor consumers principally rely on a diversified network of formal and informal outlets to satisfy their demand for food, and purchase very little from supermarkets. Moreover, Minot (1998) and Ghosh and Whalley (2004) indicate that price controls on rice production act as a revenue-raising device, by fixing producer prices and paving the way for state marketing agencies to sell output at higher prices. They argue that such controls dampen costly domestic adjustments in the face of the volatility of world prices. Furthermore, the findings from Oxfam Great Britain and Oxfam Hong Kong (2001) suggest that rice market deregulation has mixed effects on small farmers who are net sellers and on poor rural workers who buy rice on an annual basis. With respect to institutional reforms, which are closely related to trade reforms, Steer and Sen (2010) suggest that although formal institutions are developing in Vietnam, informal institutions still play an important role as the mechanisms of risk management, even when the economy becomes developed.

Many studies explore the effects of employment on poverty. Seshan (2005) examines the effects of trade liberalisation on poverty and income distribution in the rice sector and fertiliser market between 1993 and 1998. The study indicates that trade reform accounted for about half of the reduction in poverty amongst farm households. Niimi *et al.* (2007), using a multinomial logit model to evaluate the impact of trade liberalisation on poverty dynamics, conclude that trade liberalisation reduced poverty considerably over the period 1993–1998. Glewwe *et al.* (2002) and Justino *et al.* (2008) employ a model of microdeterminants of growth to investigate the impacts of price and employment on household welfare. These studies use household panel data from Vietnam over the period 1993–1998 and reveal that Vietnam gained a striking reduction in poverty during the 1990s, and trade liberalisation positively affected poverty via the labour market channel. Coello *et al.* (2010), utilising a household panel data set for 2002, 2004, and 2006, disclose that working in an export sector had a positive impact on poverty.

In summary, the studies of the relationship between trade liberalisation and poverty for Vietnam appear to support the positive impacts of trade liberalisation on poverty, especially in the 1990s. For the most part, however, they depict a partial picture and use obsolete data. No study provides the relatively adequate evaluation of the link between trade liberalisation and poverty. The impacts of trade liberalisation are multidimensional, and therefore, to be able to paint a more comprehensive picture of the trade–poverty nexus in Vietnam, the judgement of the effects of trade liberalisation on poverty should, at least, be based on all the channels pinpointed by the Winters framework.

2.7   A recapitulation

Several stylised facts of the relationship between trade, growth, and poverty are established in the literature. One of them is that trade promotes economic growth, and economic growth benefits the poor. The impacts of trade liberalisation on poverty are far from clear-cut, however. Several gaps in the literature on the trade–poverty linkage remain unexplored. First, both poverty and trade liberalisation impacts are multidimensional concepts. The measures of poverty and trade openness remain challenged and controversial. Second, most empirical studies of the relationship are claimed to be indirect. Only a few studies provide direct and compelling evidence on the link between trade and poverty. Third, trade liberalisation comprises both policy and outcomes. Studies in this vein are commonly based on the outcome-based approach. Some of them attempt to measure trade policy, to evaluate its impacts on just growth, not poverty, but are subject to several limitations. Fourth, trade liberalisation covers both international trade and internal (or domestic) trade. Nonetheless, little attention has been paid to the impacts of domestic trade on poverty. The poor probably benefit more from local trade development than from exports, which mainly depend on the world market. These two areas of trade are in fact closely related.

Fifth, the studies of the relationship appear to ignore the impacts of trade liberalisation on urban poverty. The issue of urban poverty is increasingly important in developing countries, because it tends to increase as a consequence of rural-to-urban migration. To some extent, urban poverty affects rural poverty, in the sense that urban unemployment influences rural unemployment. Sixth, the studies following the outcome-based methods tend to ignore the institutional effects of trade liberalisation, which are very case specific and important for understanding the differences in the effects of trade liberalisation on poverty amongst developing countries. Seventh, these studies appear to focus on one or two channels through which trade liberalisation affects poverty. The investigation of many facets of the impacts of trade liberalisation on poverty would provide a more rigorous evaluation of the linkage.

2.8 Conclusions

This chapter has undertaken an analytical account of the theoretical and empirical relationship between trade liberalisation and poverty. The analysis has been conducted in terms of three strands: poverty, trade liberalisation, and the trade–poverty nexus. Poverty has been recognised as a multidimensional concept that transcends the spectrum of material deprivation. The new approach to addressing poverty focuses on three fundamental facets: opportunity, empowerment, and security. This approach also emphasises the role of institutions in the alleviation of poverty. Trade liberalisation is seen as one of the most effective ways of providing the poor with opportunity, empowerment, and security. Trade policy reforms are, therefore, the *sine qua non* for the reduction of poverty. These reforms in developing countries are, however, generally inadequate and inconsistent and, as a result, the poor, on average, benefit little from trade liberalisation.

The Winters framework covers both the main effects of trade liberalisation on poverty and the main stakeholders in an economy. The argument that trade promotes growth and export-driven growth benefits people in the economy as a whole, including the poor, is still valid, in defiance of several criticisms concerning the methodology used for examining the relationship, such as the measurements of trade openness and trade policy and the problematic data. Some of the important research gaps gleaned from the review of the literature provide the motivation for our research: little attention, in the studies for Vietnam, has been paid to the role of domestic trade in poverty reduction, urban poverty, institutional effects, and a comprehensively cohesive picture of the relationship. Of the four channels in the conceptual framework, the effects of market and employment stand out as prominent and empirically verifiable. The empirical studies following these channels have, to some extent, linked trade liberalisation to poverty. Several studies on the trade–poverty link take Vietnam as a case study. They are seen mainly to support the positive role of trade liberalisation in the reduction of poverty in Vietnam. These studies, however, provide partial evidence in general and appear to have ignored the effects of institutional reforms on poverty. McCulloch *et al.* (2001) and Berg and Krueger (2003) are right in contending that each country has specific characteristics and context, and that the best way to unveil the link is to investigate the effects of trade policies on individuals or groups in a country. Trade policies in Vietnam and their impacts on the economy have specific characteristics.

Notes

1 The poverty line was originally set out at US$370 per year per person or US$1 per day per person in constant 1985 PPP prices. It was then updated to US$1.08 per day per person in 1993 PPP prices. All are referred to as the US$1/day poverty line (World Bank, 1990, 2001b).

2 See also Todaro and Smith (2009, p. 238).
3 See also United Nations (2005, p. 222).
4 See also Winters, *et al.* (2004, p. 74).
5 See also Perkins *et al.* (2006, pp. 218–229) and the United Nations (2005, p. 282).
6 Goldberg and Pavcnik (2007) define globalisation as phenomena, including flows of goods and services across borders, reductions in policy and transport barriers to trade, international capital flows, multinational activities, foreign direct investment, outsourcing, increased exposure to exchange rate vitality, and immigration. Trade liberalisation is the most common component of globalisation.
7 See Harvey *et al.* (2010) for new evidence.
8 See Todaro and Smith (2009, p. 635) for more details and discussion.
9 Solow's model is an extension of the Harrod–Domar model, developed by Harrod (1939).
10 See Mankiw *et al.* (1992) and Sachs and Larrain (1993, p. 554) for more discussion of Solow's model.
11 For more discussion about economic convergence of DCs, see Dowrick and Nguyen (1989).
12 See Kapstein (1999, p. 98) and Puntigliano and Appelqvist (2011) for more discussion.
13 See Glewwe *et al.* (2004) for more discussion.

References

Acemoglu, D., and Robinson, J. (2008). *The Role of Institutions in Growth and Development*. Commission on Growth and Development Working Paper (No. 10), 44.

Adams, J.R.R. (2004). Economic Growth, Inequality and Poverty: Estimating the Growth Elasticity of Poverty. *World Development, 32*(12), 1989–2014. DOI: 10.1016/j.worlddev.2004.08.006

Aghion, P., and Bolton, P. (1997). A Theory of Trickle-Down Growth and Development. *The Review of Economic Studies, 64*(2), 151–172.

Aitken, N.D. (1973). The Effect of the EEC and EFTA on European Trade: A Temporal Cross-Section Analysis. *The American Economic Review, 63*(5), 881–892. DOI: 10.2307/1813911

Alam, M.S. (1991). Trade Orientation and Macroeconomic Performance in LDCs: An Empirical Study. *Economic Development and Cultural Change, 39*(4), 839–848. DOI: 10.2307/1154598

Alcalá, F., and Ciccone, A. (2004). Trade and Productivity. *The Quarterly Journal of Economics, 119*(2), 613–646. DOI: 10.1162/0033553041382139

Alesina, A., Spolaore, E., and Wacziarg, R. (2003). *Trade, Growth and the Size of Countries*. Harvard Institute of Economic Research, Discussion Paper (No. 1995), 56.

Alkire, S., and Foster, J. (2011). Counting and Multidimensional Poverty Measurement. *Journal of Public Economics, 95*(7–8), 476–487. DOI: http://dx.doi.org/10.1016/j.jpubeco.2010.11.006

Alkire, S., and Santos, M.E. (2010). *Acute Multidimensional Poverty: A New Index for Developing Countries*. OPHI, Working Paper (No. 38).

Alkire, S., and Santos, M.E. (2011). *Understandings and Misunderstandings of Multidimensional Poverty Measurement*. OPHI, Working Paper (No. 43), 24.

Alkire, S., and Santos, M.E. (2013). *Measuring Acute Poverty in the Developing World: Robustness and Scope of the Multidimensional Poverty Index*. OPHI, Working Paper (No. 59), 48.

Anderson, E. (2005). Openness and Inequality in Developing Countries: A Review of Theory and Recent Evidence. *World Development, 33*(7), 1045–1063. DOI: 10.1016/j.worlddev.2005.04.003

Anderson, J. E. (1996). *Trade Reform with a Government Budget Constraint.* National Bureau of Economic Research, Working Paper Series (No. 5827).

Anderson, J. E., and Neary, J. P. (1994). *Measuring the Restrictiveness of International Trade Policy.* London: Centre for Economic Performance, London School of Economics and Political Science.

Anderson, J. E., and Neary, J. P. (2003). The Mercantilist Index of Trade Policy. *International Economic Review, 44*(2), 627–649. DOI: 10.1111/1468–2354. t01–1–00083

Anderson, K. (2003). Measuring Effects of Trade Policy Distortions: How Far Have We Come?. *The World Economy, 26*(4), 413–440. DOI: 10.1111/1467–9701.00530

Anderson, K., and Martin, W. (2005). *Agricultural Trade Reform and the Doha Development Agenda.* World Bank, Policy Research Working Paper (No. 34206).

Anderson, K., and Morris, P. (2000). The Elusive Goal of Agricultural Trade Reform. *Cato Journal, 19*(3), 385–396.

Anwar, S., and Nguyen, L. P. (2011). Foreign Direct Investment and Export Spillovers: Evidence from Vietnam. *International Business Review, 20,* 177–193.

Athukorala, P. (2010). *Trade Liberalisation and the Poverty of Nations: A Review Article.* Australian National University, Working Papers in Trade and Development (No. 2010/01), 34.

Balakrishnan, R., Steinberg, C., and Syed, M. (2013). *The Elusive Quest for Inclusive Growth: Growth, Poverty, and Inequality in Asia.* IMF, Working Paper (WP/13/152), 36.

Balassa, B. (1978). Exports and Economic Growth: Further Evidence. *Journal of Development Economics, 5*(2), 181–189. DOI: 10.1016/0304–3878(78)90006–8

Baldwin, R. E. (1989). *Measuring Nontariff Trade Policies.* National Bureau of Economic Research, Working Paper Series (No. 2978).

Baldwin, R. E. (2003). *Openness and Growth: What's the Empirical Relationship?.* National Bureau of Economic Research, Working Paper Series (No. 9578), 36.

Bandara, J. S., Athukorala, P., and Kelegama, S. (eds) (2011). *Trade Liberalisation and Poverty in South Asia.* London: Routledge.

Banerjee, A. V., and Duflo, E. (2003). Inequality and Growth: What Can the Data Say?. *Journal of Economic Growth, 8*(3), 267–299. DOI: 10.1023/a:1026205114860

Bannister, G., and Thugge, K. (2001). *International Trade and Poverty Alleviation.* IMF, Working Paper (WP/01/54), 33.

Barro, R., and Sala-i-Martin, X. (1990). *Economic Growth and Convergence across the United States.* National Bureau of Economic Research, Working Paper Series (No. 3419).

Baunsgaard, T., and Keen, M. (2005). *Tax Revenue and (or?) Trade Liberalization.* IMF, Working Paper (WP/05/112).

Baunsgaard, T., and Keen, M. (2010). Tax Revenue and (or?) Trade Liberalization. *Journal of Public Economics, 94*(9–10), 563–577. DOI: http://dx.doi.org/10.1016/j.jpubeco.2009.11.007

Berg, A., and Krueger, A. (2003). *Trade, Growth, and Poverty: A Selective Survey.* IMF, Working Paper (WP/03/30).

Berg, A., and Ostry, J. (2011). *Inequality and Unsustainable Growth: Two Sides of the Same Coin?.* IMF, Staff Discussion Note (SDN/11/08), 21.

Berg, A., Ostry, J.D., and Zettelmeyer, J. (2012). What Makes Growth Sustained?. *Journal of Development Economics, 98*(2), 149–166. DOI: http://dx.doi.org/10.1016/j.jdeveco.2011.08.002

Bhagwati, J.N. (1958). Immiserizing Growth: A Geometrical Note. *The Review of Economic Studies, 25*(3), 201–205.

Bhagwati, J.N. (1968). Distortions and Immiserizing Growth: A Generalization. *The Review of Economic Studies, 35*(4), 481–485.

Bhagwati, J.N. (1989). *Protectionism*. Cambridge: MIT Press.

Bhagwati, J.N., and Srinivasan, T.N. (2002). Trade and Poverty in the Poor Countries. *American Economic Review, 92*(2), 180–183. DOI: 10.1257/000282802320189212

Bhagwati, J.N., Srinivasan, T.N., and Henry, W.J. (1978). Value Subtracted, Negative Shadow Prices of Factors in Project Evaluation, and Immiserising Growth. *The Economic Journal, 88*(349), 121–125.

Bilal, S., Dalleau, M., and Lui, D. (2012). *Trade Liberalisation and Fiscal Adjustments: The Case of EPAs in Africa*. European Centre for Development Policy Management, Discussion Paper (No. 137), 102.

Bourguignon, F. (2003). The Growth Elasticity of Poverty Reduction: Explaining Heterogeneity across Countries and Time Periods. In T. Eichler and S. Turnovsky (eds) *Growth and Inequality* (pp. 3–26). Cambridge, MA: MIT Press.

Bourguignon, F. (2004, February 4). *The Poverty-Growth-Inequality Triangle*. Paper presented at the Indian Council for Research on International Economic Relations, Delhi.

Brown, D.J., and Srinivasan, T.N. (2007). *The Gains from Trade Liberalisation*. Yale University, Working Papers on Economic Applications and Policy (No. 24), 15.

Bruno, M., Ravallion, M., and Squire, L. (1998). Equity and Growth in Developing Countries: Old and New Perspectives on the Policy Issues. In V. Tanzi and K. Chu (eds) *Income Distribution and High-Quality Growth* (pp. 117–146). Cambridge, MA: MIT Press.

Chen, S., and Ravallion, M. (2010). The Developing World is Poorer Than We Thought, But No Less Successful in the Fight Against Poverty. *The Quarterly Journal of Economics, 125*(4), 1577–1625. DOI: 10.1162/qjec.2010.125.4.1577

Christev, A., Kupets, O., and Lehmann, H. (2005). *Trade Liberalization and Employment Effects in Ukraine*. IZA, Discussion Paper (No. 1826), 34.

Coello, B., Fall, M., and Suwa-Eisenmann, A. (2010). *Trade Liberalization and Poverty Dynamics in Vietnam 2002–2006*. Paris School of Economics, Working Paper (No.11), 43.

Collier, P., and Dollar, D. (2001). Can the World Cut Poverty in Half? How Policy Reform and Effective Aid Can Meet International Development Goals. *World Development, 29*(11), 1787–1802. DOI: http://dx.doi.org/10.1016/S0305-750X(01)00076-6

Collier, P., and Dollar, D. (2002). Aid Allocation and Poverty Reduction. *European Economic Review, 46*(8), 1475–1500.

Combes, J.L., and Saadi-Sedik, T. (2006). *How Does Trade Openness Influence Budget Deficits in Developing Countries?*. IMF, Working Paper (WP/06/3), 22.

Das, D.K. (2008). *Trade Liberalization, Employment, Labor Productivity, and Real Wages: A Study of the Organized Manufacturing Industry in India in the 1980s and 1990s*. ILO Asia-Pacific, Working Paper Series, 66.

Deardorff, A.V., and Stern, R.M. (1997). *Measurement of Non-tariff Barriers*. OECD Economics Department, Working Paper (No. 179), 118.

Deaton, A. (1989). Rice Price and Income Distribution in Thailand: A Non-parametric Ananlysis. *The Economic Journal, 99*(395), 1–37.

Deaton, A. (1997). *The Analysis of Household Surveys: A Microeconometric Approach to Development Policy.* Washington, DC: Johns Hopkins University Press.

Deaton, A. (2001). Counting the World's Poor: Problems and Possible Solutions. *World Bank Research Observer, 16*(2), 18.

Deaton, A. (2002). Is World Poverty Falling?. *Finance & Development, 39*(2), 6.

Deaton, A. (2008, February). Price Trends in India and Their Implications for Measuring Poverty. *Economic and Political Weekly,* 27.

Deaton, A. (2010). Price Indexes, Inequality, and the Measurement of World Poverty. *American Economic Review, 100*(1), 5–34.

Deolalikar, A. B., Brillantes, J. A.B., Gaiha, R., Pernia, E. M., and Racelis, M. (2002). *Poverty Reduction and the Role of Institutions in Developing Asia.* ERD, Working Paper Series (No. 10).

Dercon, S. (2006). Economic Reform, Growth and the Poor: Evidence from Rural Ethiopia. *Journal of Development Economics, 81*(1), 1–24. DOI: http://dx.doi.org/10.1016/j.jdeveco.2005.05.008

Dollar, D. (1992). Outward-Oriented Developing Economies Really Do Grow More Rapidly: Evidence from 95 LDCs, 1976–1985. *Economic Development and Cultural Change, 40*(3), 22.

Dollar, D. (2004). Reform, Growth, and Poverty. In P. Glewwe, N. Agrawal, and D. Dollar (eds) *Economic Growth, Poverty, and Household Welfare in Vietnam* (pp. 29–51). Washington, DC: World Bank.

Dollar, D., and Kraay, A. (2002). Growth is Good for the Poor. *Journal of Economic Growth, 7*(3), 195.

Dollar, D., and Kraay, A. (2004). Trade, Growth, and Poverty. *The Economic Journal, 114*(493), F22–F49. DOI: 10.1111/j.0013-0133.2004.00186.x

Dowrick, S., and Nguyen, D. T. (1989). OECD Comparative Economic Growth 1950–85: Catch-up and Convergence. *The American Economic Review, 79*(5), 1010–1030. DOI: 10.2307/1831434

Ederington, J., and Minier, J. (2008). Reconsidering the Empirical Evidence on the Grossman-Helpman Model of Endogenous Protection. *Canadian Journal of Economics, 41*(2), 16.

Edwards, S. (1992). Trade Orientation, Distortions and Growth in Developing Countries. *Journal of Development Economics, 39*(1), 31–57. DOI: http://dx.doi.org/10.1016/0304-3878(92)90056-F

Edwards, S. (1997). *Openness, Productivity and Growth: What Do We Really Know?.* National Bureau of Economic Research, Working Paper Series (No. 5978).

Esqueda, O., and Assefa, T. (2011). Purchasing Power Parity and Degree of Openness in Latin America: A Panel Analysis. *Journal of Financial and Economic Practice, 11*(2), 15.

Feenstra, R. C. (1995). *Estimating the Effects of Trade Policy.* National Bureau of Economic Research, Working Paper Series (No. 5051), 65.

Feliciano, Z. M. (2001). Workers and Trade Liberalization: The Impact of Trade Reforms in Mexico on Wages and Employment. *Industrial and Labor Relations Review, 55*(1), 95–115. DOI: 10.2307/2696188

Ferreira, F. H.G., Leite, P. G., and Wai-Poi, M. (2007). *Trade Liberalization, Employment Flows and Wage Inequality in Brazil.* World Bank, Policy Research Working Paper (No. 4108), 56.

Figuié, M., and Moustier, P. (2009). Market Appeal in an Emerging Economy: Super-markets and Poor Consumers in Vietnam. *Food Policy, 34,* 210–217.

Foster, J., Greer, J., and Thorbecke, E. (1984). A Class of Decomposable Poverty Measures. *Econometrica, 52*(3), 761–766.

Foster, J., Greer, J., and Thorbecke, E. (2010). The Foster–Greer–Thorbecke (FGT) Poverty Measures: 25 Years Later. *The Journal of Economic Inequality, 8*(4), 491–524. DOI: 10.1007/s10888–010–9136–1

Foster, N. (2008). The Impact of Trade Liberalisation on Economic Growth: Evidence from a Quantile Regression Analysis. *KYKLOS, 61*(4), 25.

Frankel, J.A., and Romer, D. (1999). Does Trade Cause Growth?. *The American Economic Review, 89*(3), 379–399.

Frankel, J.A., Stein, E., and Wei, S. (1995). Trading Blocs and the Americas: The Natural, the Unnatural, and the Super-natural. *Journal of Development Economics, 47*(1), 61–95. DOI: http://dx.doi.org/10.1016/0304–3878(95)00005–4

Fukuda, S., and Toya, H. (1995). Conditional Convergence in East Asian Countries: The Role of Exports in Economic Growth. In T. Ito and A. Krueger (eds) *Growth Theories in Light of the East Asian Experience* (vol. 4, p. 20). Chicago: University of Chicago Press.

Gallup, J.L. (2004). The Wage Labor Market and Inequality in Vietnam. In P. Glewwe, N. Agrawal, and D. Dollar (eds) *Economic Growth, Poverty, and Household Welfare in Vietnam* (pp. 53–93). Washington, DC: World Bank.

Ghose, A.K. (2000). *Trade Liberalization and Manufacturing Employment.* Employment Sector, International Labour Office Geneva, Employment Paper (No. 2000/3), 68.

Ghosh, M., and Whalley, J. (2004). Are Price Controls Necessarily Bad? The Case of Rice in Vietnam. *Journal of Development Economics, 73*(1), 215–232.

Glewwe, P., Agrawal, N., and Dollar, D. (eds) (2004). *Economic Growth, Poverty, and Household Welfare in Vietnam.* Washington, DC: World Bank.

Glewwe, P., Gragnolati, M., and Zaman, H. (2000). *Who Gained from Vietnam's Boom in the 1990s: An Analysis of Poverty and Inequality Trends.* World Bank, Policy Research Working Paper (No. 2275), 64.

Glewwe, P., Gragnolati, M., and Zaman, H. (2002). Who Gained from Vietnam's Boom in the 1990s?. *Economic Development and Cultural Change, 50*(4), 773–792.

Goldberg, P.K., and Pavcnik, N. (2004). *Trade, Inequality, and Poverty: What Do We Know? Evidence from Recent Trade Liberalization Episodes in Developing Countries.* NBER, Working Paper Series (No. 10593), 52.

Goldberg, P.K., and Pavcnik, N. (2007). *Distributional Effects of Globalization in Developing Countries.* NBER, Working Paper Series (No. 12885), 69.

Greenaway, D., Morgan, W., and Wright, P. (2002). Trade Liberalisation and Growth in Developing Countries. *Journal of Development Economics, 67*(1), 229.

Greenaway, D., and Nam, C.H. (1988). Industrialisation and Macroeconomic Performance in Developing Countries under Alternative Trade Strategies. *KYKLOS, 41*(3), 419–435. DOI: 10.1111/j.1467–6435.1988.tb01263.x

Grinspun, A. (2009). Pro-poor Growth: Finding the Holy Grail. *One Pagers No. 6.* Brasilia: United Nations Development Programme, International Policy Centre for Inclusive Growth.

GRIPS Development Forum (2003). *Linking Economic Growth and Poverty Reduction-Large-Scale Infrastructure in the Context of Vietnam's CPRGS.* Hanoi: MPI.

Grossman, G.M., and Helpman, E. (1991). Trade, Knowledge Spillovers, and Growth. *European Economic Review, 35*(2–3), 517.

Guttmann, S., and Richards, A. (2006). Trade Openness: An Autralian Perspective. *Australian Economic Papers, 45*(3), 188–203. DOI: 10.1111/j.1467–8454.2006. 00287.x

Hallaert, J.J. (2006). A History of Empirical Literature on the Relationship Between Trade and Growth. *Mondes en Développement, 3*(135), 15.

Hansson, G. (ed) (1993). *Trade, Growth and Development: The Role of Politics and Institutions.* New York: Routledge.

Harrison, A. (1996). *Openness and Growth: A Time-Series, Cross-Country Analysis for Developing Countries.* National Bureau of Economic Research, Working Paper Series (No. 5221).

Harrison, A. (2007). Globalization and Poverty: An Introduction. In A. Harrison (ed) *Globalization and Poverty* (pp. 1–30). Chicago: University of Chicago Press.

Harrison, A., and Hanson, G. (1999). Who Gains from Trade Reform? Some Remaining Puzzles. *Journal of Development Economics, 59*(1), 125.

Harrison, A., and McMillan, M. (2007). On the Links between Globalization and Poverty. *Journal of Economic Inequality, 5*(1), 123–134.

Harrison, A., and Tang, H. (2004). Trade Liberalization: Why So Much Controversy?. In *Economic Growth in the 1990s: Learning from a Decade of Reform* (pp. 133–155). Washington, DC: World Bank.

Harrison, G., Rutherford, T.F., and Tarr, D.G. (2003a). *Quantifying the Impact of Trade Reform on Poverty.* Available at GU Proquest, World Bank.

Harrison, G., Rutherford, T.F., and Tarr, D.G. (2003b). Trade Liberalization, Poverty and Efficient Equity. *Journal of Development Economics, 71*(1), 97–128. DOI: http://dx.doi.org/10.1016/S0304-3878(02)00135-9

Harrod, R.F. (1939). An Essay in Dynamic Theory. *The Economic Journal, 49*(193), 21.

Harvey, D.I., Kellard, N.M., Madsen, J.B., and Wohar, M.E. (2010). The Prebisch-Singer Hypothesis: Four Centuries of Evidence. *The Review of Economic and Statistics, 92*(2), 367–377.

Haughton, D., and Le, T.T.L. (2005). Shifts in Living Standards: The Case of Vietnam Households 1992–1998. *Phillipine Journal of Development, XXXII*(1), 79–101.

Haughton, D., and Phong, N. (2010). Multilevel Models and Inequality in Vietnam. *Journal of Data Science, 8*, 289–306.

Heo, Y., and Nguyen, K.D. (2009). Trade Liberalisation and Poverty Reduction in Vietnam. *The World Economy, 32*(6), 934.

Hertel, T.W., and Winters, L.A. (2005). Estimate the Poverty Impacts of a Prospective Doha Development Agenda. *The World Economy, 28*(8), 1057–1071.

Hiscox, M., and Kastner, S.L. (2002). *A General Measure of Trade Policy Orientations: Gravity-Model-Based Estimates for 82 Nations, 1960 to 1992.* Retrieved from http://www.is.gd/7qCqUe.

Holmes, M. (2005). New Evidence on Long-Run Output Convergence among Latin American Countries. *Journal of Applied Economics, VIII*(2), 21.

International Monetary Fund (IMF) (2004). *Vietnam: Poverty Reduction Strategy Paper.* IMF, Country Report (No. 25), 134.

International Monetary Fund (IMF) (2005). *Dealing with the Revenue Consequences of Trade Reform.* Background Paper for Review of Fund Work on Trade, 32.

International Monetary Fund (IMF) (2006). Integrating Poor Countries into the World Trading System. *Economic Issues* (37), 23.

Isik-Dikmelik, A. (2006). *Trade Reforms and Welfare: An Ex-post Decomposition of Income in Vietnam.* World Bank, Policy Research Working Paper (No. 4049), 50.

Justino, P., Litchfield, J., and Pham, H.T. (2008). Poverty Dynamics during Trade Reform: Evidence from Rural Vietnam. *Review of Income and Wealth, 54*(2), 166–192. DOI: 10.1111/j.1475–4991.2008.00269.x

Kakwani, N., Khandker, S., and Son, H. H. (2004). *Pro-poor Growth: Concepts and Measurement with Country Case Studies.* UNDP International Poverty Centre, Working Paper (No. 1), 28.

Kakwani, N., and Pernia, E. (2000). What is Pro-poor Growth?. *Asian Development Review, 18*(1), 16.

Kakwani, N., and Son, H. H. (2008). Poverty Equivalent Growth Rate. *Review of Income and Wealth, 54*(4), 643. DOI: 10.1111/j.1475–4991.2008.00293.x

Kalwij, A. S., and Verschoor, A. (2007). Not by Growth Alone: The Role of the Distribution of income in Regional Diversity in Poverty Reduction. *European Economic Review, 51*(4), 805–829. DOI: http://dx.doi.org/10.1016/j.euroecorev. 2006.06.003

Kang, W., and Imai, K. S. (2012). Pro-poor Growth, Poverty and Inequality in Rural Vietnam. *Journal of Asian Economics, 23*(5), 527–539.

Kapstein, E. B. (1999). Distributive Justice as an International Public Good: A Historical Perspective. In I. Kaul, Grunberg, I., and Stern, M.A. (eds) *Global Public Goods.* New York: Oxford University Press.

Krueger, A. O. (1978a). Alternative Trade Strategies and Employment in LDCs. *The American Economic Review, 68*(2), 270–274. DOI: 10.2307/1816703

Krueger, A. O. (1978b). *Foreign Trade Regimes and Economic Development: Liberalization Attempts and Consequences* (vol. 10). New York: National Bureau of Economic Research.

Krueger, A. O. (1982). *Trade and Employment in Developing Countries: Factor Supply and Substitution* (vol. 2). Chicago: University of Chicago Press.

Krueger, A. O. (1983). *Trade and Employment in Less Developed Countries: Synthesis and Conclusion* (vol. 3). Chicago: University of Chicago Press.

Krueger, A. O. (1997). Trade Policy and Economic Development: How We Learn. *The American Economic Review, 87*(1), 1–22. DOI: 10.2307/2950851

Krueger, A. O. (1998). Why Trade Liberalization is Good for Growth. *The Economic Journal, 108*(450), 1513–1522.

Krueger, A. O., Lary, H. B., Monson, T., and Akrasanee, N. (eds) (1981). *Trade and Development in Developing Countries: Individual Studies* (vol. 1). Chicago: University of Chicago Press.

Le, M. S. (2014). Trade Openness and Household Welfare within a Country: A Microeconomic Analysis of Vietnamese Households. *Journal of Asian Economics, 33*, 56–70.

Leamer, E. E. (1988). Measures of Openness. In R. E. Baldwin (ed) *Trade Policy Issues and Empirical Analysis* (p. 59). Chicago: University of Chicago Press.

Lenagala, C., and Ram, R. (2010). Growth Elasticity of Poverty: Estimates from New Data. *International Journal of Social Economics, 37*(12), 10.

Linnemann, H. (1966). *An Econometric Study of International Trade Flows.* Amsterdam: North Holland Publishing Company. Retrieved from http://worldcat. org/z-wcorg/database.

Litchfield, J., McCulloch, N., and Winters, L. A. (2003). Agricultural Trade Liberalization and Poverty Dynamics in Three Developing Countries. *American Journal of Agricultural Economics, 85*(5), 1285–1291. DOI: 10.1111/j.0092–5853.2003.00544.x

Little, I.M.D., Scitovsky, T., and Scott, M. (1970). *Industry and Trade in some Developing Countries: A Comparative Study.* London: Oxford University Press.

Love, P., and Lattimore, R. (2009). Protectionism? Tariffs and Other Barriers to Trade. In *International Trade: Free, Fair and Open?* (pp. 54–75). OECD Publishing.

Maggi, G., and Rodriguez-Clare, A. (1998). *Import Penetration and the Politics of Trade Protection.* NBER, Working Paper Series (No. 6711), 22.

Mankiw, N. G. (2012). *Principles of Economics* (6th ed.). Ohio: South-Western Cengage Learning.

Mankiw, N. G., Romer, D., and Weil, D. N. (1992). A Contribution to the Empirics of Economic Growth. *The Quarterly Journal of Economics, 107*(2), 407–437. DOI: 10.2307/2118477

Marchand, B. U. (2012). Tariff Pass-Through and the Distributional Effects of Trade Liberalization. *Journal of Development Economics, 99*(2), 265–281.

McCulloch, N., and Baulch, B. (2000). Tracking Pro-poor Growth: New Ways to Spot the Biases and Benefits. *ID21 Insights No. 31.* Sussex: Institute of Development Studies.

McCulloch, N., Winters, L.A., and Cirera, X. (2001). *Trade Liberalization and Poverty: A Handbook.* London: Centre for Economic Policy Research.

McKay, A. (2002). Defining and Measuring Inequality. *Inequality Briefing, 1*(1), 6.

McKinnon, R. I. (1979). Foreign Trade Regimes and Economic Development: A Review Article. *Journal of International Economics, 9*(3), 429–452. DOI: http://dx.doi.org/10.1016/0022-1996(79)90037-0

Michaely, M. (1977). Exports and Growth: An Empirical Investigation. *Journal of Development Economics, 4*(1), 49–53. DOI: 10.1016/0304-3878(77)90006-2

Milanovic, B. (2006). Global Income Inequality: A Review. *World Economics, 7*(1), 28.

Milanovic, B. (2010). *The Haves and the Have-Nots: A Brief and Idiosyncratic History of Global Inequality.* New York: Basic Books.

Minot, N. (1998). *Competitiveness of Food Processing in Vietnam: A Study of the Rice, Coffee, Seafood, and Fruit and Vegetables Subsectors.* Washington, DC: International Food Policy Research Institute.

Minot, N. (2000). Generating Disaggregated Poverty Maps: An Application to Vietnam. *World Development, 28*(2), 319–331. DOI: 10.1016/S0305–750X(99)00126–6

Minot, N. (2003, July 27–30). *Income Diversification and Poverty Reduction in the Northern Uplands of Vietnam.* Paper presented at the The American Agricultural Economics Association Annual Meeting, Montreal, CA.

Minot, N., and Baulch, B. (2005). Spatial Patterns of Poverty in Vietnam and Their Implications for Policy. *Food Policy, 30*(5–6), 461–475. DOI: 10.1016/j.foodpol.2005.09.002].

Minot, N., and Goletti, F. (1998). Export Liberalization and Household Welfare: The Case of Rice in Vietnam. *American Journal of Agricultural Economics, 80*(4), 738–749.

Myrdal, G. (1956). *An International Economy: Problem and Prospects.* New York: Harper & Brothers.

Nash, J., and Andriamananjara, S. (1999). *Have Trade Policy Reforms Led to Greater Openness in Developing Countries?.* World Bank, Policy Research Working Paper (No. 1730), 22. DOI: 10.1596/1813–9450–1730

Nash, J., and Mitchell, D. (2005). How Freer Trade Can Help Feed the Poor. *IMF Survey, Finance & Development March 2005.*

Nguyen, B. T., Albrecht, J. W., Vroman, S. B., and Westbrook, M. D. (2007). A Quantile Regression Decomposition of Urban-Rural Inequality in Vietnam. *Journal of Deveopment Economics, 83*(2), 466–490.

Nguyen, C., Tran, K. D., Ghosh, M., and Whalley, J. (2005). Adjustment Costs in Labour Markets and the Distributional Effects of Trade Liberalization: Analytics and Calculations for Vietnam. *Journal of Policy Modeling, 27*(9), 1009–1024. DOI: 10.1016/j.jpolmod.2005.06.010

Nicita, A. (2009). The Price Effect of Tariff Liberalization: Measuring the Impact on Household Welfare. *Journal of Development Economics, 89*(1), 19–27. DOI: http://dx.doi.org/10.1016/j.jdeveco.2008.06.009

Niimi, Y., Vasudeva-Dutta, P., and Winters, L. A. (2004). Storm in A Rice Bowl: Rice Reform and Poverty in Vietnam in the 1990s. *Journal of the Asia Pacific Economy, 9*(2), 170–190.

Niimi, Y., Vasudeva-Dutta, P., and Winters, L. A. (2007). Trade Liberalization and Poverty Dynamics in Vietnam. *Journal of Economic Integration, 22*(4), 819–851.

Nissanke, M., and Thorbecke, E. (2006). *A Quest for Pro-poor Globalization.* UNU-WIDER, Research Paper (No. 2006/46), 25.

Nissanke, M., and Thorbecke, E. (2007a). *Linking Globalization and Poverty.* United Nations University, Policy Brief (No. 2), 8.

Nissanke, M., and Thorbecke, E. (eds) (2007b). *The Impact of Globalization on the World's Poor: Transmission Mechanisms.* Basingstoke: Palgrave Macmillan.

Nissanke, M., and Thorbecke, E. (2008). Introduction: Globalization–Poverty Channels and Case Studies from Sub-Saharan Africa. *African Development Review, 20*(1), 19.

North, D. C. (1981). *Structure and Change in Economic History.* New York: W. W. Norton.

North, D. C. (1989). Institutions and Economic Growth: An Historical Introduction. *World Development, 17*(9), 1319–1332. DOI: http://dx.doi.org/10.1016/0305-750X(89)90075-2

North, D. C. (1991). Institutions. *Journal of Economic Perspectives, 5*(1), 97–112. DOI: 10.1257/jep.5.1.97

OECD (2001, April 25–26). *Rising to the Global Challenge: Partnership for Reducing World Poverty.* Paper presented at the DAC High Level Meeting, Paris.

OECD (2010). Import Penetration of Goods and Services. In *Measuring Globalisation: OECD Economic Globalisation Indicators 2010* (pp. 76–77). OECD Publishing.

OECD (2011). *The Impact of Trade Liberalisation on Jobs and Growth: Technical Note.* OECD, Trade Policy Papers (No. 107), 109.

Olinto, P., Beegle, K., Sobrado, C., and Uematsu, H. (2013). The State of the Poor: Where Are the Poor, Where is Extreme Poverty Harder to End, and What is the Current Profile of the World's Poor? *Poverty Reduction and Economic Management (PREM).* World Bank.

Olinto, P., Lara Ibarra, G., and Saavedra-Chanduvi, J. (2014). *Accelerating Poverty Reduction in a Less Poor World : The Roles of Growth and Inequality.* Policy Research Working Paper (No. 6855), 30.

Osmani, S. (2009). Defining Pro-poor Growth. *One Pager No. 9* (p. 1). Brasilia: United Nations Development Programme, International Policy Centre for Inclusive Growth.

Ostry, J., Berg, A., and Tsangarides, C. (2014). *Redistribution, Inequality, and Growth*. IMF, Staff Discussion Note (SDN/14/02), 30.

Oxfam Great Britain, and Oxfam Hong Kong. (2001). *Rice for the Poor and Trade Liberalization in Vietnam*. Hanoi: Oxfam.

Pacheco-Lopez, P., and Thirlwall, A.P. (2009). *Has Trade Liberalisation in Poor Countries Delivered the Promises Expected?*. Department of Economics, University of Kent, Discussion Paper (No. KDPE 0911).

Patrick, L., and Ralph, L. (2009). Protectionism? Tariffs and Other Barriers to Trade. In OECD (ed) *International Trade: Free, Fair and Open?* (pp. 54–75). OECD Publishing.

Pavcnik, N., Blom, A., Goldberg, P., and Schady, N. (2004). Trade Liberalization and Industry Wage Structure: Evidence from Brazil. *The World Bank Economic Review, 18*(3), 319–344. DOI: 10.1093/wber/lhh045

Perkins, D.H., Radelet, S., and Lindauer, D.L. (2006). *Economics of Development* (6th ed.). New York: W. W. Norton.

Pernia, E.M. (2003). *Pro-poor Growth: What is It and How is It Important?*. ERD, Policy Brief (No. 17), 11.

Phan, D., and Coxhead, I. (2010). Inter-provincial Migration and Inequality During Vietnam's Transition. *Journal of Development Economics, 91*(1), 100.

Piketty, T. (2014). *Capital in the Twenty-First Century*. Massachusetts: Harvard University Press.

Porto, G.G. (2004). *Informal Export Barriers and Poverty*. World Bank, Policy Research Working Papers (No. 3354), 39.

Porto, G.G. (2006a). *Estimating Household Responses to Trade Reforms. Net Consumers and Net Producers in Rural Mexico*. World Bank, Policy Research Working Papers (No. 3695), 50.

Porto, G.G. (2006b). Using Survey Data to Assess the Distributional Effects of Trade Policy. *Journal of International Economics, 70*(1), 140–160. DOI: http://dx.doi.org/10.1016/j.jinteco.2005.09.003

Prina, S. (2007). *Agricultural Trade Liberalization in Mexico: Impact on Border Prices and Farmers' Income*. Ohio: Department of Economics, Weatherhead School of Management, Case Western Reserve University.

Pritchett, L. (1996). Measuring Outward Orientation in LDCs: Can It Be Done?. *Journal of Development Economics, 49*(2), 307–335. DOI: http://dx.doi.org/10.1016/0304-3878(95)00064-X

Puntigliano, A.R., and Appelqvist, O. (2011). Prebisch and Myrdal: Development Economic in the Core and on the Periphery. *Journal of Global History, 6*(1), 29–52. DOI: 10.1017/S1740022811000039

Ram, R. (1985). Exports and Economic Growth: Some Additional Evidence. *Economic Development and Cultural Change, 33*(2), 415–425.

Ram, R. (1987). Exports and Economic Growth in Developing Countries: Evidence from Time-Series and Cross-Section Data. *Economic Development and Cultural Change, 36*(1), 51–72.

Ram, R. (2006). Growth Elasticity of Poverty: Alternative Estimates and a Note of Caution. *KYKLOS, 59*(4), 10.

Ram, R. (2011). Growth Elasticity of Poverty: Direct Estimates from Recent Data. *Applied Economics, 43*(19), 2433–2440.

Ravallion, M. (1990). Rural Welfare Effects of Food Price Changes under Induced Wage Responses: Theory and Evidence for Bangladesh. *Oxford Economic Papers, 42*(3), 574–585. DOI: 10.2307/2663062

Ravallion, M. (2001). Growth, Inequality and Poverty: Looking Beyond Averages. *World Development, 29*(11), 1803–1815. DOI: http://dx.doi.org/10.1016/S0305-750X(01)00072-9

Ravallion, M. (2006). Looking Beyond Averages in the Trade and Poverty Debate. *World Development, 34*(8), 1374–1392. DOI: http://dx.doi.org/10.1016/j.worlddev.2005.10.015

Ravallion, M. (2007). Economic Growth and Poverty Reduction: Do Poor Countries Need to Worry about Inequality? In S. P. Jenkins and P. Micklewright (eds) *Inequality and Poverty Re-examined* (pp. 179–186). Oxford: Oxford University Press.

Ravallion, M., and Chen, S. (1997). What Can New Survey Data Tell Us about Recent Changes in Distribution and Poverty?. *The World Bank Economic Review, 11*(2), 357–382. DOI: 10.1093/wber/11.2.357

Ravallion, M., and Chen, S. (2009). *Weak Relative Poverty.* World Bank, Policy Research Working Paper (No. 4844).

Ravallion, M., Chen, S., and Sangraula, P. (2008). *Dollar a Day Revisited.* World Bank, Policy Research Working Paper (No. 4620), 42.

Ravallion, M., and Datt, G. (2002). Why Has Economic Growth Been More Pro-poor in Some States of India than Others?. *Journal of Development Economics, 68*(2), 381–400. DOI: http://dx.doi.org/10.1016/S0304-3878(02)00018-4

Rodriguez, F., and Rodrik, D. (2001). *Trade Policy and Economic Growth: A Skeptic's Guide to Cross-National Evidence.* NBER, Working Paper Series (No. 7081), 82.

Rodrik, D. (2000). Growth Versus Poverty Reduction: A Hollow Debate. *Finance & Development, 37*(4), 8–9.

Rodrik, D. (2001). *The Developing Countries' Hazardous Obession with Global Integration.* Retrieved from http://www.is.gd/oEh3Ve.

Rodrik, D. (2002). Trade Policy Reform as Institutional Reform. In B. Hoekman, A. Mattoo, and P. English (eds) *Development, Trade, and the WTO: A Handbook* (pp. 3–10). Washington, DC: World Bank.

Rodrik, D. (2010). Diagnostics before Prescription. *Journal of Economic Perspectives, 24*(3), 33–44.

Rodrik, D. (2013). *When Ideas Trump Interests: Preferences, World Views, and Policy Innovations.* National Bureau of Economic Research, Working Paper Series (No. 19631). DOI: 10.3386/w19631

Roemer, M., and Gugerty, M. K. (1997). *Does Economic Growth Reduce Poverty?.* CAER, Harvard Institute for International Development, Discussion Paper (No. 5), 33.

Rogoff, K. (1996). The Purchasing Power Parity Puzzle. *Journal of Economic Literature, 34*(2), 647–668. DOI: 10.2307/2729217

Sachs, J. D., and Larrain, B. (1993). *Macroeconomics in the Global Economy* (1st ed.). New Jersey: Prentice Hall.

Sachs, J. D., and Warner, A. (1995). Economic Reform and the Process of Global Integration. *Brookings Papers on Economic Activity, 1995*(1), 1–118.

Salvatore, D. (1998). *International Economics* (6th ed.). USA: Prentice Hall.

Santos-Paulino, A. U. (2012). *Trade, Income Distribution and Poverty in Developing Countries: A Survey.* UNCTAD, Discussion Paper (No. 207), 36.

Sen, A. (1976). Poverty: An Ordinal Approach to Measurement. *Econometrica, 44*(2), 219–231. DOI: 10.2307/1912718

Sen, A. (2003). Development as Capability Expansion. In S. Fukuda-Parr and A. K. Shiva Kumar (eds) *Readings in Human Development* (pp. 3–16). New Delhi: Oxford University Press.

Sen, A. (1993). Capability and Well-being. In M. Nussbaum and A. Sen (eds), *The Quality of Life* (pp. 30–53). Oxford: Clarendon Press.

Sen, A. (2005). Human Rights and Capabilities. *Journal of Human Development,* 6(2), 16.

Seshan, G. (2005). *The Impact of Trade Liberalization on Household Welfare in Vietnam.* World Bank, Policy Research Working Paper (No. 3541).

Shafaeddin, S.M. (2005). *Trade Liberalization and Economic reform in Developing Countries: Structural Change or De-industrialization.* Paper presented at the The United Nations Conference on Trade and Development.

Shahbaz Akmal, M., Masood Ahmad, Q., Hussain Ahmad, M., and Sabihuddin Butt, M. (2007). An Empirical Investigation of the Relationship between Trade Liberalization and Poverty Reduction: A Case for Pakistan. *The Lahore Journal of Economics, 12*(1), 20.

Singh, T. (2002). On the Empirics of Trade and Growth Relationship in India. *International Economics, 55*(2), 17.

Singh, T. (2003). Effects of Exports on Productivity and Growth in India: An Industry-Based Analysis. *Applied Economics, 35*(7), 741–749. DOI: 10.1080/00036840210139337

Singh, T. (2010). Does International Trade Cause Economic Growth? A Survey. *The World Economy, 33*(11), 1517–1564. DOI: 10.1111/j.1467–9701.2010.01243.x

Singh, T. (2011). International Trade and Economic Growth Nexus in Australia: A Robust Evidence from Time-Series Estimators. *The World Economy, 34*(8), 1348–1394. DOI: 10.1111/j.1467–9701.2011.01341.x

Solow, R.M. (1956). A Contribution to the Theory of Economic Growth. *The Quarterly Journal of Economics, 70*(1), 31.

Son, H.H. (2007a). Interrelationship between Growth, Inequality and Poverty: The Asian Experience. *Asian Development Review, 24*(2), 37–63.

Son, H.H. (2007b). *Pro-poor Growth: Concepts and Measures.* ERD, Technical Note (No. 22), 33.

Spilimbergo, A., Londoño, J.L., and Székely, M. (1999). Income Distribution, Factor Endowments, and Trade Openness. *Journal of Development Economics, 59*(1), 77–101. DOI: http://dx.doi.org/10.1016/S0304–3878(99)00006–1

Squalli, J., and Wilson, K. (2011). A New Measure of Trade Openness. *The World Economy, 34*(10), 1745–1770.

Srinivasan, T.N., and Bhagwati, J. (2001). Outward-Orientation and Development: Are Revisionists Right?. In D. Lal and R.H. Shape (eds) *Trade, Development and Political Economy: Essays in Honour of Anne O. Krueger* (p. 334). London: Palgrave Macmillan.

Staiger, R.W. (2012). *Non-tariff Measures and the WTO.* WTO, Working Paper Series (Staff Working Paper ERSD-2012–01), 47.

Steer, L., and Sen, K. (2010). Formal and Informal Institutions in a Transition Economy: The Case of Vietnam. *World Development, 38*(11), 1603–1615. DOI: 10.1016/j.worlddev.2010.03.006

Stiglitz, J.E. (2008). Making Globalisation Work – The 2006 Geary Lecture. *The Economic and Social Review, 39*(3), 20.

Stoeckel, A., Saunders, C., and Monck, M. (2007). Trade Policy and Developing Countries: Where to Now (p. 60). Canberra: RIRDC-CIE.

Tahir, S.H., Perveen, N., Ismail, A., and Sabir, H.M. (2014). Impact of GDP Growth Rate on Poverty of Pakistan: A Quantitative Approach. *Euro-Asian Journal of Economics and Finance, 2*(2), 8.

Thirlwall, A. P. (2000). *Trade, Trade Liberalisation and Economic Growth: Theory and Evidence*. African Development Bank, Economic Research Papers (No. 63).

Thoburn, J. (2004). Globalization and Poverty in Vietnam. *Journal of the Asia Pacific Economy, 9*(2), 127–144.

Thomas, V., and Nash, J. (1991). Reform of Trade Policy: Recent Evidence from Theory and Practice. *The World Bank Research Observer, 6*(2), 219–240.

Todaro, M. P., and Smith, S. C. (2009). *Economic Development* (10th ed.). London: Pearson Education.

Topalova, P. (2010). Factor Immobility and Regional Impacts of Trade Liberalization: Evidence on Poverty from India. *American Economic Journal: Applied Economics, 2*(4), 1–41. DOI: 10.1257/app.2.4.1

Tyler, W. G. (1981). Growth and Export Expansion in Developing Countries: Some Empirical Evidence. *Journal of Development Economics, 9*(1), 121–130. DOI: 10.1016/0304-3878(81)90007-9

United Nations (UN) (2000). *A Better World for All*. New York.

United Nations (UN) (2005). *Handbook on Poverty Statistics: Concepts, Methods and Policy Use*. Washington, DC.

United Nations (UN) (2010). *The Millennium Development Goals Report 2010*. New York.

UNCTAD (2013). Non-tariff Measures To Trade: Economic and Policy Issues for Developing Countries. In *Developing Coutries In International Trade Studies* (p. 124). Geneva.

UNDP (2003). *Human Development Report 2003: Millennium Development Goals: A Compact among Nations to End Human Poverty*. New York: Oxford University Press.

United Nations Development Programme (UNDP) (2005). *What is Poverty? Concepts and Measures*. UNDP International Poverty Centre, Poverty in Focus Discussion Paper (No. 9), 1–24.

UNDP (2010). *Human Development Report 2010: The Real Wealth of Nations: Pathways to Human Development*. New York: Palgrave Macmillan.

UNDP (2014). *Human Development Report 2014: Sustaining Human Progress: Reducing Vulnerabilities and Building Resilence*. New York: Palgrave Macmillan.

United Nations Environment Programme (UNEP) (2005). *Integrated Assessment of the Impact of Trade Liberalization: A Country Study on the Viet Nam Rice Sector*. Geneva.

Wacziarg, R. (2001). Measuring the Dynamic Gains from Trade. *The World Bank Economic Review, 15*(3), 393–429. DOI: 10.1093/wber/15.3.393

Wacziarg, R., and Welch, K. H. (2008). Trade Liberalization and Growth: New Evidence. *The World Bank Economic Review, 22*(2), 45.

Watts, H. W. (1968). *An Economic Definition of Poverty*. Institute for Research on Poverty, University of Wisconsin, Discussion Papers (Nos. 5–68), 21.

White, H., and Anderson, E. (2001). Growth versus Distribution: Does the Pattern of Growth Matter?. *Development Policy Review, 19*(3), 267–289. DOI: 10.1111/1467-7679.00134

Winters, L. A. (2002). Trade Liberalisation and Poverty: What are the Links?. *The World Economy, 25*(9), 1339–1367. DOI: 10.1111/1467-9701.00495

Winters, L. A., McCulloch, N., and McKay, A. (2004). Trade Liberalization and Poverty: The Evidence So Far. *Journal of Economic Literature, XLII*(1), 72–115.

World Bank (1987). *World Development Report 1987: Barriers to Adjustment and Growth in the World Economy, Industrialization and Foreign Trade, and World Development Indicators* (p. 299). Washington, DC.

World Bank (1990). *World Development Report 1990: Poverty* (p. 274). Washington, DC.

World Bank (2001). *World Development Report 2000/01: Attacking Poverty* (p. 356). Washington, DC.

World Bank (2005). *Pro-poor Growth in the 1990s: Lessons and Insights from 14 Countries* (p. 116). Washington, DC.

World Bank (2006). *World Development Report 2006: Equity and Development* (p. 340). Washington, DC.

World Bank (2007). *World Development Report 2008: Agriculture for Development* (p. 390). Washington, DC.

World Bank (2010). *Vietnam Development Report 2010: Modern Institutions* (p. 227). Hanoi.

World Bank (2011). *Vietnam Development Report 2012: Market Economy for a Middle-Income Vietnam* (p. 90). Hanoi.

World Bank (2012a). *Well Begun, Not Yet Done: Vietnam's Remarkable Progress on Poverty Reduction and the Emerging Challenges* (p. 190). Hanoi.

World Bank (2012b). *World Development Report 2013: Jobs* (p. 422). Washington, DC.

World Bank (2014). *World Development Report 2014: Risk and Opportunity. Managing Risk for Development* (p. 362). Washington, DC.

Young, A. (1991). Learning by Doing and the Dynamic Effects of International Trade. *The Quarterly Journal of Economics, 106*(2), 369–405. DOI: 10.2307/2937942

Zafar, A. (2005). *Revenue and the Fiscal Impact of Trade Liberalisation: The Case of Neger.* World Bank, Policy Research Working Paper (No. 3500), 27.

3 Trade liberalisation and poverty in Vietnam

3.1 Introduction

Vietnam achieved remarkable outcomes in terms of the acceleration of economic growth and reduction in poverty since its transformation from a centrally planned to an open market economy. Many studies have argued that the miracle of economic growth in Vietnam is largely the outcome of its openness to trade (World Bank, 2005, 2012). Both concepts, trade policy and poverty, are multidimensional (Winters *et al.*, 2004), and the appropriateness of the measures of trade openness and poverty remains controversial (see Singh, 2010). A country-specific approach appears to be more appropriate to analyse the relationship between trade liberalisation and poverty. The literature shows several channels through which trade can affect households and poverty (see, for example, McCulloch *et al.*, 2001; Winters, 2002; Berg and Krueger, 2003; Winters *et al.*, 2004; Harrison, 2007; Nissanke and Thorbecke, 2007; Bandara, 2011; Athukorala, 2010). Of these, the Winters outline provides an analytical framework that is useful for the analysis of the relationship between trade liberalisation and poverty. Most studies seem to provide only indirect and partial evidence about the trade–growth–poverty nexus. In addition to model-based analysis, some studies attempt to examine the impacts of trade liberalisation on poverty by analytically reviewing facts and analysing data. Heo and Nguyen (2009) provide evidence on the relationship between trade liberalisation and reduction in poverty by examining the effects of trade on economic growth, market, employment, and the government revenue in Vietnam. Reports on sectors such as agriculture and textile/garment manufacture provide different angles to the relationship. The report of the United Nations Environment Programme (2005) finds that the trade reform process leads to significant changes in rice production and exports, which discernibly affect the reduction in poverty. Nadvi *et al.* (2004) find the impacts on textile and garment labourers of the integration of Vietnamese garment and textile firms into global garment and textile value chains. Even with such indirect and partial evidence, these studies provide a wealth of information on different aspects, leading to a better understanding of the relationship.

This chapter evaluates the impacts of trade liberalisation on Vietnam's economy and poverty. It uses the historical approach and compares the economic development in Vietnam before and after the liberalisation of trade. The analysis is carried out using the data drawn from various economic and social indicators for the decadal periods of the 1980s, 1990s, and 2000s from sources such as the Vietnam General Statistics Office (GSO), World Bank, IMF, ADB, and UNDP. The rest of the chapter is organized as follows. Section 3.2 provides an overview of trade liberalisation and poverty in Vietnam. Section 3.3 analyses the effects of trade liberalisation on poverty using Winters's four pathways: economic growth, market, employment, and government revenue. Section 3.4 concludes the chapter.

3.2   Taxonomy of policy reforms and economic performance

Background of Vietnam's economy

The transition of Vietnam's economy to a market economy has attracted considerable research over the last two decades. Many studies have attempted to document the history of this economic development: for instance, Vo (1990), Fforde and De Vylder (1996), Harvie and Tran (1997), Griffin (1998), Beresford and Dang (2000), Phan *et al.* (2006), Pham *et al.* (2007), and Dang (2008). Some studies divide the process of economic development into stages, based on certain criteria. Harvie and Tran (1997) and Pham *et al.* (2007) classify the economic development according to economic growth. Vo (1990) partitions the development process on the basis of the main historical and political events. This study divides the development of the economy into three broad stages, based on the main economic reforms and the level of liberalisation. These three stages of economic development roughly correspond to the last three decades: the 1980s, 1990s, and 2000s. The renovation period during 1981–1990 is marked by a comprehensive renovation programme aimed at transforming the centrally planned economy into an open market economy. The period of economic boom in the 1990s witnessed a remarkable performance of the economy. Vietnam's official membership of the WTO in 2007 marked an important milestone in the liberalisation process of the economy in the last decade. These three stages of economic reforms and development are summarised in Table A3.1.

Stage I: Renovation phase, 1981–1990

The 1980s witnessed Vietnam's efforts devoted to changing the centrally planned economy into an open market economy. After the reunification of the country, Vietnam adopted a development strategy based on central planning and inward orientation. The foundation for this strategy is the extraction of surplus from the low-productive collective agriculture production system in order to build a capital-intensive industrial sector. As a consequence, poor growth performance, combined with rapid population growth, resulted in persistent poverty and widespread malnutrition. The industrial products were not competitive in international markets, and the level of savings and investment was very low, with GDP per capita estimated to be about US$109 (World Bank, 1990). The World Bank describes the position of the economy: 'at that time, Vietnam was one of the poorest countries in the world, and with many problems: hyperinflation, famine, drastic cuts in Soviet aid, and a trade embargo by the west. For most Vietnamese, life was harsh and the future looked bleak' (2011, p. 10).

The economy was mired in its severe recession in the mid-1980s, a result of economic mismanagement. This critical situation led to the adoption of a comprehensive renovation plan, Doi Moi, declared in December 1986 by the Sixth Party Congress. Several crucial changes were made between 1986 and 1990. The domestic market was liberalised in two main ways: (1) the abolition of local trade barriers between provinces and regions, and (2) the reduction of control over foreign investment, land, foreign trade, banking activities, the private and household sectors, and agriculture. The Law on Foreign Investment in 1987 introduced an open-door policy. The Land Law in the same year, which defined households as basic production units in an agricultural economy, provided the incentives in agricultural production. In 1988, reforms were accelerated through (1) the termination of the collective method of agricultural production in favour of household production, and (2) the encouragement of the development of the nonstate sector. The removal of direct subsidies and price controls on most products, except electricity and coal, helped to reduce distortions and to establish a one-price system. These reforms brought about substantial improvements in economic performance by the end of the 1980s (Figure 3.1), laying the foundation for the economic boom in the 1990s.

Stage II: Economic boom and high growth phase, 1991–2000

Attempts to reform and integrate the economy into the world economy continued throughout the 1990s. The collapse of the Soviet Union in the early 1990s ended aid from the socialist bloc of countries (Comecon countries) on one hand and completely shifted the country's trade from the CMEA trading bloc to convertible areas on the other.[1] This decade witnessed remarkable results from the economic reforms undertaken in the previous decade. Exports boomed, and the GDP growth peaked at 9.5 per cent in 1995. Poverty declined dramatically, from over 70 per cent in the mid-1980s to 58.1 per cent in 1993, and then further to 37.4 per cent in 1998 (Figure 3.2). Many important economic relationships with other countries and trading blocs were also established in this decade, such as joining the ASEAN and the AFTA in 1995, formally applying for membership of the WTO, and signing the Vietnam–US BTA. The economy, however, experienced a slowdown from 1998 to 2000 as a consequence of the Asian financial crisis. The economy has recovered since then, becoming somewhat more stable.

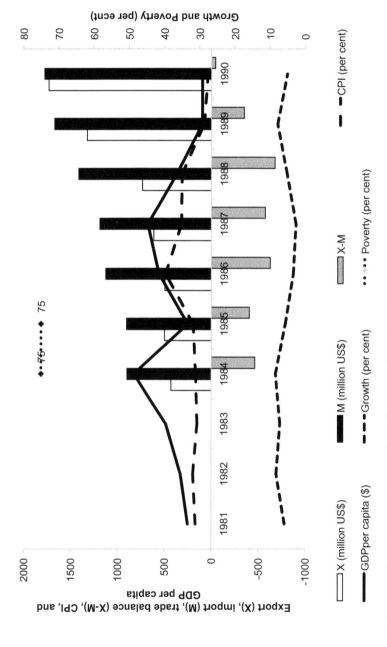

Figure 3.1 Renovation phase and economic performance, 1981–1990

Source: Author's synthesis based on data taken from the World Bank and IMF database, except for the poverty rates in the mid-1980s, which are synthesised from Dollar *et al.* (1998), Pincus and Sender (2008), and Thu Le and Booth (2013)

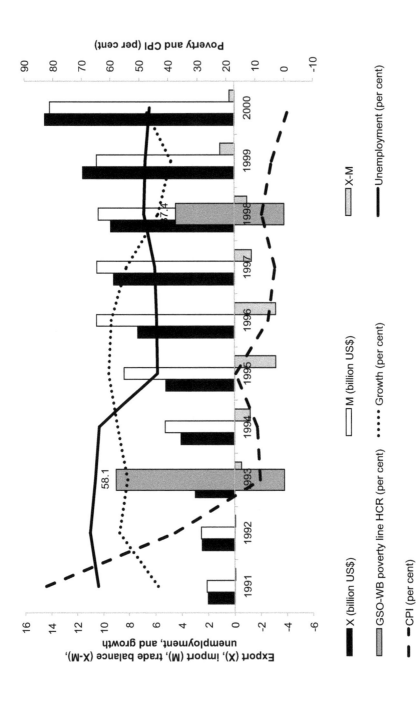

Figure 3.2 High economic performance phase, 1991–2000

Source: Author's synthesis based on data taken from the World Bank and IMF database. Data for poverty rates are from the World Bank (2012).

*Stage III: WTO membership phase and
economic performance, 2001–2010*

The Vietnamese government made considerable effort towards securing WTO membership during this period. Institutional reforms were accelerated in the very early 2000s so as to prepare for this membership. The accession to the WTO provided an opportunity to improve the underdeveloped institutional framework required for the market-based institutions that came up during the process of transition to a market economy. The efficiency of institutional reforms would thus determine whether Vietnam has been successful since its membership in the WTO. Currently, the weak institutional framework has remained an Achilles heel for Vietnam. Although the country became a member of the WTO in 2007, some important trading partners still classify Vietnam as a nonmarket economy, which brings some disadvantages in terms of exports. Vietnam's accession to the WTO is just the beginning of the long-term process of integration: many challenges still lie ahead (UNDP, 2006; Gantz, 2009). The economy was fairly stable until the mid-2000s, probably due to the continual efforts devoted to reform and to a series of laws promulgated in the 2000s (Figure 3.3). Since Vietnam adopted a socialist market economy system, with state-owned enterprises leading the economy and creating an unequal playing field against the private sector, the institutional reforms have been far from efficient. Consequently, the country has continued to face many economic problems, especially since the 2008 financial crisis.

Poverty

Poverty reduction

Vietnam was one of the poorest countries in the world before reform, with over 70 per cent of people living in poverty. The poverty rate in the 1980s was estimated to be around 75 per cent. This ratio showed a sharp fall between 1984 and 1993, although this did not seem to be connected with the distribution of income (Dollar *et al.*, 1998; Pincus and Sender, 2008; Thu Le and Booth, 2013). As a consequence of Vietnam's transition to a market economy and the resultant increase in economic growth and exports, the GDP per head increased steadily, and the rate of poverty declined throughout the three decades (Table 3.1, Figure 3.1, and Figure 3.4). Vietnam initiated poverty reduction programmes in 1998 and used both internal and external resources to reduce poverty, attaining the first goal in the MDGs for poverty reduction in 2008 and becoming a lower-middle-income country by 2010. Many challenges remain ahead, as the strategy for poverty alleviation seems unsustainable. In fact, poverty tended to increase in the late 2000s as the economy slowed down.

The characteristics of poverty in Vietnam have been reviewed in several studies, especially in the reports by the World Bank and the IMF (see World Bank, 1995,

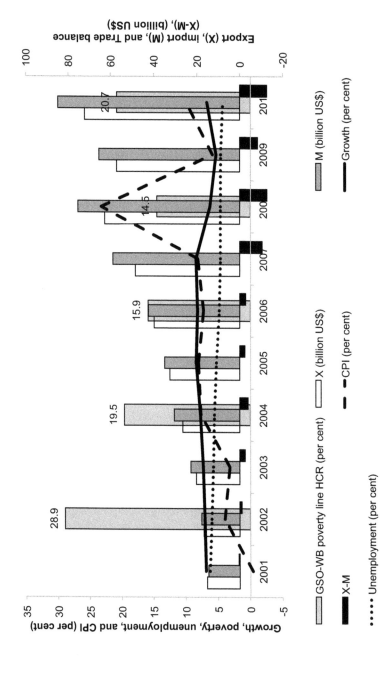

Figure 3.3 WTO membership phase and economic performance, 2001–2010

Source: Author's synthesis based on data taken from the World Bank and IMF database. Data for poverty rates are from the World Bank (2012).

1999a, 2004, 2012; CIE, 2002b; IMF, 2004). Recently, the World Bank (2012) has provided a review of poverty characteristics in Vietnam. At first, poverty is mainly found in rural areas, and this is quite similar to the general poverty pattern in the world. More than 90 per cent of the Vietnamese poor still live in rural regions, especially in the upland regions. Many are farmers (making up 65 per cent of the poor), with their livelihoods dependent on agriculture. The number of farmers who have very little or no land is increasing. The World Bank report shows that in this decade ethnic inequality has been rising, which has probably resulted in impinging on the reduction of poverty. Ethnic minority groups account for nearly half of the total poor. Poverty is also found to be associated with the low level of education: in 2010, the highest poverty incidence (nearly twice the national average) was found in households whose heads had not completed primary school. Assets such as housing and infrastructure have improved substantially since the late 1990s. Household demographic traits have little impact on poverty. Child poverty rates remain high, and children face multidimensional deprivation. The rural poor are also seen to be very vulnerable to weather shocks. Notably, existing poverty reduction and social protection programmes do not totally benefit the poor. The report indicates that urban poverty is low, concentrated in smaller cities and towns. Generally, the new methods of poverty measurement, which take into consideration not only income, but also health, education, and inequality, tend to yield higher estimates of poverty. In particular, inequality has given rise to a new dimension of poverty and has become increasingly acute (VASS, 2007, 2011).

Income inequality

The successful development of the economy in the 1990s brought about considerable reduction in overall poverty (Table 3.1), based on the traditional head count poverty ratio. Rural poverty was also reduced by half over the same period. Although Vietnam attained the first goal of the MDGs, rural poverty has yet to fulfill this first target, because the rural poverty rate is still higher than the national poverty rate. Note that most Vietnamese people live in rural areas, and most of them are poor. Income inequality has also tended to increase over the two decades, especially in urban areas. The average income of the richest is 9.2 times more than that of the poorest. This increasing income inequality is likely to erode the benefits of economic growth. Although Vietnam has become a lower-middle-income country, it should be kept in mind that the income per capita for a majority of the Vietnamese is much lower than the income per capita level reported for the country as a whole, due to high income inequality.

Vietnam has generally reduced poverty successfully over the three decades of development, at least in terms of the incidence of poverty. In addition to the impacts of economic growth and trade liberalisation on poverty, these achievements in poverty reduction in Vietnam partly result from the remarkable efforts made by the government. Reduction in poverty in the future needs a more

Table 3.1 Some indicators of poverty and economic inequality, 1993–2010

Poverty and inequality indicator	1993	1998	2002	2004	2006	2008	2010
Poverty							
Poverty rate (per cent)	58.1	37.4	23.0	18.1	15.5	13.4	14.2
Urban	25.1	9.2	10.6	8.6	7.7	6.7	6.9
Rural	66.4	45.5	26.9	21.2	18.0	16.1	17.4
Economic inequality							
Richest to poorest ratio	5.0	5.5	8.1	8.3	8.4	8.9	9.2
Gini coefficient	0.340	0.350	0.418	0.420	0.424	0.434	0.433
Urban	0.35	0.34	0.410	0.410	0.393	0.404	0.402
Rural	0.28	0.27	0.360	0.370	0.378	0.385	0.395
Gini coefficient by regions							
Red River Delta	0.32	0.32	0.390	0.390	0.395	0.411	0.409
Northeast	0.25	0.26	0.360	0.390	0.407	0.415	0.418
Northwest	0.25	0.26	0.370	0.380	0.392	0.403	0.401
North central coast	0.25	0.29	0.360	0.360	0.369	0.371	0.371
South central coast	0.36	0.33	0.350	0.370	0.373	0.380	0.393
Central highlands	0.31	0.31	0.370	0.400	0.407	0.405	0.408
Southeast	0.36	0.36	0.420	0.430	0.422	0.423	0.424
Mekong River Delta	0.33	0.30	0.390	0.380	0.385	0.395	0.398

Source: The World Bank (2004), General Statistics Office (1999, 2004, 2006, 2008, 2010, 2012)

Note: Data on poverty and Gini coefficients for 1993 and 1998 are based on expenditure; those from 2002–2010, on income.

sustainable strategy, especially with the underpinning of accelerated trade and economic growth.

Trade liberalisation

Vietnam changed development strategy from an inward-oriented to an outward-oriented strategy. Trade reforms thereby constitute a major proportion of the economic reforms undertaken in the transitional process, which occurred over the three stages of economic development overviewed. Before the reforms, export and import transactions were conducted within the CMEA area, through the state-owned enterprises. Trading prices were based, not on the market, but on agreements between Comecon governments. In this period, the

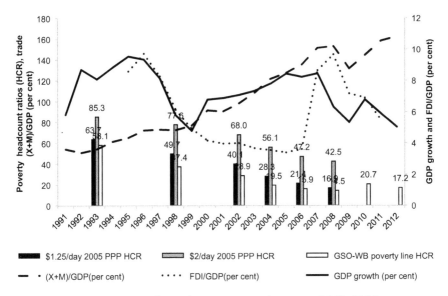

Figure 3.4 Economic growth, trade openness, and poverty, 1991–2012

Source: Data on poverty lines are from Table 3.2. Data on export, import, and GDP are from the World Economic Outlook (WEO) database, IMF.

government monopoly dominated both domestic and international trade. According to Dodsworth *et al.* (1996),

> before the reforms, foreign trade in Vietnam was subject to central decisions by the planning authorities and could be carried out only by a small number of state trading monopolies. Domestic prices were isolated from the influence of international prices through a complex system of multiple exchange rates and trade subsidies. Exports were discouraged through overvalued exchange rates and low procurement prices, while imports were impeded by an extensive system of quotas and licenses. Isolated from the world market, Vietnam relied heavily on its former CMEA partners to obtain basic commodities, such as petroleum products and fertilisers, while exporters were obliged to fulfil CMEA quotas (arranged through a system of government-to-government protocols) before they were allowed to export to the convertible currency area.
>
> (quoted in CIE, 1999)

This liberalisation of the old trade regime occurred through a series of reforms. The government gradually relaxed its controls on the prices of most goods and abolished the monopoly on trade, leaving the price decisions to the market. Only about a dozen prices remained controlled after the 1989 price reforms (Leipziger, 1992). Households were given the rights to own land, manage agricultural production, and make trade transactions across provinces. The Law on Foreign Investment in 1987 for the first time invited foreign enterprises to invest in Vietnam, opening its economy to the world economy. The relaxation of control on foreign exchange and the abolition of most quotas for imports and exports paved the way for enterprises to expand their production and enter the international markets. The 1990s witnessed a series of trade reforms, such as the introduction of the Enterprise Law 1990, the establishment of export processing zones (1991), the application of the harmonised system (HS) of tariff nomenclature (1992), the announcement of the first list of goods (1996) covered by the CEPT (where 857 tariff lines with duties were already between 0 and 5 per cent), and the termination of trade licenses (1999), allowing all legally established domestic enterprises to export and import those goods specified in their business registration certificates. Vietnam also strove to integrate into the regional and world system in this decade of the 1990s; for instance, through accessions to AFTA and WTO observer status.

The 2000s began with the signing of the Vietnam–US BTA and the action plan to implement its commitments. This agreement remains crucial to Vietnam's trade liberalisation: the United States of America continues to be the desired but difficult market for Vietnamese enterprises. The accession of Vietnam to the WTO in 2007, an important milestone in the process of trade liberalisation, brought a great opportunity for Vietnam to catch up with other countries in the region. The rest of the 2000s witnessed reforms aimed at implementing commitments to the WTO, Vietnam–US BTA, and AFTA; of these, the WTO commitments remain the cornerstone of the trade reform process.

The trade reform process has, in general, been inadequate and inefficient. Some of the forward steps have been offset by some of the backward steps, which slowed down the process of economic reforms. The inconsistency of trade reforms primarily results from the government's adoption of SOEs as the leading sector in the economy. While these enterprises are largely less inefficient than nonstate enterprises, they receive huge resources and economic rent (Dapice, 2003; IMF, 2010, 2012). Importantly, some faster trade reforms conflict with the slower reforms of the SOE sector, the SOEs' interest, and other interest groups in the economy. Another problem of trade reforms is the divergence between the government's general policy and the detailed regulations for the implementation made by line industries or interest government agencies: this divergence fails the aims of the policies towards trade liberalisation (Athukorala, 2005). The inadequacy of trade reforms may derive from an inadequate institutional framework, because trade policy reforms are, in fact, institutional reforms (Rodrik, 2002). These critical problems with the trade policies arose in the late 2000s, eroding Vietnam's drive to grow and its ability to address poverty. Generally, despite ineffective trade policy reforms, the process of trade liberalisation has had a great impact on the Vietnamese economy (World Bank, 2011), especially on poverty.

3.3   Trade liberalisation and poverty: the Winters channels

The Winters framework is utilised in this section to make an in-depth assessment of the effects of trade liberalisation on poverty in Vietnam. The high economic growth, following trade liberalisation in the 1990s, substantially contributed to the reduction in poverty. The liberalisation of agricultural production and market led to an export boom during this period. As a result of the liberalisation in agriculture and the open policies towards domestic and foreign enterprises, unemployment fell remarkably. The export boom brought about an improvement in the government budget. These effects can be observed in the process of development of the economy.

Economic growth channel

This section attempts to link trade reforms with Vietnam's economic performance in terms of economic growth, by profoundly analysing the drives for accelerating economic growth, the ground for the poverty reduction in the 1990s and the 2000s (Table 3.2). The economic overview shows that the economy faced a severe economic crisis throughout the mid and late 1980s, with low per capita income, an inflation rate of nearly 500 per cent (in 1986), persistent trade deficits, and severe shortages of basic necessities (World Bank, 1990, 1991). The reforms based on the Doi Moi were, in fact, implemented from 1989. The reforms aimed to transform the old economic management system to an open

Table 3.2 Incidence (P_0), depth (P_1), and severity (P_2) of poverty (per cent), 1993–2010

Year	GSO–WB poverty line			US$1.25/day 2005 PPP line			US$2/day 2005 PPP line		
	P_0	P_1	P_2	P_0	P_1	P_2	P_0	P_1	P_2
1993	58.1	18.5	7.9	63.7	23.6	11.0	85.3	43.0	25.2
1998	37.4	9.5	3.6	49.7	15.1	6.0	77.6	33.6	17.6
2002	28.9	7.0	2.4	40.1	11.2	4.1	68.0	27.4	13.7
2004	19.5	4.7	1.7	28.3	7.2	2.5	56.1	20.3	9.5
2006	15.9	3.8	1.4	21.4	5.3	1.9	47.2	15.9	7.1
2008	14.5	3.5	1.2	16.9	3.8	1.2	42.5	13.1	5.4
2010[1/]	20.7	5.9	2.4	..	..	..	..	..	..
2012	17.2	..	..	..	..	..	..	..	..

Source: The GSO–WB poverty head count rates are from the World Bank (2012); the dollar-a-day poverty rates are estimated by PovcalNet, World Bank.

Notes: 1/ The poverty rate in 2010 is based on the new GSO–WB poverty line, which is defined as VND 653,000 per person per month.

market economy system. Seven main reform measures were adopted in 1989: decollectivising agriculture, eliminating almost all direct subsidies and price controls, decentralising decision making to the managers of SOEs, increasing some interest rates to positive levels in real terms, tightening the budget and limiting overall credit expansion, largely devaluing the VND, and reducing restrictions on private sector activities (World Bank, 1991). Of these measures, the most striking step was the liberalisation of prices, where all domestic prices for agricultural and industrial output came to be freely negotiated between buyers and sellers (World Bank, 1990). In agricultural production, the government provided rights on arable land for farmers, who had not previously had these rights. According to Dang (2008), these rights included the use of land for cultivation and harvesting, owning the harvest and selling crops to market at market prices, transferring the rights to other farmers, having land heritage, and using land as mortgage. In the financial sector, the initial steps were taken by separating commercial banks from the routine functions of the State Bank and by establishing a state treasury (World Bank, 1990): the earlier, single state–banking system was transformed into a two-tier banking system, comprising a state bank and commercial banks.

The outward-oriented economic strategies were adopted in industry and trade. The 1987 Law on Foreign Investment paved the way for market competition between domestic and international companies. The Enterprise Law in 1990 laid the foundation for private sector development, the main drive for economic growth. In the external area, the exchange rate was largely devalued in order to close the gap between official and parallel market exchange rates. The monopoly of the state corporations on foreign trade was gradually removed, and the government granted direct foreign trade rights to some enterprises (World Bank, 1990). Other trade reforms in the 1990s included the removal of constraints on trade outside the CMEA area, the further liberalisation of foreign exchange controls, the reduction in trade quantitative controls and the increase in the use of tariff controls, the establishment of export processing zones for export promotion, the adoption of the HS to define tariffs, and Vietnam's integration into the world economy through regional and multilateral trade agreements (World Bank, 1990, 1999b; Litchfield *et al.*, 2003). Vietnam took several important steps in the 1990s and the 2000s to integrate the economy into the world economy, one of the most significant being the official membership of the WTO in 2007 as a crucial milestone in the process of trade liberalisation.

These trade-related reform measures, inter alia, brought about remarkable achievements in the 1990s. The average economic growth was nearly 8 per cent in the 1990s, peaking at 9.5 per cent in 1995 (Figure 3.4). The poverty rates, whether measured by the dollar-a-day poverty line or the GSO–World Bank poverty line, declined sharply. The share of trade volume in GDP increased dramatically, from more than 50 per cent in 1991 to 90 per cent in 2000. The trade deficit decreased, and Vietnam had a period of surplus trade balance sometime between 1999 and 2001 (Figure 3.5). The economy has experienced the moderate effects of external crises, given that it has not yet been fully

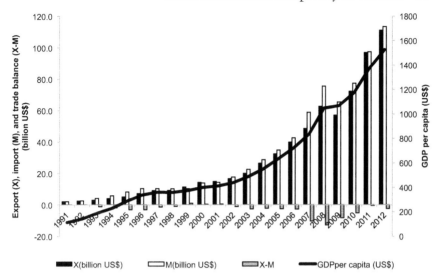

Figure 3.5 GDP per capita, export, import, and trade balance, 1991–2012
Source: The World Economic Outlook (WEO) database, IMF

integrated into the world economy. Although the impacts of the Asian financial crisis in 1997 and the global financial crisis in 2008 slowed the process of economic growth and caused foreign direct investment to fluctuate, in general the external trade and GDP per capita have shown steady increases. Poverty has declined throughout the last two decades, since Vietnam instituted economic reforms in 1986 (Figure 3.4 and Figure 3.5). The reduction of poverty in Vietnam has particularly been spectacular among 14 countries in the 1990s.[2] The decline of poverty by 7.8 per cent a year between 1993 and 2002 helped to reduce the poverty rate by more than half in this period, from 58.1 per cent to 23 per cent (World Bank, 2005).

The miracle of economic growth since the adoption of these reforms is, in fact, a predictable outcome of the process of redirecting this inward-oriented economy into an outward-oriented one. Openness, thus far, works better than autarchy in the case of Vietnam. The reform programme initiated in 1986 has not been actually radical, because many elements of the centrally planned economy are still preserved, such as the perpetuation of the leading role of state-owned enterprises in the economy. These enterprises are the main source of economic inefficiency, and their official leading role creates an unequal playing field between the state sector and the private sector.

The pursuance of high economic growth by allocating tremendous resources into inefficient state enterprises in order to achieve policy targets may have resulted in increasing income inequality. The Gini coefficients increased substantially in the 1990s and 2000s. The income gap between the poorest quintile and the richest quintile was only 4.1 times in 1998;[3] this gap nearly doubled to 8.1 times in 2002 and reached 9.2 times in 2010 (GSO, 2012). A comparison of the poverty maps between the end of the 1990s and the 2000s demonstrates that poverty has been heavily concentrated in the upland regions of Vietnam, including the northeast and northwest mountains and parts of the central highlands (World Bank, 2012). This trend is consistent with the anticipation made by Irvin (1997) that Vietnam would become less poor, but also less egalitarian. Kang and Imai (2012) argue that the effect of economic growth on poverty is higher if inequality remains unchanged. Although the relationship between inequality and economic growth is empirically inconclusive (World Bank, 2012), this inequality could be considered as an important dimension of poverty, as high inequality contributes to reduced life expectancy, poorer mental health, and higher levels of crime. The reduction in inequality arguably contributes to the reduction in poverty.

A strong link between overall economic growth and the speed of poverty reduction identified by the World Bank (2005) is highly unsustainable, however. Poor people are expected to benefit very little from high, trade-induced economic growth: the increasing inequality associated with the discrimination against the private sector and farm households may take its toll on economic growth. Although export development is relatively stable, the prices of primary exports tend to fall, and the returns from exports primarily accrue to state-owned enterprises because of their monopoly in key economic sectors of the economy. Though high economic growth theoretically generates the trickle-down effect that creates more jobs and state-owned enterprises receive immense resources, in reality they absorb a modest labour force. This phenomenon in Vietnam reflects the trend recognised by Piketty (2014) in terms of the huge wealth accumulation by the very rich, including the heads of SOEs, which is unlikely to promote growth and employment.

Market channel

The analysis of the market channel focuses on the reforms of market that could improve household welfare and contribute to poverty reduction. Before 1989, Vietnam had a dual price system: official business prices and free market prices. Price reform under the Doi Moi programme allowed buyers and sellers to negotiate freely in their transactions of agricultural and industrial goods and services. Together with other stabilisation measures, this price reform resulted in a rapid reduction in shortages and the surge and reinstatement of the supplies of many essential products. The dual price system was gradually eliminated. Exporters could sell and buy at world market prices for convertible currency exports (World Bank, 1990). Vietnam's exports generally comprise primary products, whose value added is low. Some of the exports are rice, coffee, crude oil, coal, rubber, tea, cashew nuts, and black pepper (Table 3.4). Although an important source of government revenue, the crude oil export does not directly benefit households, because of the government monopoly on oil production. Vietnam still imports petroleum due to its inability to produce enough fuel (Table 3.3). Rice and coffee are the main exports and also the main sources of household incomes.

Trade liberalisation in agricultural production, market, and exports is essential for the reduction in poverty, since the majority of Vietnamese households engage

Table 3.3 Imports of major commodities in Vietnam, 1991–2009

Year	Petroleum product		Fertilisers		Steel and irons	
	Quantity	Price	Quantity	Price	Quantity	Price
1991	2,572	189	2,425	101	113	221
1992	3,075	200	1,600	200	260	400
1993	4,095	150	925	204	656	355
1994	4,550	153	1,495	165	725	291
1995	4,969	172	1,471	230	..	..
1996	5,803	186	2,919	220	1,548	421
1997	5,947	184	2,458	173	1,320	367
1998	6,830	121	3,554	134	1,735	302
1999	7,403	142	3,782	123	2,264	259
2000	8,777	234	3,973	128	2,868	283
2001	8,998	203	3,189	127	3,938	245
2002	9,966	202	3,824	125	4,951	269
2003	9,995	243	4,119	152	4,574	362
2004	11,050	323	4,079	202	5,186	496
2005	11,478	438	2,877	223	5,524	531
2006	11,213	532	3,189	216	5,707	515
2007	12,850	600	3,792	264	8,027	637
2008	12,964	846	3,035	485	8,264	813
2009	12,706	492	4,519	313	9,749	550

Source: World Bank's Vietnam Development Reports (1998, 1999b, 2004, 2006, 2007, 2010)

Note: The quantities of the commodities are in thousand tonnes; their prices are in US dollars.

in agricultural production. The government monopoly in procurement and distribution has created serious supply shortages in the past. The government forced farmers to sell agricultural products to state enterprises at low prices to extract a surplus from agricultural production for the pursuance of its ambitious industrialisation strategy. The government also imposed restrictions on entering the agricultural market and on trading agricultural products across regions. Farmers therefore had no incentives to increase output. The end of the system based on administrative procurement pricing of most agricultural products, along with the local trade barriers after 1989, brought about rapidly expanding agricultural production and markets (World Bank, 1990). According to the World Bank (1993), Vietnam's transition into a market economy occurred without a fall in national income. The positive response of the agricultural sector to the liberalisation of price and distribution largely contributed to this success. This response to the reforms contributed to the increase in paddy production.

Table 3.4 Vietnam's exports of major commodities, 1991–2009

Year	Rice Quantity	Price	Crude oil Quantity	Price	Coal Quantity	Price	Rubber Quantity	Price	Tea Quantity	Price	Coffee Quantity	Price	Cashew nut Quantity	Price	Black pepper Quantity	Price
1991	989	228	3,917	148	1,173	41	63	789	10	1,370	94	795	30	850	16	1,080
1992	1,860	161	5,400	140	1,580	30	68	800	13	1,231	96	900	52	799	22	695
1993	1,725	210	6,153	137	1,940	36	97	763	21	1,262	122	901	48	922	20	750
1994	1,950	220	6,942	125	2,319	32	129	1,031	17	905	177	1,853	57	1,030	20	850
1995	2,052	268	7,652	134	2,800	29	130	1,392	25	1,300	200	2,475	130	1,000	18	..
1996	3,003	285	8,705	155	3,647	32	122	1,336	21	1,397	239	1,410	130	1,000	25	..
1997	3,553	245	9,574	148	3,449	32	195	981	32	1,506	389	1,261	33	4,100	23	2,727
1998	3,749	273	12,145	101	3,161	32	191	665	33	1,545	382	1,555	16	7,313	15	4,267
1999	4,508	227	14,882	141	3,260	29	265	555	36	1,250	482	1,214	18	5,978	35	3,914
2000	3,477	192	15,424	227	3,251	29	273	607	56	1,250	734	683	34	4,892	37	3,943
2001	3,729	168	16,732	187	4,290	26	308	539	68	1,150	931	420	44	3,474	57	1,601
2002	3,241	224	16,879	194	6,049	26	449	597	75	1,103	719	449	62	3,358	77	1,399
2003	3,813	189	17,143	222	7,246	25	433	872	60	1,002	749	674	84	3,390	74	1,416
2004	4,060	234	19,501	291	11,624	31	975	658	99	961	975	658	105	4,150	112	1,362
2005	5,250	199	17,967	410	17,986	37	587	1,370	88	1,103	892	824	109	4,610	109	1,381
2006	4,643	275	16,419	503	29,307	31	708	1,817	106	1,045	981	1,241	127	3,973	117	1,632
2007	4,558	327	15,062	564	31,948	31	715	1,948	114	1,143	715	2,674	153	4,287	83	3,269
2008	4,742	610	13,752	753	19,355	69	658	2,436	104	1,407	1060	1,993	165	5,510	90	3,448
2009	5,958	447	13,373	463	24,992	53	731	1,677	134	1,338	1,184	1,462	177	4,779	134	2,593

Source: World Bank's Vietnam Development Reports (1998, 1999b, 2004, 2006, 2007, 2010)

Note: The quantities of the commodities are in thousand tonnes, and their prices are in US dollars.

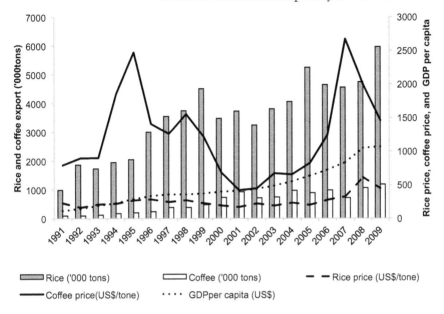

Figure 3.6 Export prices and production of rice and coffee, 1991–2009

Source: Based on Table 3.4. Data on GDP per capita are from the World Economic Outlook (WEO) database, IMF.

The significant growth of paddy production (26 per cent from 1987 to 1989) transformed Vietnam from a net rice importer before 1986 to a net rice exporter by 1989. Vietnam became the world's second largest rice exporter by 1998. The liberalised prices contributed to the efficient allocation of resources and the effective utilisation of the economy's comparative advantage.

Rice production and exports have risen steadily over the 1990s and the 2000s (Table 3.4). In contrast, rice prices showed a slower increase over the same period (Figure 3.6). This suggests that rice production and exports increased in quantity only, and that rice quality is improving slowly. Inefficient price transmission explains impoverished conditions of farm households. First, despite the liberalisation of prices, the state food enterprises still dominate the rice distribution system, squeezing farmers' profits. Farm households benefit little from the world price changes in agriculture, as these mostly accrue to state food enterprises. They have no incentives to invest their small returns to increase rice quality and productivity. The number of farm households whose rice crops exceed their home-use rice needs is rather low. Minot and Goletti (1998) observe that about one-third of Vietnamese households had net sales of rice in the 1990s. A series of surveys on farm households showed that the rice marketing system was inadequate and that farm households had almost no benefit from rice production (CIEM–IPSARD, 2007, 2011, 2013). Second, an important problem facing rice production and exports is the food security policy, which was used to prevent food shortages in the 1980s. This policy imposes quantity restrictions or quotas on rice exports to keep domestic rice prices low. Minot and Goletti (1998) point out that, although rice export liberalisation improved welfare and reduced poverty in the 1990s, rice export quotas in Vietnam drove a wedge between international and domestic rice prices. The benefits of these price differentials largely accrue to the state food enterprises. Third, residing in remote rural areas is a major barrier for poorer farm households. Around 20 per cent of the poorest communes,[4] mainly in the Mekong River Delta and the central and northern mountainous regions, are not linked to other areas by paved roads. Households have difficulty delivering products to markets or accessing inputs for their production (CIE, 2002a). The physical isolation of remote households – from having access to markets, education, and health services – has not improved much over the two decades of economic development. Poverty is increasingly concentrated in the remote areas, especially the northeast and northwest mountains and parts of the central highlands (World Bank, 2012). In the future, sustainable agricultural development involves continual efforts to remove the remaining constraints that come through the precarious policies of the CPE; these constraints are put up for one reason or another.

Coffee exports have also risen over time. The initial cost of coffee production has notably been relatively higher than that of rice production; however, coffee exports experience a wide fluctuation in world price. Most poor households cannot usually afford coffee production. Though coffee production and exports are not subject to government monopoly, the ability of coffee products to compete in the world coffee market is still low. As with rice exports, Vietnam has become the world's second largest coffee exporter in terms of volume only. Although the liberalisation of prices in agriculture in the 1990s improved household welfare and contributed to the alleviation of poverty, the existing inadequate trade policy in agriculture constrains agricultural development and exports. Despite the increase in GDP per capita, poor farm households do not seem to benefit from agricultural production and growth.

Employment channel

Trade liberalisation has contributed to the changes in the labour market and the increase in the demand for labour during the transitional period. Before Doi Moi, according to the World Bank, most of the population was employed in the public sector. However, the vast majority of Vietnamese families were not dependent on enterprises for income and subsistence, as the Vietnamese society has been largely rural and agricultural. An important goal of Vietnam's previous development strategy was its centrally planned industrialisation, which was biased towards heavy industries. This industrialisation was financed by extracting a surplus from the agricultural sector through low procurement prices for agricultural products, and by foreign assistance from the Soviet Union and other socialist countries. The government's pursuance of the capital-intensive industrialisation strategy – to lay the foundation for the acceleration of a socialist economy – consumed the country's huge resources, but generated few jobs.

The failure of the centrally planned economy to create sufficient productive jobs was one of the main motivations for the shift to a market system.

The government needed to rely on the private sector for the creation of jobs. However, the private sector is in fact not strong enough and faces many constraints and much discrimination in favour of SOEs, as noted. As a result, public sector layoffs exacerbate the existing serious unemployment problem in the short term. Due to the increasing share of the private sector, which accounts for over two-thirds of GDP, transitional unemployment during the structural adjustment is reduced. The private sector – overwhelmingly small-scale enterprises – engages in agriculture, manufacture of non-capital-intensive consumer goods, trade, and services (World Bank, 1990, 1993). This sector has been a key source of job creation. The large number of unskilled workers in the labour force is, however, the main constraint in the labour market.

As Vietnam is an agrarian economy, about 70 per cent of the Vietnamese workforce is engaged in agriculture (Figure 3.7). This ratio tends to decline over time, because of the growth of industry and trade sectors, the increase in agricultural productivity, and the accelerated rural-to-urban migration. About 1.5 million new entrants join the labour force annually. Job creation is seen as one of the main ways out of poverty (World Bank, 2007). The paradox in the labour market is that the SOEs absorb only around 9.5 per cent of total employment, despite receiving enormous resources, performing inefficiently, and competing badly in export markets. In contrast, nonstate enterprises, which typically have difficulty in accessing resources, performing efficiently, and competing well in the world market, account for more than 90 per cent of total employment (Table 3.5). In the state sector, the relatively high annual growth rate of real wages in agriculture can contribute to the reduction in poverty, since poor people are mostly engaged in agricultural activities. This sector covers only a modest part of Vietnam's employment. According to Gallup (2004), family farms and small household enterprises are the main sources of income in Vietnam, and much of the initial change from the Doi Moi occurs in these enterprises. After 1989, these enterprises belonged to the private sector. Generally, the development of the private sector, particularly micro and small household enterprises, is by far the most effective way of reducing poverty, as these are the focus of most reform plans, including trade policy reforms.

The adopted export-oriented growth strategy has had an impact on employment. A simple way to link trade liberalisation with employment is to estimate the employment elasticities of growth (EEGs), on the grounds that Vietnam's economic growth is trade induced. Even with other likely explanatory factors, these indicators mean that, for a given increase in output levels, the higher the employment elasticities of growth, the higher the rate of growth of employment. The estimates of EEGs for Vietnam have been positive at 0.35 throughout the period 1992–2006 (Table 3.5 and Figure 3.7). These indicators, however, showed an upward trend in the 1990s and a downward trend in the 2000s, somehow demonstrating an increasingly worn-out ability to absorb the growing

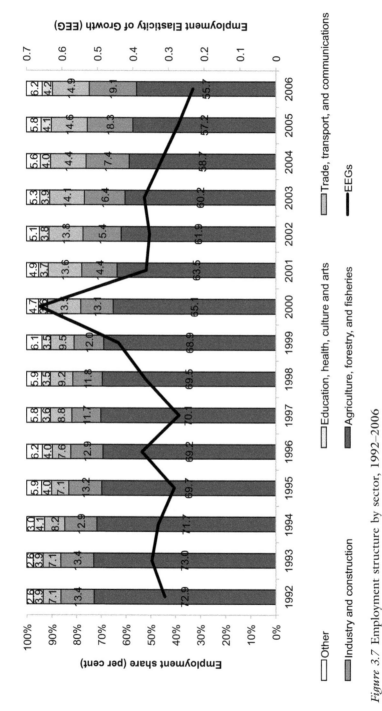

Figure 3.7 Employment structure by sector, 1992–2006

Source: International Monetary Fund (1998, 1999, 2000, 2003, 2006c, 2007)

Table 3.5 Employment and wages by sector, 1992–2006

Item	1992	1993	1994	1995	1996	1997	1998	1999	2000	2001	2002	2003	2004	2005	2006
Employment by sector															
Employment by sector (per cent)	100	100	100	100	100	100	100	100	100	100	100	100	100	100	100
State	9.4	9.0	8.7	8.8	8.8	9.5	9.6	9.5	9.3	9.3	9.5	9.9	9.9	9.5	9.2
Nonstate	90.6	90.9	91.3	91.2	91.2	90.5	90.4	90.5	90.7	90.7	90.5	90.1	90.1	90.5	90.8
Employment elasticity of growth (EEGs)															
Employment growth rate	2.70	2.80	2.90	2.70	3.50	2.20	2.10	2.10	4.50	2.50	2.50	2.70	2.50	2.30	1.9
GDP growth rate	8.70	8.08	8.83	9.54	9.34	8.15	5.77	4.77	6.79	6.90	7.08	7.34	7.79	8.44	8.23
EEGs	0.31	0.35	0.33	0.28	0.37	0.27	0.36	0.44	0.66	0.36	0.35	0.37	0.32	0.27	0.23
State sector average															
State sector average nominal wage (amount in ʻ000VND)															
Nominal wage (ʻ000VND)	177.1	274.0	390.0	478.0	543.0	642.0	697.0	729.0	850.0	954.0	1069	1247	1421	1651	..
Industry	236.3	371.0	576.0	754.0	708.0	841.0	898.0	947.0	1322	1548	1703	1925	1867	2198	..
Construction	214.4	358.0	417.0	499.0	573.0	738.0	807.0	794.0	861.0	961.0	1104	1261	1361	1960	..
Agriculture, forestry	160.2	206.0	287.0	366.0	422.0	480.0	514.0	564.0	680.0	590.0	740.0	988.0	1250	1031	..
Transportation	290.9	407.0	554.0	879.0	1018	1132	1304	1258	1525	1667	1910	2278	2433	2345	..
Trade	210.4	290.0	403.0	490.0	582.0	688.0	742.0	768.0	884.0	962.0	1127	1323	1468	1653	..
Education	114.1	214.0	349.0	310.0	329.0	405.0	451.0	501.0	615.0	725.0	783.0	1016	1115	1293	..
Science	102.4	183.0	294.0	361.0	505.0	555.0	673.0	585.0	693.0	778.0	895.0	1051	1165	1597	..
Culture, arts, and sports	115.0	194.0	311.0	347.0	400.0	453.0	540.0	520.0	607.0	718.0	815.0	994.0	1082	1321	..

(*Continued*)

Table 3.5 (Continued)

	1992	1993	1994	1995	1996	1997	1998	1999	2000	2001	2002	2003	2004	2005	2006
Public health	114.0	186.0	300.0	327.0	363.0	440.0	480.0	508.0	623.0	725.0	797.0	950.0	1024	1228	..
State management	132.3	203.0	328.0	357.0	380.0	435.0	449.0	458.0	580.0	659.0	691.0	797.0	898.0	1093	..
Financial intermediation	109.0	334.0	681.0	807.0	940.0	..	..	1142	1454	1804	1935	2321	2791	2746	..
State sector average real wage growth (per cent)															
State sector average real wage growth (per cent)	22.6	43.0	30.1	4.3	7.5	13.5	8.1	0.3	18.4	12.8	7.7	13.1	5.8	7.3	..
Industry	..	..	41.7	11.6	-11.1	14.0	6.4	1.1	41.8	17.5	5.8	9.6	-10.0	8.7	..
Construction	..	..	6.7	1.9	8.5	23.9	8.8	-5.7	10.1	12.1	10.4	10.7	0.2	33.0	..
Agriculture, forestry	..	..	27.3	8.9	8.9	9.3	6.7	5.2	22.5	-12.9	20.7	29.3	17.5	-23.8	..
Transportation	..	..	24.3	35.2	9.6	6.7	14.8	-7.5	23.2	9.7	10.2	15.6	-0.8	-11.0	..
Trade	..	..	27.3	3.6	12.3	13.6	7.4	-0.7	16.9	9.2	12.7	13.7	3.0	4.0	..
Education	..	..	47.1	-10.2	0.5	18.4	10.8	6.5	24.7	18.4	3.9	25.6	1.9	7.1	..
Science	..	..	-	-11.9	32.3	5.5	20.9	-16.6	20.3	12.8	10.6	13.7	2.9	26.6	..
Culture, arts, and sports	..	..	-	-4.8	9.0	8.8	18.7	-7.7	18.6	18.8	9.1	18.3	1.1	12.7	..
Public health	..	..	46.9	-7.0	5.0	16.4	8.8	1.5	24.5	17.0	5.6	15.6	0.1	10.8	..
State management	..	41.8	47.5	-7.3	0.7	10.1	2.8	-2.2	28.7	13.9	0.9	11.8	4.6	12.4	..
Financial intermediation	..	..	-	0.9	10.2	..	..	..	29.4	24.5	3.1	16.3	11.6	-9.2	..
Consumer price inflation	..	..	9.4	17.4	5.7	4.1	0.4	4.3	-1.6	-0.4	4.0	3.2	7.7	8.3	..

Source: Various IMF Country Reports on Vietnam (1998, 1999, 2002, 2003, 2006, 2007)

labour force since 2000. These results are consistent with those obtained by Pham *et al.* (2009) and Warren-Rodriguez (2009).

Adding to the trade–employment–poverty picture, Jenkins (2004) finds that the growth of exports has a positive effect on employment, while the increase in import competition has a negative impact on employment in Vietnam. As labour productivity rises over time, the employment effect of exporting is reduced considerably (Heo and Nguyen, 2009). McCaig (2009) identifies three labour market channels from the Vietnam-US BTA for poverty alleviation at the provincial level. Provinces that are more exposed to tariff cuts experience increases in provincial wage premiums for low-skilled workers, faster movement into wage-salaried jobs for low-skilled workers, and more rapid job growth in formal enterprises. Similarly, Fukase (2013) finds that those provinces more exposed to export increases experience a relatively larger wage growth for unskilled workers, confirming the existence of a Stolper–Samuelson-type effect.

In summary, the openness of the economy has a positive impact on employment, due to the expansion of markets. Trade liberalisation in agriculture and industry increases the demand for labourers, especially low-skilled workers, which improves incomes and reduces poverty. Discrimination against the private sector, the primary solution for unemployment, will nevertheless impinge on the employment effects of trade liberalisation. Oostendorp *et al.* (2009) find that nonfarm household enterprises, which were affected by trade liberalisation from 1993 to 2002, increased income and reduced inequality between households. In reality, these enterprises are unlikely to play their expected role in the economy, especially in urban areas. If Vietnam implements the commitments made when entering the WTO, then the minimum wage faced by domestic enterprises will be forced to rise to catch up with the minimum wage paid by foreign companies. This will take its toll on the economy's ability to create jobs (World Bank, 2007). In the labour market, the important determinant of the labour force is education, which has played a significant role in the successful development of Vietnam over the last 20 years (World Bank, 2013).

Government revenue channel

The fourth channel in Winters's framework is the impact of trade liberalisation on poverty through government revenue from trade taxes. Under the old economic system, the government allocated the state budget to economic units based on the national planning process. Surpluses generated by economic units were delivered to the national treasury. Households and the private sector were excluded from the budget allocation (World Bank, 1991). The main government revenue was largely from SOE transfers and foreign aid, and taxes on trade included only the noncommercial import tax. Trade taxes contribute to government revenue and are likely to influence public expenditure only during the transitional period. The proportions of trade taxes, tax revenue, and social expenditure in GDP peaked in the mid-1990s (Figure 3.8), probably because of the export boom and high economic growth. Simultaneously, and

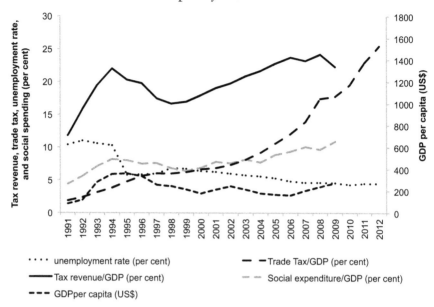

Figure 3.8 Shares of tax revenue, trade taxes, and social expenditure in GDP, unemployment rate, and GDP per capita, 1991–2012

Source: Unemployment rate and GDP per capita from World Economic Outlook (WEO) database, IMF. Trade tax/GDP from the World Bank (1998, 1999b, 2004, 2006, 2007, 2010).

interestingly, the unemployment rate dropped considerably to about 6 per cent in the mid-1990s, from over 10 per cent in the early 1990s. These results are consistent with the previous analysis of the impact of trade liberalisation on employment in the 1990s. The trade tax share declined throughout the second half of the 1990s, reflecting the implementation of the commitments to the AFTA. Meanwhile, tax revenue fell sharply in the late 1990s, probably due to the impacts of the Asian financial crisis. The steady increase in tax revenue from 1999 up until the 2008 financial crisis may have resulted from the reconstruction of the domestic tax system.

The decline in the trade tax share in GDP from 2002 to 2006 may mirror the effects of the Vietnam–US BTA in 2001 and the accelerated preparation for acceding to the WTO in 2007. The rise of the trade tax proportion after participating in the WTO may demonstrate that Vietnam is expanding export markets. Over the two decades, the employment rate tended to decline, social expenditure was little affected by the external crises and appeared to increase, and GDP per capita increased steadily. As a result, trade reforms reflected by changes in trade tax appeared unrelated to the improvement in welfare and employment. The share of social expenditure in GDP was approximately 7.8 per cent on average, and appeared to increase over time (Figure 3.9). In the government budget for social expenditure, social subsidies accounted for

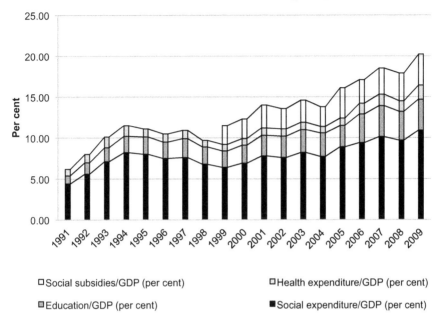

Social subsidies/GDP (per cent)   Health expenditure/GDP (per cent)

Education/GDP (per cent)   Social expenditure/GDP (per cent)

Figure 3.9 Government expenditure on health, education, and social security, 1991–2009

Source: World Bank (1998, 1999b, 2004, 2006, 2007, 2010)

about 2.9 per cent on average. Government expenditure for education averaged about 2.5 per cent. The expenditure for both social subsidies and education tended to increase slightly over time.

In addition to government spending for social security and education, its expenditure on health was very modest: only 1 per cent of GDP, on average, over the two decades. With respect to provincial budget allocation, the 2004 Budget Law marked a big milestone in the process of administrative decentralisation. The state budget allocation to provinces is based on some criteria, mainly including population, development, geography, and administration. These four criteria, which take into consideration the local poverty plight, were reflected in targeted national programmes such as the 135 programme, which aims to support disadvantaged and/or poor communes. In addition, net budget transfers, defined as the differential between the state budget that the central government provides for provinces and the tax revenue that provinces deliver to the central government, are highest for the poorest provinces. The correlation between net budget transfers and poverty rates has been positive, and has become stronger over time (World Bank, 2007).

This analysis generally identifies no significant link between trade taxes and tax revenue, or between tax revenue and social expenditure. The common prediction – that a fall in government revenue caused by the reduction of tariff barriers leads to pruning social expenditures on education, health, and social security – appears not to occur in the Vietnam case. In reality, huge efforts and resources have been contributed to reducing poverty and improving standards of living. This is discernibly consistent with what Winters conjectures: that public spending is unlikely to be reduced as a consequence of trade policy reforms.

Overall, high economic growth increased the average incomes and standards of living of households, including the poor. The liberalisation of the agricultural market helped legions of poor households to escape poverty. Industrial development, as a result of the open policy, has provided the poor with numerous opportunities of employment. The flow-on from liberalising the export sector moved through an improved trade balance to an increased government budget and on to an expanded public expenditure. Trade liberalisation, therefore, seems to have had an enormous impact on Vietnam's economy.

3.4   Conclusions

This chapter has systematically examined the effects of trade liberalisation on poverty in Vietnam over the past three decades. The analysis is carried out using the Winters analytical framework. The study provides evidence that trade liberalisation has contributed to the improvement in economic welfare and reduction in poverty in Vietnam through its effects on economic growth, market, employment, and government spending.

Five key conclusions emerge from the analysis. First, the openness of the economy has brought about fundamental changes in the outcomes of economic development, especially in terms of economic growth and poverty reduction. Second, the main drive for the export boom in the mid-1990s was the liberalisation of prices and agricultural trade. Third, unemployment declined sharply in the mid-1990s, decreasing throughout the 1990s and the 2000s. This suggests that job creation has risen along with the process of trade liberalisation. Fourth, no clear-cut relationship between trade policy reforms and public expenditure is identified. In practice, there has been an increase in the efforts and resources devoted to the reduction in poverty over time, regardless of economic situation. Fifth, the economic and trade reforms institutionalised in 1986 were not radical. Consequently, their effects on the economy have been both transient and unsustainable. The economy has shown signs of exhaustion in the more recent stages of its development.

This study's analysis of the trade–poverty relationship in Vietnam has demonstrated the crucial role of trade liberalisation in accelerating economic growth, reducing unemployment and poverty, and achieving high income. Despite these achievements, the process of trade liberalisation appears not to have been effective. In reality, farm households remain typically poor, despite the increase in the volumes of agricultural exports that have made Vietnam one of the major rice export countries in the world. This suggests the inadequacy of trade policies that are directly related to exports. Underdeveloped institutions seem to have impeded the economic development, particularly by impinging on the channels through which trade liberalisation affects welfare and poverty. Vietnam needs to take more radical and appropriate steps to reform agricultural production and market distribution, primarily by removing the monopoly of SOEs on the rice business.

Annex

Table A3.1 Three decades of trade and economic reforms in Vietnam, 1981–2010

Year	Reform type	Main trade and economic reforms
Stage I, 1981–1990: the renovation phase		
1981	Trade	• '100' Contracting (product contracting) for farm households
1985	Other	• Price, wage, and money reform
1986	Other	• The Sixth Party Congress initiated a renovation programme, Doi Moi
1987	Other	• Launched and accelerated the first Foreign Investment Law for open-door policy
		• Issue of Land Law to establish private use of allocated land in agriculture
		• Establishment of a central treasury to control the budget
1988	Trade	• Termination of government monopoly on foreign trade
		• Relaxation of restrictions on establishment of foreign trading organisations
		• Liberalisation of foreign exchange control on retention of foreign exchange
		• Permission for opening foreign currency account, and the use of transfers to pay for imports and repay foreign loans
		• Devaluation of trade and invisible payments exchange rates
		• Introduction of Law on Import and Export Duties with customs tariff
	Other	• Establishment of two-tier banking system
		• End of cooperative method of agricultural production
		• Permission of long-term land use rights for farm households
		• Adoption of Resolution 10 on agricultural land use rights of farm households
		• Official policy on encouragement of private enterprises

(Continued)

Year	Reform type	Main trade and economic reforms
1989	Trade	• Removal of two-price system, price control, and nearly all forms of direct subsidisation of production
		• Abolition of quotas for most commodities, except for 10 export and 14 import commodities
		• Unification of foreign exchange rate system
		• End of all budgetary export subsidies
1990	Trade	• Introduction of sales tax, turnover tax, and profit tax
	Other	• Amendment of Foreign Investment Law
		• Approval of Law on Central Bank, state-owned banks, and credit institutions
		• Introduction of laws on private enterprises and companies to establish legal basis for sole proprietorships, liability limited, and shareholder business entities

Stage II, 1991–2000: the economic boom phase

Year	Reform type	Main trade and economic reforms
1991	Trade	• Promulgation of regulation on setting up export processing zones (EPZ)
		• Reduction of rice export duty from 10 to 1 per cent
		• Duty exemption for imported inputs used to produce exports
		• Approval of new Law on Import and Export Duties, distinguishing normal tariffs from preferential ones
		• Private companies were entitled to export and import directly
		• Openness of foreign exchange trading floors at the state bank of Vietnam
	Other	• Ordinance on civil contracts establishes legal basis for most forms of contract
		• Banks' embarkation on providing loans to households.
1992	Trade	• Introduction of harmonised system of tariff nomenclature (HS)
		• Trade agreement with European Union
	Other	• Amendment of foreign investment law, introducing built operate transfer (BOT) concept for infrastructure projects
		• Adoption of new constitution that officially recognised the multisector economy and property rights
		• Experiments with equitisation of SOEs
		• Start of Hunger Elimination and Poverty Reduction programme (HEPR)
1993	Trade	• Removal of the United State's embargo against Vietnam
		• Introduction of 90-day duty suspension system for inputs into export production
		• Participation in Customs Cooperation Council
		• Adoption of United Nation layout key for customs declaration

	Other	• Amendments of Land Law, allowing agricultural land use rights to be transferable and use as collateral
		• Approval of Bankruptcy Law and Environment Law
1994	Trade	• Vietnam gains GATT observer status
		• Removal of export shipment licenses for all commodities except rice, timber, and petroleum
		• Elimination of import permits for all but 15 products
		• Introduction of interbank foreign exchange market
		• Expansion of export duty exemption to suspend duty payments for 90 days
	Other	• Establishment of economic courts
		• Enactment of Labour Code
		• Introduction of Law on Promotion of Domestic Investment
		• National programme for safer water and environmental sanitation launched
1995	Trade	• Vietnam joins ASEAN and accedes to protocols of AFTA membership
		• Promulgation of the 1996 list of goods under the CEPT of AFTA
		• Application for WTO member
		• Only rice left in the coverage of export quotas
		• Only seven commodities in the range of goods subject to import quota management
		• Increase of export tax rates on 11 products
		• Elimination of requirement for import permits on a by shipment basis for a wide range of consumption and capital goods
	Other	• Approval of Law on State Enterprises
		• Enactment of Civil Code to lay the foundation for market economy and legal protection of industrial property rights
1996	Trade	• Reduction of goods managed by import quota to six by the import–export policy decision for 1996
		• Lift of inward foreign exchange remittance
		• New Law on Foreign Investment reducing scope of import duty exemptions for foreign investment projects
		• Promulgation of the 1997 list of commodities under the CEPT of AFTA
	Other	• Issue of regulations on industrial property rights protection
		• Introduction of Law on State Budget

(*Continued*)

Year	Reform type	Main trade and economic reforms
1997	Trade	• Promulgation of decree allocating rice export quotas to provincial authorities, as well as agencies under central management
		• Abolition of all barriers against domestic trade in rice. Private enterprises granted licenses to rice export, subject to certain conditions
		• Prohibition of sugar imports
		• Introduction of import stamp system for antismuggling
	Other	• Promulgation of Laws on Credit Institutions, State Bank of Vietnam, Cooperatives
		• Adoption of National Action Plan for Women Advancement
1998	Trade	• Abolition of trade licenses
		• Replacement of quotas or licenses by tariff for most consumer goods
		• Amendment to import/export tax law introducing three-schedule tariff, and provision for antidumping and countervailing duty
		• Reduction of highest tariff rate to 60 per cent
		• Abolition of minimum price list for valuation of imports by foreign invested enterprises
		• Announcement of decision to allocate rice export and fertiliser import quotas to private sector enterprises
		• Exemption of export tax on rice (0 per cent)
		• Permission for opening savings account in foreign currency
		• Surrender requirements of 80 per cent of foreign exchanges
		• Permission to export products not specified in investment license for foreign-invested enterprises
		• Authorisation to forwarding and swapping exchange transactions
		• Promulgation of the 1998 list of goods under the CEPT for AFTA, completing coverage of inclusion list
	Other	• Introduction of taxpayer identification numbering system
		• Introduction of National Target Employment programme
		• Approval of Grassroots Democracy Decree
		• Introduction of the National Target Programme on Hunger Eradiation and Poverty Reduction (the 133 programme, or HEPR)
		• Introduction of the 135 programme to support most difficult communes (1998–2005)

1999	Trade	• Decree 57, liberalising rights to export and import
		• Release of new tariff with smaller range and rates
		• Surrender requirements eased to 50 per cent of foreign exchanges
		• Decree 254 to add to list of conditional imports
	Other	• Approval of New Enterprise Law
		• Introduction of value added tax (VAT)
		• Acceleration of SOE equitisation programme
2000	Trade	• Signing the Vietnam–US BTA
	Other	• New Enterprises Law comes into effective
		• Openness of the Vietnam Stock Exchange

Stage III, 2001–2010: the WTO membership phase

2001	Trade	• Introduction of the first trade policy road map for 2001–2005 (Decision 46/2001/QD-TTg)
		• The Vietnam–US BTA comes into effect
		• All domestic enterprises can now freely trade all commodities, except those prohibited or under specialized management
		• Abolition of quotas on rice exports and fertiliser imports
		• Surrender requirements eased to 40 per cent of foreign exchanges
	Other	• Ninth Communist Party Congress adopts the 10-year socioeconomic strategy 2001–2010
2002	Trade	• Decision No. 35/2002/QD-TTg to promulgate government action programme for implementation of the Vietnam–US BTA
		• Surrender requirements eased to 30 per cent of foreign exchanges
	Other	• Foreign-invested enterprises (FIEs) were granted the right to export goods beyond their permitted list
2003	Trade	• Announcement of the list of CEPT implementation 2003–2006 in accordance with the ASEAN Harmonised Tariff Nomenclature
		• Introduction of tariff rate quotas for certain agricultural products (raw and condensed milk, poultry eggs, maize, cotton, tobacco materials, and salt)
		• Only sugar and petroleum subject to quotas
2004	Trade	• Abolition of the 20 per cent VAT rate, resulting in a three-band VAT system of 0, 5, and 10 per cent
		• Removal of surrender requirements of foreign exchanges

(Continued)

Year	Reform type	Main trade and economic reforms
	Other	• Introduction of Law on Competition
		• Amendment to Credit Institution Law, Bankruptcy Law
2005	Trade	• Vietnamese Law on Competition (VLC) comes into effect
		• Introduction of Import–Export Law, Commercial Law, Intellectual Property Law
		• Acceptance of Article VIII of the IMF to maintain an exchange system free of restrictions on payments and transfers
	Other	• Introduction of Anticorruption Law, Commercial Law, Intellectual Property Law, and Environment Law
		• Amendment to Investment Law, Enterprise Law, and Education Law
2006	Other	• Introduction of Stock Market Law, Social Insurance Law, Gender Equality Law, and Residence Law
		• Amendment to Labour Code
2007	Trade	• Obtainment of WTO membership
		• Permission of trade rights for foreign traders without commercial presence in Vietnam (Decree No. 90/2007/ND-CP)
	Other	• Introduction of Personal Income Tax Law
2008	Trade	• Decree No. 75/2008/ND-CP of price management
	Other	• Reduction of corporate income tax (CIT) to 25 per cent from 28 per cent
2009	Trade	• Amendment to Law on Excise Duty, removing differentials tax between domestically produced and imported goods
	Other	• Personal income tax came into effect
		• Introduction of loyalty tax
2010	Other	• Introduction of Law of State Bank of Vietnam 2010, Nonagricultural Land Use Tax, and Environment Protection Tax
2011	Trade	• Adoption of 'Import–Export Strategy for the Period 2011–2020 with a vision towards 2030'
	Other	• Decision 732 approving the tax reform strategy for the period 2011–2020 regarding tax policy and tax management

Source: Author's synthesis based on the Centre for International Economics (1999), the National Centre for Social Sciences and Humanities (2001), Athukorala (2005), the United Nations Environment Programme (2005), Vo (2005), and the WTO (2013a, 2013b).

Notes

1 Currencies in the Comecon countries are considered to be inconvertible.
2 The countries in the World Bank research are Bangladesh, Brazil, Bolivia, Burkina Faso, El Salvador, India, Indonesia, Ghana, Romania, Senegal, Tunisia, Uganda, Zambia, and Vietnam.
3 Authors estimate the income gap in 1998, based on the data from the Vietnam living standards survey 1998 (the VLSS 1998).
4 A commune is an administrative division in rural Vietnam, which is equivalent to a ward.

References

Athukorala, P. (2005). *Trade Policy Reforms and the Structure of Protection in Vietnam*. Australian National University, Working Papers in Trade and Development (No. 2005–06).

Athukorala, P. (2010). *Trade Liberalisation and the Poverty of Nations: A Review Article*. Australian National University, Working Papers in Trade and Development (No. 2010/01), 34.

Bandara, J. S. (2011). Trade and Poverty – Theory, Evidence and Policy Issues. In J. S. Bandara, P. Athukorala, and S. Kelegama (eds) *Trade Liberalisation and Poverty in South Asia* (p. 224). London: Routledge.

Beresford, M., and Dang, P. (2000). *Economic Transition in Vietnam: Trade and Aid in the Demise of a Centrally Planned Economy*. London: Edward Elgar Publishing.

Berg, A., and Krueger, A. (2003). *Trade, Growth, and Poverty: A Selective Survey*. IMF, Working Paper (WP/03/30).

Central Institute for Economic Management, and Institute of Policy and Strategy for Agriculture and Rural Development (CIEM–IPSARD) (2007). *Characteristics of the Vietnamese Rural Economy: Evidence from a 2006 Rural Household Survey in 12 Provinces of Vietnam* (p. 262). Hanoi.

Central Institute for Economic Management, and Institute of Policy and Strategy for Agriculture and Rural Development (CIEM–IPSARD) (2011). *Characteristics of the Vietnamese Rural Economy: Evidence from a 2010 Rural Household Survey in 12 Provinces of Vietnam* (p. 289). Hanoi.

Central Institute for Economic Management, and Institute of Policy and Strategy for Agriculture and Rural Development (CIEM–IPSARD) (2013). *Characteristics of the Vietnamese Rural Economy: Evidence from a 2012 Rural Household Survey in 12 Provinces of Vietnam* (p. 350). Hanoi.

Centre for International Economics (CIE) (1999). *Vietnam's Trade Policies 1998*. Canberra.

Centre for International Economics (CIE) (2002a). *Integration and Poverty: An Economywide Analysis*. Canberra.

Centre for International Economics (CIE) (2002b). *Vietnam Poverty Analysis*. Canberra.

Dang, P. (2008). *Vietnam's Economic Mindset: A Daunting and Spectacular Road, 1975–1989*. Hanoi: Southern Intellect Publishing House.

Dapice, D. O. (2003). *Vietnam's Economy: Success Story or Weird Dualism? A SWOT Analysis*. Paper presented at the UNDP and Prime Minister's Research Commission, Hanoi.

Dodsworth, J. R., Spitaller, E., Braulke, M., Lee, K. H., Miranda, K., Mulder, C., . . . Srinivasan, K. (1996). *Vietnam: Transition to a Market Economy*. Washington, DC: IMF.

Dollar, D., Glewwe, P., and Litvack, J. (eds) (1998). *Household Welfare and Vietnam's Transition*. Washington, DC: World Bank.

Fforde, A., and De Vylder, S. (1996). *From Plan to Market: The Economic Transition in Vietnam*. Boulder, CO: Westview Press.

Fukase, E. (2013). Export Liberalization, Job Creation, and the Skill Premium: Evidence from the US–Vietnam Bilateral Trade Agreement (BTA). *World Development, 41*, 317–337. DOI: http://dx.doi.org/10.1016/j.worlddev.2012.05.035

Gallup, J. L. (2004). The Wage Labor Market and Inequality in Vietnam. In P. Glewwe, N. Agrawal, and D. Dollar (eds) *Economic Growth, Poverty, and Household Welfare in Vietnam* (pp. 53–93). Washington, DC: World Bank.

Gantz, D. A. (2009). *Non-market Economy Status and U.S. Unfair Trade Actions against Vietnam*. Arizona Legal Studies, Discussion Paper (No. 09–38), 36.

General Statistics Office (GSO) (1999). *Vietnam Living Standard Survey, 1997–1998*. Hanoi: Statistical Publishing House.

General Statistics Office (GSO) (2006). *Result of the Vietnam Household Living Standards Survey 2004*. Ho Chi Minh: Statistical Publishing House.

General Statistics Office (GSO) (2008). *Result of the Vietnam Household Living Standards Survey 2006*. Ho Chi Minh: Statistical Publishing House.

General Statistics Office (GSO) (2010). *Result of the Survey on Household Living Standards 2008*. Ho Chi Minh: Statistical Publishing House.

General Statistics Office (GSO) (2012). *Result of the Vietnam Household Living Standards Survey 2010*. Ho Chi Minh: Statistical Publishing House.

Griffin, K. B. (1998). *Economic Reform in Vietnam*. London: Palgrave Macmillan.

Harrison, A. (2007). Globalization and Poverty: An Introduction. In A. Harrison (ed) *Globalization and Poverty* (pp. 1–30). Chicago: University of Chicago Press.

Harvie, C., and Tran, V. H. (1997). *Vietnam's Reforms and Economic Growth*. London: Macmillan Publishers Limited.

Heo, Y., and Nguyen, K. D. (2009). Trade Liberalisation and Poverty Reduction in Vietnam. *The World Economy, 32*(6), 934.

International Monetary Fund (IMF) (1998). *Vietnam: Selected Issues and Statistical Annex*. IMF, Staff Country Report (No. 98/30).

International Monetary Fund (IMF) (1999). *Vietnam: Statistical Appendix*. IMF, Staff Country Report (No. 99/56).

International Monetary Fund (IMF) (2000). *Vietnam: Statistical Appendix and Background Notes*. IMF, Staff Country Report (No. 00116).

International Monetary Fund (IMF) (2002). *Vietnam: Selected Issues and Statistical Appendix*. IMF, Staff Country Report (No. 02/5).

International Monetary Fund (IMF) (2003). *Vietnam: Statistical Appendix*. IMF, Staff Country Report (No. 03/382).

International Monetary Fund (IMF) (2004). *Vietnam: Poverty Reduction Strategy Paper*. IMF, Country Report (No. 04/25), 134.

International Monetary Fund (IMF) (2006). *Vietnam: Statistical Appendix*. IMF, Staff Country Report (No. 06/423).

International Monetary Fund (IMF) (2007). *Vietnam: Statistical Appendix*. IMF, Staff Country Report (No. 07/386).

International Monetary Fund (IMF) (2010). *Vietnam: 2010 Article IV Consultation-Staff Report and Public Information Notice.* IMF, Country Report (No. 10/281).

International Monetary Fund (IMF) (2012). *Vietnam: 2012 Article IV Consultation.* IMF, Country Report (No. 12/165).

Irvin, G. (1997). Vietnam: Adjustment, Growth and Poverty. *Journal of International Development, 9*(6), 19.

Jenkins, R. (2004). Vietnam in the Global Economy: Trade, Employment and Poverty. *Journal of International Development, 16*(1), 13–28. DOI: 10.1002/jid.1060

Kang, W., and Imai, K. S. (2012). Pro-poor Growth, Poverty and Inequality in Rural Vietnam. *Journal of Asian Economics, 23*(5), 527–539.

Leipziger, D. M. (1992). *Awakening the Market: Vietnam's Economic Transition.* World Bank, Discussion Papers (No. 0157), 52.

Litchfield, J., McCulloch, N., and Winters, L. A. (2003). Agricultural Trade Liberalization and Poverty Dynamics in Three Developing Countries. *American Journal of Agricultural Economics, 85*(5), 1285–1291. DOI: 10.1111/j.0092–5853.2003. 00544.x

McCaig, B. (2009). *Exporting Out of Poverty: Provincial Poverty in Vietnam and U.S. Market Access.* Australian National University, Working Papers in Economics & Econometrics (No. 502), 56.

McCulloch, N., Winters, L. A., and Cirera, X. (2001). *Trade Liberalization and Poverty: A Handbook.* London: Centre for Economic Policy Research.

Minot, N., and Goletti, F. (1998). Export Liberalization and Household Welfare: The Case of Rice in Vietnam. *American Journal of Agricultural Economics, 80*(4), 738–749.

Nadvi, K., Bui, T. T., Nguyen, T.T.H., Nguyen, T. H., Dao, H. L., and Armas, E.B.D. (2004). Vietnam in the Global Garment and Textile Value Chain: Impacts on Firms and Workers. *Journal of International Development, 16*(1), 111–123.

National Centre for Social Sciences and Humanities (2001). *Doi Moi and Human Development in Vietnam.* National Human Development Report, Hanoi.

Nissanke, M., and Thorbecke, E. (2007). *Linking Globalization and Poverty.* United Nations University, Policy Brief (No. 2), 8.

Oostendorp, R. H., Tran, Q. T., and Nguyen, T. T. (2009). The Changing Role of Non-farm Household Enterprises in Vietnam. *World Development, 37*(3), 632–644. DOI: 10.1016/j.worlddev.2008.07.007

Pham, Q. N., Trinh, B., and Nguyen, D. T. (2007). *Economic Performance of Vietnam, 1976–2000: New Evidence from Input-Output Model.* DEPOCEN Working Paper Series (2007/13), 44.

Pham, T. H, Phung, D.T., and Nguyen, V. C. (2009). *Evaluating the Impact of the Current Economic Slow Down on Unemployment in Vietnam.* UNDP Vietnam Policy Discussion Paper, 24.

Phan, T. N., Harvie, C., and Tran, V. H. (2006). *Vietnam's Economic Transition: Policies, Issues and Prospects.* Hyderabad, India: ICFAI University Press.

Piketty, T. (2014). *Capital in the Twenty-First Century.* Massachusetts: Harvard University Press.

Pincus, J., and Sender, J. (2008). Quantifying Poverty in Vietnam: Who Counts? *Journal of Vietnamese Studies, 3*(1), 108–150. DOI: 10.1525/vs.2008.3.1.108

Rodrik, D. (2002). Trade Policy Reform as Institutional Reform. In B. Hoekman, A. Mattoo, and P. English (eds) *Development, Trade, and the WTO: A Handbook* (pp. 3–10). Washington, DC: World Bank.

Singh, T. (2010). Does International Trade Cause Economic Growth? A Survey. *The World Economy, 33*(11), 1517–1564. DOI: 10.1111/j.1467–9701.2010.01243.x

Thu Le, H., and Booth, A. L. (2013). Inequality in Vietnamese Urban–Rural Living Standards, 1993–2006. *Review of Income and Wealth.* DOI: 10.1111/roiw.12051

United Nations Development Programme (UNDP) (2006). *Discretionary Rules: Anti-dumping and Vietnam's Non-market Economy Status.* UNDP, Policy Dialogue Paper (2006/4), Hanoi.

United Nations Environment Programme (UNEP) (2005). *Integrated Assessment of the Impact of Trade Liberalization: A Country Study on the Vietnam Rice Sector.* Geneva.

Vietnam Academy of Social Sciences (VASS) (2007). *Vietnam Poverty Update Report 2006: Poverty and Poverty Reduction in Vietnam 1993–2004* (p. 60). Hanoi.

Vietnam Academy of Social Sciences (VASS) (2011). *Poverty Reduction in Vietnam: Achievements and Challenges.* Hanoi.

Vo, N. T. (1990). *Vietnam's Economic Policy Since 1975.* Singapore: ASEAN Economic Research Unit, Institute of Southeast Asian Studies.

Vo, T. T. (2005). *Vietnam's Trade Liberalisation and International Integration: Evolution, Problems, and Challenges.* ASEAN Economic Bulletin (4/2005).

Warren-Rodriguez, A. (2009). *Technical Note: Employment Elasticities* (p. 13). Hanoi: UNDP Vietnam.

Winters, L. A. (2002). Trade Liberalisation and Poverty: What are the Links?. *The World Economy, 25*(9), 1339–1367. DOI: 10.1111/1467–9701.00495

Winters, L. A., McCulloch, N., and McKay, A. (2004). Trade Liberalization and Poverty: The Evidence So Far. *Journal of Economic Literature, XLII*(1), 72–115.

World Bank (1990). *Vietnam: Stabilization and Structural Reforms* (p. 176). Washington, DC.

World Bank (1991). *Vietnam Transforming a State Owned Financial System: A Financial Sector Study of Vietnam.* Washington, DC.

World Bank (1993). *Vietnam Transition to the Market: An Economic Report* (p. 274). Washington, DC.

World Bank (1995). *Vietnam Poverty Assessment and Strategy.* Washington, DC.

World Bank (1998). *Vietnam: Rising to the Challenge?.* Hanoi.

World Bank (1999a). *Vietnam Development Report 2000: Attacking Poverty* (p. 195). Hanoi.

World Bank (1999b). *Vietnam Preparing for Take-off?: How Vietnam Can Participate Fully in the East Asian Recovery.* Hanoi.

World Bank (2004). *Vietnam Development Report 2004: Poverty* (p. 194). Washington, DC.

World Bank (2005). *Pro-poor Growth in the 1990s: Lessons and Insights from 14 Countries* (p. 116). Washington, DC.

World Bank (2006). *Vietnam Development Report 2006: Vietnam Business.* Washington, DC.

World Bank (2007). *Vietnam Development Report 2008: Social Protection* (p. 178). Hanoi.

World Bank (2010). *Vietnam Development Report 2011: Natural Resources Management* (p. 163). Hanoi.

World Bank (2011). *Vietnam Development Report 2012: Market Economy for a Middle-Income Vietnam* (p. 90). Hanoi.

World Bank (2012). *Well Begun, Not Yet Done: Vietnam's Remarkable Progress on Poverty Reduction and the Emerging Challenges* (p. 190). Hanoi.

World Bank (2013). *Vietnam Development Report 2014: Skilling up Vietnam: Preparing the Workforce for a Modern Market Economy* (p. 138). Hanoi.

World Trade Organisation (WTO) (2013a). *Trade Policy Review: Vietnam* (p. 183). Geneva.

World Trade Organisation (WTO) (2013b). *Trade Policy Review: Vietnam* (p. 21). Geneva.

4 Trade and growth elasticity of poverty

4.1 Introduction

The 1980s and 1990s witnessed the transition of several developing countries from closed or semiclosed to open and market-driven economies. Economies pursuing outward-oriented development strategies have commonly been characterised by acceleration of economic growth and reduction in poverty. Vietnam has been amongst the economies that have achieved a remarkable reduction in poverty during their process of high economic growth (World Bank, 2005). In 1986, Vietnam embarked on a renovation programme, Doi Moi, to transform its centrally planned economy (CPE) into an open, market-driven economy. The economy achieved an annual average economic growth of 8 per cent in the 1990s and 7 per cent in the 2000s. The consistently high economic growth in the 1990s and 2000s appears to have contributed to the substantial decline in poverty at both aggregate and provincial levels. The rate of poverty dropped from 58.1 per cent to 37.4 per cent over the period 1993–1998 (Figure 3.1). By the end of 2010, Vietnam became a lower-middle-income country with a per capita income of approximately US$1,130 per annum.

Although several open economies have succeeded in attaining high economic growth and low poverty, development economists acknowledge that the relationship between economic growth and poverty is difficult to establish, primarily because the poor benefit from economic growth indirectly through the trickle-down effect (Kakwani and Pernia, 2000; Pernia, 2003). Some studies provide evidence that growth is good for the poor (e.g. Dollar and Kraay, 2002, 2004). One method for examining the effects of growth on poverty is to measure the elasticity of poverty with regard to economic growth. The studies measuring such growth elasticity of poverty provide various estimates, ranging from –0.84 (Ram, 2011) to –3.12 (Ravallion and Chen, 1997). According to the World Bank (2001b) and the United Nations Development Programme (2003), a typical estimate of the growth elasticity of poverty is –2; each one per cent increase in average per capita income reduces the poverty rate by 2 per cent. Pernia (2003) estimates the elasticity for some developing countries (Korea, Laos, the Philippines, Thailand, and Vietnam) in the 1990s; for Vietnam, it was –1, a one-to-one inverse relationship between growth and poverty. This was relatively low compared with Korea

(–3.1), the Philippines (–2.5), and Thailand (–3.1). Some of the later studies, however, argue for rather low estimates of elasticity (Ram, 2006, 2011; Kalwij and Verschoor, 2007). Most of the previous studies examining the effect of growth on poverty in Vietnam used household data up until the 1990s. Contemporary evaluation of the effects of growth on poverty based on more recent data would be useful for policymakers in that it would help them devise appropriate strategies for the reduction in poverty.

This study reexamines the growth elasticity of poverty for Vietnam, using data for the 1990s and the 2000s. The study differs from the previous research on two counts. First, it uses the latest national accounts data drawn from the statistical yearbooks of Vietnam and the Vietnam Household Living Standards Surveys for the last two decades to estimate the growth elasticity of poverty. Second, it examines the elasticity of poverty with regard to growth and internal trade at the provincial level, using a provincial panel data set. The rest of the chapter includes three sections. Section 4.2 explains the methods and data used for estimating the growth elasticity of poverty. Section 4.3 estimates and analyses the effect of growth and trade on poverty. Section 4.4 concludes the chapter and draws the policy implications.

4.2 Methods and data

The growth elasticity of poverty can be estimated by the simple definition of elasticity or by regressing the log of poverty rate on the log of a measure of welfare. The common measures of welfare are income or consumption expenditure, based on a monetary approach. The estimation can be based either on survey data or on national accounts data. These different sources of data are likely to provide different results for the estimates of elasticity, both for the level of private consumption expenditure per capita and for growth. In addition, the elasticity estimates are subject to statistical errors. The advantage of using surveys is that welfare growth is directly calculated from household income or consumption per capita, whereas growth based on national accounts data captures much more than household income, including several types of spending, which do not necessarily belong to households. It may be noted that growth rates measured by survey data can also overestimate the correlation between growth and poverty reduction because of the survey measurement errors (Ravallion, 2003, 2004; Deaton, 2005).

For national accounts data, the growth elasticity of poverty is estimated by dividing the percentage change in poverty by the percentage change in per capita GDP for a certain period or periods. For household survey data, the mean per capita expenditure and poverty measure – whether it be the incidence, the depth, or the severity of poverty – are first estimated at several data points, and then the elasticity is estimated as above. However, the elasticity estimated by this method has some shortcomings. Klasen and Misselhorn (2006) point out that the percentage change in poverty reduction and growth elasticity can be easily misunderstood. If the initial poverty head count is rather low, a small absolute

Table 4.1 Pro-poor growth index by category

Classification	Pro-poor growth index (PGI)		
Anti-poor growth		PGI	<0
Weakly pro-poor growth	0<	PGI	≤0.33
Moderately pro-poor growth	0.33<	PGI	≤0.66
Pro-poor growth	0.66<	PGI	<1
Highly pro-poor growth	1≤	PGI	

Source: Kakwani and Pernia (2000)

reduction in poverty can make a large percentage change in poverty. They argue that the policymakers may be more interested in percentage point changes than in per cent changes in poverty reduction. They suggest the use of the alternative semi-elasticity measure. The method for estimating growth semi-elasticity of poverty is the same, but it uses absolute changes instead of percentage changes in poverty.

The growth elasticity of poverty is commonly used to examine whether the economic growth is pro-poor or not. According to Kakwani and Pernia (2000) and Pernia (2003), this elasticity comprises both the growth effect and the inequality effect. The total change in poverty can be decomposed into the effect of growth when the income distribution does not change and the impact of income distribution when total income is constant. The pure growth effect is negative since positive growth alleviates poverty, holding inequality constant. The inequality effect can be negative or positive depending on whether inequality is 'growth improving' or 'growth worsening'. The pro-poor growth index is the ratio of the growth elasticity of poverty to the growth effect. Whether growth is pro-poor or not depends on the values of the pro-poor growth index, as classified in Table 4.1. The remarkable development of Vietnam's economy in the 1990s, with the economy experiencing high economic growth and remarkable reduction in poverty, provides a good indication of the link between growth and poverty.

4.3   Pro-poor growth in Vietnam

The study uses Vietnam's national accounts data and the VHLSS data to estimate the growth elasticity for Vietnam. The analysis is first undertaken in terms of the conceptual definition of elasticity, and the national accounts data are used to compute the growth elasticity of poverty (GEP), growth semi-elasticity of poverty (GSEP), and the pro-poor growth index. The analysis based on the definition of elasticity is followed by the estimation of the poverty model based on the data drawn from the VHLSSs. This study then extends to analysing the impact of local trade on poverty, using a poverty regression model and the provincial panel data compiled from the VHLSSs from 1998 to 2008.

Estimates of GEP, GSEP at the aggregate level

Estimates based on national accounts data

Vietnam has had a remarkable achievement in poverty reduction. The poverty head count ratio has decreased and GDP per capita has increased steadily over the last two decades (Table 4.2). As a result of the Doi Moi reforms, poverty dropped remarkably from 58.1 per cent in 1993 to 37.4 per cent in 1998. The GEP for this period was –0.95; that is, holding other factors constant, for every 1 per cent increase in GDP per capita, poverty falls by 0.95 per cent on average. The elasticity peaked at –2.5 per cent in 2004, and then it tended to show declines. This trend is consistent with the process of economic development in Vietnam. In the early 2000s, the economy was relatively stable with low inflation. In this period, economic reforms had been accelerating to prepare for joining the WTO. The income growth benefits the poor and contributes to the reduction of poverty. In the later stages, however, the 2008 financial crisis and increasing inflation may have offset the benefits of economic growth to the poor.

The GSEP shows a similar tendency. It is generally lower than the GEP, because it uses the total absolute change rather than the total percentage change in the poverty head count ratio to compute the elasticity. For instance, on average, poverty drops by 0.55 percentage points per year based on the GSEP, instead of 0.95 per cent per year based on the GEP during the 1993–1998 period. Compared with the 1990s, both the GEP and GSEP appear to have decreased in the 2000s, probably due to the stabilisation of the economy with a lower economic growth and the rise in economic inequality. The pro-poor growth indexes of 0.73 for the 1990s or 0.66 for the 2000s suggest that the growth was pro-poor in these decades, according to the classification by Kakwani and Pernia (2000) (Table 4.1). These results suggest that Vietnam's economic growth tended to be pro-poor over the two decades.

Estimates based on VHLSS data

The study makes use of the VHLSSs to analyse the impacts of trade openness and institutional reforms on poverty, because these data are high quality and utilise large sample sizes. These nationwide surveys, conducted by the GSO, are under the technical auspices of the World Bank. The survey methodology is based on the World Bank's Living Standards Measurement Study (LSMS). Each survey round has its own core module topic, based on a basket of core module topics. Since 2002, the surveys have been conducted every two years (Table 4.3). The surveys consist of two types of data: households and communes. The data are organised into many sections, with each containing a certain subject, such as demographic traits, income and expenditure, education, health, employment, agricultural production, or communes.

The estimates, based on two different types of data sets, are likely to make some differentials in the values of the poverty indexes. Vietnam's official estimates

Table 4.2 Indicators of poverty, inequality, and the estimates of GEP, GSEP based on the national accounts data, 1993–2010

Item	1993	1998	1993–1998	2002	2004	2006	2008	2010	2002–2010
Poverty head count rate (per cent)	0.581	0.374	..	0.289	0.195	0.159	0.145	0.142	..
Gini coefficient	0.340	0.350	0.345	0.418	0.420	0.424	0.434	0.433	0.426
GDP per capita (VND bn, 1994 constant prices)	2,375.89	3,266.53	..	3,961.22	4,477.18	5,134.13	5,792.76	6,378.81	..
Total absolute change in poverty head count	..	−0.207	..	−0.085	−0.094	−0.036	−0.014	0.003	..
Total percentage change in poverty head count	..	−35.63	..	−22.73	−32.53	−18.46	−8.81	−2.07	..
Total percentage change in GDP per capita	..	37.49	..	21.27	13.03	14.67	12.83	10.12	..
GEP	..	−0.9504	−0.9504	−1.0687	−2.4971	−1.2582	−0.6864	−0.2045	−0.8334
GSEP	..	−0.5522	−0.5522	−0.3997	−0.7217	−0.2454	−0.1091	−0.0297	−0.2410
Growth effect	..	..	−1.2954	..	..	..	..	..	−1.2592
Pro-poor growth index[1]	..	..	0.7337	..	..	..	..	..	0.6619

Source: Author's estimates using data from the World Bank (2012) and the Asian Development Bank (2011, 2012, 2013).

Note: 1/ Pro-poor growth index is the ratio of GEP to growth effect.

Table 4.3 Vietnam (Household) Living Standards Surveys, 1993–2012

Survey	Household sample size	Commune/Ward coverage
VLSS 1993	4,800	150
VLSS 1998	6,000	150
VHLSS 2002	75,000	3,000
VHLSS 2004	45,945	3,063
VHLSS 2006	45,945	3,063
VHLSS 2008	45,945	3,063
VHLSS 2010	69,360	3,133
VHLSS 2012	47,000	..

Source: Author's synthesis from the World Bank (2000, 2001a), Phung and Nguyen (2004), and the General Statistics Office (2008, 2010, 2012)

of poverty head count rate are based on the income approach. This study follows the consumption or expenditure approach, assuming that consumption or expenditure is a better outcome indicator of welfare than income. Based on this approach, the incidence of poverty, calculated using expenditure data drawn from the VHLSSs, decreased from 1998 to 2006, but increased in 2008. This may reflect the economic slowdown as a result of the 2008 financial crisis. Conversely, the poverty head count indexes, estimated using income data drawn from national accounts, declined throughout the period 1998–2006 (Table 4.4). The depth and severity of poverty have the same trend as the incidence of poverty. The economy was considerably affected by the 2008 financial crisis, especially in terms of its exports (Chhibber *et al.*, 2009; Abbott and Tarp, 2011). In addition, the economic mismanagement and unsustainable development have contributed to Vietnam's economic malaise since 2008.

The estimates from 1998 to 2002 show that the incidence of poverty dropped by 0.82 per cent per year on average for every 1 per cent of growth in per capita expenditure. Over the same period, a 1 per cent increase in per capita expenditure reduced the depth and severity of poverty by about 1 per cent and 1.1 per cent, respectively. However, the growth elasticities of incidence, depth, and severity of poverty were positive in 2008, reflecting the declining benefit of growth, primarily because of high inflation and the external financial crisis, inter alia. Thus, the trend identified by the estimates of growth elasticity of poverty using the household survey data is generally similar to that estimated using national accounts data.

In summary, the estimates using national accounts and survey data show that the GEPs for Vietnam from 1998 to 2008 were below one. The estimates of the elasticity for the 1990s are similar to other studies in the same field, for instance Pernia (2003), and higher than the estimates for the 2000s. The response of poverty reduction to income growth appears to decline over time. These results

Table 4.4 Estimates of GEP based on VHLSS data, 1998–2008

Item	1998	2002	2004	2006	2008
Incidence of poverty (P_0)	0.4122	0.2940	0.1853	0.1524	0.1969
Depth of poverty (P_1)	0.1072	0.0707	0.0440	0.0380	0.0524
Severity of poverty (P_2)	0.0398	0.0245	0.0156	0.0139	0.0201
Per capita expenditure	2572.51	3476.08	4456.26	5845.60	7683.03
Percentage change in					
P_0	..	−0.2868	−0.3696	−0.1774	0.2917
P_1	..	−0.3404	−0.3773	−0.1376	0.3786
P_2	..	−0.3829	−0.3665	−0.1066	0.4464
Per capita expenditure	..	0.3512	0.2820	0.3118	0.3143
Growth elasticity of poverty incidence (GEP_0)	..	−0.8167	−1.3109	−0.5690	0.9280
Growth elasticity of poverty depth (GEP_1)	..	−0.9691	−1.3380	−0.4415	1.2046
Growth elasticity of poverty severity (GEP_2)	..	−1.0900	−1.2998	−0.3418	1.4201
GEP_0, 1998–2002 and 2002–2008	–	−0.8167	–	–	−0.2728
GEP_1, 1998–2002 and 2002–2008	–	−0.9691	–	–	−0.2146
GEP_2, 1998–2002 and 2002–2008	–	−1.0900	–	–	−0.1498

Source: Author's estimates using the VHLSSs 1998, 2002, 2004, 2006, and 2008.

mirror the economy's development over the two decades. The benefits of growth accelerate when the economy begins the transition, and decline as the economy becomes stabilised. The relationship between growth and poverty is also examined at the provincial level, based on provincial panel data from 1998 to 2008.

Provincial trade and the GEP: panel data estimates

Simple two-variable regression model

The GEP is also estimated at the provincial level to gain more insight into the effect of growth on poverty. The elasticity can be estimated by regressing the log of poverty (P) on the log of a welfare variable measured in terms of per capita income or consumption expenditure. The study follows Ravallion and Chen (1997) and estimates the log linear model specified as:

$$logP_{it} = \alpha_i + \beta logy_{it} + \gamma_t + \varepsilon_{it};\ i = 1,...,\ N\ and\ t = 1,\ ...,\ T_j \tag{4.1},$$

where α_i is a fixed effect that accounts for the time differences amongst countries or provinces, β is the elasticity of poverty with respect to mean consumption expenditure represented by y_{it}, γ_t is the trend rate of change over time t, and ε_{it} is the white noise error term. The dependent variable is a measure of poverty (P). The study uses the poverty head count rates of provinces, including the incidence (P_o), or depth (P_1), or severity (P_2) of poverty. Thus, the corresponding growth elasticities of poverty are GEP_o, GEP_1, and GEP_2. These measures of poverty for provinces are provided in the appendix (Table A4.1). The independent variable is the provinces' real per capita expenditure (RPCE), measured in log (RPCE).

The study also measures the impact of the local trade transaction on poverty, or the internal trade elasticity of poverty (TEP). The independent variable used for this purpose is the provincial total real sales per capita (RPCT), measured in log (RPCT). The trade elasticities of poverty corresponding to the measures of poverty are TEP_o, TEP_1, and TEP_2. The model is estimated for a panel of 58 provinces. The data used for the estimation are aggregated from the five waves of the VHLSSs, with each giving 58 provinces. These data thus include 290 panel observations. As the model uses the provincial panel data, it does not take into account the effect of the trend rate of change over time (γ_t).

The results obtained from the simple pooled regression for the estimates of GEP are presented in Table 4.5. These results demonstrate that both growth and local trade are pro-poor. The growth elasticity of poverty incidence is estimated to be –1.5. This means, holding other things constant, every 1 per cent increase in per capita expenditure reduces poverty by 1.5 per cent on average. The absolute value of the estimate of elasticity for rural areas (1.5 per cent) exceeds the absolute value for urban areas (1.2 per cent). Thus, the impact of growth on poverty is greater in the rural areas than in the urban areas. Most Vietnamese households live in rural areas, and poverty is largely found in rural regions. As growth has a greater impact on the poor, sustaining high economic growth is the most appropriate strategy for the alleviation of poverty. In addition to the effect of growth, provincial trade also shows a pro-poor effect; poverty drops by 0.8 per cent for a one-percentage rise in total real sales per capita. This analysis suggests that both income growth and local trade contribute to the reduction in provincial poverty.

As regards the depth of poverty, both growth and local trade have almost the same impacts as on the incidence of poverty. However, the effects of growth and trade on the severity of poverty are lower. For every 1 per cent increase in per capita expenditure and total real sales per capita, the severity of poverty drops by 0.9 per cent and 0.5 per cent, respectively. The impact of growth on the depth and severity of poverty is also greater in rural areas than in urban areas. Growth and local trade are associated with the reduction in the incidence, depth, and severity of poverty at the provincial level. The results also suggest that the rural poor benefit more from growth than their urban counterparts do.

In summary, the analysis of the growth and local trade elasticity of poverty indicates that, aside from growth, local trade development is crucial to the reduction in poverty. In fact, the development of trade in provinces brings about the development of infrastructure, market places, and communication. More

Table 4.5 Pooled OLS estimates of GEP and TEP by province, 1998–2008

Sector/item	Coefficient	p-value	Adjusted R^2
Growth and trade elasticity of the incidence of poverty			
Overall GEP_0	−1.493***	0.000	0.60
Rural GEP_0	−1.542***	0.000	0.59
Urban GEP_0	−1.203***	0.000	0.27
TEP_0	−0.844***	0.000	0.51
Growth and trade elasticity of the depth of poverty			
Overall GEP_1	−1.466***	0.000	0.56
Rural GEP_1	−1.532***	0.000	0.56
Urban GEP_1	−1.039***	0.000	0.21
TEP_1	−0.813***	0.000	0.45
Growth and trade elasticity of the severity of poverty			
Overall GEP_2	−0.910***	0.000	0.39
Rural GEP_2	−0.989***	0.000	0.43
Urban GEP_2	−0.498***	0.000	0.10
TEP_2	−0.490***	0.000	0.30

Source: Author's estimates using the VHLSSs 1998, 2002, 2004, 2006, and 2008

Notes: ***, **, and * significant at 1 per cent, 5 per cent, and 10 per cent level, respectively.

GEP_0, GEP_1, and GEP_2 are estimated by regressing $logP_0$, $logP_1$, and $logP_2$ on $log(RPCE)$, respectively.

TEP_0, TEP_1, and TEP_2 are estimated by regressing $logP_0$, $logP_1$, and $logP_2$ on $log(RPCT)$, respectively.

significantly, trade development shortens the distances from commercial centres to the remote areas where most poor people live, and the transmission of prices from one place to another is more effective. Local trade development is believed to be the result of local institutional reforms that help to reduce the institutional dimension of poverty. Therefore, internal trade development, to some extent, is more important to the poor than international trade, which largely depends on the world market.

Multiple regression model

The impacts of growth and local trade on poverty reduction are further analysed using an extended multiple regression model or a poverty regression model that examines concurrently the effects of both real per capita expenditure and local trade on poverty. The simple regression model for the growth elasticity of poverty is extended to take into account the effects of real per capita expenditure, local trade, agricultural production, and inflation on the incidence of provincial poverty (P). Following Ravallion and Chen (1997) and Ravallion (2006), the extended equation (4.1) is specified as follows:

$$logP_{it} = \alpha_i + \beta_1 logy_{it} + \beta_2 logPT_{it} + \beta_3 logAGO_{it} + \beta_4 logCPI_{it} + \gamma_t + \varepsilon_{it} \quad (4.2),$$

where *PT* is provincial total real sales, *AGO* is total real agricultural output, and *CPI* is consumer price index. Equation (4.2) is first estimated using the simple pooled OLS regression, and then using the fixed and random effects models. Model (4.2) is estimated using a household panel data set constructed from the VHLSS data.

The results show that the growth of per capita expenditure is significantly associated with poverty reduction (Table 4.6). The incidence of poverty is reduced by 1.36 per cent on average for each 1 per cent of growth in real per capita expenditure, holding other things constant and controlling for local trade transactions, agricultural production, and inflation. This implies that growth helps to reduce poverty in the provinces. The growth of expenditure per head also has a similar effect on the depth and severity of poverty. This indicates that growth also helps to mitigate income gaps amongst the poor. In addition to growth, local trade transaction also helps provinces to alleviate poverty; for a 1 per cent rise in total real sales, the incidence of poverty drops by 0.24 per cent. However, local trade does not affect the depth and severity of poverty.

In contrast to expectation, agricultural output has no effect on the incidence of poverty. This may reflect the inadequacy of the agricultural production, primarily due to low productivity and the government's monopoly on rice distribution. However, agricultural production helps provinces to reduce the depth and severity of poverty. A 1 per cent increase in real agricultural output decreases the depth of poverty by 0.16 per cent and the severity of poverty by 0.2 per cent. Thus,

Table 4.6 Pooled OLS estimates of the poverty model
(Dependent variable: log of poverty head count)

Independent variable	Incidence of poverty		Depth of poverty		Severity of poverty	
	Coefficient	p-value	Coefficient	p-value	Coefficient	p-value
log(y)	−1.3588***	0.000	−1.7932***	0.000	−1.1938***	0.000
log(PT)	−0.2432***	0.001	−0.0177	0.780	0.0576	0.318
log(AGO)	−0.0008	0.990	−0.1625***	0.002	−0.1997***	0.000
log(CPI)	4.8625***	0.000	6.7675***	0.000	4.0610***	0.000
Constant	15.9831***	0.000	17.2133***	0.000	11.2418***	0.000
R^2	0.689		0.668		0.487	
Number of observations	290		290		290	

Source: Author's estimates using the VHLSSs 1998, 2002, 2004, 2006, and 2008

Notes: ***, **, and * significant at 1 per cent, 5 per cent, and 10 per cent level, respectively.

agricultural activities continue to be the underpinning for the very poor, in the sense that agriculture helps to lessen inequality between the poor. As expected, inflation is a chronic obsession for poor households. The higher consumer price index is associated with the higher incidence, depth, and severity of poverty. Growth of expenditure per head, local trade, agricultural production, and inflation are seen to be the important factors in explaining the reduction of poverty in provinces.

The pooled OLS model may face the problem of observed and unobserved heterogeneity, where the disturbances may not have the same variance but vary across individuals and/or are related to each other. The use of the fixed or random effects model can help to tackle the potential problem of heterogeneity. These results are consistent with those obtained from the fixed and random effects models (Table 4.7). The random effects model is found to be more efficient than the fixed effects model. The χ^2 value in the Hausman test is 6.67, small enough to accept the null hypothesis that the individual effects are uncorrelated with other regressors in the model (Greene, 2012). Hence, the test suggests that the random effects model is preferable to its fixed effects counterpart. The impacts of the explanatory variables in the random effects model are similar to those in the simple pooled OLS regression model; however, their magnitude is a little lower. The results from the fixed and random effect models further suggest the signifi-cant role of growth and local trade in reducing poverty in the provinces. These

Table 4.7 Fixed and random effects estimates of poverty
(Dependent variable: log of poverty head count)

Independent variable	Fixed effects model		Random effects model	
	Coefficient	p-value	Coefficient	p-value
log(y)	−1.5989***	0.000	−1.2320***	0.000
log(PT)	0.2414**	0.032	−0.2092***	0.003
log(AGO)	0.0950	0.578	0.0036	0.953
log(CPI)	2.3125***	0.000	3.9311***	0.000
Constant	13.4281***	0.000	14.6675***	0.000
F/Wald statistic	83.44***		495.97***	
R^2	0.594		0.561	
Sum of squared errors (SSE)	38.6310			
Standard errors of the estimates ($\hat{\sigma}_v$)	0.4116		0.4116	
Variance component of group ($\hat{\sigma}_u$)	0.5725		0.2129	
Variance of random effect (θ)			0.3460	
F-test (fixed effect)	4.09			
LM-test (random effect)			35.21	
Hausman test	$\chi^2(4) = 6.67$; Prob $> \chi^2 = 0.1376$			
Number of observations	290		290	

Source: Author's estimates using the VHLSSs 1998, 2002, 2004, 2006, and 2008

Notes: ***, **, and * significant at 1 per cent, 5 per cent, and 10 per cent level, respectively.

results also show a less active role than was expected for agricultural production, probably not because of its lack of importance, but because it is underdeveloped.

The above analysis of the growth elasticity of poverty demonstrates that growth helps to reduce poverty in Vietnam. The pro-poor growth index suggests that growth is pro-poor; more interestingly, that rural poor households benefit more from growth than their urban counterparts complies with the definition of pro-poor growth, and with the finding by Deaton (2003). The estimates of the elasticity measure obtained from the regression models, based on provincial aggregate data, also show similar results. In addition to growth, provincial trade also helps provinces alleviate poverty. The variable of total real sales explains the impact of local trade on poverty. The analysis of the pooled regression and random effects estimates also confirms the trend identified in the analysis of the definition-based growth elasticity of poverty. The growth and the internal trade help provinces to reduce poverty, whereas inflation does the opposite. Unexpectedly, agricultural production shows no impact on the incidence of poverty.

4.4   Conclusions

The Vietnamese economy achieved remarkable outcomes in economic growth and poverty reduction following the liberalisation of the economy and trade since the late 1980s. This chapter has measured the responsiveness of poverty to economic growth by estimating the growth elasticity of poverty over two decades of economic development. The estimates are based on both national accounts data and the VHLSS data. The findings are consistent with other, similar studies: for instance, Ram (2006, 2011) and Kalwij and Verschoor (2007). More interestingly, growth has a greater impact on rural poverty than on urban poverty, suggesting that sustaining high economic growth is an essential prerequisite for the alleviation of rural poverty. The analysis also shows that growth, and thereby the effect of growth on poverty, tends to dissipate over time. The chapter has estimated the panel data models to analyse the relationship between income growth, internal trade, and poverty. The results suggest that growth of welfare and internal trade are typically pro-poor in Vietnam. These results raise some concerns about the insignificant role of agriculture in the reduction of poverty, and about the obsession of inflation, which can largely offset the benefits of growth to the poor.

The results suggest the need to maintain high economic growth to achieve a further reduction in poverty. Several studies have underlined the tough challenges ahead, and have raised concerns regarding the poor quality of economic growth and unsustainable poverty reduction (IMF, 2006b; World Bank, 2012). Faced with many economic problems resulting from economic mismanagement and unsustainable economic development, Vietnam may possibly be unable to replicate the miracle of economic development of the 1990s. Although Vietnam comes second in the world in terms of rice export, farm households benefit little from agricultural production, possibly due to the inadequate trade policies in agriculture. Sustained agricultural development is the key to helping farm households to benefit from growth and to escape poverty. Therefore, maintaining high economic growth and accelerating trade reforms in agriculture to sustain agricultural production and contain inflation are crucial to an effective poverty reduction strategy.

Annexe

Table A4.1 Incidence, depth, and severity of poverty head count ratio across provinces and regions, 1998–2008

Province	1998			2002			2004			2006			2008		
	Po	P1	P2	Po	P1	P2	Po	P1	P2	Po	P1	P2	Po	P1	P2
Hanoi	0.04	0.01	0.00	0.12	0.01	0.00	0.07	0.00	0.00	0.08	0.01	0.00	0.01	0.00	0.00
Hai Phong	0.17	0.03	0.01	0.23	0.03	0.01	0.10	0.01	0.00	0.03	0.00	0.00	0.05	0.00	0.00
Vinh Phuc	0.78	0.25	0.10	0.38	0.07	0.02	0.17	0.03	0.01	0.13	0.01	0.00	0.14	0.03	0.01
Ha Tay	0.45	0.11	0.04	0.29	0.07	0.02	0.12	0.02	0.00	0.10	0.02	0.00	0.15	0.03	0.01
Bac Ninh	0.64	0.17	0.06	0.14	0.02	0.00	0.03	0.00	0.00	0.04	0.00	0.00	0.04	0.01	0.00
Hai Duong	0.29	0.06	0.02	0.26	0.04	0.01	0.10	0.01	0.00	0.06	0.01	0.00	0.09	0.01	0.00
Hung Yen	0.38	0.07	0.02	0.19	0.04	0.01	0.13	0.03	0.01	0.04	0.01	0.00	0.14	0.02	0.01
Ha Nam	0.44	0.08	0.02	0.33	0.07	0.02	0.24	0.03	0.01	0.15	0.03	0.01	0.20	0.04	0.01
Nam Dinh	0.20	0.03	0.01	0.30	0.05	0.01	0.17	0.03	0.01	0.09	0.01	0.00	0.09	0.02	0.01
Thai Binh	0.44	0.09	0.02	0.38	0.07	0.02	0.14	0.02	0.00	0.06	0.01	0.00	0.14	0.03	0.01
Ninh Binh	0.17	0.03	0.01	0.35	0.06	0.02	0.18	0.03	0.01	0.09	0.01	0.00	0.05	0.01	0.00
Ha Giang	0.72	0.19	0.07	0.77	0.20	0.07	0.58	0.14	0.05	0.52	0.09	0.03	0.64	0.17	0.07
Cao Bang	0.69	0.14	0.04	0.60	0.12	0.04	0.33	0.08	0.03	0.37	0.08	0.03	0.51	0.16	0.07
Lao Cai	0.40	0.12	0.04	0.57	0.13	0.05	0.55	0.13	0.05	0.42	0.07	0.02	0.52	0.14	0.06
Bac Kan	..	..	..	0.74	0.22	0.09	0.50	0.12	0.05	0.43	0.08	0.02	0.38	0.10	0.03
Lang Son	0.84	0.23	0.08	0.44	0.09	0.03	0.38	0.05	0.01	0.23	0.04	0.01	0.29	0.04	0.01

Tuyen Quang	0.47	0.06	0.02	0.43	0.08	0.03	0.25	0.05	0.02	0.25	0.05	0.02	0.27	0.05	0.02
Yen Bai	0.52	0.19	0.09	0.48	0.09	0.03	0.36	0.05	0.02	0.27	0.04	0.01	0.26	0.05	0.02
Thai Nguyen	0.20	0.03	0.01	0.27	0.05	0.02	0.21	0.03	0.01	0.09	0.01	0.00	0.13	0.02	0.00
Phu Tho	0.81	0.25	0.10	0.43	0.09	0.03	0.19	0.04	0.01	0.15	0.02	0.01	0.19	0.04	0.01
Bac Giang	0.78	0.27	0.12	0.40	0.07	0.02	0.18	0.03	0.01	0.12	0.01	0.00	0.19	0.04	0.01
Quang Ninh	0.17	0.03	0.01	0.12	0.01	0.00	0.07	0.00	0.00	0.11	0.02	0.01	0.08	0.02	0.01
Lai Chau	..	..	..	0.80	0.25	0.12	0.72	0.30	0.15	0.74	0.25	0.12	0.70	0.24	0.11
Dien Bien	-	-	-	-	-	-	0.67	0.20	0.09	0.74	0.21	0.08	0.63	0.17	0.07
Son La	0.53	0.14	0.05	0.67	0.18	0.07	0.52	0.12	0.04	0.33	0.06	0.02	0.43	0.08	0.03
Hoa Binh	0.59	0.12	0.03	0.66	0.20	0.09	0.56	0.13	0.05	0.41	0.09	0.03	0.39	0.08	0.03
Thanh Hoa	0.38	0.08	0.02	0.50	0.10	0.03	0.36	0.07	0.03	0.25	0.05	0.01	0.26	0.05	0.02
Nghe An	0.46	0.13	0.05	0.45	0.09	0.03	0.28	0.07	0.03	0.29	0.07	0.03	0.27	0.07	0.03
Ha Tinh	0.53	0.12	0.04	0.43	0.10	0.04	0.35	0.06	0.02	0.26	0.05	0.02	0.29	0.06	0.02
Quang Binh	0.47	0.09	0.03	0.38	0.08	0.02	0.30	0.06	0.02	0.21	0.05	0.02	0.19	0.04	0.01
Quang Tri	0.69	0.17	0.06	0.46	0.11	0.04	0.33	0.06	0.02	0.22	0.04	0.01	0.21	0.04	0.01
Thua Thien Hue	0.31	0.06	0.02	0.33	0.06	0.02	0.18	0.02	0.01	0.14	0.02	0.01	0.13	0.02	0.01
Da Nang	0.39	0.09	0.03	0.11	0.00	0.00	0.13	0.00	0.00	0.00	0.00	0.00	0.00	0.00	0.00
Quang Nam	0.13	0.03	0.01	0.42	0.10	0.04	0.30	0.08	0.03	0.16	0.03	0.01	0.22	0.04	0.01
Quang Ngai	0.40	0.15	0.08	0.37	0.11	0.05	0.27	0.06	0.03	0.11	0.03	0.01	0.24	0.06	0.02
Binh Dinh	0.31	0.06	0.02	0.30	0.05	0.01	0.15	0.02	0.01	0.11	0.02	0.00	0.07	0.01	0.00
Phu Yen	0.28	0.07	0.03	0.25	0.05	0.02	0.15	0.03	0.01	0.10	0.01	0.00	0.26	0.04	0.01

(Continued)

Table A4.1 (Continued)

	1998			2002			2004			2006			2008		
	P0	P1	P2	P0	P1	P2	P0	P1	P2	P0	P1	P2	P0	P1	P2
Khanh Hoa	0.32	0.10	0.05	0.14	0.02	0.00	0.14	0.02	0.01	0.11	0.02	0.00	0.17	0.02	0.01
Kon Tum	0.97	0.45	0.23	0.58	0.10	0.03	0.46	0.08	0.03	0.48	0.05	0.01	0.44	0.09	0.04
Gia Lai	0.67	0.33	0.20	0.73	0.22	0.11	0.51	0.13	0.05	0.50	0.13	0.06	0.54	0.16	0.08
Dak Lak	0.39	0.08	0.03	0.53	0.13	0.05	0.32	0.09	0.04	0.17	0.05	0.02	0.22	0.05	0.02
Dak Nong	-	-	-	-	-	-	0.23	0.06	0.03	0.20	0.03	0.01	0.07	0.02	0.01
Lam Dong	0.38	0.07	0.02	0.50	0.10	0.04	0.26	0.05	0.02	0.10	0.02	0.01	0.21	0.03	0.01
HCMC	0.02	0.00	0.00	0.03	0.00	0.00	0.00	0.00	0.00	0.00	0.00	0.00	0.00	0.00	0.00
Ninh Thuan	0.53	0.23	0.11	0.52	0.14	0.06	0.42	0.11	0.05	0.38	0.10	0.05	0.30	0.07	0.03
Binh Phuoc	0.05	0.00	0.00	0.29	0.06	0.02	0.09	0.02	0.01	0.07	0.02	0.01	0.04	0.01	0.00
Tay Ninh	0.18	0.04	0.01	0.21	0.04	0.01	0.11	0.01	0.00	0.08	0.01	0.00	0.10	0.02	0.01
Binh Duong	0.09	0.01	0.00	0.18	0.03	0.01	0.03	0.00	0.00	0.03	0.00	0.00	0.01	0.00	0.00
Dong Nai	0.13	0.02	0.01	0.12	0.01	0.00	0.04	0.01	0.00	0.02	0.00	0.00	0.04	0.01	0.00
Binh Thuan	0.23	0.05	0.02	0.23	0.04	0.01	0.11	0.01	0.00	0.14	0.01	0.00	0.05	0.01	0.01
Ba Ria-Vung Tau	0.21	0.05	0.02	0.14	0.01	0.00	0.06	0.01	0.00	0.03	0.01	0.00	0.02	0.00	0.00
Long An	0.31	0.07	0.02	0.18	0.03	0.01	0.10	0.01	0.00	0.10	0.01	0.00	0.13	0.02	0.00
Dong Thap	0.33	0.07	0.02	0.31	0.05	0.02	0.08	0.01	0.00	0.04	0.01	0.00	0.10	0.02	0.00
An Giang	0.33	0.07	0.02	0.18	0.03	0.01	0.13	0.02	0.00	0.03	0.01	0.00	0.15	0.02	0.01
Tien Giang	0.26	0.05	0.01	0.13	0.02	0.00	0.08	0.01	0.00	0.06	0.01	0.00	0.08	0.02	0.00
Vinh Long	0.21	0.05	0.02	0.22	0.03	0.01	0.11	0.01	0.00	0.04	0.00	0.00	0.11	0.01	0.00

Ben Tre	0.30	0.05	0.01	0.14	0.02	0.01	0.13	0.02	0.01	0.05	0.01	0.00	0.13	0.03	0.01
Kien Giang	0.39	0.07	0.02	0.24	0.05	0.01	0.22	0.03	0.01	0.06	0.01	0.00	0.09	0.02	0.00
Can Tho	0.29	0.06	0.02	0.28	0.05	0.01	0.15	0.02	0.01	0.06	0.01	0.00	0.04	0.01	0.00
Hau Giang	–	–	–	–	0.05	–	0.12	0.02	0.01	0.09	0.01	0.00	0.22	0.02	0.01
Tra Vinh	0.58	0.14	0.05	0.31	0.05	0.01	0.19	0.04	0.02	0.17	0.02	0.00	0.15	0.03	0.01
Soc Trang	0.55	0.17	0.07	0.32	0.06	0.02	0.22	0.04	0.01	0.14	0.01	0.00	0.18	0.03	0.01
Bac Lieu	0.21	0.04	0.01	0.28	0.04	0.02	0.23	0.04	0.02	0.17	0.03	0.01	0.21	0.04	0.01
Ca Mau	0.25	0.06	0.01	0.31	0.07	0.02	0.19	0.03	0.01	0.18	0.03	0.01	0.24	0.05	0.02
Region															
Red River Delta	0.26	0.05	0.02	0.23	0.05	0.01	0.11	0.02	0.01	0.07	0.01	0.00	0.09	0.02	0.01
Northeast	0.50	0.13	0.05	0.37	0.09	0.03	0.25	0.06	0.02	0.20	0.04	0.01	0.24	0.06	0.02
Northwest	0.67	0.19	0.07	0.60	0.21	0.09	0.54	0.18	0.08	0.47	0.15	0.06	0.45	0.14	0.06
North central	0.43	0.10	0.03	0.38	0.09	0.03	0.26	0.06	0.02	0.21	0.05	0.02	0.21	0.05	0.02
South central coast	0.33	0.09	0.04	0.24	0.06	0.02	0.16	0.04	0.01	0.08	0.02	0.01	0.14	0.03	0.01
Central highlands	0.55	0.21	0.10	0.45	0.14	0.06	0.28	0.08	0.03	0.22	0.06	0.02	0.22	0.07	0.03
Southeast	0.13	0.03	0.01	0.14	0.03	0.01	0.06	0.01	0.01	0.05	0.01	0.01	0.05	0.01	0.00
Mekong River Delta	0.32	0.07	0.02	0.21	0.04	0.01	0.13	0.02	0.01	0.08	0.01	0.00	0.12	0.02	0.01

Source: Authors' estimate from the VHLSSs

Note: Figures in the table are ratios.

References

Abbott, P., and Tarp, F. (2011). *Globalization Crises, Trade, and Development in Vietnam.* UNU-WIDER, Working Paper (No. 2011/20), 30.

Asian Development Bank (ADB) (2011). *Key Indicators for Asia and the Pacific 2011* (42nd ed.). Mandaluyong City, PH.

Asian Development Bank (ADB) (2012). *Key Indicators for Asia and the Pacific 2012* (43rd ed.). Mandaluyong City, PH.

Asian Development Bank (ADB) (2013). *Key Indicators for Asia and the Pacific 2013* (44th ed.). Mandaluyong City, PH.

Chhibber, A., Ghosh, J., and Palanivel, T. (2009). *The Global Financial Crisis and the Asia-Pacific Region: A Synthesis Study Incorporating Evidence from Country Case Studies.* Sri Lanka: UNDP.

Deaton, A. (2003, January). Prices and Poverty in India, 1987–2000. *Economic and Political Weekly*, 7.

Deaton, A. (2005). Measuring Poverty in a Growing World (or Measuring Growth in a Poor World). *The Review of Economics and Statistics, LXXXVII*(1), 19.

Dollar, D., and Kraay, A. (2002). Growth is Good for the Poor. *Journal of Economic Growth, 7*(3), 195.

Dollar, D., and Kraay, A. (2004). Trade, Growth, and Poverty. *The Economic Journal, 114*(493), F22–F49. DOI: 10.1111/j.0013–0133.2004.00186.x

General Statistics Office (2008). *Result of the Vietnam Household Living Standards Survey 2006.* Ho Chi Minh: Statistical Publishing House.

General Statistics Office (2010). *Result of the Survey on Household Living Standards 2008.* Ho Chi Minh: Statistical Publishing House.

General Statistics Office (2012). *Result of the Vietnam Household Living Standards Survey 2010.* Ho Chi Minh: Statistical Publishing House.

Greene, W. H. (2012). *Econometric Analysis* (7th ed.). Boston: Prentice Hall.

International Monetary Fund (IMF) (2006b). *Vietnam: Poverty Reduction Strategy Paper – Annual Progress Report.* IMF, Country Report (No. 06/340), 160.

Kakwani, N., and Pernia, E. (2000). What is Pro-poor Growth?. *Asian Development Review, 18*(1), 16.

Kalwij, A. S., and Verschoor, A. (2007). Not by Growth Alone: The Role of the Distribution of Income in Regional Diversity in Poverty Reduction. *European Economic Review, 51*(4), 805–829. DOI: http://dx.doi.org/10.1016/j.euroecorev.2006.06. 003

Klasen, S., and Misselhorn, M. (2006). *Determinants of the Growth Semi-Elasticity of Poverty Reduction.* Paper presented at the German Development Economics Conference, Berlin.

Pernia, E. M. (2003). *Pro-poor Growth: What is It and How is It Important?.* ERD, Policy Brief (No. 17), 11.

Phung, D. T., and Nguyen, P. (2004). *Vietnam Household Living Standards Survey (VHLSS), 2002 and 2004: Basic Information* (p. 50). Vietnam: General Statistics Office of Vietnam.

Ram, R. (2006). Growth Elasticity of Poverty: Alternative Estimates and a Note of Caution. *KYKLOS, 59*(4), 10.

Ram, R. (2011). Growth Elasticity of Poverty: Direct Estimates from Recent Data. *Applied Economics, 43*(19), 2433–2440.

Ravallion, M. (2003). Measuring Aggregate Welfare in Developing Countries: How Well Do National Accounts and Surveys Agree?. *Review of Economics and Statistics*, *85*(3), 645–652. DOI: 10.1162/003465303322369786

Ravallion, M. (2004). *Pro-poor Growth: A Primer*. World Bank, Policy Research Working Paper (No. 3242).

Ravallion, M. (2006). Looking Beyond Averages in the Trade and Poverty Debate. *World Development*, *34*(8), 1374–1392. DOI: http://dx.doi.org/10.1016/j.worlddev.2005.10.015

Ravallion, M., and Chen, S. (1997). What Can New Survey Data Tell Us about Recent Changes in Distribution and Poverty?. *The World Bank Economic Review*, *11*(2), 357–382. DOI: 10.1093/wber/11.2.357

United Nations Development Programme (UNDP) (2003). *Human Development Report 2003: Millennium Development Goals: A Compact among Nations to End Human Poverty*. New York: Oxford University Press.

World Bank (2000). *Viet Nam Living Standards Survey (VNLSS), 1992–93: Basic Information* (p. 41). World Bank, Poverty and Human Resources Division.

World Bank (2001a). *Vietnam Living Standards Survey (VLSS), 1997–98: Basic Information* (p. 70). World Bank, Poverty and Human Resources Division.

World Bank (2001b). *World Development Report 2000/01: Attacking Poverty* (p. 356). Washington, DC.

World Bank (2005). *Pro-poor Growth in the 1990s: Lessons and Insights from 14 Countries* (p. 116). Washington, DC.

World Bank (2012). *Well Begun, Not Yet Done: Vietnam's Remarkable Progress on Poverty Reduction and the Emerging Challenges* (p. 190). Hanoi.

5 Farm households' perceptions of agricultural market and policy

5.1 Introduction

The majority of people in developing countries engage in agricultural production and market. This characteristic is the key to the strategy for tackling poverty. It can be linked to trade liberalisation through the Winters framework that postulates four main pathways that link trade policy with household welfare and poverty. Several studies have examined the effects of market on households and poverty as conceptualised in the Winters framework. The market effects relate to the price mechanism and market distribution system. Most developing countries are agrarian economies, and agricultural prices and market distribution matter greatly to the poor. By altering the prices of tradable goods and the market distribution system, trade liberalisation has a considerable impact on poverty (Deaton, 2008). One of the most important conditions for the outward-oriented strategy to be successful is to maintain macroeconomic stability, which is indirectly beneficial for the poor (Bhagwati and Srinivasan, 2002). Trade policy can cause price distortion, resulting from trade monopoly, distributional channels, transaction costs, and other institutional costs. The poor are unlikely to benefit from trade liberalisation, due primarily to the ineffectiveness of the price transmission to households. Several studies provide evidence on the impacts of prices and market distribution on welfare and income distribution (Deaton, 1989; Minot and Goletti, 1998; Porto, 2004; Winters *et al.*, 2004; Seshan, 2005; Isik-Dikmelik, 2006; Justino *et al.*, 2008; Nicita, 2009; Marchand, 2012).

Deaton (1989) studies the case of Thailand and concludes that higher prices for rice were likely to benefit rural households at all levels of living. Ravallion (1990) investigates the dynamics of wage formation in Bangladesh and suggests that the rural rich were likely to gain and the rural poor lose from a rise in the relative price of food staples. Minot and Goletti (1998) use the multimarket spatial-equilibrium model to simulate the effects of export liberalisation on paddy and rice prices, and find that the liberalisation in rice exports raised food prices, thereby increasing the average real income and reducing the incidence of poverty in Vietnam in the 1990s. Using the decomposition technique and the framework by Deaton (1997) for net benefit ratio (NBR), Isik-Dikmelik (2006) finds that the growth in Vietnam was pro-poor on the whole, and that the poorer and net buyer households benefited more from growth than the other groups did. Seshan (2005) uses a multi-output production function to examine the trade–poverty linkage in Vietnam, revealing that trade liberalisation explained about half the reduction in the incidence of poverty.

McCulloch *et al.* (2001) point out two factors that can block price transmission. First, weak infrastructure can attenuate or block price transmission due to high transport costs. Consequently, remote, poor households are insulated from the price effect of trade policy (Winters *et al.*, 2004). Second, changes in domestic marketing arrangements can isolate farm households from the markets, where the elimination of market institutions makes them suffer substantial income losses. Winters *et al.* (2004) also observe that trade policy is totally ineffective for farm households in the case of a market dominated by some sole state purchasers of export crops, whose business strategy is deliberately to isolate farmers from world price changes. The issue of price transmission is most important in agriculture where many export crops, especially those of small farmers, are sold via state or private agents at prices far less than the free-on-board export prices. Such issues of price transmission and market distribution, resulting from a trade policy, can explain why the majority of farm households in some developing countries are on the whole still poor, even though the countries may be open and leading rice exporters. The literature generally shows the likely market effects of trade liberalisation on poverty. Although similar studies on Vietnam are based on more advanced estimation methods and large data sets, they have yet to explain the reason why most Vietnamese farm households remain poor. Several similar studies for Vietnam that focus on the price effects on poverty appear to ignore the market distribution aspect of trade liberalisation and farmers' perception of trade policy.

The primary objective of this chapter, motivated by Winters's framework and the case-specific approach, is to examine the farmer's perception of trade policy based on a case study. Such an analysis is intended to empirically verify the 'market channel' of Winters, using firsthand data collected through the primary field survey conducted. It is, as such, intended to glean deeper insights into the impacts of trade policy on farm households in Vietnam. The analysis differs from the previous studies on three counts. First, it is based on the primary field survey of farm households conducted in three provinces in Vietnam. These provinces, located in different regions, account for a major proportion of the agricultural exports of Vietnam. As the farm households in these provinces are intensively involved in agricultural production and trade, the information collected through the primary survey is expected to reveal many real facets of trade policy in agriculture. Second, other similar surveys on households, such as the Vietnam Household Living Standard Surveys (VHLSS), conducted by the Vietnamese General Statistics Office (GSO), or the Vietnam Access to Resources Household Survey (VARHS), undertaken by the Institute of Policy and Strategy for Agriculture and Rural Development (IPSARD), focus on agricultural production and/or poverty in general, and thus appear to lose a specialised focus on how farmers perceive the trade policy in agriculture. The chapter focuses on the market distribution system in agriculture, which is presumably the key to understanding the persistence of poverty amongst farm households in Vietnam. Third, while other studies focus on analysing data on farm production and trade, this study analyses the primary survey data on farmer perceptions about trade policy, agricultural production, and welfare. This analysis attempts to elucidate the hypotheses that farm households suffer from inadequate trade policies in agriculture and that better awareness of trade policy contributes to economic welfare. An analysis based on the field interviews with farmers who directly engage in agricultural production and trade is the most effective way to provide adequate answers for the question of why farm households remain poor in one of the major rice export economies of the world. Other groups, such as local authorities, traders, and exporters, tend to conceal their business from the public, because of their own vested interests.

The rest of this chapter is designed as follows. Section 5.2 overviews the production and distribution systems of rice and coffee in Vietnam. Section 5.3 discusses the research methods and collection of primary data. Section 5.4 analyses the results of the primary field survey. Section 5.5 concludes the chapter and provides policy implications.

5.2   Rice and coffee markets in Vietnam: an overview

The inadequacy of agricultural trade policy impinging on farm households lies primarily in Vietnam's internal trade system. Since the transition from a centrally planned to an open market economy began in 1986, Vietnam has been striving to reform its centrally planned trading system. The repercussion of the centrally planned economy still affects the current performance of the market-based economy; for instance, typically inefficient SOEs legally play a leading role in the economy and receive a great deal of economic rent. Food SOEs are the main legitimate rice exporters. While state intervention, in terms of its regulation of food security, is useful, some of the interventions undertaken, in terms of fixing export quotas and issuing trade licenses, as well as setting cumbersome customs procedures, tend to impede the efficiency of the agricultural markets and reduce the incomes from rice and coffee production for farmers.

Compared to coffee production, rice production is more important, in that it helps to ensure food security and income. Liberalisation in agricultural trade has, over the last two decades, led to successful agricultural production, which has significantly contributed to the reduction in poverty. Tran *et al.* (2013) identify three principal hindrances to the development of rice production in Vietnam: small and fragmented land, low profit rice production for farmers, and the reduction in rice land. These features clearly signify unsustainable rice production, which prevents the country from competing with other rice producers in the world, such as Thailand, India, and, more recently, Myanmar. The World Bank (2010) shows that, from 2006 to 2011, world rice prices have fluctuated highly, but the rice prices of Thailand have tended to be considerably higher than the rice prices of Vietnam. Vietnam's rice competitiveness tends to worsen, as the other agrarian countries focus increasingly on agricultural development. The government has allocated extensive resources to inefficient, industrial state, chaebol-like companies, neglecting the country's primary comparative advantage. Both rice and coffee are the strategic exports, but each has its own market characteristics. *The Economist* elaborates:

> . . . Vietnam's rice farmers are being left behind. Part of the problem is that Vietnamese rice strains tend to be of low or middling quality – a contrast to the premium varieties grown in Thailand. The costs of fuel, fertilisers and pesticides are rising. And Vietnam's rice-exporter sector is dominated by state-owned firms with links to corrupt officials. Some farmers, especially in the country's north, are finding it more profitable to let their land lie fallow.
>
> (2014)[1]

The Mekong River Delta, the biggest rice production area in Vietnam, produces the majority of export crops. This region accounted for half of the national rice production in the marketing year 2011/2012 (USDA, 2012b). The rice market in this region is more typical than other rice markets in Vietnam, such as the Red River Delta or the central region. Generally, the main participants in the rice market are farmers, private merchants/traders, and rice exporters, who are primarily state-owned food enterprises and who may gain the most in the agricultural value chain. Luu (2002) observes that private merchants were very diverse, including paddy private assemblers, private wholesalers, private rice millers or polishers, and private retailers. According to Young *et al.* (2002) and Tran *et al.* (2013), 95 to 96.5 per cent of Vietnamese rice farmers, on average, sold their paddy crops to traders, not to final exporters. Export prices were typically twice as much as farm-gate prices. More particularly, poor households preferred selling crops to other private households. The same did not hold true for richer households, who tended to sell crops to private traders and/or enterprises (CIEM–IPSARD, 2007, 2013).

Tran *et al.* (2013) also report that over 200 rice exporters in Vietnam are SOEs. Big exporters, mostly SOEs, account for more than 70 per cent of the total rice exports. Most importantly, farmers gain almost nothing from their production; for instance, in 2008, when the export price increased by US$470 per tonne, the farm-gate price rose by only US$100 per tonne. Farmers bear the increasing input costs, especially fertiliser, which typically accounts for 45 per cent of the total input cost. The existence of numerous rice intermediaries or rice middlemen, although declining (CIEM–IPSARD, 2011), is typical of the rice market in Vietnam. These middlemen discernibly squeeze a share of farmers' profit and impoverish farm households.

Vietnam is also amongst the leading coffee producers in the world, with coffee exports reaching 1.26 million metric tonnes of coffee beans in the marketing year 2011/2012 (USDA, 2012a). Robusta, the main coffee crop in Vietnam, accounts for about 90 per cent of the total coffee production. Coffee cultivation is suitable to only some highland areas and temperatures, such as Buon Ma Thuot, Dak Lak, Bao Loc, and Lam Dong provinces; so these regions specialise in growing coffee. Coffee is in demand in both the domestic market and the export markets. Main participants in the coffee market are farmers, middlemen or agents, processing or export companies, and domestic retailers. According to Roldan-Perez *et al.* (2009), agents and middlemen were buying approximately 90 per cent of the coffee output. Unlike the rice market, the coffee market is more liberalised, with the participation of a wide range of companies, from private to state-owned enterprises. The presence of many trading intermediaries, a common characteristic of the two markets, adds to the inadequacy of trade policy, and potentially attenuates farm income and impoverishes farm households. The issues of trade policy in the rice and coffee sector are further elaborated upon in the following sections, which analyse farmers' perceptions, as well as their experience of trade policy in agriculture, using the information collected through the field survey on farm households in the An Giang, Dong Nai, and Dak Lak provinces of Vietnam. These are the most appropriate regions, as the farm households in these regions are substantially involved in trading farm crops.

5.3 Research methods and data

Socioeconomic and geographical characteristics of the surveyed provinces

The surveyed fields, which should be dominated by, or at least involved in, agricultural trade activities, and which should contain some contrastive characteristics, are selected in a way that allows comparisons between regions in terms of trade performance, welfare, and perception of trade policy. For the field survey, the study is focused on three provinces in Vietnam, each covering around 100 households: An Giang, Binh Duong, and Dak Lak. Some economic and social characteristics of the provinces are presented in Table 5.1. These provinces contain some differences in terms of economic development and trade policy.

An Giang is at the heart of the Mekong River Delta, in the southwest of Vietnam. Located about 190 kilometres from HCMC, it has an area of 3,536.8

Table 5.1 Key economic indicators of An Giang, Dak Lak, and Dong Nai, 2010

Indicator	An Giang	Dak Lak	Dong Nai
Area (square kilometre)	3,536.76	3,536.8	5,907.236
Population (1,000 people)	2,149.5	1,910	2,569.442
GDP growth (per cent)	10.12	12.2	13.5
GDP per capita (US$)	1,141	794.973	1,542.6
Export (million US$)	700	620.229	7,546
Poverty rate (per cent)	9.16	10.34	2.93
PCI/PCI ranking	61.94/14th	57.2/38th	59.49/25th
Main export commodities	Rice	Coffee	Manufactures

Source: Statistics offices of An Giang, Dak Lak, and Dong Nai

square kilometres, and had a population of about 2,273,150 in 2010. Agricultural land accounted for the largest area (approximately 281,862 hectares), of which 82 per cent was dominated by rice farms. Most areas in this province are relatively flat, crisscrossed by the networks of canals, irrigation channels, and small rivers. In 2010, its GDP per capita was estimated to be US$1,141, a little lower than the national GDP per capita.[2] Its export value was approximately US$700 million; its two biggest export earners were rice and seafood. Its poverty rate fell from 13.15 per cent in 2006 to 9.16 per cent in 2010. An Giang's provincial competitiveness index (PCI)[3] in the same year was 61.94, ranked 14th in the total of 64 provinces of Vietnam. An Giang best represents a large rice-export region, but with disadvantageous infrastructure.

In common with An Giang, Dak Lak is basically an agricultural province. It is the largest province in the central highlands of Vietnam, with its average population of 1,910,000 residing in an area of 13,125 square kilometres in 2010. Located about 350 kilometres from HCMC, its economy relies largely on agriculture and forestry, with coffee cultivation being the primary activity. About 82.64 per cent of its area is cultivated; agricultural land accounts for 26 per cent of the cultivatable area. In contrast to An Giang, Dak Lak is a highland region with hills and mountains. In recent years, its provincial GDP annual growth has averaged 11.9 per cent, and its GDP per capita reached US$794.973 in 2010.[4] This GDP per head has been rather low, compared to the national GDP per capita. Its exports were US$620.229 million in 2010, with coffee being the main export commodity. With nearly 111,000 households having climbed above the national poverty line each year, the poverty rate had fallen to just 10.34 per cent in 2010. Dak Lak's PCI in 2010 was 57.20, ranked 38th in the PCI classification. Its coffee export and its highland characteristics make Dak Lak distinctly different from An Giang and Dong Nai.

Dong Nai, a typically industrial province with virtually perfect infrastructure, is also quite different from the other two provinces surveyed in the study. Located in the southeast of Vietnam, adjacent to HCMC, its natural area of 5,907.236 square kilometres had a population of about 2,569,442 in 2010. Its GDP grew to 13.5 per cent in 2010, with GDP per capita being US$1,542.60. Its economic structure was dominated by industry: the industrial share in GDP was 57.2 per cent, compared with the shares of 34.2 per cent of service and 8.6 per cent of agriculture. Its export turnover was US$7,546 million in the same year. This wealthy province had a poverty rate of only 2.93 per cent at the end of 2010. In addition, its PCI was 59.49, ranked 25th in the 2010 PCI classification. Industry and trade contributed considerably to Dong Nai's economic development.

The survey is conducted in the fields where the agricultural trade policy is most likely to affect farm households' production. The characteristics of local economy, geography, and society in the provinces usually do not mirror the real plights of farm households. As rice and coffee are the main export products, farm households involved in rice and coffee production potentially suffer most from trade policy. Differences in infrastructure, export commodity, and trade performance should provide important insights into the characteristics of trade policy and poverty across the provinces.

Sample selection and questionnaire design

The scope of the field survey is confined to evaluating the effects of trade policy from the farmers' points of view; it does not attempt to examine the effects of trade policy on the economy as a whole. Farm households that own and cultivate land are the study's units of analysis, as they engage in trade-related activities and largely constitute the poor in Vietnam. The underlying assumptions of the study are that poor households are more likely to be farm households and that the impacts of trade policy on a household are the same for every individual within the household. In terms of the sampling frame, the survey was intended to be directed at farm households who are cultivating their lands, and at rural or sub-urban areas where farm households are mostly involved in trading their crops, as the analyses of these areas are the primary objectives of the study. Although the selection of the survey fields was not random, as the research focuses on farmers' perception of trade policy, the participants within a survey field were randomly selected. A sample of about 300 households was randomly drawn from the local administrative list of households.

The design of the protocol for the survey was grounded on the purpose of the study, the literature on survey methodology, the VHLSSs, peer advice, and Vietnamese farmers' common level of education. In addition to the mainstream of the protocol, the survey also proposed paying attention to other opinions, if any, in order to support the study's later analysis. The difficulty in designing the questionnaire was how to express questions in a manner that farmers with little or no education could understand. The questionnaire comprises 39 closed and open-ended questions. The main contents cover general information, economic characteristics, agricultural production, occupation, and trade and trade policy.

The questionnaire also includes a cover letter with three functions: (1) the participants in the survey were explicitly advised that participation is totally voluntary, that private household information is kept secret, and that the data are solely used for the research project; (2) each participant's consent was requested; and (3) full information was provided about the project and contact persons. This kind of protocol can allow for soliciting information beyond the mainstream questions in the form of field notes; it really consumes more time, however, for interviews and for the data processing to categorise opinions. To measure farm households' assessment of some issues, a 10-point rating scale ranging from 1 (the lowest) to 10 (the highest), familiar to the Vietnamese farmers from their school years, was used to quantify opinions.[5]

Survey fieldwork

Participants were anonymously chosen from the local administrative list of households. The field survey was then conducted by directly interviewing the farm households. The face-to-face method was really time consuming and costly; furthermore, some interviews failed because the chosen farm households had little or no information or gave biased information, which could cause some data quality problems. Much more time was needed to evaluate and double-check the questionnaire information. The survey collected 329 questionnaires with relatively complete information.

The survey procedure as explained and conducted helps the study with reliability and validity, but can be only partially generalised due to the nonrandom selection of the provinces. The survey potentially faces two shortcomings. First, it cannot capture the whole impact of the trade policy in agriculture, primarily due to the limitation of the farmers' knowledge. Vietnamese farmers, especially those living in remote areas, generally have had little education. They do not know or care much about government policies or Vietnam's socioeconomic issues. On the one hand, this could attenuate the quality of their response; on the other hand, what the farmers tell are true stories. Second, the survey considered the farm households as the units of analysis, ignoring every individual in a household. The data thus did not capture the details of individuals. Despite the data quality concerns, the survey in fact amassed a great deal of useful and interesting information, which is analysed in the next section.

5.4   Field survey results and analysis

The welfare of farm households can be affected by both non-trade- and trade-related factors. Therefore, in addition to the trade-focused variables, the survey contains non-trade-related variables for general information, which provide the foundation for other parts of the survey. The study uses descriptive analytical methods to examine the primary survey data. The analysis of the survey results begins with providing general household characteristics; it then analyses the trade-related factors from the perception of farm households.

Provincial development: some socioeconomic characteristics

The field survey focused on two main export products of Vietnam. Of 329 surveyed farm households, about 40 per cent were from An Giang (Table 5.2), one of the key rice production provinces in Vietnam. It was expected to contain rich information about rice production and business. Dong Nai and Dak Lak accounted for 60 per cent of the sample, equally divided between the two. Coffee

Table 5.2 Main production of surveyed farm households (per cent)

Province	Paddy	Coffee	Cashew	Pepper	Fruit	Corn	Vegetables	Total
An Giang	38.6	0	0	0	0.6	0	0.6	39.8
Dong Nai	24.9	0	1.5	1.8	0	1.8	0.3	30.4
Dak Lak	0	29.8	0	0	0	0	0	29.8
Total	63.5	29.8	1.5	1.8	0.6	1.8	0.9	100

exports from Dak Lak, one of the leading coffee production provinces, account for a considerable proportion of Vietnam's total coffee exports.

Beside rice as the main crop, the farmers in An Giang and Dong Nai also grew cashews, pepper, fruit, corn, and vegetables. All of these products are exportable, especially cashews, pepper, and some fruit; however, they are not Vietnam's main export products. The data thus captured only the main products on which trade policy can impinge. The data covered several key topics: household demographics, education, expenditure, agricultural production, occupation, and trade policy.

As with the majority of Vietnamese households in this sample, heads of families were predominantly male. In fact, male farmers were more knowledgeable than their female counterparts. Respondents were relatively young, with an average age of 46 (Table 5.3). Participants who are male or of middle age may provide better information than those who are female or in other ages. Household size in the sample was typically a family with four or more members. Moreover, farm households in Dong Nai had more members than those in the other provinces; interestingly enough, that province's dependent ratio was the highest amongst the provinces surveyed. An Giang had the lowest dependent proportion, which may suggest a greater need for labour. These results suggest that the characteristic of a province's production may relate to its household composition.

At the primary educational level, Dong Nai had the highest ratio of respondents attaining primary school education, while this proportion in Dak Lak was lowest. However, Dak Lak had the highest proportion of people who had attained the lower secondary educational level, nearly twice as high as those of the other provinces. This province also had the highest ratio of people with an upper secondary education, more than twice as high as that of Dong Nai, and 1.5 that of An Giang (Figure 5.1). The proportion of people who complete post-secondary education (such as vocational training, college, and university) was low. The proportion of people with vocational training was almost zero in Dak Lak, very small in An Giang, and highest in Dong Nai.

These results are reasonable, because industry is typical of Dong Nai, where numerous industrial factories are located. People in this province have the advantage, over those in the other provinces, of obtaining training. However, the

Table 5.3 Demographic characteristics of surveyed households

Province	Total households	Head gender (per cent)		Average age (year)	Average household size (person)	Household composition (per cent)	
		Female	Male			Children	Adult
An Giang	131	17.6	82.4	44.2	4.4	14.5	85.5
Dong Nai	100	41	59	48.1	4.7	18.5	81.5
Dak Lak	98	16.3	83.7	47.3	4.5	17.0	83.0
Total	329	24.3	75.7	46.3	4.5	16.5	83.5

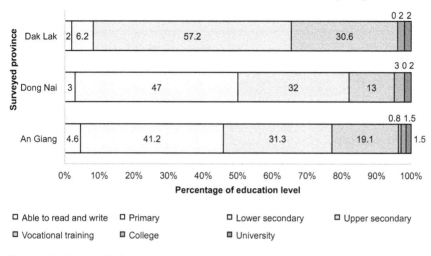

Figure 5.1 Levels of education

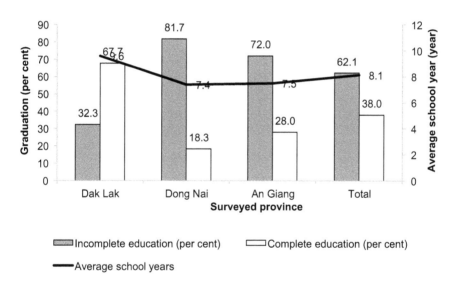

Figure 5.2 Graduation and schooling years

percentage of college education was almost zero in Dong Nai and highest in Dak Lak. An Giang had the lowest number of people with a university education, reflecting the fact that it was amongst the provinces having the lowest level of education in Vietnam. Although An Giang was one of the leading rice-production provinces, its farmers are generally poor, and low profits from rice production probably bring about low investment in education. Conversely, high profits from coffee production in Dak Lak contribute to the higher level of education. Graduation is an important achievement in education. Figure 5.2 shows that the proportion of

Table 5.4 Per capita expenditure and main income sources

Item	An Giang	Dong Nai	Dak Lak	Total
Average per capita expenditure (million VND)	9.6	6.6	16.0	10.6
Main income source (per cent)	100	100	100	100
Farming	80.2	92	67.3	79.9
Farming and extra work	13.7	8	32.7	17.6
Others	6.1	0	0	2.4

respondents who finished their education was lowest in Dong Nai and highest in Dak Lak. The farmers surveyed in Dak Lak were generally better educated than those in An Giang and Dong Nai.

With respect to income and expenditure, Dak Lak had the highest level of average expenditure per capita amongst the surveyed provinces, probably because coffee production might be more productive than rice production. Engaging in farming accounted for 80 per cent of the farm households' sources of income. In addition, the proportion of farm households earning a living from farming and extra work was highest in Dak Lak and lowest in Dong Nai (Table 5.4). If combined with the status quo of education, where the respondents in Dak Lak were better educated, then better educated people did not rely solely on farming; rather, they were highly capable of finding extra jobs. The preliminary picture of education and welfare shows that the poor had low levels of education and may not afford higher education.

The most important factor that affects household income or expenditure is inflation. The poor households have really been dismayed by accelerating inflation in recent years. Increasing prices of goods and services, especially food staples, have significantly reduced their already small real incomes. Amongst the causes of inflation, the change in sugar price stands out as particularly noteworthy in Vietnam. Sugar used to be a strictly protected product. The sugar industry has remained inefficient, providing little labour, despite the government's continued support for increasing its competition levels (Dapice, 2003). Consequently, the Vietnamese have borne the burden of poor trade policies in the sugar industry, with high and frequently fluctuating sugar prices. Not surprisingly, the farm households surveyed have seen the sugar price change substantially in the last decade (Figure 5.3). The performance of the sugar industry, an instance of the inadequacy of Vietnam's trade policy, has impinged on household welfare.

The success in the reduction of poverty in Vietnam partly results from the effects of poverty reduction programmes. The survey also considered the Hunger Eradication and Poverty Reduction (HEPR) programme, an important national programme in Vietnam's social and economic development policy, which helps poor households to escape poverty. It was not really effective, however, as access to this programme was not always easy. The data show that, on average, only

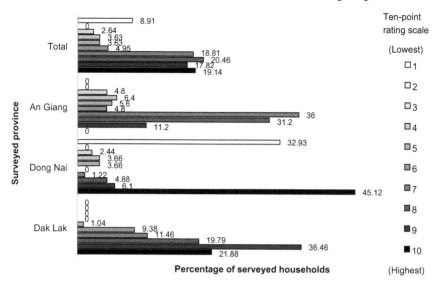

Figure 5.3 Assessment of sugar price change (per cent)

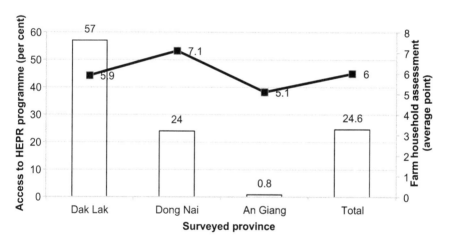

Figure 5.4 Access to poverty reduction programmes and household assessment

Note: The assessment of the usefulness of the poverty reduction programme ranges between 1 (lowest) and 10 (highest), using the 10-point rating scale.

25 per cent of the respondents had access to the local poverty reduction programme, which was chiefly the preferential credit programme (Figure 5.4). The allocation of the programme resources appears uneven across the surveyed provinces. In An Giang, the farm households that probably needed capital most for

agricultural production had extremely low access to the programme. On the contrary, the better-off farm households in Dak Lak had generous access to credit, even though their need for capital support was not as great as that of the farm households in Dong Nai. Figure 5.4 also indicates that poor farm households in Dong Nai assessed the programme highly, with their average evaluation of the programme being 7.1 per cent, compared with 5.1 per cent in An Giang and 5.9 per cent in Dak Lak. In summary, the HEPR programme, which was most expected to support the poor, performed less effectively than expected. These results suggest that huge resources for poverty reduction were inefficiently used and allocated, and were, therefore, wasted.

The analysis of the general information shows some important characteristics of poor households in the provinces. The poor in An Giang had a lower level of education than those in Dong Nai and Dak Lak. Although Dong Nai is an industrial province, poor households in this province had a lower level of expenditure than households in the other provinces. This may suggest a high level of income inequality in the industrial and urban regions. The inadequacy of trade policy has brought about souring and unstable prices for several products, such as sugar. The government efforts to support the poor through the poverty reduction programmes proved less effective. Low education, low income, major concern over inflation, and weak support are some important crosscutting characteristics of farm households in the surveyed provinces.

Trade policy perceptions

Agricultural trade is the main activity of farm households in Vietnam. Data provided by other household surveys may conceal the real plight of farmers in rural Vietnam, as they ignore farmers' perceptions of trade in agriculture. Farmer awareness of agricultural trade constitutes a major part of this survey. Aspects of agricultural trade in Vietnam are revealed in the following analysis of seven main factors: agricultural production; occupation; market distribution; difficulties in agricultural production; desired support from government; the role of cooperation amongst enterprises, banks, scientists, and government; and overall remarks on agricultural business.

Agricultural production

The production of rice and coffee represents Vietnam's main agricultural activity. The analysis of some characteristics of agricultural production allows for better understanding of trade activities and trade policy in agriculture. The surveyed provinces, especially An Giang and Dak Lak, are predominantly rice and coffee producers. In reality, land for cultivation, which is a fundamental requirement of agricultural production, has not been planned for efficient agricultural production in that the cultivatable land is a patchwork of tiny plots. Each household has its own area and has itself managed the production. Different households may have different targets and methods for production, and thus different productivity. This is one of the reasons for low quality and productivity of rice.

The farm households in An Giang owned the largest land area, as compared to the other provinces, with their average land area per capita being 0.25 hectares. Compared with An Giang, the other rice-growing area, Dong Nai, was lowest on the index (0.13 hectares), as shown in Table A5.2. An Giang's rice productivity (tonne per hectare) was 42.6 per cent higher than that of Dong Nai. The farm households in An Giang invested more in rice production than those in Dong Nai, as the production cost per hectare in An Giang was typically 51.9 per cent higher than that in Dong Nai. Coffee production, the main product of Dak Lak, generally requires more capital resources than rice production at the beginning. In rice production, the profit per tonne was more than twice as high as the cost per tonne. In coffee production, the profit per tonne was more than three times as high as the production cost. Given these differences in production between rice and coffee, coffee production tends to be more productive than rice production in Vietnam. However, it suits only some areas, such as the highlands. Coffee growing is unlikely to be a feasible option for the majority of the poor.

The fertiliser was, inter alia, a crucial factor making up rice productivity. Among the inputs for agricultural production, fertiliser typically accounted for about 60 per cent, followed by the cost of seed (about 16 per cent, on average) (Figure 5.5). While farmers use several kinds of fertiliser, NPK (nitrogen, phosphorus, potassium) and Kali fertilisers are the ones that are most commonly used. The prices of these fertilisers fluctuated highly. The ratio of the difference between the highest price and the lowest price (the range) of the NPK to its average price can reach 97 per cent, especially in An Giang and Dong Nai, where farmers mostly need fertiliser for rice crops (Table A5.3). These ratios for Kali and other fertilisers can exceed 100 per cent. Vietnam imports some fertilisers due to the limited and unstable supply of domestically produced fertilisers. Farmers frequently endure the government's mismanagement of fertiliser importation,

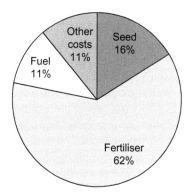

Figure 5.5 Cost composition of agricultural production (per cent), 2011

Note: The sample for this figure covers 71 households who provided details of paddy cost production, including 16 in An Giang and 55 in Dong Nai.

Table 5.5 Assessment of access to fertiliser

Item	An Giang	Dong Nai	Dak Lak	Total
Perception of fertiliser price change[1/] ...		9.8	9.7	9.7
Access to fertiliser purchase[2/]	6.3	6.5	8.7	7.1
Reasons for possibly difficult access (percentage of surveyed households choosing the answer)[3/]				
Shortage supply	5.3	1.0	0	2.4
High price	95.4	100	100	98.8
Import limitation	0.8	0	0	0.3
Low quality	6.1	0	0	2.7
Unreasonable market	6.8	0	0	2.7
Other reasons[4/]	0	10	0	3.0

Notes:
1/ The perception of fertiliser price change ranges from 1 (lowest) to 10 (highest), using a 10-point rating scale. This question was not in the questionnaire for An Giang, and was added later to the questionnaire for Dong Nai and Dak Lak.
2/ The access to purchasing fertiliser ranges from 1 (most difficult) to 10 (easiest), using a 10-point rating scale.
3/ The total percentages do not add to 100 per cent in each province, as a respondent can choose one or more answers.
4/ Other stated reasons included high price fluctuation, unstable market price, extreme price fluctuation, too-high price fluctuation, and unexpectedly up-and-down market price. These opinions were unpopular in the sample.

which causes supply shortage and raises prices. This consequential rise in the cost of agricultural production substantially affects poor farm households.

As fertiliser was one of the farmers' main concerns, especially at the beginning of a crop, changes in fertiliser price strongly impacted the farmers: their average assessment of the level of fertiliser price change is 9.7 points (Table 5.5). The purchase of fertiliser was not always easy for many: their estimate of the difficulty of access to fertiliser purchase was as high as 7.1 points on the rating scale of 1 to 10. When asked about the possible difficulties in buying fertiliser, nearly 99 per cent of the respondents quoted the high price as their main consideration. The extreme price fluctuation was also quoted as a major impediment to fertiliser purchase. Mismanagement of the fertiliser market may result in low and unpredictable productivity, low-quality rice, uncertain rice supply, and low prices.

When evaluating profitability in agricultural business, almost all the farmers in the An Giang and Dak Lak provinces stated that their agricultural production was profitable. The number of farm households in Dong Nai that were reported to be profitable accounted for only 32.5 per cent of the sample of the province. The difference between the average crop price that the farmers desired to sell at and the one they actually sold at was considerable, with the average percentage change being 16 per cent in An Giang, 27 per cent in Dong Nai, and 17 per cent in Dak Lak (Table 5.6). Although crops were reported to be profitable, the farmers may

Table 5.6 Perception of agricultural business

Item	An Giang (n = 126)	Dong Nai (n = 80)	Dak Lak (n = 92)
Perception of profit (per cent)			
Profitable	100.0	32.5	100.0
Not profitable	0.0	67.5	0.0
Average real price (VND)	6,202.8	5,915.0	49,243.5
Average desired price (VND)	7,250.4	7,530.0	57,630.4
Average percentage change (per cent)	15.9	27.3	17.1

Note: n denotes the sample size in each province.

not gain the benefits that they desire. Moreover, their profits have yet to take inflation into consideration.

The results indicate that agricultural production in Vietnam was unsustainable. Prices of fertiliser, the main input to agricultural production, were perceived to be very high, with extreme fluctuation, whilst rice and coffee crops were sold at lower prices than were expected. The profits the farmers received may not correspond to what they deserved. The small profits probably make them lack incentives to invest in agricultural production to increase productivity. They grew rice perhaps because they had no better choices. In reality, the convoluted distribution of the crops was a cause for low profits. As a consequence, the farm households did not rely altogether on farming as the main source of income. Rather, they had to find an extra job to feed their typically large family.

Occupation

Employment is one of the most visible effects of trade liberalisation. If farmers have good harvests and rice prices are high, they have a high demand for labour to do farm services. Small farm households are busy with their own harvests and crop sales. The unsustainable agricultural production may result in an unstable source of income in rural areas. Farm households had no choice but to find other jobs, or extra jobs, which may not be relevant to agriculture. The younger people tend to find jobs in the industrial or urban sectors. The older people tend to work for richer households in the same or neighbouring regions. Of the three provinces, Dong Nai had the largest proportion of farm households with a second job (Table 5.7). There are more opportunities for finding jobs in Dong Nai than in the other provinces, because numerous enterprises are located there. This province also has the highest ratio of household members working in export sectors. However, the survey results show that finding jobs in Dong Nai was more difficult than in the other provinces, suggesting a more competitive labour market in this province (Figure 5.6).

Table 5.7 Perception of occupation

Item	An Giang	Dong Nai	Dak Lak	Total
Extra work (percentage of households in each province)	35.9	41	33.7	36.8
Perception of difficulty in finding job[1]	4.6	2.4	3.7	3.7
Household members working in export sector (percentage of households in each province)	2.3	6.0	0.0	2.7
Residence near an industrial park[2]	35.9	62.0	100.0	62.9

Notes:
1/ Based on a 10-point rating scale, ranging from 1(most difficult) to 10 (easiest). The figures in the table are averaged.
2/ Households residing within a 50-kilometre radius from an industrial park.

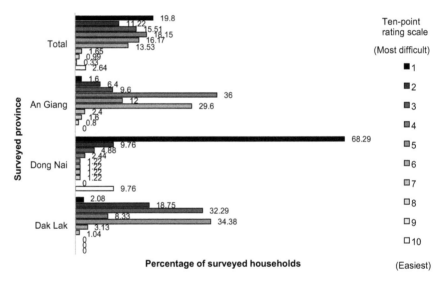

Figure 5.6 Perception of finding jobs (per cent)

The farm households surveyed worked in low-income jobs, probably due to low qualifications or inadequate training. The percentage of respondents living near industrial parks was 62 per cent in Dong Nai, compared with 36 per cent in An Giang. Although the households surveyed in Dak Lak mostly lived near an industrial park, the chance to work in export enterprises was low, as this province had few industrial parks, compared with Dong Nai or An Giang. The results suggest that the farm households in An Giang may have a better opportunity for finding jobs than those in Dong Nai and Dak Lak. Likewise, famers' jobs in An Giang are low income, and primarily comprised of agricultural or other services.

The opportunity for finding a job for farm households depends primarily on the state of crops and the rice market, an individual's qualification or education, local business development, and geography. Remote households are typically poor, because of both their low level of education and the poor development of local businesses. A high rate of rural employment is secured only when crops are successful and rice prices are high. In reality, these two conditions seldom occur at the same time. Farm households in industrial provinces have more opportunities for finding jobs beyond the farm, especially in the export sectors. This signifies the employment effect of trade openness on poverty. Low education may also prevent poor households from having jobs, especially good jobs. As low-income work continues to be the most likely option for poor households, their chance of escaping poverty remains very slim.

Markets for rice and coffee

Farmers need to have appropriate prices from their crop sales. The survey results show that farm households had almost no idea about the rationale for selling their crop. About 84 per cent of the respondents sold their crop for the reason of convenience, and this ratio was highest in Dak Lak (Table 5.8). Other recognised reasons, such as urgent need of money, no choice, or cash payment, suggest that the crop distribution was poorly organized. Some surveyed farmers stated that state food companies, the main rice exporters, never bought crops directly from them, but rather purchased crops only from private merchants/traders or rice agents. Since farmers simply process rice in the paddy after harvesting, their crops are of low quality. They are unable to carry out more complicated rice processing, due to the lack of knowledge and investment in machinery or equipment.

Farmers had no option but to sell their crops directly from paddy to private rice/coffee traders for low prices, as their continuing main concern was to somehow receive money as soon as possible. This meant that they had no chance to consider other possibilities, even though they knew that they lost money when selling crops to private traders. The survey results suggest that farmers mostly

Table 5.8 Stated reasons for selling crops (percentage of total households)

Reason	An Giang	Dong Nai	Dak Lak	Total
Urgent need of money	37.4	58.0	31.6	41.9
Convenience	74.0	83.0	98.0	83.9
No choice	21.4	23.0	0.0	15.5
Other reasons[1]	4.6	0.0	0.0	1.8

Notes:
- The total percentages do not add to 100 per cent in each province, as a respondent can choose one or more answers.
- 1/ These stated reasons: good price, state firms only bought export paddy and not farm gate paddy, no state agent, cash payment.

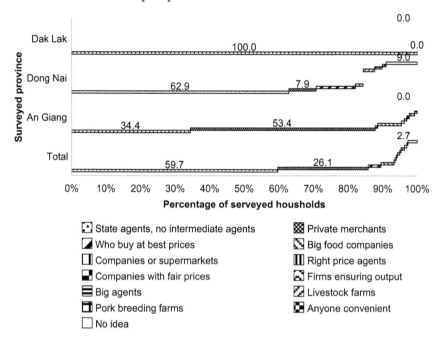

Figure 5.7 Revealed preference for distribution channels for crops (per cent)

desired to sell crops to state food enterprises, believing that they would have most returns via this distributional channel (Figure 5.7). Farmers perceived that private rice traders are just middlemen making great profits by collecting paddy from farm growers and processing paddy to sell output to rice exporters. They also reckoned that selling crops to rice exporters is the best option, because they would receive better prices without these middlemen. The results demonstrate that farmers also sold crops to many buyers, mostly private rice/coffee traders.

In reality, state food companies, the main legitimate rice exporters, seldom bought crops directly from farmers for export. All the respondents reported that they traded with the private rice traders, who almost altogether controlled this lucrative market segmentation. By nature, private rice traders always find ways to lower price as much as possible, to squeeze farmers' profits. The existence of a variety of trading intermediaries mirrors the poor trading system for two of Vietnam's leading export commodities. As a consequence, although the world rice prices tend to increase and Vietnam frequently comes first or second in rice export in the world, farm households in this country typically remain poor. In the last three years, rice and coffee have seen their prices change dramatically: the change of rice price was from about 42 per cent to about 52 per cent and coffee price approximately 151 per cent (Table 5.9). Although rice prices tend to grow, input cost for agricultural production, especially the fertiliser cost, has also risen.

To further examine farmers' perceptions of the fluctuation in the rice or coffee market in Vietnam, the farmers were asked to explain the reasons why prices of

Table 5.9 Rice market price fluctuations

Item	An Giang	Dong Nai	Dak Lak
Lowest price in last 3 years (VND, average)	4,146.0	3,856.2	14,076.9
Highest price in last 3 years (VND, average)	6,425.4	5,567.9	49,384.6
Price change (per cent)	51.9	42.3	150.8

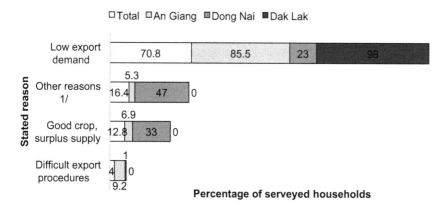

Figure 5.8 Stated reasons for the lowest price (since last three years)

Notes: 1/ These reported reasons: firms could not borrow from state banks, so they had no plan to purchase; too many agents; private merchants' unfair prices; low-quality paddy and rice; surplus supply when harvesting; low inflation; food security; unstable market price; private merchants' purchases; price fluctuation or due to market prices; not many livestock farms; no idea; unknown.

rice or coffee have been lowest within the last three years. The options offered for this question focused on market factors, export, trade policy, and open responses. The results suggest that export demand played a crucial role in rice and coffee production, especially in An Giang and Dak Lak (Figure 5.8). Notably, however, the farmers in An Giang recognised the difficulties relevant to export procedure as being a reason for the lowest rice price over the last three years. Export demand for rice is the external factor, which is mostly beyond government control. What the Vietnamese government can do is attempt to forecast the world demand as specifically as possible. The government can also reform customs procedures to smooth rice export, as well as other exports, as customs procedures appear to be far from efficient and often make export enterprises difficult. The rice export shipments are occasionally delayed due to the cumbersome export procedures. Such a halt to rice exports may cause difficulties for farmers at the beginning of the rice supply chain. The mismanagement of rice distribution and export, such as poorly planned procurement and storage of rice, poor market forecast, and inefficient customs procedures, lowers the rice quality and farmers' profits. Lower profit may also result in other identified difficulties in agriculture, such as the lack of capital and low productivity.

Identified difficulties in agricultural production

The analysis of difficulties in rice or coffee production can help to disclose other aspects of agricultural production and trade. Producing rice or coffee is a complicated process, especially in developing countries with low technology support. Farmers in these countries work very hard and face numerous difficulties. The results suggest that the inadequate availability of capital was the farmers' major concern, as about 80 per cent of the respondents quoted capital shortage as their main difficulty in agricultural production (Figure 5.9). In addition to lack of capital, labour shortage may curb agricultural production. The results show that lack of labour considerably concerned the farmers in Dong Nai and Dak Lak, because people, especially the youth, probably preferred working in manufacturing factories to improve their income or migrating to urban areas to look for better opportunities. Most of the farmers in Dong Nai claimed that they did not profit from agricultural production. For those in Dak Lak, coffee production relied substantially on the weather. Most importantly, more than 88 per cent of the respondents in An Giang stated that the rice market was unpredictable. The uncertainty of the rice market suggests the unsustainable development of agriculture in Vietnam. As well, most of the farmers in Dak Lak said that they lacked the technical knowledge needed for coffee production.

In summary, the difficulties facing the farm households reveal the inadequacy of Vietnam's trade system in agriculture. The chronic lack of capital results from

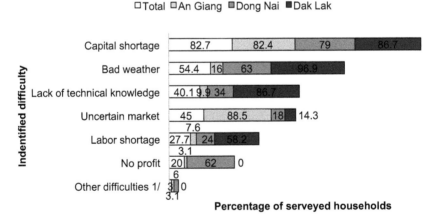

Figure 5.9 Identified difficulties in agricultural production (per cent)

Notes: 1/ Other identified difficulties were downgraded lands due to continual production, lack of after-crop technique, high input prices, no drying yards, land shortage, increasing population, small profit, high fluctuation of fertiliser and bio protection drugs, low-quality paddy.

having low profit and almost no access to bank loans. Lack of capital potentially leads to low productivity, because no investment is made in production. Lack of technical supports also lowers productivity. Most importantly, if farmers are uncertain about the market, they are unable to plan their production, and are vulnerable to numerous risks in agricultural production. Low income in the agricultural sector causes legions of people to migrate to urban areas, where most factories are located, to earn a living. The process of rural-to-urban migration creates shortage of labour in rural areas, threatening agricultural production. Farmers are, therefore, mired in agricultural woes and need lots of support from the government.

Farmers' expectations of support from the government

The analysis of the farmers' perceptions of agricultural difficulties, combined with the understanding of the farmers' expectations of support from the government, further demystifies the inadequacy of trade policies in rice or coffee. Based on the perceived difficulties in agricultural production, the farmers had the desire for wide-ranging support from the government, of which special lending, organisation of purchase system, stabilisation of fertiliser, and fuel market were most crucial. About 80 per cent to 90 per cent of the respondents in An Giang and Dak Lak expected to have access to a preferential bank loan, whereas the farmers in Dong Nai said that they did not need that much (Figure 5.10). The farmers in An Giang and Dak Lak also recognised the importance of smoothing export procedures to encourage rice production, as they experienced the bottleneck of crop distribution due to the delayed export shipments. Customs procedures concerned the Dong Nai farmers less than the An Giang and Dak Lak farmers, since the scale

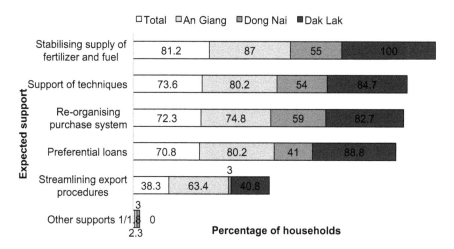

Figure 5.10 Expected support from the government (per cent)

Notes: 1/ Other desired supports consisted of building local rice storages, market-driven regional planning, providing poor households with seeds, banks' providing insufficient lending quota for agriculture, no comment.

of agricultural production in Dong Nai was relatively small and simple, and the rice crops were primarily for home consumption. More than 70 per cent of the respondents considered that the existing procurement of rice and coffee needed to be reorganized, as they regularly sold crops with unfair prices. More than 80 per cent of the respondents also hoped to have a stabilised supply of fertiliser and fuel, the two main inputs into agricultural production. They really needed the supporting knowledge of agricultural techniques to increase productivity.

The whole process of agricultural production of rice and coffee, from input market and rice cultivation to output market and export, needs support. The highest need for support is to stabilise the supply of fertiliser and fuel. High and unpredictable prices of fertilisers really concern rice and coffee growers. The desired supports perceived by the farmers suggest that both agricultural input and output markets are mismanaged, and this whole process of production – from input to production, distribution, and export – needs to be reformed. The farmers' concerns about export procedures signal the real obstacle for Vietnam's export road to the world market.

Cooperation between enterprises, banks, scientists, and government

The Vietnamese government has initiated multiagency cooperation between farmers, enterprises, banks, scientists, and authorities to support farmers. In this scheme, farmers are the main stakeholders, responsible for producing the rice, coffee, or other agricultural products. Enterprises, which are mainly responsible for output distribution and export, need to play a more active role in supporting farmers. They can approach farmers to order products prior to crops and can provide them with facilities and/or finance. Banks formally provide farmers with bank loans and banking services. The Vietnam Bank for Agriculture and Rural Development, as its name suggests, specialises in providing agricultural development support. Poor farmers with small plots of land have very restricted access to credit such as this, since they have poor assets as collateral. In this alliance, scientists are increasingly important to farm households. Farmers require knowledge of more advanced techniques for cultivation, because they are typically less educated. Technology in agriculture constitutes the underpinning for successful agricultural development. The last, very important stakeholders in the cooperation are the local and central authorities. The government, which can directly help farmers through agricultural programmes, should coordinate the cooperation to work, facilitating it among stakeholders. The effectiveness of the cooperation between firms, banks, scientists, and authorities in supporting farmers would contribute to the development of agriculture in Vietnam.

The respondents, on the whole, thought highly of the useful role of the cooperation in supporting farmers. More than 80 per cent of farm households surveyed considered that the operation of this cooperation would be very useful for farmers (Figure 5.11). The highest evaluation of the cooperation came from the An Giang farmers, probably because they are most engaged in farm activities. Only 63 per cent of the farmers in Dong Nai thought that it was important. The

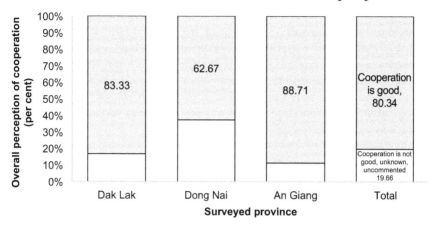

Figure 5.11 Overall perception of the cooperation (per cent)

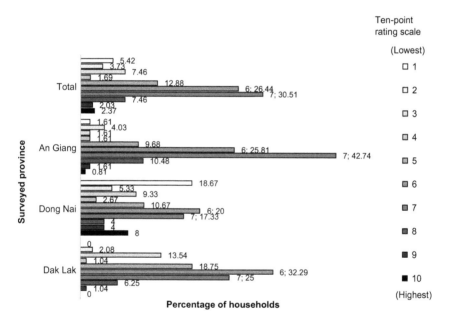

Figure 5.12 Assessment of cooperation

farmers in this province did not think highly of its role, because rice production is, in fact, not the province's main activity. Despite its theoretical and practical usefulness, the cooperation appeared to be more form than content. Its performance was modest in the farmers' points of view. In the farmers' evaluation of its operation, using a 10-point rating scale, the average and mode mark was 5.7 and 7, respectively (Figure 5.12, see also Table A5.8).

Whilst the respondents in An Giang gave the usefulness of cooperation the highest mark, those in Dong Nai found its role least useful. Surprisingly, not many farmers surveyed knew of the existence of the cooperation, possibly because of its dim role in supporting farmers, or the farmers' lack of knowledge. In addition, the farmers, especially those in Dong Nai, who gave their opinion of the cooperation claimed that it almost did not exist in reality. Its existence was seasonal and far more form than content. They downgraded its role because this alliance failed in four ways: to control rice prices, to provide farmers with access to agricultural policy and information, to provide farmers access to formal bank loans, and to forge a close relationship with farmers.

The establishment of the cooperation is most appropriate for supporting farmers and developing agriculture. Contrary to expectation, it did not perform as would have been expected. Its faded function to support farmers suggests the inconsistent trade policies in agriculture. Each stakeholder in the cooperation, apart from farmers, may not play the role as expected. Its dim role can be ascribed to the government, responsible for coordinating its operation. Without government coordination, other stakeholders cannot fully cooperate. The government itself resists decisive reforms, as it still maintains SOEs' monopoly of rice.

Agricultural business pre- and post-2000: an overall assessment

At the end of the questionnaire, the farmers were asked to evaluate agricultural business overall before and after the year 2000. The aim of this question is to assess farmers' recognition of the changes in their business environment over two decades. The year 2000 milestone is more meaningful than the year 2007, when Vietnam became an official member of the WTO, because farmers did not have much knowledge of the WTO and its impacts on the economy and their business. After the year 2000, the economy was relatively stable and performed well as a result of the economic reforms that were initiated in the 1990s and that accelerated after 2000 to prepare for participating in the WTO. Farmers could realize changes in the economy before and after that time.

The farmers were asked to compare the two periods with three degrees of assessment: 'better', 'unchanged', and 'worse'. Nearly 77 per cent of the respondents thought that their farm business was better after 2000 (Figure 5.13). The

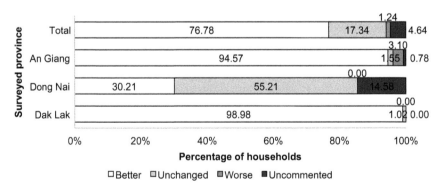

Figure 5.13 Assessment of agricultural business, before and after 2000

percentage of farmers with positive perspectives was highest in Dak Lak and lowest in Dong Nai. The reasons for being better were diverse: 17.1 per cent of the respondents in An Giang reasoned that farm business was better for an improvement in technique and productivity; 72.9 per cent for high demand, price, and good export; and 7.8 per cent for the role of the government in supporting farmers, which coincided with the viewpoint of 55.1 per cent of the respondents in Dak Lak (Table A5.10). The rest of the farmers surveyed gave varied remarks, generally relevant to the government policies, the development of the economy, market stabilisation, and integration of the economy into the world economy.

For most of the Dong Nai farmers, farm business was unchanged after the year 2000. 45 per cent of them reasoned that rice prices were still low and agricultural production had small or no profit. Some of the farmers in Dong Nai had no idea of the change, probably due to their low education or indifference. Some of the respondents in An Giang considered that farm business was worse after the year 2000, primarily owing to poor management in agriculture, high inflation, and poor harvest. Although the farmers' overall perspective is that agricultural business has improved over the two decades, a considerable number of the farmers had not noticed any changes. This implies that several farmers did not really benefit from agricultural growth and trade reforms.

Generally, the analysis has depicted several aspects where trade policies in agriculture proved to be inadequate. Farmers' perceptions of agricultural trade policies suggest a range of weaknesses in agricultural production and business in Vietnam. The weak cooperation amongst farmers, enterprises, banks, scientists, and government can help to explain the sluggish development of agriculture and the low-income farming. Although the surveyed farmers' attitude towards the multiagency cooperation for supporting farm households and farm business was, on the whole, positive, many of them, especially poor farm households, appeared to be left behind in the process of economic development.

5.5   Conclusions

This chapter has analysed many facets drawn from the primary field survey regarding the effects of trade policies on rice and coffee production and markets from the points of view of the farmers. The field survey was conducted in three provinces in Vietnam: An Giang, Dong Nai, and Dak Lak. Overall, the production and distribution of rice and coffee is, to a large extent, liberalised but mismanaged. The farmers faced several risks in relation to crop distribution, inflation, capital shortage, unstable supply of fertiliser and fuel, and rice export delays. They also lacked support from the multiagency cooperation system proposed by the government to be the farmers' primary sources of support. In An Giang, private rice traders' domination in rice procurement from farmers can be typical of rice distribution in Vietnam. The farmers in this province seem to suffer most from the local poor trade system, as most of them felt displeased when trading with private rice traders. As they are the big rice producers, they desired to reorganize the distributional system to stabilise the rice market. The key challenge for An

Giang is to reform the rice distribution system to smooth rice exports and to take most benefits for farmers.

Compared to the rice situation in An Giang, coffee production in Dak Lak was more profitable. Similar to An Giang, coffee exporters bought coffee crops from coffee agents or private traders who had collected these crops from the growers. Consequently, the difference between farm-gate prices and the prices at which private traders sold coffee crops to coffee exporters was claimed to be considerable. However, compared with the rice agents in An Giang, coffee agents in Dak Lak are large businesses, able to use their market power to defer payments for coffee farmers until they receive payments from coffee exporters. Coffee growers, therefore, face the risk of default by coffee agents. Dak Lak needs to reform its coffee distribution system to secure payment for coffee production.

The Dong Nai farm households differ from those in both An Giang and Dak Lak: they engaged in less productive, small-scale agricultural production. As Dong Nai is a typical industrial province, agriculture plays a minor role in its economic development. Nonetheless, the farm households in this province are still poor. They had limited knowledge about trade policies and the role of the multiagency cooperation system in supporting agricultural production. Rice crops were mainly domestically consumed, and rice market distribution was similar to that in An Giang. Had trade policy been efficient and consistent, and given that Dong Nai has the advantage of being adjacent to HCMC, Dong Nai farmers would have been very capable, quality rice producers, the same as those in An Giang. Trade policy reforms in agriculture could be made consistent so that all farmers could have the same access to the resources for agricultural production.

The agricultural trading system in each province has its own flaws. The farm households suffer from what continues to be an inadequate trade policy, especially with respect to rice and coffee market distribution. Reforming the internal trading system in agriculture is the most appropriate way for improving the welfare of farm households. More significantly, the identified relationship between farmers' perceptions of trade policy and welfare can provide a new direction for future research on the trade–poverty nexus. It also suggests that the trade policy reforms in agriculture require farmers be fully apprised of changes in trade policies, and that better perception of trade policy can help farmers to decide rationally how to distribute their crops and gain the most from this output distribution. This three-province case study of agricultural trade has pinpointed the problems with Vietnam's internal agricultural trade system that dampen farmers' incentives to improve agricultural production. It also suggests that the effectiveness of trade policy reforms lies in farmers' comprehension of trade policy.

Annexe

Table A5.1 Education level of surveyed farm households (per cent)

Education level	An Giang	Dong Nai	Dak Lak
Total	100	100	100
Able to read and write	4.6	3.0	2.0
Primary	41.2	47.0	6.1
Lower secondary	31.3	32.0	57.1
Upper secondary	19.1	13.0	30.6
Vocational training	0.8	3.0	0.0
College	1.5	0.0	2.0
University	1.5	2.0	2.0

Table A5.2 Indicators of agricultural production

Productivity indicator	An Giang (rice)	Dong Nai (rice)	Dak Lak (coffee)	Total
Average land area per household (hectare)	1.0	0.53	0.96	0.8
Average land area per head (hectare)	0.25	0.13	0.21	0.20
Tonne per hectare	6.7	4.7	3.8	
Cost per hectare (million VND)	12.3	8.1	81.9	
Cost per tonne (million VND)	1.9	1.8	13.8	
Revenue per tonne (million VND)	6.3	6.3	49.3	
Profit per tonne (million VND)	4.4	4.5	35.5	
Sample observation	127	82	98	329

Table A5.3 Fertiliser price change

Fertiliser	Total	An Giang	Dong Nai	Dak Lak
NPK	n = 298	n = 116	n = 85	n = 97
Average price	12,687.8	11,958.2	13,183.5	13,125.8
Standard deviation	106.3	157.2	164.6	200.8
Maximum	20,000	18,000	20,000	15,000
Minimum	7,660	7,660	10,000	10,000
Range/average price (per cent)	97.3	86.5	75.9	38.1
Kali	n = 276	n = 101	n = 78	n = 97
Average price	12,769.2	12,896.8	12,801.7	12,610.3
Standard deviation	87.3	169.9	201.7	64.4
Maximum	20,000	20,000	18,000	13,500
Minimum	6,000	7,200	6,000	8,000
Range/average price (per cent)	109.6	99.2	93.7	43.6
Other fertiliser	n = 277	n = 115	n = 66	n = 96
Average price	12,385	16,261.7	9,240.2	9,903.1
Standard deviation	253.5	154.3	596.0	106.1
Maximum	20,000	20,000	15,000	11,000
Minimum	2,300	10,909.1	2,300	3,000
Range/average price (per cent)	142.9	55.9	137.4	80.8

Note: n denotes the corresponding sample size.

Table A5.4 Cost structure of rice production

Cost structure per hectare per crop (per cent)	An Giang (n = 16)	Dong Nai (n = 55)
Seed	14.9	17.4
Fertiliser	66.3	57.5
Fuel	10.8	11.1
Other costs	8.0	14.0

Note: n denotes the effective sample size in each province.

Table A5.5 Identified difficulties in agricultural production (per cent)

Difficulty	An Giang	Dong Nai	Dak Lak	Total
Capital shortage	82.4	79.0	86.7	82.7
Labour shortage	7.6	24.0	58.2	27.7
No profit	3.1	62.0	0.0	20.0
Bad weather	16.0	63.0	96.9	54.4
Uncertain market	88.5	18.0	14.3	45.0
Lack of technical knowledge	9.9	34.0	86.7	40.1
Other difficulties[1]	3.1	6.0	0.0	3.0

Notes:
- The total percentages do not add to 100 per cent in each province, as a respondent can choose one or more answers.
- 1/ Other identified difficulties were downgraded lands due to continual production, lack of after-crop technique, high input prices, no drying yards, land shortage, increasing population, small profit, high fluctuation of fertiliser and bioprotection chemicals, low-quality paddy.

Table A5.6 Access to fertiliser

Item	An Giang	Dong Nai	Dak Lak	Total
Perception of fertiliser price change[1]	..	9.8	9.7	9.7
Access to fertiliser purchase[2]	6.3	6.5	8.7	7.1
Reasons for possible difficult access (percentage of surveyed households choosing the answer)[3]				
• Shortage supply	5.3	1.0	0.0	2.4
• High price	95.4	100	100	98.8
• Import limitation	0.8	0.0	0.0	0.3
• Low quality	6.1	0.0	0.0	2.7
• Unreasonable market	6.8	0.0	0.0	2.7
• Other reasons[4]	0.0	10.0	0.0	3.0

Notes:
- 1/ The perception of fertiliser price change ranges from 1 (lowest) to 10 (highest) using a 10-point rating scale. This question was not in the questionnaire for An Giang, and just added later to the questionnaire for Dong Nai and Dak Lak.
- 2/ The access to purchasing fertiliser ranges from 1 (most difficult) to 10 (easiest) using a 10-point rating scale.
- 3/ The total percentages do not add to 100 per cent in each province, as a respondent can choose one or more answers.
- 4/ Other stated reasons included high price fluctuation, unstable market price, extreme price fluctuation, too high price fluctuation, unexpectedly up-and-down market price. These opinions were patchy.

Table A5.7 Desired distributional channels for crop sales

Distributional channel	An Giang	Dong Nai	Dak Lak	Total
Total	100	100	100	100
State agents, no intermediate agents	34.4	62.9	100	59.7
Private merchants	53.4	7.9	0.0	26.1
Who buy at best prices	0.8	11.2	0.0	3.7
Big food companies	6.9	2.2	0.0	3.7
Companies or supermarkets	0.8	0.0	0.0	0.3
Right price agents	0.8	0.0	0.0	0.3
Companies with fair prices	0.8	0.0	0.0	0.3
Firms ensuring output market	1.5	0.0	0.0	0.7
Big agents	0.8	0.0	0.0	0.1
Livestock farms	0.0	3.4	0.0	1.0
Pork breeding farms	0.0	2.2	0.0	0.7
Anyone convenient	0.0	1.1	0.0	0.3
No idea	0.0	8.9	0.0	2.7

Table A5.8 Cooperation between farmers, enterprises, banks, scientists, and government

Assessment and opinion	An Giang	Dong Nai	Dak Lak	Total
Assessment of the association (point)	6.3	4.7	5.8	5.7
Opinions about the association (percentage of surveyed households choosing the answer)				
• Private merchants' purchase with unfair price	0.8	0.0	3.1	1.2
• Difficult access to agricultural policy and information due to administrative procedures	3.1	1.0	3.1	2.4
• No coalition in reality, formalism, seasonal combination, real desire for an actual coalition	3.1	26.0	3.1	10.0
• Difficult access to bank credit and food firms to sell crops	4.6	11.0	2.0	5.8
• No really close relationship with farmers	3.1	0.0	11.2	4.6
• Other remarks[1]	0.0	10	6.1	4.9

Notes: 1/ Other remarks include: access to government has been difficult; the government's support for farmers has been slow to come; the government has not provided farmers with support, nor even approached them; the government did not ensure output market and prices would be appropriate; farmers suffered from high inflation; farmers wanted the government to stabilise market price, to support farmers in planting technique, and to lend farmers capital preferentially; application of new planting techniques to agricultural production has been ineffective and slow; farmers desired extension training with regard to planting techniques; farmers expected that cooperation would promote exchange of knowledge regarding planting techniques; respondent did not understand the cooperation issue.

Table A5.9 Expected support from the government (per cent)

Type of support/reform	An Giang	Dong Nai	Dak Lak	Total
Preferential loans	80.2	41.0	88.8	70.8
Streamlining export procedures	63.4	3.0	40.8	38.3
Reorganising purchase system	74.8	59.0	82.7	72.3
Stabilising supply of fertiliser and fuel	87.0	55.0	100.0	81.2
Support of techniques	80.2	54.0	84.7	73.6
Other supports[1]	2.3	3.0	0	1.8

Notes:
- The total percentages do not add to 100 per cent in each province, as a respondent can choose one or more answers.
- 1/ Other desired supports consisted of building local rice storages, market-driven regional planning, providing poor households with seeds, banks' overly small lending quota for agriculture, no comment.

Table A5.10 Overall assessment of agricultural business, pre- and post-2000

Assessment and reason	An Giang	Dong Nai	Dak Lak	Total
Better	94.6	30.2	99.0	76.8
• Improving technique and productivity, reducing after-harvesting loss, mechanising agriculture, building drying houses and warehouses, modern yielding machine	17.1	0.0	0.0	6.8
• High demand and prices, good export	72.9	10.4	1.0	32.5
• Increased quality of rice and paddy	4.7	0.0	0.0	1.9
• Government policies, supports of technique, loan, market, procedures	7.8	0.0	55.1	19.8
• Opening agricultural technical training courses	0.8	6.3	1.0	2.5
• Others[1]	3.1	17.7	25.5	14.2
Unchanged	1.6	55.2	1.0	17.3
• Supply surplus	0.8	0.0	0.0	0.3
• Frequent and high fluctuation of production materials' prices, high costs	0.8	1.0	0.0	0.6
• Low rice price, no or small profit	0.0	45.8	0.0	13.6

(*Continued*)

Table A5.10 (Continued)

Assessment and reason	An Giang	Dong Nai	Dak Lak	Total
• High inflation	0.0	2.1	0.0	0.6
• Others[2]/	0.0	3.1	2.0	1.5
Worse	3.1	0.0	0.0	1.2
• Bad agricultural management	0.8	0.0	0.0	0.3
• High inflation	0.8	0.0	0.0	0.3
• Poor harvest	1.6	0.0	0.0	0.6
No idea/comment	0.8	14.6	0.0	4.6

Notes:
- The numbers in the table are the percentage of surveyed households choosing a particular answer.
- 1/ Quoted as saying crops easily sell, but at a low price level; the improving cooperation; organising purchase outlets; smooth export; developing economy; the opening of many livestock farms; development of breeding farm; many local cashew plants; good seeds suitable to land and climate; before 2000, being a farmer was difficult due to market prices, but after 2000 prices were relatively stable, although not good enough; the impact of market mechanism; better but still slow outcomes; the government should provide more support for farmers; more progress, and the government was more attentive; more socialised policy; easier trading; progress, but still low; engaging globalisation; more stable prices; change of market mechanism; relatively stable, but need to pay more attention to farmers; structure of market is easier; low effectiveness; a little better agricultural business; need close connection with farmers; many changes of purchase system; it suits a general trend of society.
- 2/ Other stated reasons for being unchanged include higher rice prices and relatively stable, but need to pay more attention to farmers.

Notes

1 Retrieved from http://www.economist.com/node/21594338.
2 Vietnam's GDP per capita in 2010 was US$1,174 (IMF, 2012).
3 The Provincial Competitiveness Index (PCI) was constructed by the Vietnam Chamber of Commerce and Industry (VCCI) and the project for Vietnam Competitiveness Initiative (VNCI) in 2005 to assess and rank the business environment and policies for private sector development across provinces in Vietnam. It is based on differences in geography, infrastructure, market size, and local administration. This index is detailed in Chapter 8.
4 This indicator was estimated by using the IMF's exchange rate of 19,498 VND (the Vietnamese currency unit) per USD in 2010 (IMF, 2012).
5 The 10-point grade is universally used in Vietnam's educational system to assess study.

References

Bhagwati, J. N., and Srinivasan, T. N. (2002). Trade and Poverty in the Poor Countries. *American Economic Review*, *92*(2), 180–183. DOI: 10.1257/000282802320189212

Central Institute for Economic Management, and Institute of Policy and Strategy for Agriculture and Rural Development (CIEM–IPSARD) (2007). *Characteristics of the Vietnamese Rural Economy: Evidence from a 2006 Rural Household Survey in 12 Provinces of Vietnam* (p. 262). Hanoi.

Central Institute for Economic Management, and Institute of Policy and Strategy for Agriculture and Rural Development (CIEM–IPSARD) (2011). *Characteristics of the Vietnamese Rural Economy: Evidence from a 2010 Rural Household Survey in 12 Provinces of Vietnam* (p. 289). Hanoi.

Central Institute for Economic Management, and Institute of Policy and Strategy for Agriculture and Rural Development (CIEM–IPSARD) (2013). *Characteristics of the Vietnamese Rural Economy: Evidence from a 2012 Rural Household Survey in 12 Provinces of Vietnam* (p. 350). Hanoi.

Dapice, D. O. (2003). *Vietnam's Economy: Success Story or Weird Dualism? A SWOT Analysis.* Paper presented at the UNDP and Prime Minister's Research Commission, Hanoi.

Deaton, A. (1989). Rice Price and Income Distribution in Thailand: A Non-Parametric Analysis. *The Economic Journal*, *99*(395), 1–37.

Deaton, A. (1997). *The Analysis of Household Surveys: A Microeconometric Approach to Development Policy.* Washington, DC: Johns Hopkins University Press.

Deaton, A. (2008, February). Price Trends in India and Their Implications for Measuring Poverty. *Economic and Political Weekly*, 27.

International Monetary Fund (IMF) (2012). *Vietnam: 2012 Article IV Consultation.* IMF, Country Report (No. 12/165).

Isik-Dikmelik, A. (2006). *Trade Reforms and Welfare: An Ex-Post Decomposition of Income in Vietnam.* World Bank, Policy Research Working Paper (No. 4049), 50.

Justino, P., Litchfield, J., and Pham, H. T. (2008). Poverty Dynamics during Trade Reform: Evidence from Rural Vietnam. *Review of Income and Wealth*, *54*(2), 166–192. DOI: 10.1111/j.1475–4991.2008.00269.x

Luu, T.D.H. (2002). *The Organization of the Liberalized Rice Market in Vietnam.* PhD thesis, University of Groningen, Groningen, NL.

Marchand, B. U. (2012). Tariff Pass-Through and the Distributional Effects of Trade Liberalization. *Journal of Development Economics, 99*, 265–281.

McCulloch, N., Winters, L. A., and Cirera, X. (2001). *Trade Liberalization and Poverty: A Handbook*. London: Centre for Economic Policy Research.

Minot, N., and Goletti, F. (1998). Export Liberalization and Household Welfare: The Case of Rice in Vietnam. *American Journal of Agricultural Economics, 80*(4), 738–749.

Nicita, A. (2009). The Price Effect of Tariff Liberalization: Measuring the Impact on Household Welfare. *Journal of Development Economics, 89*(1), 19–27. DOI: http://dx.doi.org/10.1016/j.jdeveco.2008.06.009

Porto, G. G. (2004). *Informal Export Barriers and Poverty*. World Bank, Policy Research Working Papers (No. 3354), 39.

Ravallion, M. (1990). Rural Welfare Effects of Food Price Changes under Induced Wage Responses: Theory and Evidence for Bangladesh. *Oxford Economic Papers, 42*(3), 574–585. DOI: 10.2307/2663062

Roldan-Perez, A., Gonzalez-Perez, M., Huong, P. T., and Tien, D. N. (2009, May). *Coffee, Cooperation and Competition: A Comparative Study of Columbia and Vietnam*. Paper presented at the Virtual Institute of the United Nations Conference on Trade and Development, Geneva, CH.

Seshan, G. (2005). *The Impact of Trade Liberalization on Household Welfare in Vietnam*. World Bank, Policy Research Working Paper (No. 3541).

The Economist (2014, January 18). Against the Grain – Vietnam's Farmers are Growing a Crop That No Longer Pays Its Way. Retrieved from http://www.economist.com/news/asia/21594338-vietnams-farmers-are-growing-crop-no-longer-pays-its-way-against-grain.

Tran, C. T., Do, L. H., and Le, N. M. (2013). *Who Has Benefited from High Rice Prices in Vietnam?* (p. 63). Hanoi: OXFAM–GROW–IPSARD.

United States Department of Agriculture (USDA) (2012a). *Vietnam 2012 Coffee Annual GAIN Report*. Washington, DC.

United States Department of Agriculture (USDA) (2012b). *Vietnam Grain and Feed Annual 2012 GAIN Report*. Washington, DC.

Winters, L. A., McCulloch, N., and McKay, A. (2004). Trade Liberalization and Poverty: The Evidence So Far. *Journal of Economic Literature, XLII*(1), 72–115.

World Bank (2010). *Vietnam Rice, Farmers and Rural Development: From Successful Growth to Sustainable Prosperity*. Hanoi.

Young, K. B., Wailes, E. J., Cramer, G. L., and Tri Them, N. (2002). *Vietnam's Rice Economy: Developments and Prospects* (vol. 968). Fayetteville: Arkansas Agricultural Experiment Station, Division of Agriculture, University of Arkansas.

6   Rural poverty and employment

6.1   Introduction

Trade liberalisation stimulates economic growth, and that economic growth in turn benefits everyone in the economy, including the poor. This is one of the major pathways through which trade liberalisation affects poverty. Historically, trade liberalisation was considered to be an engine of growth for many countries, especially developing countries. Vietnam attained remarkable achievements in economic growth and poverty reduction after transforming a centrally planned economy into an open market economy in 1986. High economic growth in the 1990s and the 2000s appears to have contributed to the substantial reduction in poverty over the two decades in this country. Although several other countries also achieved high economic growth and reduced poverty considerably, the relationship between trade liberalisation and poverty has been far from confirmed. The persistence of poverty amongst a considerable proportion of people in the transitional or liberalised developing economies also calls into question the impacts of trade liberalisation on poverty in reality. In fact, the context of trade policy in a country is important to understand its impacts. The focus of recent research on the relationship appears to have shifted to examining the impacts at the microeconomic level.

Many pathways through which trade influences households and poverty have been identified in the literature on the trade–poverty nexus. The impacts of trade liberalisation are claimed to be enormous and pervasive, but to a large extent difficult to vet empirically (McCulloch *et al.*, 2001). The transmission channels suggested by Winters cover the main impacts of trade liberalisation and stakeholders in the market economy, and, more importantly, these can be empirically verified. For the employment channel, several studies have shown that the employment generation effects of trade are largely positive (for example, Krueger, 1983; World Bank, 2001; Niimi *et al.*, 2007; Justino *et al.*, 2008; Athukorala, 2010; Coello *et al.*, 2010). These studies suggest, to some degree, the positive impacts of trade liberalisation on poverty through employment. Since rural households mostly engage in agricultural production and trade, the practical way for linking trade openness with poverty at the microeconomic level would be first to establish the trade-related variables taken from the household characteristics of agricultural production and employment, and then to examine their impacts on household welfare and poverty.

This chapter, based on the Winters framework, examines the effects of trade liberalisation on poverty in Vietnam, with a particular focus on the employment effect. The analysis is carried out using panel data models estimated over the period 2002–2006. The research undertaken in this chapter differs from the previous studies on Vietnam in several respects. First, the sample period used is not only more recent, but also more appropriate for studying the effects of trade liberalisation: in this period, the economy was somewhat stable, and reforms were accelerating. Second, the study examines more facets of the impacts of trade liberalisation than other studies in the field: for instance, poverty dynamics under trade liberalisation, and the effects of internal trade on welfare and poverty. Third, these impacts are examined using both continuous and discrete modelling approaches and panel data. The rest of the chapter is organised into three sections. Section 6.2 explains the research methods and the data used in the study, including the basis of the microdeterminants of growth, the decomposition technique for the evaluation of the returns of household traits on welfare, and the multinomial logit model for the analysis of poverty dynamics. Section 6.3 analyses the results of the model regressions, encompassing the results of the decomposition analysis, the model of microdeterminants of growth, the fixed and random effects models, and the multinomial logit model. Section 6.4 concludes the chapter by drawing policy implications.

6.2   Methods and data

The microeconomic impacts of trade liberalisation on poverty are examined under different approaches. The practical way of linking trade liberalisation with poverty at the microeconomic level is to construct a set of trade-related variables based on household characteristics of employment and agricultural production. The effects of these variables on household welfare and poverty are thereafter examined using panel regression models. For these general empirical strategies, the study employs both continuous and discrete approaches to analyse the effects of trade liberalisation on welfare and poverty, using both cross-sectional data and panel data.

Methods

Both continuous and discrete approaches use a model of microdeterminants of growth that is based on an income equation. The study first employs the model of microdeterminants of the growth of household welfare. The cross-sectional household data drawn from the VHLSSs are used to decompose the determinants of household welfare in order to provide an explanation of how household welfare is explained by a wide range of household characteristics. Second, the model of microdeterminants of the growth of household welfare is also used to analyse the impacts of trade liberalisation, using a wide-form panel data set constructed from the VHLSSs. Third, the impacts are further examined using the fixed effects model and a long-form panel data set also taken from the VHLSSs. Fourth, the study analyses poverty dynamics using a multinomial logit model and the wide-form panel data set to explain the change in poverty over the period 2002–2006.

Microeconomic determinants of economic growth

Ravallion (1998) and Haughton and Khandker (2009) consider that static regression analysis is by far the most widespread tool used to identify the contributions of different variables to poverty. This method of poverty analysis is based on the income equation that postulates real consumption (income) as a function of observed household characteristics. Using this approach, two common types of model are used to analyse poverty: levels regression and binary regressand. The levels regression model is used to explain the level of expenditure or income per capita. The dependent variable in this model – a function of characteristics of individuals, households, communities, and regions – is a continuous quantitative variable. The binary regressand model is used to account for whether a household is poor, using a logit or probit regression. In this method, the dependent variable is a discrete qualitative variable, and the independent variables are similar to those in the levels regression model. While the continuous approach faces concern about its inability to distinguish between poor and nonpoor households, the discrete method is confronted with the possibility of losing information, because of the use of a binary dependent variable. Some similar studies for Vietnam employ both approaches: for instance, Glewwe *et al.* (2002) and Justino *et al.* (2008).

The model specification used in this study follows Glewwe *et al.* (2000) and Justino *et al.* (2008). Both those studies are based on the model of microdeterminants of growth, estimated using a panel data set over the period 1993–1998. Their main aim is to attempt to capture the determinants of household welfare and the dynamics of poverty under the impact of a wide range of variables, in order to assess progress of poverty reduction in Vietnam during the 1990s. This study uses more recent data, and constructs both long- and wide-form panel data sets to analyse the impacts of trade liberalisation on welfare and poverty in Vietnam from 2002 to 2006. The model of microdeterminants of growth can be expressed in a simple log linear form:

$$log\,(y_i) = \beta X_i + U_i \tag{6.1}$$

where y_i is commonly real per capita consumption expenditure (RPCE), X_i is a vector of independent variables, β is a vector of estimated parameters, and U_i is a vector of the error term. The dependent variable is the real consumption expenditure per capita, measured in logarithm (log of RPCE). The study follows the monetary approach to measuring welfare and poverty.[1] Real consumption expenditure per capita is used as a proxy for welfare, assuming that consumption is a better outcome indicator than income is. The independent variables are the conventional characteristics of individuals, households, communities, and regions.

Several alternative sets of independent variables are used to explain household welfare. In the studies of trade liberalisation and welfare, these are commonly divided into two broad groups: non-trade-related and trade-related variables. Haughton and Khandler (2009) split the former variables into four general groups of characteristics: regional, community, household, and individual. Ravallion (1998) classifies them as internal (households and individuals) and external or area characteristics. This study also organises the independent variables into two broad groups: the non-trade-related variables measure household and regional characteristics, and the trade-related variables measure local trade liberalisation and institutional reforms. The former group covers the subgroups of variables measuring the characteristics of households and household heads, such as demographic traits, education, occupation, household agricultural production, and regional difference. The study draws on Glewwe and Hall (1998), Glewwe *et al.* (2002), and Niimi *et al.* (2007) to choose the independent variables: these are selectively confined to predetermined variables that are likely to be exogenous to per capita expenditure.

The first group of these variables, used to measure demographic traits of households and heads of household, or heads, includes household size, ethnicity, gender, age, marital status, and household composition. The second group, employed to quantify the impacts of human capital, comprises the school years of household heads, their spouses, and their parents, along with the proportions of household members with technical or post-secondary diplomas. All educational variables should have a positive impact on welfare. The third group, which aims to measure the impacts of occupation by household heads, includes four kinds of dummy variables (leader or business owner, professional, white collar, and skilled worker) with the unskilled as the reference category. Employment is expected to have a positive effect on welfare. The fourth group, used to measure agricultural production, encompasses rice productivity, net rice production, and total quantity of fertiliser. These agricultural variables should be positively associated with rural income.

The fifth group is used to measure household assets. Instead of using the variables of household assets such as house, remittance, and savings, which are obviously endogenous, this study uses some housing characteristics, such as access to electricity and safe drinking water, to explain rural welfare. These variables, relevant to essential living conditions, should have a positive impact on welfare. Moreover, as pointed out by Perkins *et al.* (2006), access to safe water is vital for rural households to meet nutritional needs. The model takes the impacts of community characteristics into account in the sixth group of variables: communes with roads suitable for vehicles or paved roads, and proximity to paved roads, commune schools, post offices, markets, electricity, and clinics. All commune characteristics should be positively associated with rural welfare. The model also includes a set of dummy variables indicating household location, with the reference being the north central region, widely considered as the poorest region in Vietnam.[2] Households in this region are expected to be worse off than those in the other regions.

Setting the trade-related variables is the key to investigating the impacts of trade liberalisation on household welfare and poverty. Cross-country studies use various methods to measure trade openness, such as tariff and nontariff barriers, as well as the ratios of exports to GDP and of trade volume (exports plus imports) to GDP. As pinpointed in the literature, none of these is optimal, however. These measures of trade openness may not link up with welfare and poverty at the household level. According to Justino *et al.* (2008), to evaluate the impacts of trade openness on household welfare, some specific household characteristics can be linked to trade reforms. These linkages can be based on Winters's pathways, as discussed in Chapter 2. Agricultural production and employment are important trade-induced factors in the framework.

Drawn on Niimi *et al.* (2007), the trade-related variables in this study include rice crops, rice productivity, the ratio of export sector employment (seafood, food processing, garment, shoes, rubber, and plastic products), the ratio of import-competing sector employment (textiles, leather, chemical, metals, and machinery), the ratio of manufacturing employment, the total retail sales per capita, and the changes of these variables. Trade openness includes both external and internal trade. The study focuses on internal trade, measured by the total retail sales per capita or trade transaction: the total value of retail sales that a province attains over a year, divided by its population. This variable measures local trade transaction, which is expected to be the key to improving welfare and reducing poverty. Local trade transaction can also reflect the level of internal trade and production activities. The study also draws on Justino *et al.* (2008), where the trade-related variables are measured at the commune level or the provincial level, except for rice crops and rice productivity. Hence, they are exogenous to per capita expenditure measured at the household level. In the case of rice crops and rice productivity, note that changes are likely to be endogenous to the change in per capita expenditure, because, as income increases, farm households tend to invest more in agricultural production to obtain a higher level of output and productivity. Some main descriptive statistics of the variables used in the panel data models are summarised in Table 6.1.

Decomposition of the growth of household welfare

The household welfare is first analysed using the decomposition technique suggested by Wodon (2000). Wodon (2000) argues that a change in per capita expenditure over a period can be decomposed into two components: one derives from the changes in household characteristics, and the other from the changes in the returns on those characteristics (the gains from the endowments of the characteristics). In particular, denoting X_M as the mean characteristics of households, the growth in per capita expenditure, y, between year t and $t+1$ can be decomposed as follows:

$$Growth \approx E^{t+1}\left(logy\right) - E^t\left(logy\right) = \left(\beta^{t+1} - \beta^t\right)X_M^t + \beta^t\left(X_M^{t+1} - X_M^t\right) + R \quad (6.2)$$

Table 6.1 Descriptive statistics of the model variables

Variables	Unit	Wide panel 2002–2006, n = 904				Long panel 2002–2004–2006 n = 2,469	
		2002		2006			
		Mean	Std. dev.	Mean	Std. dev.	Mean	Std. dev.
Dependent variable							
Real expenditure per capita	'000VND	2,476.38	1,240.42	4,379.32	2,419.83	3,370.62	1,999.934
Demographic characteristics							
Household size	Person	4.704	1.607	4.442	1.643	4.554	1.618
Head ethnicity (Kinh)	Binary	0.811	0.392	0.813	0.390	0.813	0.390
Head gender (male)	Binary	0.843	0.364	0.832	0.374	0.838	0.369
Head age	Year	46.184	12.932	49.191	12.480	47.775	12.691
Heads with spouse	Binary	0.856	0.351	0.846	0.361	0.853	0.355
Proportion of children	Per cent	12.738	15.610	22.390	21.537	18.025	19.397
Proportion of elderly	Per cent	8.064	19.083	10.840	22.827	9.527	21.126
Proportion of females	Per cent	41.760	17.103	49.921	17.349	46.211	17.838
Human capital							
Head years of school	Year	6.653	3.340	6.837	3.333	6.888	3.280
Spouse years of school	Year	5.285	3.792	5.340	3.867	5.405	3.866
Technical diploma ratio	Per cent	1.736	7.934	35.731	29.150	22.846	27.780
Postsecondary ratio	Per cent	2.260	9.421	31.330	28.710	20.155	26.434

Occupation							
Head business owner/leader	Binary	0.001	0.033	0.022	0.147	0.014	0.117
Head professional	Binary	0.018	0.132	0.012	0.110	0.014	0.118
Head white collar	Binary	0.003	0.058	0.002	0.047	0.002	0.049
Head skilled worker	Binary	0.110	0.312	0.147	0.354	0.134	0.341
Agricultural production							
Total land area	m2	9,624.37	20,723.2	9,166.80	17,241.7	9,222.93	17,690.63
Rice productivity	Kg/m2	0.453	0.139	0.491	0.109	0.477	0.119
Rice crops	Kg	3,237.53	5,537.33	2,329.98	3,969.21	2,323.26	4,115.172
Selling state firms crops	Binary	0.004	0.066	0.002	0.047	0.003	0.053
Net rice producers	Binary	0.513	0.500	0.407	0.492	0.487	0.500
Household assets							
Land use rights	Binary	0.918	0.274	0.718	0.450	0.850	0.357
Total living area	m2	57.361	48.105	58.750	27.162	57.890	31.266
Electricity access	Binary	0.826	0.379	0.958	0.201	0.899	0.301
Remittance	'000VND	1,027.08	3,252.41	2,576.04	6,873.43	1,885.72	5,185.099
Commune characteristics							
Commune paved roads	Binary	0.864	0.343	0.893	0.310	0.892	0.310
Commune remote areas	Binary	0.180	0.385	0.174	0.379	0.175	0.380
Primary school	Binary	0.899	0.301	0.982	0.132	0.953	0.212
Lower secondary school	Binary	0.045	0.208	0.920	0.271	0.627	0.484

(*Continued*)

Table 6.1 (Continued)

| Variables | Unit | Wide panel 2002–2006, n = 904 | | | | Long panel 2002–2004–2006 n = 2,469 | |
| | | 2002 | | 2006 | | | |
		Mean	Std. dev.	Mean	Std. dev.	Mean	Std. dev.
Upper secondary school	Binary	0.004	0.066	0.158	0.365	0.095	0.294
Post office	Binary	0.371	0.483	0.879	0.326	0.706	0.456
Daily market	Binary	0.350	0.477	0.674	0.469	0.441	0.497
National electricity network	Binary	0.913	0.283	0.988	0.110	0.957	0.203
Clinic	Binary	0.993	0.081	0.993	0.081	0.996	0.067
Openness to trade							
Commune export labour ratio	Per cent	2.384	5.030	2.948	6.686	2.837	6.150
Commune import labour ratio	Per cent	1.062	3.496	1.173	3.693	1.204	4.017
Commune industrial labour ratio	Per cent	5.762	8.604	7.030	11.234	6.769	10.682
Province export labour ratio	Per cent	3.615	2.863	3.763	2.752	3.661	2.649
Province import labour ratio	Per cent	1.395	1.301	1.321	1.129	1.365	1.321
Province industrial labour ratio	Per cent	6.918	4.145	7.154	3.711	7.106	4.017
Total retail sales per capita	mVND	2.215	1.292	4.491	2.518	3.216	2.141

The first term on the right side of equation (6.2) explains the effect of the changes in returns over time. The second term represents the impact of the changes in household characteristics. R is the residual, which is small, on average. This decomposition is useful for assessing both the impact of household characteristics on welfare, and the returns on household endowments over a certain period. The more important question – how to explain the movement in poverty under the impacts of the characteristics of households and communes – is discussed in the following section.

Determinants of poverty: a multinomial logit model

A multinomial logit (MNL) model is used to investigate the characteristics that enable households to escape poverty, paying particular attention to trade-related factors. The MNL model analyses the probability that a given household falls into a particular poverty state over the period 2002–2006: being poor in 2002 and remaining poor in 2006 (P → P: outcome 1), being poor in 2002 and becoming nonpoor in 2006 (P → NP: outcome 2), being nonpoor in 2002 and becoming poor in 2006 (NP → P: outcome 3), and being nonpoor in 2002 and remaining nonpoor in 2006 (NP → NP: outcome 4). The probability that household i is in state j can be expressed as:

$$Prob\left(Y_i = j\right) = \frac{e^{\beta_j' x_i}}{\sum_{k=1}^{4} e^{\beta_k' x_i}}; j = 1,2,3,4 \tag{6.3}$$

where Yi is the outcome experience, the state of poverty over the period, by household i, x_i is the vector of characteristics for household i, and β_j is the vector of coefficients on the x_i vector. In other words, each state j has a set of β_k. To estimate these sets of β_k, one set must be chosen as the base category and set to zero, and the other sets estimated in relation to this benchmark set. In most similar studies, such as Glewwe *et al.* (2002), Niimi *et al.* (2007), and Justino *et al.* (2008), outcome 1 (being poor in both years) is usually chosen as the base category (all of its coefficients are set to zero).

The coefficients of the MNL model are difficult to interpret directly (Greene, 2012). Therefore, the results are usually presented in a form of marginal effects, known as relative risk ratios (RRR) or odds ratios. RRR is explained as the ratio of the probability of each outcome to the probability of the base outcome, or the impact of a variable on the relative risk ratio. For instance, the relative risk ratio for outcome 2 for a change in each variable x is calculated as:

$$\frac{Prob\left(Y = 2\right)}{Prob\left(Y = 1\right)} = e^{\beta_2' x} \tag{6.4}$$

where $e^{\beta_2'}$ is the odds ratio for a unit change in variable x. An RRR less than one means that an increase in variable x raises the probability of the household being in the base category, or decreases the probability of the household being in the relevant state, and vice versa. However, the MNL model is based on the assumption of independence from irrelevant alternatives (IIA), which states that the odds ratios in the MNL model are independent of the other alternatives (Greene, 2012). Baulch and Dat (2010), however, consider that the four unordered states of poverty transition used in the MNL model are ordered states in nature. Even with these likely shortcomings, the MNL model is still a useful tool to analyse poverty dynamics.

Data

The study uses the VHLSSs from 2002, 2004, and 2006, with their sample sizes of about 45,945 households over 3,063 communes/wards, which are representative of regions, urban areas, rural areas, and provinces. However, about 30,000 households of the VHLSS 2002 and 9,000 households of the VHLSS 2004 and 2006 cover data on income and expenditure. The surveys consist of two types of data: households and communes. The data are organised into many sections, with each containing a certain subject, such as demographic traits, income and expenditure, education, health, employment, agricultural production, or communes. This study compiles the data from different sets of questionnaires to gather relevant variables. The samples used in the analysis of the study include 19,881 households for the VHLSS 2002, 4,464 households for the VHLSS 2004, and 4,384 households for the VHLSS 2006. According to Le and Pham (2009), data from these surveys can be used to form longitudinal panels, with 3,931 households common to both the 2002 and 2004 surveys, 4,193 households common to both the 2004 and 2006 surveys, and 1,844 households common to the 2002, 2004, and 2006 surveys. These panels constitute the short and wide kinds of panel data (Hill *et al.*, 2007; Kennedy, 2008; Greene, 2012). From these panel data sets, this study constructs the wide form and the long form of the panel data used for the analysis, encompassing 904 and 823 rural households, respectively.

6.3   Analysis of results

The results of the decomposition are first analysed to provide an overview of the determinants of the growth of household welfare in the model of microdeterminants of growth. This model then uses the wide panel data to analyse the effects of trade-related variables, with a focus on employment. These trade-related variables are also examined in the fixed and random effects models, using the long panel data. Finally, poverty dynamics are analysed using the multinomial logit model and the wide panel data.

Decomposition of growth of household expenditure: cross-sectional estimates

The estimates of the determinants and decomposition of the growth of household welfare aim at analysing the general factors that affect household welfare.

The microdeterminants of the growth of household welfare are estimated using the cross-sectional data drawn from the VHLSS 2002 and VHLSS 2006, to compare the impacts of the household characteristics on rural household welfare. Table 6.2 presents the results of the OLS estimates of the cross-sectional regressions for equation (6.1). Overall, most of the coefficients are statistically significant and have expected signs. With the mean of the variance inflation factor (VIF) being 4.75 for the 2002 regression and 9.1 for the 2006 regression, multicollinearity is not a major problem for the models. The use of robust standard errors also helps the regressions to eliminate the issue of heteroskedasticity. These results help to illustrate the effects of household and commune characteristics on welfare. The coefficients explain percentage changes in per capita expenditure associated with household characteristics.

The groups of variables pointed out in the literature are the important determinants of household welfare. These are demographic characteristics, education, employment, agricultural production, assets, geography, and commune infrastructure. The demographic attributes (household size, ethnicity, and household composition) have expected and consistent effects on welfare in both results. The insignificance of gender of household heads may indicate that gender inequality tends to be minor in Vietnam; women do play an increasing role in the society. Most women are employed in the textile and garment sectors, which absorb a considerable labour force. As expected, household size and the dependent ratio tend to mitigate welfare significantly. An additional member in a household, on average, decreased household expenditure per capita by 7.8 per cent and 6.4 per cent for the two regressions, respectively, holding all other things constant. For household composition, the negative impact of dependent ratios appears to rise from 2002 to 2006. Importantly, belonging to Kinh, the major ethnicity in Vietnam, has a considerable impact on welfare. The coefficient of 0.2162 attached to the variable 'heads' ethnicity (Kinh)' in the 2006 regression indicates that per capita expenditure of Kinh households was typically 24.1 per cent higher than that of other households.[3] This suggests income inequality amongst ethnicities, favouring Kinh, with the inequality effect tending to increase slightly over the period.

Human capital, in terms of education levels and especially technical training, has a significant and consistent effect on household welfare over the period. One year added to heads' years of school typically increased expenditure per head by 2.1 per cent in 2002 and 3.1 per cent in 2006, *ceteris paribus*. For heads' spouses, the effect is smaller; 1.6 per cent in 2002 and 3.4 per cent in 2006. As predicted, heads' employment has a significant impact on welfare: per capita expenditure of households where heads were skilled labourers was 11.7 per cent higher than that of the unskilled in 2006, whereas this ratio for heads as professionals was 21.4 per cent in the same year. Hence, these effects appear to increase by the level of qualification.

Agricultural production is the main activity in rural areas. The results show that having land has a significant, positive impact on welfare. The small returns on land may reflect low agricultural productivity. The inclusion of the rice distribution dummy aims to take into consideration the impact of selling crops to state-owned food enterprises as an important distributional channel. This variable is

Table 6.2 OLS estimates of the impacts of household characteristics on real per capita expenditure

Independent variable	2002		2006	
[Cross–sectional regressions, VHLSS 2002 and 2006] [Dependent variable: log of RPCE]				
	Coefficient	*p–value*	*Coefficient*	*p–value*
Constant term	6.7946***	0.000	7.7024***	0.000
Demographic Characteristics				
Household size	–0.0777***	0.000	–0.0637***	0.000
Head ethnicity (Kinh)	0.1955***	0.000	0.2162***	0.000
Head gender (male)	0.0089	0.447	–0.0165	0.501
Head age	0.0248***	0.000	0.0053	0.138
Head age square	–0.0002***	0.000	0.0000	0.283
Heads with spouse	–0.0412***	0.005	–0.1736**	0.016
Proportion of children	–0.0016***	0.000	–0.0051***	0.000
Proportion of elderly	–0.0012***	0.000	–0.0017***	0.000
Proportion of females	0.0009***	0.000	–0.0004	0.193
Human capital (reference is no education)				
Head years of school	0.0214***	0.000	0.0313***	0.000
Head primary school	0.0257**	0.029	0.0483	0.378
Head lower secondary school	0.0084	0.636	0.0108	0.852
Head upper secondary school	0.0363	0.160	–0.0066	0.920
Head university	0.1868***	0.000	0.0283	0.627
Head technical school	0.1207***	0.000	0.0735***	0.001
Spouse years of school	0.0163***	0.000	0.0343***	0.000
Spouse primary school	–0.0224*	0.072	–0.0650	0.313
Spouse lower secondary school	–0.0374**	0.048	–0.1285*	0.059
Spouse upper secondary school	–0.0193	0.495	–0.1760**	0.023
Spouse university	0.2716***	0.000	–0.1016	0.150
Spouse technical school	0.1494***	0.000	0.1541***	0.000
Occupation (reference is unskilled head)				
Head leader	0.1691***	0.002	0.1615***	0.000
Head professional	0.1755***	0.000	0.1942***	0.000
Head white collar	0.1309***	0.000	0.1589**	0.011
Head skilled work	0.1060***	0.000	0.1106***	0.000

Agricultural production

Total land area	0.0000***	0.000	0.0000***	0.000
Net rice producers	−0.0147**	0.013	0.0328**	0.011
Selling state firms crops	−0.0182	0.660	0.0501	0.744
Household assets				
Land use rights	−0.0004	0.971	−0.0282**	0.039
Total living area	0.0016***	0.000	0.0039***	0.000
Electricity access	0.1771***	0.000	0.0992***	0.001
Own drinking water tap	0.2327***	0.000	0.0714***	0.009
Community characteristics				
Proximity to paved roads	−0.0034***	0.004	0.0012*	0.087
Remote areas	−0.0523***	0.000	−0.0918***	0.000
Primary school	−0.1553***	0.000	−0.0357	0.421
Lower secondary school	−0.1369***	0.000	0.0050	0.839
Upper secondary school	−0.1383***	0.001	0.0233	0.171
Post office	−0.0095	0.152	−0.0279*	0.093
Daily market	0.0315***	0.000	−0.0091	0.439
National electricity grid	−0.0270**	0.040	−0.0448	0.280
Clinic	−0.0572***	0.003	−0.0142	0.781
Geography (reference is North Central)				
Red River Delta	0.0969***	0.000	0.1777***	0.000
Northeast	0.1388***	0.000	0.1303***	0.000
Northwest	0.1181***	0.000	0.0480	0.159
South central coast	0.1023***	0.000	0.1759***	0.000
Central highlands	0.1339***	0.000	0.2138***	0.000
Southeast	0.3719***	0.000	0.3568***	0.000
Mekong River Delta	0.3950***	0.000	0.3381***	0.000
R^2	0.425		0.474	
Number of observations	19,881		4,384	

Note: ***, **, and * significant at 1 per cent, 5 per cent, and 10 per cent level, respectively.

nevertheless insignificant. In fact, most farmers were unable to sell crops directly to the state food firms, the legitimate rice exporters, which are expected to help farmers to receive more profits from their crops. The results of the housing features, such as total living areas, access to electricity, and safe drinking water (the proxies for household assets), also show important influences on rural welfare. Commune characteristics, however, play almost no role in explaining rural welfare, likely mirroring slow improvement in rural public infrastructure. In the results, location affects household welfare considerably. Households in remote areas and north central Vietnam appear to be worse off than those in other regions. Households residing in the southeast or the Mekong Delta River are much better off.

The results of decomposition presented in Table 6.3 demonstrate that the changes in returns to demographic variables are negative, accounting for the largest share of the change in per capita expenditure over the period. The rise in dependent ratios and household size could be a reason for the fall in welfare. A decrease of returns correlates with increased head age, which suggests that households with younger heads fare better. Compared with other household characteristics, demographic characteristics contribute considerably to the drop in standards of living over the period. Among variables that raise welfare, education contributes the most. In particular, the return from investment in education (school years) of both heads and spouses increases over time, and spouses' education brings more return than that of heads. In regard to occupation, the returns on employment change very little over the period. Particularly, professional and skilled works contribute most to the return on employment.

Amongst agricultural variables, the returns on households as net rice producers increase over time. The returns on acquiring land and selling state food firms crops have become stable over the period. In reality, land is becoming less available for cultivation, to make room for inefficient industrial areas and apartments that are part of the growth of foreign investment. Added to this, many farmers withdraw from farming due to loss or unprofitability. These could be the reasons for the decrease in returns on owning the land use rights certificate, one of the most valuable household assets. As illustrated in Table 6.3, total living areas contribute significantly to the increase of welfare over time, compared with access to electricity and possession of a drinking water tap.

The returns on commune schools, as well as on health centres, rise, while those on local market, post office, and power public services fall over the period. Primary schools in particular play an important role in welfare improvement. The results also suggest that households in the Red River Delta, South Central Coast, and central highlands are better off than those in the other regions. The decrease in the return on living in the Mekong River Delta is worth noting, since this region produces the largest rice crops in Vietnam. Overall, changes in the return on household characteristics are relatively small over the period, with education the most important determinant of household welfare. As analysed in the following sections, trade liberalisation is also expected to improve welfare.

Model of microeconomic determinants of growth: a wide panel analysis

This section makes use of the microdeterminants of growth and the wide-form panel data between 2002 and 2006 to explain the change in household

Table 6.3 Decomposition of growth of per capita expenditure, 2002–2006

Independent variable	2002		2006		Return	Characteristics
	Coefficient	Mean	Coefficient	Mean		
Constant term	6.7946	–	7.7024	–	0.9079	0.0000
Demographic total					-0.7280	0.0106
Household size	-0.0777	4.6429	-0.0637	4.4491	0.0648	0.0151
Head ethnicity (Kinh)	0.1955	0.8111	0.2162	0.7828	0.0168	-0.0055
Head gender (male)	0.0089	0.8171	-0.0165	0.8298	-0.0207	0.0001
Head age	0.0248	47.1439	0.0053	48.1090	-0.9191	0.0239
Head age square	-0.0002	2421.77	0.0000	2481.80	0.3439	-0.0108
Heads with spouse	-0.0412	0.8284	-0.1736	0.8451	-0.1097	-0.0007
Proportion of children	-0.0016	12.0315	-0.0051	23.5525	-0.0419	-0.0188
Proportion of elderly	-0.0012	11.2435	-0.0017	10.8681	-0.0062	0.0004
Proportion of females	0.0009	43.0431	-0.0004	50.9906	-0.0560	0.0069
Human capital total					0.1120	0.2007
Head years of school	0.0214	6.3946	0.0313	6.8070	0.0636	0.0088
Head primary school	0.0257	0.2530	0.0483	0.2719	0.0057	0.0005
Head lower secondary school	0.0084	0.2941	0.0108	0.3588	0.0007	0.0005
Head upper secondary school	0.0363	0.0677	-0.0066	0.0933	-0.0029	0.0009
Head university	0.1868	0.0128	0.0283	0.2660	-0.0020	0.0473
Head technical school	0.1207	0.0427	0.0735	0.3244	-0.0020	0.0340

(Continued)

Table 6.3 (Continued)

Independent variable	2002		2006		Return	Characteristics
	Coefficient	Mean	Coefficient	Mean		
Spouse years of school	0.0163	4.9810	0.0343	5.3691	0.0894	0.0063
Spouse primary school	-0.0224	0.2217	-0.0650	0.2443	-0.0094	-0.0005
Spouse lower secondary school	-0.0374	0.2346	-0.1285	0.2849	-0.0214	-0.0019
Spouse upper secondary school	-0.0193	0.0423	-0.1760	0.0552	-0.0066	-0.0002
Spouse university	0.2716	0.0083	-0.1016	0.2543	-0.0031	0.0668
Spouse technical school	0.1494	0.0255	0.1541	0.2808	0.0001	0.0381
Occupation total					0.0013	0.0050
Head leader	0.1691	0.0023	0.1615	0.0219	0.0000	0.0033
Head professional	0.1755	0.0241	0.1942	0.0135	0.0005	-0.0019
Head white collar	0.1309	0.0121	0.1589	0.0059	0.0003	-0.0008
Head skilled work	0.1060	0.1141	0.1106	0.1551	0.0005	0.0043
Agricultural production total					0.0210	-0.0006
Total land area	0.0000	8471.08	0.0000	8169.04	0.0011	-0.0010
Net rice producers	-0.0147	0.4120	0.0328	0.3937	0.0196	0.0003
Selling state firms crops	-0.0182	0.0042	0.0501	0.0021	0.0003	0.0000
House assets total					0.0335	0.0345
Land use rights	-0.0004	0.9004	-0.0282	0.7240	-0.0251	0.0001
Total living area	0.0016	55.1484	0.0039	59.4040	0.1261	0.0069
Electricity access	0.1771	0.8129	0.0992	0.9437	-0.0634	0.0232
Own drinking water tap	0.2327	0.0259	0.0714	0.0447	-0.0042	0.0044
Community characteristics total					0.1074	-0.1567
Proximity to paved roads	-0.0034	0.6190	0.0012	0.5215	0.0028	0.0003
Remote areas	-0.0523	0.2070	-0.0918	0.1975	-0.0082	0.0005

Primary school	-0.1553	0.8337	-0.0357	0.9751	0.0997	-0.0220
Lower secondary school	-0.1369	0.0458	0.0050	0.9181	0.0065	-0.1194
Upper secondary school	-0.1383	0.0037	0.0233	0.1286	0.0006	-0.0173
Post office	-0.0095	0.3609	-0.0279	0.8791	-0.0066	-0.0049
Daily market	0.0315	0.3489	-0.0091	0.6277	-0.0142	0.0088
National electricity grid	-0.0270	0.9129	-0.0448	0.9772	-0.0162	-0.0017
Clinic	-0.0572	0.9751	-0.0142	0.9920	0.0430	-0.0010
Geography total					0.0152	-0.0247
Red River Delta	0.0969	0.2426	0.1777	0.2858	0.0196	0.0042
Northeast	0.1388	0.1737	0.1303	0.1975	-0.0015	0.0033
Northwest	0.1181	0.0440	0.0480	0.0591	-0.0031	0.0018
South central coast	0.1023	0.0829	0.1759	0.0972	0.0061	0.0015
Central highlands	0.1339	0.0690	0.2138	0.0427	0.0055	-0.0035
Southeast	0.3719	0.0769	0.3568	0.0333	-0.0012	-0.0162
Mekong River Delta	0.3950	0.1804	0.3381	0.1407	-0.0103	-0.0157
Grand total					0.4702	0.0687
Change in log expenditure					0.5389	0.5389
Percentage change					0.8725	0.1275

Note: The results of decomposition in this table are estimated using the results of Table 6.2.

expenditure per head under the employment effects of trade liberalisation. Panel data can generate more precise estimates of the change in household expenditure than single, cross-sectional data (Glewwe and Hall, 1998; Glewwe *et al.*, 2002; Baltagi, 2005). The regression of the change in per capita expenditure on household characteristics in 2002 operates as a base model, covering initial and predetermined characteristics. More importantly, these characteristics are likely to be exogenous to the change in the dependent variable (log of RPCE). Compared with the models in the previous section, the base model has some changes. The set of dummy variables representing head and spouse education is replaced by the proportions of technical and post-secondary education in a household, due to the considerable reduction in the panel sample. A similar change is also made to dummy variables of occupation. Additions to the model include some variables of agricultural production and other household incomes such as rice crops, rice productivity, and remittance, because they are exogenous to the change in per capita expenditure over the period. The base model is then added to, one at a time, with the change variables relating to trade and employment explained in the methods section.

In the base regression results (Model 1, Table 6.4), the difference in location has a significant impact on rural welfare change. Households in remote areas and in north central are consistently worse off, whereas those residing in the Red River Delta, central highlands, and Mekong River Delta are better off, as expected. Compared with the north central region, per capita expenditure in the above regions is higher on average: 10.7 per cent for the Red River Delta, 26 per cent for the central highlands, and 20.1 per cent for the Mekong River Delta, holding all other things constant. Spouse education also has a significant impact on welfare improvement: an additional school year of spouse's education typically increased the change in per capita expenditure by 1.7 per cent over the period. Other variables of education have no effect on welfare change. Concerning occupation, skilled heads have no impact on welfare change. As expected, the higher the unskilled to household adults ratio, the lower welfare improvement is. With respect to household assets, only land use rights significantly affect the change in per capita expenditure. For commune variables, only remote areas and upper secondary schools have expected and significant effects on welfare change. Demographic characteristics either have no impact or have unexpected impacts on welfare change. Generally, not many household characteristics significantly affect rural welfare improvement over time, perhaps due to the somewhat small panel sample.

Compared with the base regression, the regressions with the change variables are better in terms of the explanatory power of the model (R^2). The impacts of other variables are almost the same as those in the base regression. For instance, the change in rice crops over the period is significant, but the impact of this variable is relatively small. Most importantly, the change in rice productivity has a significant impact on the change in per capita expenditure. On average and *ceteris paribus*, a one-unit change in rice productivity increased the change in per capita expenditure by 45.3 per cent, other things being unchanged.

Table 6.4 OLS estimates of trade effects on changes in real per capita expenditure

[Wide-form panel VHLSS 2002–2006]

[Dependent variable: change of log of RPCE]

Independent variable	Model 1 (base)	Model 2	Model 3	Model 4	Model 5	Model 6
Constant term	0.1465 (0.580)	0.1238 (0.638)	-0.0136 (0.959)	0.1723 (0.521)	0.1530 (0.557)	0.1685 (0.526)
Demographic						
Log of household size	0.1872*** (0.001)	0.1858*** (0.001)	0.1889*** (0.000)	0.1884*** (0.001)	0.1925*** (0.000)	0.1969*** (0.000)
Head ethnicity (Kinh)	-0.0454 (0.360)	-0.0441 (0.364)	-0.0724 (0.143)	-0.0447 (0.367)	-0.0433 (0.385)	-0.0356 (0.475)
Head gender (male)	-0.0107 (0.892)	-0.0029 (0.971)	-0.0006 (0.994)	-0.0065 (0.934)	-0.0049 (0.950)	0.0060 (0.935)
Head age	0.0097 (0.243)	0.0103 (0.216)	0.0117 (0.161)	0.0095 (0.254)	0.0092 (0.266)	0.0082 (0.322)
Head age square	-0.0001 (0.319)	-0.0001 (0.297)	-0.0001 (0.202)	-0.0001 (0.333)	-0.0001 (0.341)	-0.0001 (0.396)
Heads with spouse	-0.0943 (0.293)	-0.0956 (0.281)	-0.1158 (0.195)	-0.0960 (0.280)	-0.1017 (0.251)	-0.1113 (0.195)
Proportion of children	0.0028** (0.026)	0.0027** (0.029)	0.0026** (0.035)	0.0028** (0.025)	0.0029** (0.018)	0.0028** (0.024)
Proportion of elderly	0.0012 (0.333)	0.0011 (0.363)	0.0015 (0.242)	0.0012 (0.343)	0.0012 (0.351)	0.0013 (0.319)

(*Continued*)

Table 6.4 (Continued)

Independent variable	Model 1 (base)	Model 2	Model 3	Model 4	Model 5	Model 6
Human capital						
Head years of school	0.0055 (0.354)	0.0046 (0.437)	0.0044 (0.461)	0.0056 (0.349)	0.0050 (0.403)	0.0054 (0.363)
Spouse years of school	0.0166*** (0.005)	0.0161*** (0.007)	0.0166*** (0.005)	0.0165*** (0.006)	0.0173*** (0.004)	0.0173*** (0.004)
Technical diploma ratio	0.0017 (0.693)	0.0017 (0.704)	0.0018 (0.693)	0.0018 (0.678)	0.0021 (0.633)	0.0019 (0.646)
Postsecondary ratio	-0.0030 (0.466)	-0.0028 (0.489)	-0.0028 (0.492)	-0.0030 (0.456)	-0.0032 (0.419)	-0.0032 (0.399)
Occupation						
Head skilled work	-0.0557 (0.287)	-0.0461 (0.367)	-0.0426 (0.411)	-0.0513 (0.329)	-0.0452 (0.389)	-0.0481 (0.360)
Unskilled-to-adults ratio	-0.0011*** (0.008)	-0.0011** (0.011)	-0.0011** (0.011)	-0.0012*** (0.007)	-0.0012*** (0.004)	-0.0012*** (0.006)
Agricultural production						
Total land area	-0.0000*** (0.001)	-0.0000*** (0.001)	-0.0000*** (0.001)	-0.0000*** (0.000)	-0.0000*** (0.001)	-0.0000*** (0.001)
Rice productivity	-0.0708 (0.516)	-0.0518 (0.632)	0.2759* (0.078)	-0.0784 (0.474)	-0.0783 (0.474)	-0.0693 (0.523)
Rice crops	0.0000 (0.661)	0.0000** (0.014)	0.0000 (0.847)	0.0000 (0.674)	0.0000 (0.725)	0.0000 (0.729)
Selling state firms crops	-0.1712 (0.537)	-0.1724 (0.505)	-0.1807 (0.518)	-0.1541 (0.567)	-0.1661 (0.542)	-0.1479 (0.582)
Net rice producers	-0.0248 (0.427)	-0.0274 (0.379)	-0.0269 (0.388)	-0.0248 (0.426)	-0.0224 (0.476)	-0.0289 (0.352)

House assets and other incomes

Land use rights	0.0899*	0.0928*	0.0833*	0.0849*	0.0927*	0.0877*
	(0.060)	(0.056)	(0.079)	(0.077)	(0.054)	(0.066)
Total living area	-0.0002	-0.0002	-0.0001	-0.0002	-0.0002	-0.0002
	(0.444)	(0.531)	(0.579)	(0.436)	(0.385)	(0.498)
Electricity access	-0.0514	-0.0553	-0.0496	-0.0497	-0.0577	-0.0545
	(0.295)	(0.249)	(0.311)	(0.312)	(0.236)	(0.265)
Remittance	-0.0000***	-0.0000***	-0.0000***	-0.0000***	-0.0000***	-0.0000***
	(0.000)	(0.000)	(0.001)	(0.000)	(0.000)	(0.000)
Community characteristics						
Paved roads	0.0464	0.0433	0.0432	0.0439	0.0523	0.0480
	(0.273)	(0.303)	(0.305)	(0.300)	(0.220)	(0.258)
Remote areas	-0.1234***	-0.1331***	-0.1146***	-0.1214***	-0.1207***	-0.1154***
	(0.003)	(0.001)	(0.006)	(0.004)	(0.004)	(0.006)
Primary school	0.0773	0.0769	0.0610	0.0784	0.0735	0.0757
	(0.177)	(0.175)	(0.280)	(0.173)	(0.204)	(0.183)
Lower secondary school	0.0696	0.0582	0.0397	0.0768	0.0726	0.0766
	(0.389)	(0.480)	(0.625)	(0.345)	(0.368)	(0.342)
Upper secondary school	0.2707*	0.2634*	0.2851*	0.2866*	0.2202	0.2684*
	(0.077)	(0.083)	(0.061)	(0.065)	(0.170)	(0.081)
Post office	-0.0164	-0.0207	-0.0154	-0.0152	-0.0252	-0.0127
	(0.617)	(0.526)	(0.640)	(0.643)	(0.440)	(0.697)
Daily market	0.0110	0.0037	0.0080	0.0090	0.0170	0.0075
	(0.766)	(0.921)	(0.828)	(0.806)	(0.644)	(0.836)

(*Continued*)

Table 6.4 (Continued)

Independent variable	Model 1 (base)	Model 2	Model 3	Model 4	Model 5	Model 6
National electricity grid	-0.0016 (0.981)	0.0003 (0.996)	0.0105 (0.879)	-0.0022 (0.975)	-0.0031 (0.964)	-0.0001 (0.999)
Clinic	-0.1462 (0.203)	-0.1535 (0.174)	-0.1519 (0.160)	-0.1633 (0.165)	-0.1321 (0.222)	-0.1539 (0.192)
Geography (reference is North Central)						
Red River Delta	0.1021** (0.020)	0.1047** (0.017)	0.0877** (0.047)	0.1018** (0.020)	0.1034** (0.017)	0.0946** (0.030)
Northeast	0.0169 (0.700)	0.0215 (0.623)	0.0101 (0.818)	0.0215 (0.625)	0.0095 (0.832)	0.0213 (0.630)
Northwest	0.1149 (0.124)	0.1153 (0.120)	0.1116 (0.126)	0.1157 (0.121)	0.1104 (0.140)	0.1231 (0.103)
South central coast	0.0299 (0.589)	0.0288 (0.603)	0.0187 (0.739)	0.0346 (0.533)	0.0268 (0.629)	0.0328 (0.557)
Central highlands	0.2311*** (0.002)	0.2301*** (0.002)	0.2270*** (0.002)	0.2322*** (0.002)	0.2260*** (0.003)	0.2272*** (0.003)
Southeast	0.1399* (0.092)	0.1361 (0.104)	0.1602* (0.063)	0.1393* (0.091)	0.1255 (0.137)	0.1310 (0.111)
Mekong River Delta	0.1835*** (0.002)	0.1386** (0.029)	0.1797*** (0.003)	0.1833*** (0.002)	0.1860*** (0.002)	0.1951*** (0.001)
Change variables						
Rice output change		0.0000*** (0.006)				

	(1)	(2)	(3)	(4)	(5)	(6)
Rice productivity change			0.4530*** (0.002)			
Change of commune ratio of export employment				0.0026 (0.237)		
Change of commune ratio of import employment					0.0066* (0.066)	
Change of commune ratio of manufacturing employment						0.0034** (0.047)
R^2	0.120	0.130	0.130	0.122	0.126	0.127
Number of observations	904	904	904	904	904	904

Notes: – ***, **, and * significant at 1 per cent, 5 per cent, and 10 per cent level, respectively.

- p-values are in parentheses.

The inclusion of employment in the export and import sectors at the commune level aims to relate trade liberalisation to welfare. In these two trade employment variables, only employment in the import-competing sectors has a significant and expected impact.

Rural household heads' low education is actually a major hindrance to export or import employment. In fact, not many export or import firms build factories in rural areas because of poor infrastructure. The change in the ratio of commune industrial employment is significantly and positively associated with welfare change, as expected. Although the number of export or import firms is likely to be small in rural regions, other local manufacturing enterprises could help to improve rural welfare. In summary, the variables measuring the employment effects of trade liberalisation have a positive effect on welfare improvement in rural areas, suggesting a positive relationship between trade liberalisation and poverty. The role of trade and employment will be more important if they can help the poor to escape poverty.

Fixed effects model

This analysis has used the wide panel data set over the period 2002–2006 to examine the impacts of trade liberalisation on rural welfare. The analysis goes a step further by exploring a long panel data set to test fixed effects. The fixed effects analysis uses a panel data set of 823 rural households over three waves of the VHLSSs: 2002, 2004, and 2006. This section begins by comparing the pooled OLS model with the fixed effects model, using dummy variables or the least square dummy variable (LSDV) model. The latter uses a set of time dummy variables, with 2002 as the reference. It then discusses the use of the fixed effects model and the random effects model in examining the impacts of trade liberalisation on welfare.

Pooled OLS versus LSDV fixed effects model

The purpose of using the fixed effects in the model of microdeterminants of growth to investigate the employment effects is to tackle the potential problem of observed and unobserved heterogeneity that may arise in the pooled OLS model. The estimates of the determinants of rural household welfare using the pooled OLS model and the LSDV fixed effects model are presented in Table 6.5. The explanatory variables are almost the same as those in the previous models. Each coefficient explains a percentage change in per capita expenditure associated with a household characteristic. These household characteristics on average accounted for about 56 per cent and 59 per cent of the change in per capita expenditure for the pooled OLS model and the LSDV fixed effects model, respectively. Therefore, the LSDV fixed effects model is a little better than the pooled OLS model. The impacts of household demographic characteristics on welfare are almost the same in the two models. Household size and the dependent ratios have a negative impact on per capita expenditure, head age is positively associated with welfare,

Table 6.5 Estimates of the pooled OLS and fixed effects models for the impacts of trade liberalisation on real per capita expenditure

	[Long-form panel 2002–2006] [Dependent variable: log of RPCE]			
Independent variable	*Pooled OLS model*		*LSDV fixed effects model*	
	Coefficient	*p-value*	*Coefficient*	*p-value*
Constant term	6.6723***	0.000	6.9150***	0.000
Demographic characteristics				
Household size	–0.0883***	0.000	–0.0804***	0.000
Head ethnicity (Kinh)	0.1169***	0.000	0.1450***	0.000
Head gender (male)	0.0126	0.715	–0.0062	0.854
Head age	0.0257***	0.000	0.0193***	0.000
Head age square	–0.0002***	0.000	–0.0001***	0.001
Heads with spouse	–0.0604	0.150	–0.0475	0.246
Proportion of children	–0.0021***	0.000	–0.0027***	0.000
Proportion of elderly	–0.0022***	0.000	–0.0018***	0.001
Proportion of females	0.0005	0.315	0.0000	0.933
Human capital				
Head years of school	0.0190***	0.000	0.0177***	0.000
Spouse years of school	0.0173***	0.000	0.0163***	0.000
Technical diploma ratio	0.0021***	0.004	0.0015**	0.034
Postsecondary ratio	–0.0012	0.128	–0.0016**	0.050
Occupation (reference is the unskilled)				
Head leader	0.2891***	0.000	0.2406***	0.000
Head professional	0.2677***	0.000	0.2810***	0.000
Head white collar	0.2032**	0.012	0.2057***	0.010
Head skilled work	0.0762***	0.000	0.0761***	0.000
Head wage work	–0.0213	0.258	–0.0287	0.108
Head self–farmed business	–0.0448	0.113	–0.0528*	0.057
Head self–business, nonfarm	0.1234***	0.000	0.1179***	0.000
Agricultural production				
Total land area	0.0000***	0.000	0.0000***	0.000
Rice productivity	0.2826***	0.000	0.1907***	0.002
Selling state firms crops	0.1241	0.489	0.1647	0.369
Net rice producers	0.0039	0.810	0.0304*	0.057

(*Continued*)

Table 6.5 (Continued)

Independent variable	Pooled OLS model		LSDV fixed effects model	
	Coefficient	p-value	Coefficient	p-value
House assets and other incomes				
Land use rights	–0.0484**	0.020	–0.0062	0.757
Total living area	0.0027***	0.000	0.0027***	0.000
Access to electricity	0.1472***	0.000	0.1200***	0.000
Remittance	0.0000***	0.000	0.0000***	0.000
Community characteristics				
Paved roads	–0.0026	0.913	0.0092	0.690
Remote areas	–0.0254	0.249	–0.0388*	0.072
Primary school	0.0319	0.370	–0.0147	0.664
Lower secondary school	0.1844***	0.000	0.0505*	0.084
Upper secondary school	0.0758***	0.002	0.0566**	0.018
Post office	–0.0060	0.751	–0.0307	0.108
Daily market	0.0501***	0.001	0.0053	0.741
National electricity network	–0.0118	0.787	–0.0159	0.700
Clinic	–0.1795***	0.004	–0.1684***	0.010
Geography (reference is North Central)				
Red River Delta	0.0948***	0.000	0.1360***	0.000
Northeast	0.1324***	0.000	0.1238***	0.000
Northwest	0.0810	0.102	0.0695	0.147
South central coast	0.0968***	0.002	0.1184***	0.000
Central highlands	0.1410***	0.000	0.1628***	0.000
Southeast	0.2380***	0.000	0.2997***	0.000
Mekong River Delta	0.3335***	0.000	0.3738***	0.000
Trade and employment				
Commune ratio of export employment	0.0011	0.358	0.0006	0.626
Commune ratio of import employment	0.0047**	0.013	0.0054***	0.002
Commune ratio of industrial employment	0.0016*	0.065	0.0019**	0.022
Province trade per capita	0.0348***	0.000	0.0153***	0.000
Time dummy (reference is year 2002)				
Year 2004			0.1477***	0.000
Year 2006			0.3827***	0.000
Adjusted R²	0.556		0.588	
Number of observations	2,469		2,469	

Note: ***, **, and * significant at 1 per cent, 5 per cent, and 10 per cent level, respectively.

and head gender has, again, no impact. The effects of education on welfare in the LSDV fixed effects model are similar to those in the pooled OLS model. The school years of heads and spouses and the proportion of technical or vocational training have a positive impact on welfare. However, the proportion of post-secondary education has a negative effect in the LSDV fixed effects model, and no impact in the pooled OLS model. This suggests that technical training is more important than general education for welfare improvement in rural areas.

In the LSDV fixed effects model, the dummy variables used to explain the impacts of occupation are a little better than those in the pooled OLS model. Heads working as leaders, professionals, white collars, and skilled workers appear to improve welfare, compared with the unskilled. Heads involved in self-business also fare better than the others. In terms of agricultural production, total land areas and rice productivity play an important role in welfare improvement. As with the previous models, selling crops to state food enterprises has no impact on per capita expenditure. In the results, the positive significant impact of household net rice producers who most likely had surplus in rice production and sold their crops makes the difference between the two models. The effect is more obvious in the LSDV fixed effects model. These results also demonstrate that household assets and other incomes positively affect welfare, as expected. In the pooled OLS regression, having a certification of land use rights, although significant, is unexpectedly negative. It is insignificant in the LSDV fixed effects model, however.

The impacts of commune characteristics are in contrast to expectation: communes with paved roads, grid electricity, a clinic, and a post office play no part in explaining welfare. However, commune secondary schools have a positive impact on welfare, and in the pooled OLS model, commune daily markets play an important role in improving welfare. As expected, households living in remote communes are worse off than those in other communes, as shown in the LSDV fixed effects model. Residing in different regions also affects welfare. The results suggest that households in all regions, except the northwest, are better off than those in the north central region. Hence, the location effect in this regression is roughly similar to those in the previous regressions.

Of special interest in Table 6.5 is the impact of the variables measuring trade and employment. Both results demonstrate that the commune ratios of employment in the import-competing sectors and the manufacturing sectors have a significant positive impact on welfare. These results are consistent with those in the regressions analysing the impacts of trade liberalisation on welfare growth using the wide panel data. In these results, using total sale value per capita to measure local trade transaction also shows a significant positive effect on welfare. Finally, the commune ratio of employment in the export sectors is insignificant. As noted, manufacturing export sectors need highly skilled workers, and farmers are unlikely to meet this labour demand. Generally, the results of the two models are roughly similar. However, if the fixed effects exist in the data, the fixed effects model will be preferred. The *F* test for fixed effects based on loss of 'goodness of fit' for a significant group fixed effect can help to identify whether the fixed effects are present in the panel data or not (Greene, 2012).

$$F(n-1, nT-n-k) = \frac{\dfrac{\left(R^2_{LSDV} - R^2_{Pooled}\right)}{n-1}}{\dfrac{\left(1 - R^2_{LSDV}\right)}{nT-n-k}} \qquad (6.5)$$

The *F* ratio is 98.2, which is large enough to reject the null hypothesis that all LSDV parameters equal zero, except the reference dummy; thus, the fixed effects model significantly increases goodness of fit. Therefore, the LSDV fixed effects model is preferred to the pooled OLS model in terms of explaining the impacts of trade and employment and of econometric criteria. The comparison is also extended to discuss the alternative selection between fixed effects and random effects models.

Within fixed versus random effects models

The study also estimates the within fixed effects and random effects models. Unlike the LSDV fixed effects model, the within fixed effects model does not use dummy variables. Instead, it uses the deviations from the means of the group, or the time period. The fixed effects model allows individual effects to be correlated with regressors, whereas the random effects model assumes that individual effects are not correlated with any regressor. The fixed effects model also cannot estimate the effects of the time-invariant variables (Baltagi, 2005); these are the variables, such as ethnicity, gender, school years, and living areas, whose values are unchanged over the period 2002–2006. The random effects model can include these time-invariant variables. The Hausman test can determine which model is more appropriate.

The analysis of fixed effects and random effects models first tests the poolability of panel data, using the Chow test extension (Baltagi, 2008). The poolability test examines whether the panel data are poolable or not, so that the slopes of regressors are the same across the total data period from 2002 to 2006. The null hypothesis is that the slope of a regressor is the same, regardless of individuals, for all *k* regressors: $H_o: \beta_{ik} = \beta_k$. Note that slopes are constant in fixed and random effects models; only intercepts and error variances change.

$$F\left[(n-1)(k+1), n(T-k-1)\right] = \frac{\dfrac{\left(e'e - \sum e'_i e_i\right)}{(n-1)(k+1)}}{\dfrac{\sum e'_i e_i}{n(T-k-1)}} \qquad (6.6)$$

where $e'e$ is the sum of squared errors (SSE) of the pooled OLS, $e'_i e_i$ is the SSE of the pooled OLS for group *i*, *n* is the group sample ($n = 823$), and *T* is the observed period ($T = 3$). If the null hypothesis is rejected, the panel data are not poolable. In this case, each wave of data in the panel may have its own slopes of regressors, and fixed or random effects are no longer appealing. The test is conducted by regressing OLS models for each wave of data in the panel. The null hypothesis is that all slopes of regressors are the same across the period, H_o: β_{2002} = β_{2004} = β_{2006}. The F-statistic for this test is -0.157, small enough not to reject the null hypothesis.[4] The result of the test means that the panel data can be pooled to proceed with fixed and random effects models.

The estimates of both the within fixed effects and random effects models are presented in Table 6.6. Compared with the pooled OLS model, the random effects model is preferable. This can be tested by the Breusch–Pagan LM test, which examines whether individual- or time-specific variance components are zero, H_o: $\sigma_u^2 = 0$. The LM-statistic using the chi-squared distribution (χ^2) with one degree of freedom (Greene, 2012) is:

$$LM = \frac{nT}{2(T-1)} \left[\frac{\sum_{i=1}^{n} (T\bar{e}_i)^2}{\sum_{i=1}^{n} \sum_{t=1}^{T} e_{it}^2} - 1 \right]^2 \qquad (6.7)$$

The LM-statistic is 313.1 (Prob. > χ^2 = 0.000). The result of the test rejects the null hypothesis in favour of the random effects model.

In the within fixed effects model, the time-invariant variables are wiped out, while the random effects model allows for estimating the time-constant variables (Greene, 2012). The random effects model is thereby usually preferred. Hence, in the fixed effects model, the time-constant variables, such as gender, ethnicity, and regions, are excluded. However, the Hausman test is used to decide which effect is more significant, and which model is better. The null hypothesis is that the individual effects are uncorrelated with other regressors in the model. The Hausman statistic is 195.6, which is large enough to reject the null hypothesis. Therefore, the Hausman test suggests that the fixed effects model is favoured over the random effects model, as it controls for unobservable, individual-specific effects that are correlated with per capita expenditure. Actually, the random effects model assumes exogeneity of all the regressors with the random individual effects (Baltagi, 2005), which is not usually the case.

In the random effects model, internal trade and commune employment in the import-competing sectors and in the manufacturing sectors are significantly and positively associated with per capita expenditure. Nevertheless, its results are less efficient than those of its fixed effects counterpart. In the fixed effects estimates, local trade and commune manufacturing employment have a significant and positive impact on per capita expenditure. These results are consistent with those in the pooled OLS and LSDV fixed effects models. Commune manufacturing employment also has a positive effect on rural welfare, as found in the model using the wide panel data. Provincial trade and industrial employment thus prove to be crucial to rural household welfare.

In conclusion, the analysis of the determinants of rural household welfare has demonstrated that, apart from conventional household characteristics relevant to demographics, human capital, employment, agricultural production, household assets, location, and commune infrastructure, it is evident that trade-related

Table 6.6 Estimates of fixed effects and random effects models for the impacts of trade liberalisation on real per capita expenditure

[Long-form panel 2002–2006]
[Dependent variable: log of RPCE]

Independent variable	Within fixed effects model		Random effects model	
	Coefficient	p-value	Coefficient	p-value
Constant term	6.4670***	0.000	6.3986***	0.000
Demographic characteristics				
Household size	–0.1076***	0.000	–0.0955***	0.000
Head ethnicity (Kinh)	Omitted	–	0.0850***	0.006
Head gender (male)	Omitted	–	0.0499	0.209
Head age	0.0468***	0.000	0.0333***	0.000
Head age square	–0.0004***	0.000	–0.0003***	0.000
Heads with spouse	–0.0539	0.240	–0.0921**	0.043
Proportion of children	–0.0011**	0.026	–0.0014***	0.001
Proportion of elderly	–0.0007	0.393	–0.0018***	0.003
Proportion of females	0.0025***	0.000	0.0011**	0.028
Human capital				
Head years of school	Omitted	–	0.0161***	0.000
Spouse years of school	Omitted	–	0.0169***	0.000
Technical diploma ratio	0.0020***	0.004	0.0021***	0.001
Postsecondary ratio	–0.0021***	0.004	–0.0017**	0.012
Occupation (reference is unskilled head)				
Head leader	0.1802**	0.012	0.2702***	0.000
Head professional	0.0492	0.612	0.2287***	0.001
Head white collar	–0.1320	0.365	0.0735	0.584
Head skilled work	–0.0037	0.884	0.0443**	0.043
Head wage work	0.0382*	0.082	–0.0004	0.982
Head self–farmed business	–0.0047	0.873	–0.0270	0.285
Head self–business, nonfarm	0.0866***	0.001	0.1181***	0.000
Agricultural production				
Total land area	0.0000***	0.000	0.0000***	0.000
Rice productivity	0.2328***	0.002	0.3016***	0.000
Net rice producers	0.0078	0.639	0.0044	0.771
House assets and other incomes				
Total living area	0.0006**	0.029	0.0018***	0.000
Access to electricity	0.0971***	0.002	0.1287***	0.000

Remittance	0.0000***	0.000	0.0000***	0.000
Community characteristics				
Paved roads	−0.0415	0.130	−0.0212	0.374
Primary school	0.0811**	0.022	0.0715**	0.028
Lower secondary school	0.1423***	0.000	0.1736***	0.000
Upper secondary school	0.0340	0.242	0.0650***	0.009
Post office	−0.0033	0.852	−0.0047	0.777
Daily market	0.0617***	0.000	0.0665***	0.000
Clinic	−0.0476	0.643	−0.1250	0.197
Geography (reference is North Central)				
Red River Delta	Omitted	–	0.0724**	0.020
Northeast	Omitted	–	0.1353***	0.000
Northwest	Omitted	–	0.0698	0.202
South central coast	Omitted	–	0.0781*	0.050
Central highlands	Omitted	–	0.1309**	0.010
Southeast	Omitted	–	0.2038***	0.001
Mekong River Delta	Omitted	–	0.3071***	0.000
Trade and employment				
Commune ratio of export employment	−0.0001	0.948	0.0009	0.489
Commune ratio of import employment	0.0027	0.223	0.0036*	0.064
Commune ratio of industrial employment	0.0023**	0.037	0.0018**	0.044
Province trade per capita	0.0832***	0.000	0.0509***	0.000
R^2	0.551		0.522	
Number of observations	2,469		2,469	

Note: ***, **, and * significant at 1 per cent, 5 per cent, and 10 per cent level, respectively.

factors play an important role in explaining welfare change. The decomposition of the microdeterminants of growth shows that education is the most important determinant of welfare. The simulation of the impacts of trade liberalisation indicates that rice output, rice productivity, and commune employment in both import-competing sectors and manufacturing sectors improve rural welfare. The analysis of the fixed effects and random effects models, using the long-form panel data, further suggests the significant role of commune employment and local trade in rural welfare improvement.

Poverty dynamics: the multinomial logit model

Understanding the change in poverty over time is very significant for policymakers to monitor progress in poverty reduction. This section examines the determinants of the movement of poverty. Households' transitional states of poverty can be divided into four groups: being poor in both years (chronic poverty), being poor in 2002 but becoming not poor in 2006 (poverty escape), being not poor in 2002 but becoming poor in 2006 (falling into poverty), and being not poor in both years. Policymakers perhaps should pay more attention to the determinants of poverty escape. The poverty transition over the period 2002–2006 can be captured by a matrix of poverty transition, using the panel data of 904 households (Table 6.7).

For Vietnam as a whole, the share of households remaining poor in both years was 13.6 per cent. Meanwhile, households who escaped poverty accounted for 23.1 per cent. The percentage of households falling into poverty over the period was rather small; only 3.2 per cent of households were not poor in 2002 but poor in 2006. Furthermore, 60.1 per cent of households continued to be 'not poor' in both years. These indicators reflect the achievements of Vietnam in the reduction of poverty in this period. The analysis of poverty dynamics can be broken into regions. The prosperous regions, such as the Red River Delta, southeast, and Mekong River Delta, have the lowest percentage of households being poor in both years. The most successful poverty reduction belongs to the central highlands (42.2 per cent of households escaping poverty), the north central region (30.6 per cent), and the northwest (24.4 per cent). Note that the north central region is commonly considered to be the poorest region in Vietnam. Although a major rice production region, the Mekong River Delta has both the lowest percentage of poverty-escaped households and the highest percentage of households remaining 'not poor' in both years. To some extent, this may suggest that poverty reduction programmes might not perform well in this region.

Neither the matrix of poverty movement nor the models of microdeterminants of growth using the continuous dependent variable are likely to answer two important questions: (1) what are the determinants of households' escape from poverty, and (2) does trade liberalisation play any part in poverty movements? The multinomial logit (MNL) model is used to investigate the characteristics that enable households to escape poverty, paying particular attention to trade-related factors. The analysis of a multinomial logit model can provide important insights into these questions. The results of the estimates of the multinomial logit model are presented in Table 6.8. The base model (Model 1) is almost the same as that in the previous section. Five trade-related variables are added to the base model: the changes in rice productivity measured at the household level; in the employment ratios of export, import, and manufacturing sectors; and in the trade per capita measured at the provincial level over the period. In the extended model, the changes in rice productivity and the export employment ratio are positively associated with the escape from poverty. The ratio of export employment and the provincial trade per capita also help households not to fall into poverty. None of the change variables are positively associated with the likelihood of households falling into poverty in 2006.

Table 6.7 Poverty dynamics over 2002–2006: a matrix of transition (per cent)

Vietnam and regions	Poor 2006	Nonpoor 2006
Whole Vietnam		
Poor 2002	13.61	23.12
Nonpoor 2002	3.21	60.07
Red River Delta		
Poor 2002	4.00	21.78
Nonpoor 2002	1.78	72.44
Northeast		
Poor 2002	23.20	23.20
Nonpoor 2002	0.49	49.17
Northwest		
Poor 2002	48.78	24.39
Nonpoor 2002	4.88	21.95
North central		
Poor 2002	19.44	30.56
Nonpoor 2002	3.47	46.53
South central coast		
Poor 2002	9.78	22.83
Nonpoor 2002	3.26	64.13
Central highlands		
Poor 2002	24.44	42.22
Nonpoor 2002	2.22	31.11
Southeast		
Poor 2002	0.00	23.53
Nonpoor 2002	8.82	67.65
Mekong River Delta		
Poor 2002	2.82	11.27
Nonpoor 2002	2.11	83.80

Source: Author's estimates based on the data drawn from the VHLSSs

The results of the multinomial logit regression can be explained through the impacts of the variables on the relative risk ratio (RRR), which is the ratio of the probability of a given outcome to the probability of a base outcome (here, households being poor in both years). The estimates of RRR are provided in Table 6.9, demonstrating the impact of each household characteristic on the RRR for the other states of poverty movement. According to Glewwe *et al.* (2002), the impact of a variable being less than one means that the variable raises the

Table 6.8 Estimates of multinomial logit model of poverty movement, 2002–2006

Independent variable	P → NP		NP → P		NP → NP	
	Model 1	Model 2	Model 1	Model 2	Model 1	Model 2
Constant term	-3.8752** (0.035)	-5.4204*** (0.007)	4.0578 (0.235)	-4.4221 (0.241)	-7.4540 (0.000)	-8.2889*** (0.000)
Demographic characteristics						
Household size	-0.0688 (0.470)	-0.0663 (0.500)	-0.7419*** (0.000)	-0.7449*** (0.000)	-0.5374*** (0.000)	-0.5500*** (0.000)
Head ethnicity (Kinh)	0.9746*** (0.005)	0.7619** (0.037)	1.2237* (0.084)	1.0921 (0.112)	1.8532*** (0.000)	1.6591*** (0.000)
Head gender (male)	0.7190 (0.218)	0.7413 (0.267)	1.1501 (0.117)	1.3310 (0.148)	0.3503 (0.482)	0.4417 (0.449)
Head age	0.1590** (0.021)	0.1754** (0.015)	0.1734 (0.141)	0.2096 (0.128)	0.2042*** (0.001)	0.2140*** (0.001)
Head age square	-0.0016** (0.021)	-0.0018** (0.013)	-0.0013 (0.282)	-0.0016 (0.258)	-0.0016*** (0.008)	-0.0017*** (0.010)
Heads with spouse	-0.7240 (0.272)	-0.8995 (0.234)	-0.8348 (0.349)	-1.0380 (0.303)	-0.0650 (0.912)	-0.2575 (0.704)
Proportion of children	0.0228* (0.076)	0.0199 (0.119)	-0.0359 (0.120)	-0.0429* (0.087)	0.0354*** (0.005)	0.0348*** (0.005)
Proportion of elderly	0.0034 (0.799)	0.0047 (0.719)	-0.0234 (0.163)	-0.0247 (0.194)	-0.0163 (0.224)	-0.0168 (0.198)
Human capital						
Head years of school	-0.0048 (0.922)	-0.0015 (0.977)	-0.0338 (0.719)	-0.0523 (0.585)	0.0466 (0.374)	0.0649 (0.226)

	(1)	(2)	(3)	(4)	(5)	(6)
Spouse years of school	0.0825 (0.127)	0.0990* (0.082)	0.1723* (0.072)	0.2153** (0.030)	0.1390** (0.013)	0.1589*** (0.007)
Technical diploma ratio	1.1884*** (0.000)	1.1295*** (0.000)	1.1119*** (0.000)	1.0554*** (0.000)	0.2958*** (0.007)	0.2292** (0.032)
Postsecondary ratio	−0.1431*** (0.000)	−0.1322*** (0.007)	−0.0388 (0.547)	−0.0336 (0.612)	0.8124*** (0.000)	0.8311*** (0.000)
Occupation						
Head skilled work	0.1685 (0.795)	0.3281 (0.644)	1.7620** (0.046)	1.7314* (0.067)	0.2382 (0.706)	0.4246 (0.541)
Unskilled–to–adult ratio	−0.0036 (0.341)	−0.0021 (0.587)	0.0060 (0.209)	0.0068 (0.187)	−0.0068* (0.068)	−0.0063* (0.096)
Agricultural production						
Total land area	−0.0000 (0.191)	−0.0000 (0.262)	0.0000 (0.281)	0.0000 (0.313)	0.0000** (0.012)	0.0000** (0.011)
Selling state firms crops	−1.2484** (0.037)	−1.1298 (0.115)	0.2038 (0.843)	0.4201 (0.727)	15.9963*** (0.000)	16.0721*** (0.000)
Net rice producers	0.5601* (0.057)	0.4530 (0.145)	1.1597** (0.011)	1.0113** (0.029)	1.2392*** (0.000)	1.1591*** (0.000)
Rice productivity	0.0238 (0.979)	2.2250 (0.103)	−0.6953 (0.759)	−1.7061 (0.535)	0.2842 (0.744)	1.2356 (0.377)
House assets and other incomes						
Land use rights	−0.1611 (0.667)	−0.1683 (0.676)	−0.9553 (0.155)	−1.0868 (0.108)	0.3434 (0.398)	0.3216 (0.456)
Total living area	0.0074 (0.198)	0.0087 (0.163)	0.0067 (0.343)	0.0037 (0.636)	0.0152*** (0.005)	0.0154** (0.010)

(Continued)

Table 6.8 (Continued)

Independent variable	P → NP		NP → P		NP → NP	
	Model 1	Model 2	Model 1	Model 2	Model 1	Model 2
Electricity access	0.2453 (0.540)	0.2921 (0.480)	0.4124 (0.561)	0.5839 (0.450)	0.6977* (0.078)	0.7146* (0.080)
Remittance	0.0003 (0.108)	0.0003* (0.096)	0.0004*** (0.006)	0.0005*** (0.005)	0.0004*** (0.007)	0.0004*** (0.008)
Commune characteristics						
Paved roads	0.1574 (0.667)	0.1298 (0.723)	−0.0471 (0.949)	−0.0430 (0.953)	0.3144 (0.411)	0.2454 (0.517)
Remote areas	−0.8463* (0.010)	−0.7681** (0.023)	−0.4992 (0.376)	−0.6444 (0.261)	−0.9906*** (0.002)	−1.0017*** (0.003)
Primary school	0.0374 (0.931)	−0.2044 (0.647)	−1.7113** (0.037)	−1.8313** (0.023)	0.2368 (0.682)	−0.0643 (0.913)
Lower secondary school	0.3403 (0.703)	0.0920 (0.914)	−1.8079 (0.212)	−1.7502 (0.230)	0.8964 (0.328)	0.7055 (0.420)
Upper secondary school	15.8143*** (0.000)	15.4471*** (0.000)	−1.9532* (0.066)	−2.4901** (0.046)	15.8245*** (0.000)	15.1953*** (0.000)
Post office	−0.2916 (0.351)	−0.3370 (0.304)	−0.1372 (0.815)	−0.1912 (0.761)	−0.2334 (0.452)	−0.3095 (0.342)
Daily market	−0.1770 (0.598)	−0.2495 (0.477)	0.5650 (0.309)	0.4908 (0.382)	0.2230 (0.492)	0.1176 (0.727)
National electricity grid	0.3332 (0.468)	0.2459 (0.595)	0.2040 (0.811)	0.0407 (0.963)	1.1703** (0.022)	0.9751* (0.065)

Geography

North Central	−0.9489**	−0.6364*	−0.8239	−1.1583*	−2.0730***	−1.6483***
	(0.012)	(0.099)	(0.232)	(0.099)	(0.000)	(0.000)

Change variables in trade and employment

Rice productivity		3.4511**		−2.1865		1.7331
		(0.012)		(0.368)		(0.194)
Province ratio of export employment		0.2631**		−0.0982		0.3404***
		(0.024)		(0.600)		(0.004)
Province ratio of import employment		−0.2007		0.2730		−0.1134
		(0.484)		(0.522)		(0.684)
Province ratio of manufacturing employment		−0.0392		0.0508		0.0107
		(0.682)		(0.782)		(0.910)
Province trade per capita		0.1878		0.2555		0.3026**
		(0.160)		(0.194)		(0.018)
Pseudo R^2	0.270	0.288	0.270	0.288	0.270	0.288
Number of observations	904	904	904	904	904	904

Notes: − ***, **, and * significant at 1 per cent, 5 per cent, and 10 per cent level, respectively.

- p-values are in parentheses.

- Model 1 and Model 2 are with and without trade-related variables, respectively.

Table 6.9 Estimates of the probability of poverty movement (odds ratios), 2002–2006

Independent variable	P → NP(RRR)		NP → P(RRR)		NP → NP(RRR)	
	Model 1	Model 2	Model 1	Model 2	Model 1	Model 2
Demographic characteristics						
Household size	0.9336	0.9359	0.4762***	0.4748***	0.5843***	0.5770***
Head ethnicity (Kinh)	2.6502***	2.1424**	3.3997*	2.9805	6.3800***	5.2548***
Head gender (male)	2.0523	2.0987	3.1586	3.7849	1.4194	1.5554
Head age	1.1723**	1.1917**	1.1893	1.2332	1.2265***	1.2387***
Head age square	0.9984**	0.9982**	0.9987	0.9984	0.9984***	0.9983***
Heads with spouse	0.4848	0.4068	0.4340	0.3542	0.9370	0.7729
Proportion of children	1.0230*	1.0201	0.9647	0.9580*	1.0360***	1.0354***
Proportion of elderly	1.0034	1.0048	0.9769	0.9756	0.9838	0.9833
Human capital						
Head years of school	0.9952	0.9985	0.9668	0.9490	1.0477	1.0671
Spouse years of school	1.0860	1.1040*	1.1880*	1.2402**	1.1491**	1.1722***
Technical diploma ratio	3.2817***	3.0942***	3.0400***	2.8732***	1.3442***	1.2576**
Postsecondary diploma ratio	0.8667***	0.8762***	0.9619	0.9670	2.2532***	2.2960***
Occupation						
Head skilled work	1.1836	1.3883	5.8241**	5.6488*	1.2690	1.5289
Unskilled-to-adult ratio	0.9964	0.9979	1.0061	1.0068	0.9932*	0.9938*
Agricultural production						
Total land area	1.0000	1.0000	1.0000	1.0000	1.0000**	1.0000**

Selling state firms crops	0.2870**	0.3231	1.2261	1.5222	8853007***	9550779***
Net rice producers	1.7508*	1.5730	3.1890**	2.7492**	3.4529***	3.1869***
Rice productivity	1.0241	9.2532	0.4989	0.1816	1.3287	3.4404
House assets and other incomes						
Land use rights	0.8512	0.8451	0.3847	0.3373	1.4097	1.3794
Total living area	1.0074	1.0087	1.0067	1.0037	1.0153***	1.0156**
Electricity access	1.2780	1.3392	1.5104	1.7931	2.0092*	2.0433*
Remittance	1.0003	1.0003*	1.0004***	1.0005***	1.0004***	1.0004***
Community characteristics						
Paved roads	1.1705	1.1386	0.9539	0.9579	1.3694	1.2781
Remote areas	0.4290*	0.4639**	0.6070	0.5250	0.3714***	0.3673***
Primary school	1.0381	0.8151	0.1806**	0.1602**	1.2672	0.9377
Lower secondary school	1.4054	1.0964	0.1640	0.1737	2.4507	2.0248
Upper secondary school	7380283***	5111921***	0.1418*	0.0829**	7456107***	3974208***
Post office	0.7471	0.7139	0.8718	0.8260	0.7918	0.7338
Daily market	0.8378	0.7792	1.7595	1.6336	1.2498	1.1248
National electricity grid	1.3955	1.2788	1.2263	1.0415	3.2230**	2.6514*

(*Continued*)

Table 6.9 (Continued)

Independent variable	P → NP(RRR)		NP → P(RRR)		NP → NP(RRR)	
	Model 1	Model 2	Model 1	Model 2	Model 1	Model 2
Geography						
North Central	0.3872**	0.5292*	0.4387	0.3140*	0.1258***	0.1924***
Rice productivity		31.5344**		0.1123		5.6579
Province ratio of export employment		1.3010**		0.9065		1.4055***
Province ratio of import employment		0.8181		1.3139		0.8928
Province ratio of manufacturing employment		0.9615		1.0521		1.0108
Province trade per capita		1.2066		1.2911		1.3534**
Pseudo R^2	0.270	0.288	0.270	0.288	0.270	0.288
Number of observations	904	904	904	904	904	904

Notes: ***, **, and * significant at 1 per cent, 5 per cent, and 10 per cent level, respectively.

- Model 1 and Model 2 are with and without trade-related variables, respectively.

relative probability of being in the base state (being poor in both years), whereas the impact greater than one implies that the variable decreases the relative probability of being in the base state, and increases the relative probability of being in the relevant state.

In the extended model, with the added change variables, the results of demographic variables show that being of Kinh ethnicity increased the relative probability of escaping poverty by 114 per cent, and a one-year increase in the age of the household head raised this relative probability by 19.2 per cent. For variables measuring education, the education of spouses and the proportion of household members with a technical diploma increased the relative probability of lifting households out of poverty by about 10.4 per cent (at the 0.1 significance level) and 209 per cent, respectively. However, the proportion of those with post-secondary education reduced the relative probability by 12.4 per cent. Therefore, technical training once again proves to be more important than general education in rural regions.

In contrast to expectation, the variables measuring occupation, agricultural production, and assets play an insignificant role in poverty reduction. This could in part result from the relatively small panel data. In this period, both domestic and overseas remittance contribute little – only 0.03 per cent – to raising the relative probability of escaping poverty. Regarding commune characteristics, commune high schools are very important for poor households to escape poverty, with a corresponding very high impact. In addition, residing in remote communes decreases the relative probability of escaping poverty. Other commune characteristics are insignificant. In terms of geography, the probability of lifting households out of poverty was 47.1 per cent lower in the north central region, compared with the other regions.

Most importantly, amongst the change variables relating to local trade and employment, the very high impact of rice productivity demonstrates its importance to poverty reduction, given a small number of variables in the model that help to boost the relative probability of escaping poverty. Moreover, the employment ratio in the export sector increased the relative probability of moving out of poverty by 30.2 per cent. As can be seen, not many household characteristics impact the poverty movements of households. However, many play a part in keeping households from falling into poverty, as shown in the last column of Table 6.9. Of particular interest, once again, are the changes in the employment ratio of the export sectors and in the internal trade per capita that raised the probability of not becoming poor by 40.6 and 35.3 per cent, respectively. Note that the provincial trade per capita is used to measure the level of local trade transaction, which is highly expected to help the poor to escape poverty. This variable also has a significant impact on rural welfare in the fixed effects analysis. Therefore, amongst the factors that explain the transition of poverty, statistically significant impacts on the relative probability are evident for trade-related variables, especially employment and internal trade.

6.4 Conclusions

This chapter has examined the effects of trade liberalisation on the welfare and poverty of rural households in Vietnam. These impacts are analysed using both continuous and discrete panel data modelling approaches. The models based on these approaches utilise both wide and long forms of the panel data over the period 2002–2006. Overall, the results provide evidence for the impacts of trade liberalisation on rural household welfare, poverty, and poverty dynamics. The decomposition of the determinants of growth of household welfare shows that the returns on net rice production increase over time. The variable of net rice producer is trade related, as farm households having a surplus in rice production tend to engage more in trade activities for their crops. The continuous approach, based on the model of the microdeterminants of growth and the wide form of panel data, indicates that working in the import-competing sector has a significant impact on the growth of household welfare. This finding is reasonable because rural households are generally low-skilled labourers. They may not be capable of working in the export sectors or in the economic sectors that require highly skilled qualification. The fixed effects model also demonstrates the significant impact of manufacturing employment and local trade transaction on rural welfare. Local trade also plays a role in keeping households from falling into poverty in the multinomial logit model. Also in this model, export employment helps the poor to escape poverty. These findings suggest that the trade liberalisation effect, especially job creation and internal trade development, is crucial to any improvement in rural standards of living and poverty reduction.

Policies aiming to boost local employment in the import-competing and industrial sectors, and to develop local trade, would help rural households to improve welfare and keep from falling into the poverty trap. The problems with trade liberalisation in Vietnam lie in both internal and external trade. On the external side, the market forecast and direction, especially for the world rice and coffee markets, are not efficient enough to help Vietnam to compete with numerous rice exporters in the world. On the internal side, the monopoly of the rice market by some big state food companies, along with the disorganised market distribution of rice and coffee, largely squeeze farmers' agricultural profits. Thus farmers, on the whole, have little profit and thereby no incentives to improve agricultural productivity. Consequently, the probability of remaining chronically poor over a period is considerable. The reorganisation of agricultural production and trade can help, both to provide more local employment and to develop local trade.

Notes

1 See the UNDP (2005) for more discussion about the approaches to measuring poverty.
2 This region includes Thanh Hoa, Nghe An, Ha Tinh, Quang Binh, Quang Tri, and Thua Thien Hue province, located in the poorest resource region in Vietnam.

3   The percentage increase is calculated as $e^{0.2162} - 1 = 0.2414$. This calculation is used for all dummy variables used in this study.
4   The F-statistic is negative, because the time periods are rather smaller than the number of parameters.

References

Athukorala, P. (2010). *Production Networks and Trade Patterns in East Asia: Regionalization or Globalization?*. ADB, Working Paper Series on Regional Economic Integration (No. 56), 76.

Baltagi, B. H. (2005). *Econometric Analysis of Panel Data* (3rd ed.). London: John Wiley & Sons Ltd.

Baltagi, B. H. (2008). *Econometrics* (4th ed.). Berlin: Springer.

Baulch, B., and Dat, V. H. (2010). *Poverty Dynamics in Vietnam, 2002–2006*. World Bank, Policy Research Working Paper (No. 64278), 1–35.

Coello, B., Fall, M., and Suwa-Eisenmann, A. (2010). *Trade Liberalization and Poverty Dynamics in Vietnam 2002–2006*. Paris School of Economics, Working Paper (No. 11), 43.

Glewwe, P., Gragnolati, M., and Zaman, H. (2000). *Who Gained from Vietnam's Boom in the 1990s: An Analysis of Poverty and Inequality Trends*. World Bank, Policy Research Working Paper (No. 2275), 64.

Glewwe, P., Gragnolati, M., and Zaman, H. (2002). Who Gained from Vietnam's Boom in the 1990s?. *Economic Development and Cultural Change, 50*(4), 773–792.

Glewwe, P., and Hall, G. (1998). Are Some Groups More Vulnerable to Macroeconomic Shocks Than Others? Hypothesis Tests Based on Panel Data from Peru. *Journal of Development Economics, 56*(1), 181–206. DOI: 10.1016/s0304-3878(98)00058-3

Greene, W. H. (2012). *Econometric Analysis* (7th ed.). Boston: Prentice Hall.

Haughton, J., and Khandker, S. R. (2009). *Handbook on Poverty and Inequality*. Washington, DC: World Bank.

Hill, R. C., Griffiths, W. E., and Lim, G. C. (2007). *Principles of Econometrics*. New York: Wiley.

Justino, P., Litchfield, J., and Pham, H. T. (2008). Poverty Dynamics during Trade Reform: Evidence from Rural Vietnam. *Review of Income and Wealth, 54*(2), 166–192. DOI: 10.1111/j.1475–4991.2008.00269.x

Kennedy, P. (2008). *A Guide to Econometrics* (6th ed.). Cambridge, MA: MIT Press.

Krueger, A. O. (1983). *Trade and Employment in Less Developed Countries: Synthesis and Conclusion* (vol. 3). Chicago: University of Chicago Press.

Le, D. T., and Pham, T. H. (2009). *Construction of the Panel Data Vietnam Household Living Standard Surveys (VHLSS) 2002–2006*. Hanoi: Mimeo, Indochina Research and Consulting.

McCulloch, N., Winters, L. A., and Cirera, X. (2001). *Trade Liberalization and Poverty: A Handbook*. London: Centre for Economic Policy Research.

Niimi, Y., Vasudeva-Dutta, P., and Winters, L. A. (2007). Trade Liberalization and Poverty Dynamics in Vietnam. *Journal of Economic Integration, 22*(4), 819–851.

Perkins, D. H., Radelet, S., and Lindauer, D. L. (2006). *Economics of Development* (6th ed.). New York: W. W. Norton.

Ravallion, M. (1998). Poor Areas. In A. Ullah and D.E.A. Giles (eds) *Handbook of Applied Economic Statistics* (pp. 63–91). New York: Marcel Dekker, Inc.

United Nations Development Programme (UNDP) (2005). *What is Poverty? Concepts and Measures.* Poverty in Focus-UNDP International Poverty Centre, 24.

Wodon, Q.T. (2000). Microdeterminants of Consumption, Poverty, Growth, and Inequality in Bangladesh. *Applied Economics, 32*(10), 1337–1352. DOI: 10.1080/000368400404498

World Bank (2001). *World Development Report 2000/01: Attacking Poverty* (p. 356). Washington, DC.

7 Urban poverty and employment

7.1 Introduction

Studies on the trade–poverty relationship commonly focus on rural poverty, considering that poverty is predominantly a rural phenomenon; urban poverty, as such, has not received matching attention. Macours and Swinnen (2008) observe that urban poverty is generally lower than rural poverty, and largely moves in the same direction as rural poverty. The difference between urban and rural poverty varies strongly across countries. Urban poverty, in fact, tends to be more and more severe as individual countries become increasingly integrated into the world economy. Urban poverty is different from rural poverty in several respects. The primary concern of the urban poor usually relates to the living and working conditions in towns and cities, such as housing, occupation, income inequality, and pollution. In contrast, their rural counterparts worry mostly about income and starvation. The measures of urban poverty that utilise the income- or expenditure-based approach may therefore be inadequate. The urban poor tend to be the first victims of the economic slowdown, as unemployment is the primary cause of poverty, especially in urban areas. The immediate effects of unemployment on urban people may be more severe than those on their rural counterparts, as the economic shocks often originate from the centres of business and commerce, which are largely located in urban areas. With an increasing rate of rural-to-urban migration in developing and/or transitional economies, rural poverty becomes closely related to urban poverty. The World Bank (2011b) conjectures that the growth and reduction in the poverty of small towns will help Vietnam to reduce rural poverty.

The empirical evidence on the effects of trade and growth on urban poverty is sketchy and mixed. Goldberg and Pavcnik (2005) examine whether trade reforms in Colombia could account for the reduction in poverty between 1984 and 1995, using short- and medium-run links through which trade reforms could impact poverty. Nonetheless, the study finds no evidence on the relationship between tariff reductions and poverty. Kabeer and Tran (2006) examine the impacts of globalisation on gender and poverty in Vietnam, based on a survey of workers in HCMC and Hanoi. The study finds that most workers in the garment industry were female. They primarily migrated from the countryside and worked in firms, regardless of the working conditions and wages. This finding may support the view that the effects of the reduction in urban poverty are transmitted to rural poverty. Dercon and Shapiro (2007) consider that location and access to particular types of jobs matter to the urban poor. Datt and Ravallion (2011) investigate the effect of economic growth on poverty in India, using a new series of consumption-based measures over 50 years. They reveal that urban economic growth in the post-reform period significantly benefited the rural, as well as the urban, poor. In terms of income inequality, Liu (2008) finds that urban inequality declined in the 1990s, and that the changing returns on regional factors and physical assets underpinned that decline in inequality in Vietnam. In developing countries and transitional economies, the impacts of trade liberalisation on urban poverty are, therefore, as important as those on rural poverty. The open policy and urbanisation of Vietnam, as well as the increasing rural-to-urban migration, may worsen poverty in urban areas. Although many studies conducted for Vietnam focus on the impacts of trade liberalisation on rural poverty (Seshan, 2005; Niimi *et al.*, 2007; Justino *et al.*, 2008), little attention has been paid to the trade–poverty relationship in urban areas (Glewwe *et al.*, 2002).

The main focus of this chapter is to examine the effects of trade liberalisation on urban poverty that operate through the creation of employment. It attempts to shed more light on this relationship in urban regions of Vietnam. The analysis is undertaken using a case study of poverty in HCMC and Hanoi, the two largest cities in Vietnam. The trade–poverty linkages are examined by analysing the effects of employment on urban welfare, based on a panel data set and the fixed effects model. It is assumed that the employment effects of trade liberalisation on urban welfare are transmitted to the urban poor: the poor migrants from the countryside account for a considerable proportion of the urban population, as reported by Haughton *et al.* (2010). The rest of the chapter is organized as follows. Section 7.2 provides an overview of urban poverty in Vietnam, as well as a case study of poverty in HCMC and Hanoi. This section also descriptively analyses the relationship between employment and poverty in Vietnam. Section 7.3 uses a panel data model to examine the employment effect on urban household welfare. Section 7.4 concludes the chapter and suggests some policy implications.

7.2   Urban poverty in Vietnam: an overview

About one-third of the Vietnamese population lives in urban areas. Urban areas have better infrastructure and more effective institutions than are available to rural areas. Hence, the urban poor are likely to benefit more rapidly from trade liberalisation than their rural counterparts, or at least they may receive fewer negative effects of trade liberalisation than the rural poor. In urban regions, however, income disparity could be more severe than in rural regions. Assuming that a rise in inequality worsens poverty, the new trend of poverty in Vietnam is associated with the increase in inequality, especially in urban areas.

Scale and characteristics of urban poverty

The transition of the Vietnamese economy to an outward- and market-oriented economy has been associated with the remarkable reduction in urban poverty in the 1990s. Urban poverty was reduced by more than half, with the urban poverty rate dropping from about 25 per cent to below 10 per cent, while rural poverty was halved in the same period (see Table 7.1). While the incidence of poverty in urban regions was always lower than that in rural areas, the urban Gini coefficients, having increased over time, were invariably higher than those in rural regions in the 2000s.

Since urban areas are presumably more commercial than rural areas, trade liberalisation could have more rapid and positive impacts on urban poverty than on rural poverty. According to the World Bank (2012), the urban poor accounted for only 8.6 per cent of the poor in Vietnam. Moreover, the urban poverty rate is 6 per cent, whereas the rural poverty rate is 27 per cent. One of the reasons why urban poverty is becoming important is that the process of urbanisation in Vietnam is accelerating, and the urban infrastructure is not catching up with the increasing urban population.

Table 7.1 Poverty incidence and poverty distribution (per cent), 1999–2009

Poverty indicator	1999		2009		1999–2009	
	P_1	P_d	P_1	P_d	P_1	P_d
Poverty incidence/Distribution by region						
Northern midlands	58.1	20.9	26.2	25.2	−31.9	4.3
Red River Delta	33.0	21.1	8.5	14.5	−24.5	−6.6
North central/Central coast	43.1	28.0	18.8	30.8	−24.3	2.8
Central highlands	43.8	6.4	21.3	9.5	−22.5	3.1
Southeast	8.3	3.0	2.4	3.0	−5.9	−0.1
Mekong River Delta	35.8	20.7	11.4	17.1	−24.4	−3.6
(Pmax–Pmin)/Pmin	600.0	824.0	991.7	938.3	391.7	114.4
Poverty incidence/Distribution by city class						
Special cites	15.9	23.5	3.3	17.5	−12.6	−6.0
Class-I cities	29.9	19.6	7.9	16.3	−22.0	−3.4
Class-II cities	31.6	12.4	12.5	17.3	−19.1	4.9
Class-III towns	38.9	24.7	13.6	28.5	−25.3	3.8
Class-IV provincial towns	39.4	19.7	15.7	20.4	−23.7	0.7
(Pmax–Pmin)/Pmin	147.8	99.1	375.8	75.0	228.0	−24.1

Source: Authors' synthesis based on data from the World Bank (2011b).

Notes: P_1 is poverty incidence, measured by poverty head count ratio; P_d is poverty distribution, the national share of poor people in an area; P is either poverty incidence or poverty distribution.

The cities in Vietnam are divided into five groups. In the World Bank's classification in 2009 (World Bank, 2011b, 2012), the country had 2 special cities, 5 class-I cities, 12 class-II cities, 40 class-III towns, 47 class-IV provincial towns, and 625 class-V small townships. Except for the special cities (HCMC and Hanoi) and the class-I cities, other smaller cities and towns are located in the rural-like urban areas. People in smaller cities and towns appear to have less access to basic urban services, such as electricity and water. Hence, the poverty rate in these cities and towns has recently shown a tendency to increase over time. In 1999, the poverty rate in class-IV provincial towns was nearly three times that of the special cities.[1] However, this gap was substantially narrowed in 2009 (Table 7.1). Across the whole country, the poverty rate in the poorest regions in 1999 was about seven times that in the richest regions. This gap appears to have become significantly wider in 2009. Poverty declined in both areas, but poverty in the richest regions fell more rapidly. As observed by the World Bank (2011b), the benefits of economic growth were evenly distributed across regions in the country. This probably suggests that, among other things, local trade openness in the richer regions widens the regional disparity in Vietnam.

In 2010, urban poverty was seen to be negatively correlated with city size: smaller cities had a higher poverty rate. The largest cities had a poverty rate of 1.9 per cent, whereas the poverty rate in the smallest cities was 11.2 per cent (Table 7.2). The depth and severity of poverty also decreased in bigger cities. Thus, small cities and towns are likely to harbour most of the urban poor. They accounted for only 43 per cent of the urban population, but covered over 70 per cent of the urban poor. HCMC and Hanoi, the two big special cities making up 32 per cent of the urban population, had a poverty rate of 11 per cent (World Bank, 2012). These cities are in fact the most commercial and industrial cities in Vietnam.

Table 7.2 Poverty by city size, 2010

Indicator	Special city	Class-I	Class-II	Class-III	Class-IV,V	Rural
	Extra large	Large	Medium	Small	Extra small	
Number of cities in category	2	7	14	45	634	
Average population (1,000)	4,075	467	225	86	11	..
Per cent of total population	9.5	3.8	3.7	4.5	8.1	70.4
Per cent of urban population	32.1	12.9	12.4	15.3	27.3	..
Poverty rate (per cent)	1.9	3.8	4.2	5.8	11.2	25.6
Poverty gap (per cent)	0.4	0.6	0.7	1.1	2.4	6.8
Share of urban poor	11.0	8.8	9.2	5.9	55.0	..

Source: World Bank (2012)

The International Monetary Fund (2004) reported some differences between urban poverty and rural poverty in Vietnam. The inflow of unregistered migrants from rural regions increased as a result of the process of industrialisation and urbanisation. These migrants had difficulty in securing permanent registration for residence, so were unable to secure stable jobs and income. Added to this, the changing economic and ownership structure in the state sector led to labour shedding, resulting in labour redundancy in the urban areas. The urban poor were also more vulnerable, since they relied primarily on a cash income. Most of them worked in the informal sector, which had unstable jobs and low and unstable incomes. In such plights, they mostly lived in the urban areas with poor infrastructure and had poor access to basic services.

These characteristics of urban poverty have shown little change over time. More recent studies show that, similar to the rural poor and the general poor, the urban poor had many children (see Table 7.3). They were also often unemployed, probably because of low education. The ethnic poor did not even understand the general language. They typically had few assets or no valuable assets. They also had poor access to information and weak social relationships. Beyond the characteristics common to both poor areas are further traits found only in the urban poor areas. Most importantly, the urban poor were likely to have more access to information on prices and markets. They had, on average, more sick dependents than their rural counterparts had, and were more likely to be unable to work (e.g., being disabled) or to be outside the working age.

Table 7.3 Rural versus urban poverty: a comparison

Characteristics	Rural poor	Urban poor
Demography	• They had many children, especially babies.	• They had many children and/or sick household members as dependents.
Employment	• They lacked household labourers. • They had no jobs. • They lacked opportunities for nonagricultural employment. • Agriculture-based livelihoods • They were self-subsistence farmers or worked for other farmers. • They worked for others in mountainous fields. • Major livelihoods depended on paddy fields.	• They worked as informal labourers or street vendors with low and uncertain income. • They were often out of working ages or unable to work.

(*Continued*)

Table 7.3 (Continued)

Characteristics	Rural poor	Urban poor
Assets	• They lacked productive assets. • They maintained no livestock husbandry or kept only one animal. • They had limited investment in forestry. • They had low-quality land, including fields and one-crop terraces. They used land inefficiently. Their land had low productivity. They lacked efforts to reclaim state-provided land.	• They largely had both one bicycle and one television. • Few of them had motorbikes, except those in big cities. • They had corrugated metal–roofed, one-story houses. • They had a strong demand for borrowing from the Bank for Social Policy. Not many had actual access to subsidised credit.
Education	• The ethnic poor had limited understanding of Vietnamese. • They were unable to absorb technical knowledge or even make efforts to learn. • They had no interest in utilisation of technical advancements, or if they did, they were slow to use them, or applied them inefficiently.	• Their education was lower than the secondary level.
Connectivity	• They lived in isolated, remote areas. • They had poor access to information. • They lacked information on prices and markets.	
Institutional capital	• They were controlled by brokers who bought products at low prices and then sold them at considerably higher prices.	
Social inclusion	• They had weak social relationships and were involved in several social problems, such as alcoholism and gambling.	• They seldom participated in social activities.

Source: Authors' synthesis based on the Oxfam UK and ActionAid (2010) and Vietnam Academy of Social Sciences (2011)

With respect to human capital, the education achievement of the urban poor was on average lower than secondary level. They did informal jobs, for example as street vendors and construction assistants. Although they tended to abstain from social activities, unlike the rural poor, they did not usually engage in social problems, such as alcoholism or gambling (VASS, 2011). The main reason why they did not participate in social activities is that, according to a survey of urban poverty on households in HCMC and Hanoi reported by Haughton *et al.* (2010), the urban poor had neither time nor interest in doing so. This suggests that either social organisations do not fulfill their role in supporting poor households in urban areas, or the urban poor are unlikely to think highly of their role, due mainly to their low education, or both. The low level of education and the limited access to information are likely to be the main causes of urban poverty.

Studies by the World Bank (2012) and Haughton *et al.* (2010) suggest that the rapid urbanisation in Vietnam is likely to increase urban poverty, based on the dimensions of poverty beyond income. In the process of urbanisation, rural-to-urban migration puts pressure on urban infrastructure, which is slowly improved, to provide basic services. In addition to poor urban basic services, low education and low access to information are the primary causes of urban poverty. More significantly, the analysis reveals that, because the urban poor apparently had more access to information on prices and markets than their rural counterparts had, they did not have problems with the system of market distribution. This suggests that they should benefit more from trade liberalisation. Since remittance from working in urban areas constitutes a considerable part of household incomes, urban poverty in one way or another affects rural poverty. The issues of urban poverty will be better understood by looking closely at the case of HCMC and Hanoi.

Urban poverty: the case of HCMC and Hanoi

Most urban households live in rural-like or semi-urban areas, and urban poverty is largely found in the more rural-like regions of urban areas. Urban households in smaller towns or cities are, therefore, not much different from rural households. However, urban households in large cities, like HCMC and Hanoi, are quite different from rural households. The analysis of poverty in HCMC and Hanoi should provide more insight into the issues of urban poverty, as HCMC is the largest city and Hanoi is the second largest city in Vietnam. For most of the dimensions of poverty, urban poverty is generally less extreme than rural poverty. Using the urban poverty survey, a more recent survey of poor households in HCMC and Hanoi in 2009, Haughton *et al.* (2010) reported that poor households in HCMC were better off than those in Hanoi in terms of income. Conversely, they were worse off than those in Hanoi with respect to the other dimensions of poverty, according to the MPI.

Poverty in the two cities can be compared through different income poverty lines (Figure 7.1). Five income poverty lines are used in this analysis: the 2009

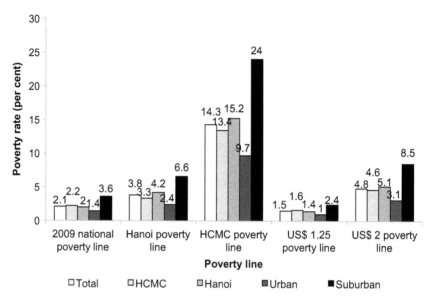

Figure 7.1 Income poverty ratios by poverty line and region, UPS 2009
Source: Based on the UPS 2009 data

national poverty line, the Hanoi poverty line, the HCMC poverty line, and the two international poverty lines, US$1.25, and US$2.[2] Hanoi is a little poorer than HCMC by the head count method. The difference in the incidence of poverty between urban and suburban areas within cities is considerable; the suburban poverty rates are more than twice the urban poverty rates, suggesting significant income inequality within cities. In the multidimensional approach to measuring poverty, the poverty rates for all the social poverty dimensions of HCMC were higher than those of Hanoi (Figure 7.2). According to Haughton *et al.* (2010), although being better off than Hanoi by the traditional head count method, HCMC was poorer than Hanoi in the multidimensional indexes. The results seem altogether reasonable, because HCMC is believed to be more open and dynamic than Hanoi, and its economic performance is better than that of Hanoi. However, as a consequence of rapid development and urbanisation, the quality of its living conditions is thereby worse than that of Hanoi. This finding also implies that openness to trade and investment helps to improve welfare in urban areas, based on the monetary approach.

In addition to the difference in the head count poverty rates, the data also show that income inequality appears to increase in the two cities. The difference in poverty between urban and suburban areas is very significant (Figure 7.1), suggesting that there is a major difference in the standards of living between the central districts and the outskirts. Compared to Vietnam as a whole, although

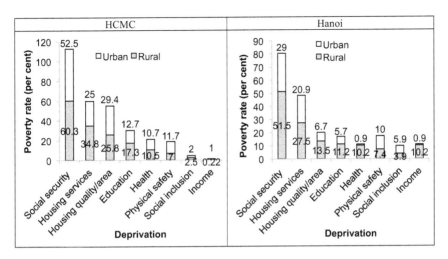

Figure 7.2 Poverty head count by deprivation in HCMC and Hanoi, 2009

Source: Based on the data drawn from Haughton *et al.* (2010)

Table 7.4 Gini coefficients by income in Vietnam and major cities, 2002–2010

| Country/city | VHLSS | | | | | UPS 2009 |
	2002	2004	2006	2008	2010	2009
Vietnam	0.418	0.420	0.424	0.434	0.433	..
HCMC	0.360	0.382	0.376	0.338	..	0.372
Hanoi	0.365	0.367	0.345	0.352	..	0.370

Source: Based on the data collected from General Statistics Office (2012) and Haughton *et al.* (2010)

the Gini coefficients of the two cities are lower than the national Gini coefficients in the 2000s, the Gini coefficients of the cities in 2009 are, on average, higher than those in the previous years (Table 7.4). Increasing income inequality in urban areas probably offsets the advantage that urban people have over their rural counterparts.

Urban poverty is primarily derived from the degree of access people have to some basic living conditions, such as total living areas, drinking water source, type of toilet, and power connection, which reflect the standards of living in urban areas. The living area per head of the richest quintile (Quintile 5) nearly doubled that of the poorest quintile (Quintile 1) (Table 7.5). The poorest, who may have the larger household size, lived in smaller areas, and vice versa. Living area per capita of the households in HCMC was larger than that of the Hanoi households. This indicates that the HCMC households were wealthier

Table 7.5 Main housing characteristics, UPS 2009

City and income quintile	Average living area per person (square metre)	Private tap water	Private direct connection with national electric grid
Total two cities	17.0	58.3	81.2
HCMC	17.7	52.5	77.0
Hanoi	15.7	70.6	90.1
Income quintile			
Quintile 1 (poorest)	13.3	43.3	82.8
Quintile 2	13.0	54.3	81.9
Quintile 3	12.7	54.7	79.1
Quintile 4	18.1	59.3	76.8
Quintile 5 (richest)	25.5	75.0	85.4

Source: Based on the data drawn from Haughton *et al.* (2010)

than the Hanoi households. Just more than half the sample had private access to safe drinking water, and this proportion increased as incomes rose. Besides living area and safe drinking water, more than 80 per cent of the households had a direct connection with the national electric grid. The percentage of households having private access to safe drinking water and electricity was lower in HCMC. Generally, compared with the rural poor, the urban poor have better living conditions, which can help them to maintain health and work more productively. These data also suggest the discernible inequality in having access to basic urban services.

The inequality is also reflected in terms of urban education. The proportion of people who are illiterate or have no degree appears to be lower as income rises, and vice versa (Figure 7.3). The poor are unable to afford the higher levels of education, such as university and postgraduate education. Most households in the sample attained primary and secondary levels. Hence, the poor's ability to earn a living is low, because they generally lack sufficient education. The difference between income groups is also reflected in the occupations in which people engage. People in lower-income quintiles had jobs that required lower qualification, whereas those in higher-income groups did jobs requiring higher education levels. The percentage of the unskilled was very high in the poorest group, and lower in groups with higher income levels. Analogously, the proportion of professionals with high qualifications amongst the richest group was very high. These figures suggest that education and occupation are closely correlated in urban areas.

People with little to no education are not likely to find a good job, or even a job. The results further indicate that the percentage of people who are business owners or leaders was very low in the poorest quintile (0.4 per cent), compared

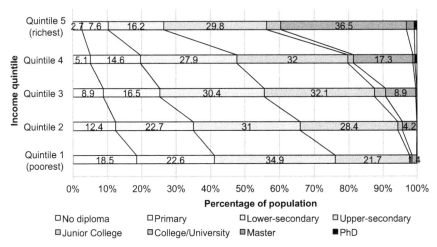

Figure 7.3 Education of the urban poor (per cent) by quintile, UPS 2009

Source: Based on the data drawn from Haughton *et al.* (2010)

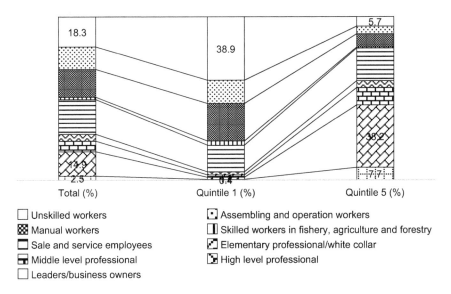

Figure 7.4 Main occupations of urban individuals (per cent), UPS 2009

Source: Based on the data drawn from Haughton *et al.* (2010)

with that in the richest quintile (7.6 per cent) (Figure 7.4). As widely believed, the development of private household microenterprises is the most effective way to reduce poverty. Low education, however, could limit the entrepreneurial ability to start up a business. The insufficient educational backgrounds of the poor also imply that the development of private household enterprises is difficult in

Vietnam. Consequently, poor people's capability of escaping poverty is expected to be low. Thus, the development of the private sector, which is promising to be an effective way to reduce poverty, is likely to depend on a small group of richer and/or educated people.

In conclusion, in accordance with the overall trend in the reduction in poverty, urban poverty appears to decline in Vietnam, based on the monetary approach. The increasing income inequality, however, indicates that the reduction in poverty in urban areas is unsustainable. The descriptive analysis of the main characteristics of urban households reveals that human capital, occupation, and living conditions significantly varied across income groups. The urban poor are expected to benefit more from trade liberalisation than the rural poor, especially from employment, because trade is mostly centred on urban areas with better infrastructure and higher density of population. The analysis suggests that they had no problem with either price transmission or market distribution. Thus, the effects of price and market distribution are likely to be less meaningful to urban households than to their rural counterparts, and so too probably is the revenue effect of trade liberalisation. Urban households generally enjoy considerable advantages in terms of better infrastructure and institutions. Overall, amongst the effects of trade liberalisation, employment greatly affects urban welfare. Access to particular types of jobs also matters to the urban poor, as noted by Dercon and Shapiro (2007).

Employment effects of trade liberalisation in urban areas

Unlike rural poor households, the urban poor have more opportunities to have jobs and to benefit from price changes, economic growth, and institutional reforms. Urban areas with more openness to trade and investment, and better infrastructure and communication are highly attracted to industrial factories, which can provide better chances of finding good jobs. The employment structure varies according to the level of urbanisation and trade (Table 7.6). Nationally, the agricultural sector (including forestry and fishery) accounted for 54 per cent of employment in 2009. The high ratios of agricultural employment are found in the northern midlands, the Mekong River Delta, and the Red River Delta. It may be noted that the northern midlands is not the centre of agricultural production, but it is a region of low population density, where most people engage in agriculture. The growth of employment in the agricultural sector in Vietnam is lowest compared with other sectors over a decade (4.2 per cent). Two main reasons can be taken into account. First, cultivable land is becoming scarce, and this increases the number of landless people. Second, agricultural production has been modernised to allow for the use of more machinery and less labour. The southeast region absorbs most of the labour in industry, manufacturing, and services. In fact, it is the most urbanised and commercial region in Vietnam. In this region, manufacturing demonstrates the highest rate of growth of employment over a decade (119 per cent), compared with other sectors. Trade, urbanisation,

Table 7.6 Employment by sector and region (per cent)

Sector	Region						Total
	Northern midlands	Red River Delta	North central/ Central coast	Central highlands	Southeast	Mekong River Delta	
Employment share, percentage of total for each region, 2009							
1. Agriculture, forestry, fishery	76.2	48.8	6.9	74.1	19.4	58.2	54.0
2. Industries, construction	9.3	24.8	16.2	7.6	40.2	15.2	20.3
3. Mining, quarrying	0.6	1.1	0.8	0.2	0.3	0.2	0.6
4. Manufacturing	4.8	16.0	8.9	4.1	32.6	10.2	13.7
5. Construction	3.5	7.1	6.0	2.9	6.5	4.5	5.5
6. Commerce/services	14.5	26.4	22.9	18.3	40.4	26.6	25.8
Employment growth, 1999–2009 (per cent)							
1. Agriculture, forestry, fishery	22.1	−14.8	4.1	36.5	4.5	3.1	4.2
2. Industries construction	161.0	155.1	107.4	106.6	117.1	106.5	125.0
3. Mining, quarrying	136.9	27.9	76.9	323.4	79.9	117.2	60.5
4. Manufacturing	151.1	155.5	72.0	72.9	119.0	79.0	110.7
5. Construction	297.7	216.6	205.7	170.1	114.3	209.0	190.7
6. Commerce/services	70.4	97.7	68.6	89.4	84.1	69.5	79.7

Source: Based on the data from the World Bank (2011b)

Table 7.7 Employment structure by sector and city class (per cent)

Sector	City class					Total
	Special cities	Class-I cites	Class-II cites	Class-III cites	Class-IV cites	
Employment share by sector for each class (per cent), 2009						
1. Agriculture, forestry, fishery	17.2	41.4	54.7	57.0	61.7	54.0
2. Industries, construction	35.5	23.6	21.4	19.3	15.5	20.3
3. Mining, quarrying	0.2	0.3	1.6	1.1	0.7	0.6
4. Manufacturing	27.4	15.5	13.9	12.6	10.0	13.7
5. Construction	7.1	7.0	5.4	5.2	4.3	5.5
6. Commerce/services	47.3	35.0	23.9	23.7	22.8	25.8
Employment growth 1999–2009 (per cent)						
1. Agriculture, forestry, fishery	–19.9	2.3	27.8	17.9	0.2	4.2
2. Industries, construction	90.1	94.5	148.8	164.1	81.8	125.0
3. Mining, quarrying	113.6	38.5	63.0	80.0	51.1	60.5
4. Manufacturing	87.4	80.6	142.0	151.9	66.0	110.7
5. Construction	104.7	137.4	224.4	242.6	144.3	190.7
6. Commerce/services	89.4	70.7	98.7	96.2	48.4	79.7

Source: Based on the data from the World Bank (2011b)

industry, and employment therefore provide urban people with an advantage over their rural counterparts.

A similar trend is also found for the structure of employment in cities. The ratio of employment in the agricultural sector, including forestry and fishery, was lowest in special cities (17.2 per cent) and highest in the class-IV cities (61.7 per cent) (Table 7.7). In contrast, the proportion of employment in the sectors of industry, manufacturing, and services was highest in special cities and lowest in the class-IV cities. Nevertheless, the same does not hold true for the growth of employment. The growth rates of employment in these sectors (industry, manufacturing, and services) were found to be highest in the class-II and III cities. This indicates that workers in the cities, be they residents or migrants, have low levels of qualification and/or training. They are, for the most part, unable to meet the larger cities' demand for high-qualification workers. Generally, the larger cities are likely to absorb most of the labour in the industrial and service sectors, whereas smaller cities appear to direct labour into the agricultural sector, including forestry and fishery.

The structure of urban employment shows the impact of the level of commercialisation and urbanisation on employment. Larger cities with high levels of commercialisation and urbanisation absorb more labour in manufacturing and services. These sectors typically provide higher levels of wages. Middle cities appear to open more job opportunities for workers with low qualifications and/or training. Middle and smaller cities are thereby more likely to help the urban poor, who have generally less education and primarily live in smaller cities. The employment effects of trade liberalisation on urban welfare and poverty are further examined using regression analysis.

7.3   Employment and welfare: a fixed effects analysis

Background of the model

The model of microdeterminants of growth is used to analyse the impacts of trade liberalisation on urban poverty. The model specification here is the same as the model used in Chapter 6. Real consumption expenditure per capita is used as a proxy for welfare. The independent variables are alternatively the conventional characteristics of individuals, households, and communities. The independent variables encompass two groups: non-trade- and trade-related variables. The non-trade-related variables consist of demographic characteristics, education, employment, and geography. The trade-related variables include employment in the export sectors, the import-competing sectors, the manufacturing sectors, and provincial trade per capita, or total retail sales per capita. Urban commune employment in the export sectors is defined as the ratio of labour working in the export sectors, including seafood, food processing, garment, shoes, rubber, and plastic products; commune employment in the import-competing sectors as the ratio of labour working in textiles, leather, chemical, metals, and machinery; and commune employment in industry as the ratio of labour working in the manufacturing sector. Provincial trade per capita measures local trade transactions, which are expected to be the key to improving welfare and reducing poverty. Although these proxies are still indirect for investigating the impacts of trade liberalisation on welfare and poverty, they are expected to throw more light on the effects of employment on urban welfare and poverty.

The fixed effects model is estimated using a panel data set of urban households, constructed from the VHLSSs for 2002, 2004, and 2006. The panel data covers 1,122 panel households for three waves, each with 374 observations. Unlike rural data, urban data do not include information on agricultural production and communes. This data set includes both poor and nonpoor households. As noted in Chapter 3, studies of the trade–poverty link, following the levels regression approach and using rural household data, have usually assumed that these effects on welfare will discernibly affect poverty, as most rural households are poor. In the case of a study of this relationship for Vietnam using urban household data, this assumption is still valid for two main reasons. First, most cities and towns in Vietnam are more rural-like regions where most poor households reside (World Bank, 2012). Second, a considerable proportion of urban poor households migrate from rural areas. This study therefore assumes that the effects of urban employment on urban household welfare are transmitted to the urban poor.

Analysis of results

Pooled OLS versus LSDV fixed effects model

The study first estimates a simple pooled OLS model, and then the LSDV fixed effects model. The LSDV fixed effects model is actually the OLS model with a set of dummies generated for the waves of the panel data. Both regressions, based on model (6.1), provide almost similar results in terms of values and expected signs of the coefficients (Table 7.8). In particular, the results of demographic traits, occupation, and geography are consistent across the two regressions. The pooled OLS results for education appear to be better than those of the LSDV fixed effects regression. The LSDV fixed effects regression, however, provides better results overall than those of the pooled OLS regression in terms of the explanatory power (adjusted R^2) of the regression and the level of significance of the coefficients. More importantly, the LSDV fixed effects results for the trade-related impacts appear to be better than those in the pooled OLS regression. The analysis is therefore based on the results of the LSDV fixed effects model.

The results suggest that most household demographic characteristics, such as household size, gender, spouse, and dependent ratios, have significant and expected impacts on welfare (Table 7.8). Ethnicity no longer affects welfare, however, probably because other ethnic groups in Vietnam live mainly in rural areas. The negative significant effect of the gender variable suggests that, holding other things constant, urban women now play a more important role in society than do their rural counterparts. Age also has no impact on welfare; although urban areas may have more demand for younger labourers, older people may be more appropriate to work in rural areas. The results also show that there is, in general, no improvement in welfare with household heads having spouses, signifying that jobs are relatively scarce in urban areas, as a result of the increasing rural-to-urban migration; therefore, spouses may largely become dependent in households. As expected, household size and dependent ratios, such as the ratios of children and elderly, decrease welfare.

The results suggest that education is a significant determinant of urban welfare. Increased number of school years completed helps urban people to improve their earnings. The ratios of household members with a technical diploma and postsecondary diploma are significant, but have unexpected signs, such as reflecting the surplus of labourers with diplomas in urban areas. A technical diploma is more useful for welfare improvement in rural areas than in urban regions, as shown in Chapter 6. In contrast, urban areas need real abilities and experience to work, rather than just qualifications. In addition to human capital, occupation also demonstrates an important role in improving urban welfare. Household heads who are leaders, professional labourers, or white-collar workers are better off than the unskilled. However, skilled workers receive no significantly different benefits as compared to the unskilled. Compared with other types of occupation, wage

Table 7.8 Estimates of pooled OLS and fixed effects models for the impacts of trade liberalisation on real per capita expenditure in urban areas, 2002–2006

		[Dependent variable: log of RPCE]			
Independent variable	*Expected sign*	*Pooled OLS model*		*LSDV fixed effects model*	
		Coefficient	*p-value*	*Coefficient*	*p-value*
Constant term		7.6666***	0.000	7.7974***	0.000
Demographic characteristics					
Household size	–	–0.1048***	0.000	–0.0961***	0.000
Head ethnicity (Kinh)	+	0.0917	0.142	0.0788	0.195
Head gender (male)	+	–0.0896***	0.008	–0.0851***	0.009
Head age	+	0.0125	0.142	0.0073	0.380
Head age square	+	–0.0000	0.714	–0.0000	0.954
Heads with spouse	+	–0.1533***	0.009	–0.1785***	0.002
Proportion of children	–	–0.0024***	0.009	–0.0035***	0.000
Proportion of elderly	–	–0.0034***	0.001	–0.0030***	0.002
Proportion of females	–	0.0003	0.738	0.0001	0.907
Human capital					
Head years of school	+	0.0471***	0.000	0.0451***	0.000
Spouse years of school	+	0.0352***	0.000	0.0358***	0.000
Parent years of school	+	0.0251***	0.000	0.0193**	0.020
Technical diploma ratio	+	0.0001	0.813	–0.0013**	0.048
Postsecondary diploma ratio	+	0.0021***	0.001	–0.0020***	0.001
Occupation (reference is the unskilled)					
Head leader	+	0.5648***	0.000	0.5094***	0.000
Head professional	+	0.1942***	0.000	0.2246***	0.000
Head white collar	+	0.1065	0.115	0.1098*	0.096
Head skilled work	+	0.0701**	0.049	0.0484	0.171
Head wage work	+	–0.0411	0.313	–0.0433	0.283
Head self–farmed business	+	–0.1156***	0.001	–0.1314***	0.000
Head self–business, nonfarm	+	0.0464	0.219	0.0412	0.263
Geography (reference is north central region)					
Red River Delta	+	0.0081	0.889	0.0484	0.381
Northeast	+	0.0163	0.779	0.0239	0.661

(*Continued*)

Table 7.8 (Continued)

Independent variable	Expected sign	Pooled OLS model		LSDV fixed effects model	
		Coefficient	p-value	Coefficient	p-value
Northwest	+	0.0389	0.693	0.0216	0.820
South central coast	+	0.0605	0.300	0.0837	0.127
Central highlands	+	−0.0325	0.662	−0.0450	0.523
Southeast	+	0.1143*	0.054	0.1721***	0.003
Mekong River Delta	+	0.0418	0.463	0.0586	0.278
Trade and employment					
Commune ratio of export labour	+	0.0012	0.538	0.0016	0.386
Commune ratio of import labour	+	0.0055*	0.053	0.0055**	0.043
Commune ratio of industrial labour	+	−0.0017	0.275	−0.0018	0.247
Province trade per capita	+	0.0524***	0.000	0.0421***	0.000
Time dummy (reference year: 2002)					
Year 2004	+			0.1483***	0.000
Year 2006	+			0.2800***	0.000
Adjusted R^2		0.533		0.553	
Number of observations		1,122		1,122	

Note: ***, **, and * significant at 1 per cent, 5 per cent, and 10 per cent level, respectively.

labour is insignificant, which appears somewhat odd. In practice, the general wage level in Vietnam is rather low, compared to other neighbouring countries. Meanwhile, living in urban areas with much higher living costs than rural areas is still difficult for wage workers. In addition to wage employment, self-farm business has a significant negative impact on urban welfare. This is reasonable, because farming may not be very suitable for urban areas. Self-businesses unrelated to farming also have no influence on urban welfare. They are often in the form of micro or household enterprises that generally face severe competition in urban areas. Amongst the regional effects taken into account, only the southeast is significantly different from the north central region (the reference region). This finding is also rational, as the southeast region is generally more dynamic than other regions in Vietnam. The results in general suggest that the regional effects are not significant in urban areas.

With respect to the impacts of trade liberalisation, amongst the trade-related variables, the commune ratio of employment in the import sectors and provincial trade per capita stand out as consistently significant in both pooled OLS and LSDV fixed effects regressions. This implies that the import-competing sectors in urban areas are growing up as a consequence of trade liberalisation, and have an increasing demand for labour. In addition, the level of trade in provinces consistently shows an important role in welfare improvement. Theoretically, trade liberalisation could have either external impacts, such as export earnings, or internal impacts, such as local trade development, or both. In reality, local trade is probably more important than exports for three main reasons. First, exports largely depend on the world market, which potentially has numerous risks and shocks that are possibly harmful to the poor. Second, the poor may not benefit from exports due to inadequate trade policies, such as the high costs of imported products, which are likely to result from nontariff barriers. Third, the development of local trade leads to the improvement in local infrastructure, which shortens the distances to remote areas where most poor households live. In summary, there is evidence for the favourable effects of trade liberalisation on welfare in urban areas, but these effects appear not to be as strong as expected. The expectation that the effects of trade liberalisation in urban areas are higher than in rural areas may also be unreasonable, because urban areas already have a higher level of trade liberalisation and welfare. The improvement of welfare under the impacts of trade liberalisation may thereby lessen.

Within fixed versus random effects model

The results from the fixed effects model can be compared to those of the random effects model. The effects of the trade-related variables in both within fixed and random effects models are consistent with those in the pooled OLS and LSDV fixed effects models (Table 7.9). The results of the random effects regression appear to be better in terms of the level of significance of the coefficients. The Hausman test, however, lends support to the within fixed effects model; the Hausman statistic is 86.6, which is large enough to reject the null hypothesis that the individual effects are not correlated with other regressors in the model.

Although the results from the within fixed effects model appear less effective than those from the LSDV fixed effects model, the estimates of the impacts of trade liberalisation in both are consistent. The results from the LSDV fixed effects model also appear to be better than those of the pooled OLS model and the random effects model. These results show that both employment in the import-competing sectors and local trade per capita helped urban households to improve welfare. More importantly, local trade in provinces demonstrates a consistent and significant impact on urban welfare. Contrary to expectation, employment in both export and industrial sectors is insignificant. The results from the models, whether it be the pooled OLS, LSDV fixed effects, within fixed effects, or random effects, have suggested evidence for the effects of employment on urban welfare.

Table 7.9 Estimates of fixed and random effects models of the impacts of trade liberalisation on real per capita expenditure in urban areas, 2002–2006

		[Dependent variable: log of RPCE]			
Independent variable	*Expected sign*	*Within fixed effects model*		*Random effects model*	
		Coefficient	*p-value*	*Coefficient*	*p-value*
Constant term		7.4167***	0.000	7.3325***	0.000
Demographic characteristics					
Household size	–	–0.1042***	0.000	–0.1103***	0.000
Head ethnicity (Kinh)	+	Omitted	–	0.1213*	0.098
Head gender (male)	+	Omitted	–	–0.0867*	0.054
Head age	+	0.0445**	0.013	0.0233**	0.016
Head age square	+	–0.0004**	0.029	–0.0001	0.191
Heads with spouse	+	–0.0940	0.176	–0.1706**	0.015
Proportion of children	–	–0.0002	0.828	–0.0011	0.204
Proportion of elderly	–	–0.0008	0.529	–0.0031***	0.001
Proportion of females	–	0.0000	0.985	–0.0002	0.830
Human capital					
Head years of school	+	Omitted	–	0.0465***	0.000
Spouse years of school	+	Omitted	–	0.0336***	0.000
Parent years of school	+	Omitted	–	0.0272**	0.009
Technical diploma ratio	+	0.0024***	0.001	0.0009	0.127
Postsecondary ratio	+	0.0005	0.477	0.0017***	0.006
Occupation (reference is the unskilled)					
Head leader	+	0.1225	0.221	0.3992***	0.000
Head professional	+	–0.0563	0.462	0.1138**	0.046
Head white collar	+	–0.0345	0.693	0.0291	0.704
Head skilled work	+	0.0622	0.181	0.0624	0.108
Head wage work	+	0.0743	0.140	0.0194	0.638
Head self–farmed business	+	0.0360	0.464	–0.0664*	0.070
Head self–business, nonfarm	+	0.0445	0.355	0.0509	0.182
Geography (reference is north central region)					
Red River Delta	+	Omitted	–	0.0097	0.899
Northeast	+	Omitted	–	0.0185	0.811

Northwest	+	Omitted	–	0.0597	0.614
South central coast	+	Omitted	–	0.0656	0.401
Central highlands	+	Omitted	–	–0.0312	0.739
Southeast	+	Omitted	–	0.1108	0.157
Mekong River Delta	+	Omitted	–	0.0475	0.523
Trade and employment					
Commune ratio of export labour	+	0.0009	0.742	0.0010	0.596
Commune ratio of import labour	+	0.0096***	0.006	0.0071**	0.011
Commune ratio of industrial labour	+	–0.0012	0.564	–0.0015	0.309
Province trade per capita	+	0.0559***	0.000	0.0536***	0.000
Adjusted R^2		0.315		0.294	
Number of observations		1,122		1,122	

Note: ***, **, and * significant at 1 per cent, 5 per cent, and 10 per cent level, respectively.

7.4 Conclusions

This chapter has examined the impacts of trade liberalisation on urban poverty in Vietnam, using the 2009 urban poverty survey (UPS) data and the VHLSS panel data set for the period from 2002 to 2006. Urban poverty increasingly matters to Vietnam's economic development because of the rapid growth of urban population and the rising inequality in income. The surge in urban population exceeds the provision of urban essential services and infrastructure. The large cities, such as HCMC and Hanoi, have witnessed the rapid growth of urban population in the past few years, as a result of the adoption of the open door policy and the liberalisation of trade. The analysis based on the case study of urban poverty in HCMC and Hanoi reveals that demographic characteristics, human capital, occupation, and living conditions change across income groups. These cases of HCMC and Hanoi also suggest the increase in inequality amongst different income groups. Compared with rural households, urban households benefit more from economic growth and development, in terms of education, health care, living standards, institutional reforms, and employment. More importantly, urban households tend to be affected less by the adverse effects of trade liberalisation, such as the uneven price transmission or the revenue effects.

Amongst the effects of trade liberalisation, trade-induced employment in urban areas matters greatly to urban households. The analysis of the panel data of urban households from 2002 to 2006 shows that local trade and employment in the import-competing sectors improved urban welfare. Local trade per capita has a consistent impact on welfare in urban areas. By and large, the study provides evidence for the effects of trade liberalisation on urban welfare, especially the employment effects. These effects are, however, weaker than expected. It should be noted that most of the urban households in Vietnam are located in the rural-like urban areas. A considerable number of them, those who are poor, migrate from the actually rural areas. The impacts of trade liberalisation on urban welfare are, therefore, significant for the reduction in urban poverty. The study suggests that the development of local markets and local production, especially small and medium private enterprises, will be the key to improving urban standards of living and reducing urban poverty. The reduction of urban poverty, by developing small and medium private enterprises to absorb the employment surplus from agriculture, is a very strategic policy for addressing poverty in the long run in Vietnam.

Notes

1 See the World Bank (2011b) for details of the classification of cities in Vietnam.
2 The national poverty line was issued in 2006 and converted to 2009 values using consumption price indexes, which was equivalent to VN$4.778 million per person per year; the Hanoi poverty line was VN$6 million for urban areas, applied for the period 2009–2013; the HCMC poverty line was VN$12 million, applied for the period 2009–2015; and the two international poverty lines, US$1.25 and US$2 per day per head, were equivalent to VN$4.135 million and VN$6.612 million per person per year, respectively.

References

Datt, G., and Ravallion, M. (2011). Has India's Economic Growth Become More Pro-poor in the Wake of Economic Reforms?. *The World Bank Economic Review,* 25(2), 33.

Dercon, S., and Shapiro, J.S. (2007). *Moving On, Staying Behind, Getting Lost: Lessons on Poverty Mobility from Longitudinal Data.* Global Poverty Research Group, Working Paper (No. 075), 51.

General Statistics Office (2012). *Result of the Vietnam Household Living Standards Survey 2010.* Ho Chi Minh: Statistical Publishing House.

Glewwe, P., Gragnolati, M., and Zaman, H. (2002). Who Gained from Vietnam's Boom in the 1990s?. *Economic Development and Cultural Change,* 50(4), 773–792.

Goldberg, P.K., and Pavcnik, N. (2005). *The Effect of the Colombian Trade Liberalisation on Urban Poverty.* NBER, Working Paper Series (No. 11081), 47.

Haughton, J., Loan, N.T.T., and Linh, N.B. (2010). *Urban Poverty Assessment in Ha Noi and Ho Chi Minh City.* Hanoi: UNDP.

International Monetary Fund (IMF) (2004). *Vietnam: Poverty Reduction Strategy Paper.* IMF, Country Report (No. 04/25), 134.

Justino, P., Litchfield, J., and Pham, H.T. (2008). Poverty Dynamics during Trade Reform: Evidence from Rural Vietnam. *Review of Income and Wealth,* 54(2), 166–192. DOI: 10.1111/j.1475-4991.2008.00269.x

Kabeer, N., and Tran, T.V.A. (2006). *Globalization, Gender and Work in the Context of Economic Transition: The Case of Vietnam.* UNDP, Vietnam Policy Dialogue Paper (No. 2), 40.

Liu, A.Y.C. (2008). Changes in Urban Inequality in Vietnam: 1992–1998. *Economic Systems, 32*(4), 410–425. DOI: 10.1016/j.ecosys.2007.10.002

Macours, K., and Swinnen, J.F.M. (2008). Rural-Urban Poverty Differences in Transition Countries. *World Development, 36*(11), 2170–2187.

Niimi, Y., Vasudeva-Dutta, P., and Winters, L.A. (2007). Trade Liberalization and Poverty Dynamics in Vietnam. *Journal of Economic Integration, 22*(4), 819–851.

Oxfam UK and ActionAid (2010). *Participatory Monitoring of Urban Poverty in Vietnam: Third Round Synthesis Report.* United Kingdom: Oxfam.

Seshan, G. (2005). *The Impact of Trade Liberalization on Household Welfare in Vietnam.* World Bank, Policy Research Working Paper (No. 3541).

Vietnam Academy of Social Sciences (VASS) (2011). *Poverty Reduction in Vietnam: Achievements and Challenges.* Hanoi.

World Bank (2011b). *Vietnam Urbanization Review: Technical Assistance Report* (p. 263). Hanoi.

World Bank (2012). *Well Begun, Not Yet Done: Vietnam's Remarkable Progress on Poverty Reduction and the Emerging Challenges* (p. 190). Hanoi.

8 Institutional reforms and poverty

8.1 Introduction

Institutions play an important role in the acceleration of economic growth and the transmission of its effects across the economy. The literature on the trade–poverty relationship shows that institutions are crucial to the impacts of trade liberalisation on poverty (Rodrik, 2002). Acemoglu and Robinson (2012) conflate experiences of the development of nations and suggest that a country's own institutions determine its success or failure. Vietnam transitioned into the market economy from the CPE with an underdeveloped institutional system. Its weak institutional framework rendered resource allocation inefficient and dampened the business incentives. The establishment of a business involved 11 administrative procedures and took 45 days in 2006. The number of procedures and the length of time to start up a business in 2010 were 11 and 39, respectively. In 2014, it took on average 34 days and 10 procedures to start up a business in Vietnam, compared with an average of 37.8 days and 7 procedures, respectively, in East Asia and the Pacific.[1] Although having made considerable progress in institutional reforms, Vietnam has been somewhat less attractive to foreign investors. Inadequate institutions made business costly, dampening the business environment and thereby the employment creation. Consequently, the poor may benefit only modestly from the liberalisation of trade and the acceleration of economic growth. Many studies on the trade–poverty link for Vietnam have yet to address the institutional effects on welfare. Generally, although institutions have been an important dimension of poverty, only few studies have taken into consideration the effects of institutional reforms on household welfare and poverty (see, for instance, Dollar and Kraay, 2003).

This chapter demystifies the impacts of institutions on household welfare in Vietnam. It focuses on rural areas because of the high incidence of poverty often found in these areas. The research undertaken in this chapter differs from previous similar studies in several respects. First, it draws on the contention of Abbott *et al.* (2009) that those models using cross-country data or focusing more on tariff changes as a key element of reforms may be flawed and may have failed to incorporate the influence of institutional reforms. Second, it uses internal trade transaction and indexes of institutional reforms to capture the effects of institutional reforms on welfare that appear to have been ignored by the previous studies in the field. Both institutional reforms and local trade openness are discernibly important to rural household welfare. The chapter sheds more light on the institutional effects of trade liberalisation on rural welfare in Vietnam. The impacts of local trade openness and institutional reforms on rural welfare are investigated at the provincial level, using the model of microdeterminants of growth. The model is estimated on the household survey data over the period 2006 to 2010. The rest of the chapter is organized as follows. Section 8.2 explains the model and the methodology used to estimate the model. Section 8.3 analyses the results of the model. Section 8.4 concludes the chapter and draws some policy implications.

8.2   Methods and data

Methods

The model specification used in the study draws on Glewwe *et al.* (2000) and Justino *et al.* (2008). Both of these studies use the model of microdeterminants of growth and attempt to capture the determinants of household welfare and the dynamics of poverty in Vietnam during the 1990s, under the impact of a wide range of variables. These studies, however, neither focus on nor capture institutional effects, because the data used in these studies contain no information about institutions. This study does not need to draw any distinction between poor and nonpoor households, as it focuses on rural households that primarily constitute the poor in Vietnam. The study differs from other similar studies in that it analyses the impacts of institutional reforms and local trade openness on rural household welfare at the provincial level and it uses more recent data.

The dependent variable in the model used in the study is per capita income, measured in logarithm (log of per capita income). The study follows the monetary approach to measuring welfare and poverty.[2] Income per capita is used as a proxy for welfare, because income may better reflect the potential household wealth. According to Deaton and Zaidi (2002) and Haughton and Khandker (2009), both income and consumption are in fact the main alternatives for measuring welfare. The independent variables are the conventional characteristics of individuals, households, communities, and regions. The study organises the independent variables into two broad groups: the non-trade- and trade-related variables. The non-trade-related variables measure household and regional characteristics, whereas the trade-related variables measure local trade liberalisation and institutional reforms. The former group covers the subgroups of variables measuring the characteristics of households and household heads, such as demographic traits, education, occupation, household agricultural production, and regional difference.

In the non-trade-related variables, drawn on Glewwe and Hall (1998), Glewwe *et al.* (2002), and Niimi *et al.* (2007), the predetermined variables are chosen to avoid the possible problem of endogeneity. These variables are not likely to be determined by the current level of incomes (Glewwe *et al.*, 2002; Niimi *et al.*, 2007). According to Glewwe and Hall (1998), the characteristics of household heads that are determined by the age of adulthood, such as age, education, and occupation, are assumed to be exogenous. The variables that measure agricultural production, such as rice productivity, net rice producers, and fertiliser used in agricultural production, are assumed to be exogenous, because they depend primarily on farm technology, land quality, and weather. Household assets, such as durable goods, savings, and houses, are considered to be endogenous. Access to electricity and safe drinking water are chosen as household assets. These variables are assumed to be exogenous, as they depend largely on regional characteristics, rather than on household incomes. Regardless of income levels, people tend to acquire electricity and safe water for the sake of health, if these basic needs are available in the region where they live.

The first group of variables, used to measure demographic traits of households and household heads, includes household size, ethnicity, gender, age, marital status, and household composition. The second group, employed to quantify the impact of human capital, comprises the school years of household heads, spouses, and their parents, as well as the proportion of household members with a technical diploma or post-secondary diploma. All education variables are expected to have a positive impact on welfare. The third group, which measures the impact of occupation by household heads, includes four kinds of dummy variables (leader or business owner, professional, white collar, and skilled worker), with the unskilled being the reference category. Employment is expected to have a positive effect on welfare. The fourth group, used to measure agricultural production, encompasses rice productivity, the net rice producer, and the total quantity of fertiliser. Net rice producers are farm households that have a surplus in rice production in a year. These agricultural variables should be positively associated with rural income.

The fifth group is used to measure household assets. The study uses some housing characteristics, such as access to electricity and safe drinking water, to explain rural welfare, instead of using the variables of household assets such as house, remittance, and savings, which are obviously endogenous. These variables, relevant to essential living conditions, are expected to have a positive impact on welfare. As pointed out by Perkins *et al.* (2006), access to safe water is vital for rural households to meet nutritional needs. The sixth group of non-trade-related variables is used to measure the difference in household location. These geographical dummies are used to indicate whether a particular household is located in an urban or a rural region, and in the north central region or the other regions.[3] The north central region is widely considered to be the poorest region in Vietnam. Households in rural regions and in the north central region are expected to be worse off than those in the other regions.

Construction of the trade-related variables is the key to investigating the impacts of trade liberalisation on household welfare and poverty. Various methods have been used to measure trade openness, including tariff and nontariff barriers, as well as ratios of exports to GDP, and of trade volume (exports plus imports) to GDP (see Singh, 2010). The literature shows that none of these is optimal, however, as these measures of trade openness may not link up with welfare and poverty at the household level. To evaluate the impacts of trade liberalisation on household welfare and poverty, according to Justino *et al.* (2008), some specific household characteristics can be linked to trade reforms. These linkages can be based on the Winters pathways, as explained in the review of literature. The trade-related variables include commune employment, provincial trade, and institutional reforms. Employment can reflect a region's level of trade and industrial activities, as well as its level of development of the labour market. The use of employment as a measure of trade openness should be interpreted with caution, as a high level of employment could also result from factors other than trade. Another measure of trade openness is the provincial or local trade. Although trade openness includes both external trade and internal trade, this chapter focuses on internal trade only, as measured by total retail sales per capita, or trade transaction. Local trade transactions can reflect the level of internal trade and production activities.

Studies by Dollar and Kraay (2003), Levchenko (2004), Gaiha and Imai (2005), and Kandil (2009) have attempted to measure institutions. Levchenko (2004) uses the Herfindahl index as a proxy for institutional dependence. Kandil (2009) measures institutional quality using six separate indicators of governance: voice and accountability, political stability, government effectiveness, regulatory quality, rule of law, and control of corruption. This study uses the PCI to measure institutional reforms. This index was constructed in 2005 to assess the business environment and the policies on private sector development across provinces, covering nine or 10 component indexes. It has been used in the studies by Tran *et al.* (2008) and Dang (2010, 2013). These studies, however, do not focus on the impacts of institutions and trade openness on welfare. By virtue of its aims and components, the PCI is most appropriate for measuring the quality of institutions and institutional reforms in the provinces. In terms of the empirical strategy, drawn on Justino *et al.* (2008), this study measures trade-related variables at the commune or provincial level; therefore, these variables are likely to be exogenous to household income, which is measured at the household level. The details of measurement and the main descriptive statistics of the model variables are provided in Table 8.1.

Data

Vietnam Household Living Standards Surveys (VHLSSs)

The study utilises the large sample data drawn from the VHLSSs (2006 and 2010) to estimate the model. The VHLSSs cover about 45,945 households over 3,063 communes/wards (VHLSS 2006), and about 69,360 households over 3,133 communes/wards (VHLSS 2010). Such comprehensive coverage is representative of regions, urban areas, rural areas, and provinces in Vietnam. The surveys consist of two types of data: households and communes. The data in the VHLSSs are organised into many sections, each containing a certain subject, such as demographic traits, income and expenditure, education, health, employment,

Table 8.1 Descriptive statistics of the model variables

Variable	Unit	Variable type	Descriptive statistics			
			2006		2010	
			Mean	Std. dev.	Mean	Std. dev.
Per capita income	'000 VND	Cont.	6087.740	4932.347	12422.60	12121.77
Household size	Person	Cont.	4.445	1.629	4.199	1.504
Head ethnicity (Kinh)		Binary	0.785	0.411	0.731	0.443
Head gender (male)		Binary	0.824	0.381	0.847	0.360
Head age	Year	Cont.	48.207	12.966	47.249	13.015
Heads with spouse		Binary	0.843	0.366	0.856	0.352
Proportion of children	Per cent	Cont.	23.517	21.127	22.510	21.148
Proportion of elderly	Per cent	Cont.	10.900	22.689	9.337	20.672
Head years of school	Year	Cont.	6.804	3.406	6.833	3.462
Spouse years of school	Year	Cont.	5.364	3.910	5.445	3.955
Parent years of school	Year	Cont.	0.248	1.288	0.299	1.504
Technical diploma ratio	Per cent	Cont.	37.385	29.588	16.304	21.531
Postsecondary diploma ratio	Per cent	Cont.	33.444	29.724	12.882	19.593
Head business owner/leader		Binary	0.021	0.142	0.016	0.125
Head professional		Binary	0.014	0.117	0.012	0.109
Head white collar		Binary	0.006	0.078	0.002	0.049
Head skilled worker		Binary	0.158	0.364	0.324	0.468
Rice productivity	Kg/m2	Cont.	0.486	0.116	0.485	0.120

Variable	Unit	Type				
Household net rice producers	Kg	Cont.	3590.665	6967.646	1302.439	1010.484
Total used fertiliser quantity	Kg	Cont.	527.275	827.461	522.182	872.149
Access to electricity		Binary	0.946	0.227	0.960	0.196
Access to safe drinking water		Binary	0.052	0.222	0.079	0.269
North central region		Binary	0.138	0.345	0.137	0.344
Urban areas		Binary	0.060	0.238	0.079	0.270
Commune industry labour ratio	Per cent	Cont.	6.747	10.707	10.008	15.726
Commune wage labour ratio	Per cent	Cont.	21.926	14.501	15.890	14.143
Provincial total sales per capita	mVND	Cont.	4.711	2.652	12.121	6.862
Provincial competitiveness index	Per cent	Cont.	51.710	6.502	57.317	4.561
Market entry costs	Per cent	Cont.	7.359	0.774	6.585	0.644
Land access	Per cent	Cont.	5.898	0.767	5.843	1.189
Transparency	Per cent	Cont.	5.302	1.145	5.675	0.696
Time costs	Per cent	Cont.	4.472	0.755	6.272	0.950
Informal charges	Per cent	Cont.	6.263	0.711	6.216	0.745
Provincial leadership proactivity	Per cent	Cont.	4.881	1.312	5.064	1.266
Business support services	Per cent	Cont.	5.000	1.220	5.802	0.898
Labour training	Per cent	Cont.	5.102	1.262	5.253	0.585
Legal institutions	Per cent	Cont.	3.692	0.773	4.729	0.959

Source: Authors' calculation, based on the VHLSSs 2006 and 2010

agricultural production, and communes. As the data on communes are not yet available in the VHLSS 2010, the effects of commune characteristics cannot be observed. The data from different sets of questionnaires are compiled to gather relevant variables. The samples used in the analysis for the study comprised 4,680 households for the VHLSS 2006 and 4,221 households for the VHLSS 2010.

Data for trade-related variables

The data collected from the VHLSSs are supplemented with the data drawn from other sources to have some proxies for local trade openness and institutional reforms. These proxies are measured in terms of the ratios of industrial employment and wage employment at the commune level, the provincial total retail sales per capita, and the PCI. First, industrial employment is the commune proportion of labour working in the industrial sector, such as seafood, food processing, garment and shoes, and rubber and plastic products, measured at the commune level (Niimi *et al.*, 2007). Wage employment is the ratio of labour receiving wages as working to the commune sample. These ratios are calculated from the VHLSS data.

Second, the provincial total retail sales per capita are the total value of retail sales that take place in a province over a year, divided by the population of the province (Table 8.2). This variable measures the level of trade transactions, and thereby their level of openness to trade and investment in provinces. The data for the variable are taken from various issues of the statistical yearbooks of Vietnam, published by the GSO.

Third, the PCI, developed in 2005 by the VCCI and the project for the VNCI, was constructed to assess and rank the business environment and the policies towards private sector development across provinces in Vietnam. The PCI rates provinces on a 100-point scale, using the survey data on the enterprise perceptions of the local business environment. It also employs credible and comparable data from officials and other sources relevant to local conditions (USAID and VCCI, 2006, 2010). The PCI 2006 was constructed using 10 subindexes that capture the key dimensions of the local business environment: market entry costs, land access and security of tenure, transparency and access to information, time costs of regulatory compliance, informal charges, SOE-biased competition environment, proactivity of provincial leadership, private sector development services, labour training, and legal institutions. The PCI 2010, comprising nine subindexes, is conceptually the same as the PCI 2006, except for the absence of the component index of SOE-based competition environment. This 2006 subindex is excluded for ease of comparison. The classification of provinces, based on the PCI 2006 and PCI 2010, is shown in Figure 8.1.

The PCI, by virtue of its components, can capture institutional and thus trade reforms. It is the most appropriate index to represent the provincial level of trade openness and institutional reforms. Some studies of Vietnam have used this index to compare the provincial performance and reforms. This study uses it in conjunction with household data to examine the provincial welfare and poverty. Based

Table 8.2 Provincial per capita income, head count poverty rate, trade, and the PCI

Province	Poverty rate (per cent)		Mean per capita income (1,000 VND)		Sales per capita (million VND)		PCI	
	2006	2010	2006	2010	2006	2010	2006	2010
Hanoi	1	2	14047.00	31339.60	17.526	34.756	50.34	55.73
Hai Phong	2	3	10257.55	21906.52	7.679	18.572	49.98	54.64
Vinh Phuc	3	5	7925.83	16462.49	4.215	16.355	61.27	61.73
Ha Tay	6	-	8039.00	-	6.874	-	40.73	-
Bac Ninh	4	1	8417.83	20808.44	5.051	16.650	54.79	64.48
Hai Dương	3	5	8415.75	16763.15	3.179	7.205	52.70	57.51
Hung Yen	4	4	8817.36	19753.39	3.786	8.710	55.97	49.77
Ha Nam	5	2	6369.22	15961.27	4.018	9.087	47.27	52.18
Nam Định	4	5	8105.59	15892.80	2.746	6.460	48.89	55.63
Thai Binh	9	7	6710.29	17633.71	2.986	8.027	50.54	60.04
Ninh Binh	4	7	6860.91	15839.26	3.957	11.825	55.82	62.85
Ha Giang	31	47	4668.38	8524.91	1.572	3.448	48.49	53.94
Cao Bang	21	40	7090.00	10075.18	2.892	7.240	46.63	53.55
Lao Cai	22	25	6472.80	13171.88	3.488	8.975	64.11	67.95
Bac Kan	11	18	5642.71	12012.71	2.587	5.955	48.73	51.49
Lang Son	2	24	6396.22	11673.00	4.366	12.605	49.64	50.20
Tuyen Quang	16	30	6014.05	11393.47	3.481	8.007	47.21	57.90
Yen Bai	16	21	6314.42	12211.37	2.552	7.113	56.85	60.16
Thai Nguyen	8	12	7596.58	15203.02	3.597	7.850	52.71	56.54
Phu Tho	4	6	7159.85	13988.69	2.919	7.507	54.42	52.47
Bac Giang	4	9	7038.21	14455.93	2.070	4.788	55.99	58.02
Quang Ninh	5	5	11486.58	21776.41	10.622	21.757	53.25	64.41
Lai Chau	36	50	3801.65	8887.31	1.336	3.582	36.76	51.77
Đien Bien	35	48	4435.64	10648.24	2.514	6.634	42.28	55.12
Son La	17	25	6313.47	13699.52	2.576	7.355	45.22	49.26
Hoa Binh	16	22	6073.16	11744.11	1.943	6.133	50.17	49.89
Thanh Hoa	14	17	5918.14	11462.78	2.589	6.998	45.30	55.68
Nghe An	15	17	5880.92	13434.93	3.179	9.451	54.43	52.38
Ha Tinh	20	15	5743.26	13381.28	3.733	11.919	42.35	57.22
Quang Binh	12	15	5772.29	13771.90	4.274	11.269	47.90	55.22
Quang Tri	20	16	5828.82	13390.82	6.090	15.778	52.18	61.61

(*Continued*)

Table 8.2 (Continued)

Province	Poverty rate (per cent)		Mean per capita income (1,000 VND)		Sales per capita (million VND)		PCI	
	2006	2010	2006	2010	2006	2010	2006	2010
Thua Thien-Hue	12	5	7424.09	12583.91	6.268	13.369	50.53	61.31
Đa Nang	0	2	14377.68	28622.44	13.355	36.797	75.39	69.77
Quang Nam	11	11	6404.67	13165.81	3.348	9.936	56.42	59.34
Quang Ngãi	7	12	6333.68	12325.31	5.385	14.139	44.20	52.21
Binh Đinh	5	1	7834.86	18018.52	6.513	15.097	66.49	60.37
Phu Yen	4	7	7671.90	13779.02	4.476	10.796	54.93	58.18
Khanh Hoa	5	11	9003.13	14797.83	10.810	24.943	55.33	56.75
Kon Tum	7	15	6358.83	16496.47	3.158	8.325	41.38	57.01
Gia Lai	20	14	6678.00	15471.57	3.883	10.069	53.06	53.65
Đak Lak	9	9	7201.06	16211.93	4.001	14.897	51.65	57.20
Đak Nong	6	9	8505.33	14081.88	4.079	10.319	38.91	48.91
Lam Đong	13	9	8311.73	17990.47	6.337	16.831	52.25	58.26
HCMC	0	0	19660.48	40682.26	21.056	50.579	63.39	59.67
Ninh Thuan	12	7	6671.20	16114.47	4.809	11.292	45.82	56.61
Binh Phuoc	4	2	9931.37	20684.90	5.580	13.765	46.29	57.24
Binh Duong	1	1	10046.55	16737.24	11.441	28.162	76.23	57.93
Đong Nai	0	2	15818.11	48728.61	9.140	28.090	64.64	65.72
Binh Thuan	0	1	11645.48	22956.87	7.269	22.221	52.66	59.49
BaRia-Vung Tau	2	4	8089.27	16986.76	9.169	14.029	55.95	58.45
Long An	0	4	12603.30	22974.36	5.078	23.079	50.40	60.55
Đong Thap	5	4	9158.46	18638.85	5.621	12.432	58.13	62.74
An Giang	1	7	8486.57	16946.50	9.045	16.019	60.45	67.22
Tien Giang	2	3	8831.19	18812.84	6.347	22.838	52.18	61.94
Vinh Long	3	4	8823.03	17751.44	6.735	12.812	64.67	59.63
Ben Tre	3	7	8246.96	18764.00	5.089	16.589	53.11	63.40
Kien Giang	3	8	8611.77	16418.59	7.536	12.372	51.27	63.11
Can Tho	3	10	9337.77	16417.26	11.105	17.574	58.30	58.90
Hau Giang	0	0	11982.47	19897.83	5.239	27.196	52.61	62.46
Tra Vinh	10	5	8563.27	15351.68	4.982	15.870	56.83	63.91
Soc Trang	4	16	8092.55	13549.49	5.545	8.517	55.34	65.80
Bac Lieu	5	7	6685.22	16811.92	7.436	16.751	42.89	61.49
Ca Mau	2	7	7698.84	18711.47	8.101	13.732	43.99	58.20

Source: Authors' calculations using data from the VHLSSs 2006 and 2010, the GSO, and the VCCI

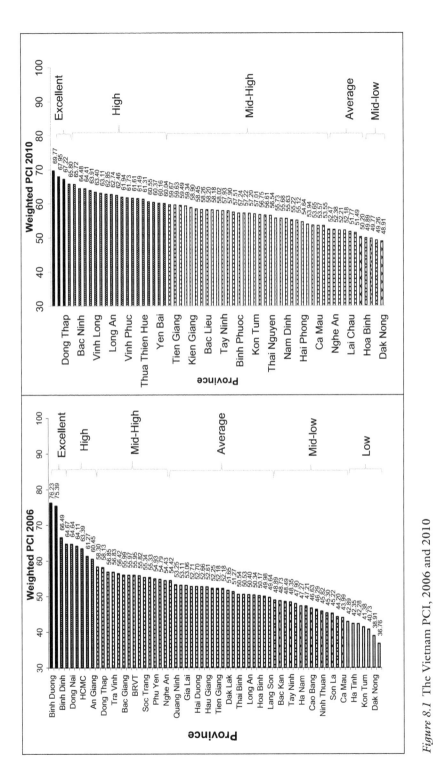

Figure 8.1 The Vietnam PCI, 2006 and 2010

Source: Based on the data collected from the USAID and Vietnam Chamber of Commerce and Industry (2006, 2010)

on the PCI, provinces are classified as excellent, high, mid-high, average, mid-low, and low performing. The index helps provinces to identify their competitive strengths and weaknesses and accordingly formulate strategies to enhance their level of competitiveness in nurturing trade and private business. The improvements in provincial competitiveness would provide motivation for the increase in the level of trade liberalisation and the quality of institutions, which would eventually help to raise the standards of living of local households.

8.3   Results and discussions

The model 6.1, as specified in Chapter 6, is estimated using the data collected from the VHLSS 2006 and VHLSS 2010 to analyse the changes in the impacts of local trade openness and institutional reforms on the welfare of rural households over the two points in time (2006 and 2010). In terms of institutional reforms, the model uses both the overall PCI and the PCI by component. The results from the estimates of model (6.1) suggest that most of the coefficients are statistically significant and have the expected signs (Table 8.3 and Table 8.4). The model has only a minor issue of multicollinearity, given that the mean of the variance inflation factor (VIF) is around 2 for the 2006 regression and 1.7 for the 2010 regression. The robust standard errors are used to eliminate the possible problem of heteroscedasticity. The following analysis shows the impacts of each group of the variables on rural welfare. The non-trade-related variables provide a broad picture of the determinants of rural welfare. The trade-related variables provide a clearer focus on the impacts of trade openness and institutional reforms on household welfare. The coefficients explain the percentage changes in per capita income associated with the household characteristics. The analysis begins with the regression results based on the overall PCI, and then follows with the results based on the PCI by component.

Regression results based on the overall PCI

The results of the impacts of household demographic characteristics on welfare could be different from those in the previous analyses, as the data were updated and included the variables of institutional reforms. These results show that only gender and household heads with spouses fail to affect welfare; the other variables do have an impact on welfare, to varying degrees (Table 8.3). The insignificance of the gender of head is also found in several similar studies, for instance, Glewwe *et al.* (2002), Niimi *et al.* (2007), and Justino *et al.* (2008). This result reinforces the findings obtained in Chapter 6. Theoretically, Haughton and Khandker (2009) assert that the households headed by men are better off than those headed by women. The World Bank (2012), however, observes that the female head-ship has become less correlated with poverty in Vietnam. Although this result is somewhat counter to expectation, it suggests that the issue of gender inequality appears to be minor in Vietnam: in reality, women are increasingly important in Vietnamese society. The results also show that the variable of household heads

Table 8.3 Cross-sectional OLS estimates of overall impact of institutional reforms and local trade on per capita income, 2006 and 2010

[Dependent variable: log of per capita income]

Independent variable	Expected sign	2006		2010		Coef. change
		Coefficient	p-value	Coefficient	p-value	(7) = (5) – (3)
(1)	(2)	(3)	(4)	(5)	(6)	(7) = (5) – (3)
Constant term		7.8723***	0.000	8.1939***	0.000	0.3216
Household and individual characteristics						
Household size	–	-0.0575***	0.000	-0.0655***	0.000	-0.0080
Head ethnicity (Kinh)	+	0.1177***	0.000	0.2402***	0.000	0.1225
Head gender (male)	+	-0.0177	0.558	-0.0096	0.786	0.0020
Head age	+/–	0.0026***	0.002	0.0046***	0.000	0.0020
Heads with spouse	+/–	-0.0570	0.128	-0.0479	0.265	0.0002
Proportion of children	–	-0.0046***	0.000	-0.0044***	0.000	0.0002
Proportion of elderly	–	-0.0024***	0.000	-0.0030***	0.000	-0.0006
Human capital						
Head years of school	+	0.0225***	0.000	0.0224***	0.000	-0.0001
Spouse years of school	+	0.0087***	0.003	0.0153***	0.000	0.0066
Parent years of school	+	0.0191***	0.003	0.0133**	0.010	-0.0058
Technical diploma ratio	+	0.0040***	0.000	0.0025***	0.000	-0.0015
Postsecondary diploma ratio	+	-0.0043***	0.000	-0.0022***	0.003	0.0021
Occupation (reference category is the unskilled)						
Head business owner/leader	+	0.2102***	0.000	0.2632***	0.000	0.0529
Head professional	+	0.2958***	0.000	0.3701***	0.000	0.0743
Head white collar	+	0.2578***	0.001	0.0497	0.703	-0.2081

(*Continued*)

Table 8.3 (Continued)

Independent variable	Expected sign	2006		2010		Coef. change
		Coefficient	p-value	Coefficient	p-value	
(1)	(2)	(3)	(4)	(5)	(6)	(7) = (5) − (3)
Head skilled worker	+	0.1066***	0.000	0.1493***	0.000	0.0427
Agricultural production						
Rice productivity	+	0.2207***	0.000	0.4214***	0.000	0.2007
Household net rice producers	+	0.0000***	0.000	0.0001***	0.000	0.0000
Total used fertiliser quantity	+	0.0001***	0.000	0.0001***	0.001	0.0000
House characteristics						
Access to electricity	+	0.0564**	0.038	0.0454	0.266	−0.0111
Access to safe drinking water	+	0.0771**	0.015	0.1369***	0.000	0.0598
Geography						
North central region	−	−0.1863***	0.000	−0.2613***	0.000	−0.0750
Urban areas	+	0.1157***	0.000	0.1543***	0.000	0.0386
Provincial/commune trade and institutional reforms						
Commune ratio of industrial labour	+	0.0058***	0.000	0.0013**	0.021	−0.0045
Commune ratio of wage labour	+	0.0011**	0.041	0.0063***	0.000	0.0052
Provincial total sales per capita	+	0.0216***	0.000	0.0064***	0.000	−0.0152
Provincial competitiveness index	+	0.0046***	0.000	−0.0031	0.131	−0.0016
Adjusted R^2		0.38		0.41		
Number of observations		4,680		4,221		

Notes: ***, **, and * significant at 1 per cent, 5 per cent, and 10 per cent level, respectively.

Table 8.4 Cross-sectional OLS estimates of specific impacts of institutional ...

[Dependent variable: log of per capita income]						
		2006		*2010*		
Independent variable	*Expected sign*	*Coefficient*	*p-value*	*Coefficient*	*p-value*	*Coef. change*
(1)	*(2)*	*(3)*	*(4)*	*(5)*	*(6)*	*(7) = (5) – (3)*
Constant term		7.6113***	0.000	8.3762***	0.000	0.7649
Household and individual characteristics						
Household size	–	–0.0576***	0.000	–0.0670***	0.000	–0.0094
Head ethnicity (Kinh)	+	0.1122***	0.000	0.2270***	0.000	0.1147
Head gender (male)	+	–0.0132	0.663	–0.0069	0.845	–
Head age	+/–	0.0026***	0.001	0.0046***	0.000	0.0020
Heads with spouse	+/–	–0.0768**	0.041	–0.0730*	0.083	0.0038
Proportion of children	–	–0.0046***	0.000	–0.0044***	0.000	0.0002
Proportion of elderly	–	–0.0022***	0.000	–0.0028***	0.000	–0.0006
Human capital						
Head years of school	+	0.0237***	0.000	0.0242***	0.000	–0.0005
Spouse years of school	+	0.0110***	0.000	0.0183***	0.000	0.0074
Parent years of school	+	0.0188***	0.003	0.0130**	0.012	–0.0057
Technical diploma ratio	+	0.0041***	0.000	0.0026***	0.000	–0.0016
Postsecondary diploma ratio	+	–0.0045***	0.000	–0.0023***	0.002	0.0023
Occupation (reference category is the unskilled)						
Head business owner/leader	+	0.2078***	0.000	0.2617***	0.000	0.0539
Head professional	+	0.2855***	0.000	0.3594***	0.000	0.0739
Head white collar	+	0.2354***	0.004	0.0619	0.645	–
Head skilled worker	+	0.1187***	0.000	0.1516***	0.000	0.0329
Agricultural production						
Rice productivity	+	0.2914***	0.000	0.4184***	0.000	0.1270
Household net rice producers	+	0.0000***	0.001	0.0001***	0.000	0.0000
Total used fertiliser quantity	+	0.0001***	0.000	0.0001***	0.002	0.0000

(*Continued*)

Table 8.4 (Continued)

Independent variable	Expected sign	2006 Coefficient	2006 p-value	2010 Coefficient	2010 p-value	Coef. change (7) = (5) − (3)
(1)	(2)	(3)	(4)	(5)	(6)	(7) = (5) – (3)
House characteristics						
Access to electricity	+	0.0434	0.119	0.0363	0.370	–
Access to safe drinking water	+	0.0688**	0.031	0.1249***	0.000	0.0561
Geography						
North central region	–	-0.1778***	0.000	-0.2227***	0.000	-0.0449
Urban areas	+	0.1052***	0.000	0.1533***	0.000	0.0480
Provincial/commune trade and institutional reforms						
Commune industry labour ratio	+	0.0063***	0.000	0.0020***	0.001	-0.0042
Commune wage labour ratio	+	0.0007	0.199	0.0062***	0.000	0.0055
Provincial total sales per capita	+	0.0269***	0.000	0.0110***	0.000	-0.0159
Market entry costs	+	0.0092	0.367	-0.0006	0.969	–
Land access	+	0.0342***	0.003	0.0183*	0.063	-0.0159
Transparency	+	-0.0168**	0.049	-0.0194	0.170	–
Time costs	+	-0.0383***	0.000	-0.0111	0.345	–
Informal charges	+	0.0495***	0.000	0.0386**	0.022	-0.0110
Provincial leadership proactivity	+	-0.0096	0.212	0.0146	0.144	–
Business support services	+	0.0154*	0.094	-0.0070	0.634	–
Labour training	+	0.0078	0.284	-0.0501**	0.038	–
Legal institutions	+	0.0191*	0.058	0.0020	0.841	–
Adjusted R^2		0.38		0.41		
Number of observations		4,680		4,221		

Note: ***, **, and * significant at 1 per cent, 5 per cent, and 10 per cent level, respectively.

who live with spouses has no impact on household welfare. Household heads may be the primary source of income, and spouses may largely become dependents. As expected, the household size and the dependency ratios appear to diminish welfare significantly. An additional member in a household decreased, on average, the household income per capita by 5.8 per cent in 2006, holding other things constant. This percentage increased to 6.6 per cent in 2010, probably a sign of the economic slowdown, as a consequence of the 2008 financial crisis. The effects of dependency have shown a decline over time. A one-percentage rise in the proportion of children reduced per capita income by 0.5 per cent in 2006 and 0.4 per cent in 2010.

The dummy variable indicating whether a household head belongs to the Kinh, the major ethnicity in Vietnam, has a considerable effect on rural welfare. The coefficient of 0.1177 attached to the variable 'Heads' ethnicity (Kinh)' means that, holding other factors unchanged, per capita income of Kinh households is typically 12.5 per cent higher than that of other households.[4] The effect of this variable doubled in 2010. This suggests the widening income inequality amongst ethnicities in favour of the Kinh. The age of household heads has a positive and significant impact on welfare. A one-year increase in the age of household heads raised the per capita income by 0.3 per cent in 2006 and 0.5 per cent in 2010, on average, and holding other things equal. This analysis shows that the household demographic characteristics are the important determinants of rural welfare.

Education has a consistently significant impact on rural welfare over the period. One year added to household heads' school years typically increased the income per head by more than 2 per cent. This effect is greater than that in rural areas but smaller than that in urban areas. The effect of school years is smaller for spouses and parents of household heads. The proportion of household members having a technical diploma is positively associated with a rise in per capita income; accordingly, per capita income, on average, rose about 0.3 per cent for a one-percentage increase in the share of members with a technical diploma. The ratio of post-secondary qualifications of general education shows the opposite. This suggests that technical training plays a more important role in welfare improvement than general training, which is inefficient and lags behind. The provision of education is thus crucial to the improvement in rural welfare. The results are consistent with other similar studies (see, for example, Ravallion, 2013; Nguyen, 2004), suggesting that education is the key to alleviating rural poverty.

As predicted, employment of household heads has a significant impact on rural welfare. On average, and other things being constant, the per capita income of household heads who were business owners or leaders was 23.4 per cent in 2006 and 30.1 per cent in 2010, both of which are higher than that of the unskilled (the reference category in the model). For professionals, these impacts, which were even higher, rose from 34.4 per cent in 2006 to 44.8 per cent in 2010. The effect of skilled labourers on welfare was smaller, but appeared to increase over time. The impact of white-collar employment was insignificant in 2010, probably mirroring the rise in unemployment from 2010 onwards in Vietnam. The results further indicate that the jobs requiring higher qualifications were associated with higher income, and the effect of qualification on income increased over the period. Employment, which is closely related to education, is increasingly an important factor for the improvement in rural welfare.

Agricultural production continues to be the main activity in rural areas. The results show that the agricultural factors, such as rice productivity, surplus in rice production, and total quantity of fertiliser used in agricultural production, have a significant impact on rural welfare. The net rice production, as well as the total quantity of fertiliser, appears to be relatively less important than rice productivity for the improvement in welfare. A one-unit increase in rice productivity, on average, raised income per head by 22.1 per cent in 2006, holding other things constant. The effect of rice productivity nearly doubled in 2010, possibly reflecting the increase in the level of technology in agricultural production. The improvement in rice productivity helps farm households to increase their incomes.

The above analysis demonstrates the important role of the non-trade-related variables in improving rural welfare. As regards the impacts of the trade-related variables, the results indicate that the provincial trade openness and institutional reforms had a significant impact on rural welfare, especially in 2006. As expected, the proportion of industrial employment helped to improve rural incomes. On average and *ceteris paribus*, a one-percentage rise in the ratio of commune industrial employment increased the per capita income by 0.6 per cent in 2006 and 0.1 per cent in 2010. This sharp decline in the impact possibly reflects the economic slowdown in the late 2000s. The effect of commune wage labour appeared to increase over time. In a time of economic recession, people are likely to diversify jobs, as industrial employment is declining.

For local trade, total retail sales per head are significantly and consistently associated with welfare improvement, although this impact falls over time. Per capita income increased by 2.2 per cent for a one-million-VND increase in total sales per capita. The impact of provincial trade declined sharply in 2010, presumably because of the economic downturn. In addition to these effects of employment and local trade per capita, the PCI had a positive and significant impact on rural welfare in 2006. This was notably just before Vietnam joined the WTO.[5] On average, and other things being equal, the per capita income rose by 0.5 per cent for one percentage point increase in the PCI. The results clearly reflect the efforts to reform institutions towards membership of the WTO. These institutional reforms discernibly helped provinces to improve welfare. The effect of institutional reforms became insignificant in 2010, possibly suggesting the slowdown in institutional reforms after Vietnam's becoming a member of the WTO. The slow pace of institutional reforms could have contributed to the economic recession since 2010.

Regression results based on the PCI by component

The above analysis is based on the regression model estimated using the overall PCI. The regression model is also estimated using the PCI by component, so as to glean deeper insight into the effects of institutional reforms. The results obtained from the model estimated using the non-trade-related and trade-related variables (Table 8.4) are almost the same as those in the former regression, estimated using the overall PCI (Table 8.3). Market entry costs have no impact on welfare, suggesting that firms' entry into or withdrawal from a market is no longer an important issue. More importantly, the results show that access to land has a consistent and significantly positive effect on welfare over time. Access to land is very important for a farm household to cultivate and for an entrepreneur to establish or expand a business. In the components of the PCI, the informal charges demonstrate a positive and significant impact on household welfare. In the weak institutional system, informal costs, such as unofficial customs fees and charges, are a major burden, deterring enterprises from starting up or expanding business.

The business support services and legal institutions were found significant only in the results for 2006. This seems to arise from the difference in the speed and efficiency of institutional reforms before 2006 and after 2006, to 2010, which is similar to the results using the overall PCI. Other components of the PCI, such as transparency, time costs, and provincial leadership's proactivity, have either no impact or unexpected impacts. Amongst the PCI components, access to land and informal costs are the important determinants of rural welfare over the period.

In summary, analysis of the above results shows that, in addition to the effects of conventional household characteristics, such as demographic traits, education, employment, agricultural production, household assets, and geography, there is evidence that the provincial trade openness and institutional reforms have a positive impact on rural welfare. The support for the significant impacts of internal trade openness and institutional reforms make the study more useful and straightforward in explaining institutional effects on welfare. The impact of institutional reforms on welfare in 2010 was insignificant, and this points towards the sluggish progress in institutional reforms in the period from joining the WTO to the late 2000s. This impact of institutional reforms in 2010 underlines the need for sustained policy efforts in this direction.

8.4 Conclusions

The chapter has combined the VHLSS data with the Vietnam PCI in a model of microdeterminants of growth of household income to examine the effects of local trade and institutional reforms on rural welfare. It provides evidence that local trade and institutional reforms improved rural welfare, and thereby contributed to the reduction of poverty in Vietnam. This finding is striking, given that most rural households are poor. Several proxies for institutional reforms have a notably significant impact on per capita income, making the analysis a direct explanation for the important role of institutional factors in household welfare. The changing impacts, especially of provincial trade openness and institutional reforms from 2006 to 2010, which reflect the pace and efficiency of institutional reforms in Vietnam, are useful for policymakers. Institutional reforms and local trade openness are found to be appropriate for improving rural household welfare and reducing poverty.

The results suggest that institutional reforms in Vietnam have progressed slowly since the accession to the WTO. The sluggish process of institutional reforms impedes the pathways through which trade liberalisation affects welfare, given that trade policy reforms accompany institutional reforms. Poor households are unlikely to benefit from trade liberalisation, if it is unaccompanied by adequate institutional reforms. Stagnant or sluggish trade reforms and institutional reforms dampen business incentives, and bring about unemployment. In fact, the economy has not taken advantage of having WTO membership, primarily because of the slow pace of reforms.

The analysis suggests the crucial role of local trade and institutional reforms in the improvement in rural welfare and reduction in poverty. It predicts that the slow progress of institutional reforms will hinder the development of enterprises, and thereby preclude farm households from benefiting from employment. Although considered to be a successful case in terms of the improvement in economic growth and reduction of poverty in the 1990s, Vietnam is unlikely to sustain previous success in the future, without accelerating its trade and institutional reforms. The acceleration of its trade and institutional reforms in rural areas is one of the inevitable ingredients for the acceleration of economic growth and reduction of poverty in Vietnam.

Notes

1 The data are taken from the World Bank's 'Doing Business in Vietnam', retrieved from http://www.doingbusiness.org/data/exploreeconomies/vietnam/.
2 For more discussions about the approaches to measuring poverty, see UNDP (2005), Ravallion (1992), and Deaton and Zaidi (2002).
3 The north central region includes Thanh Hoa, Nghe An, Ha Tinh, Quang Binh, Quang Tri, and Thua Thien Hue province, located in the poorest resource region in Vietnam (see Table 8.2).
4 The percentage increase is calculated as $e^{0.1177} - 1 = 0.1249$. As noted, a similar method is used for all the dummy variables used in the study.
5 Vietnam became an official member of the World Trade Organization in January 2007, after more than 10 years of preparation and negotiation.

References

Abbott, P., Bentzen, J., and Tarp, F. (2009). Trade and Development: Lessons from Vietnam's Past Trade Agreements. *World Development, 37*(2), 341–353.

Acemoglu, D., and Robinson, J.A. (2012). *Why Nations Fail: The Origins of Power, Prosperity, and Poverty* (1st ed.). New York: Crown Publishers.

Dang, D.A. (2010). *Trade Liberalization and Institutional Quality: Evidence from Vietnam*. MPRA, Working Paper (No. 31485), 42.

Dang, D.A. (2013). How Foreign Direct Investment Promote Institutional Quality: Evidence from Vietnam. *Journal of Comparative Economics, 41*(4), 1054–1072. DOI: http://dx.doi.org/10.1016/j.jce.2013.05.010

Deaton, A., and Zaidi, S. (2002). *Guidelines for Constructing Consumption Aggregates for Welfare Analysis*. LSMS, Working Paper (No. 135), 128.

Dollar, D., and Kraay, A. (2003). Institutions, Trade, and Growth. *Journal of Monetary Economics, 50*(1), 133.

Gaiha, R., and Imai, K.S. (2005). *Do Institutions Matter in Poverty Reduction? Prospects of Achieving the MDG of Poverty Reduction in Asia.* Economics Discussion Paper (No. 0506), 48.

Glewwe, P., Gragnolati, M., and Zaman, H. (2000). *Who Gained from Vietnam's Boom in the 1990s: An Analysis of Poverty and Inequality Trends.* World Bank, Policy Research Working Paper (No. 2275), 64.

Glewwe, P., Gragnolati, M., and Zaman, H. (2002). Who Gained from Vietnam's Boom in the 1990s?. *Economic Development and Cultural Change, 50*(4), 773–792.

Glewwe, P., and Hall, G. (1998). Are Some Groups More Vulnerable to Macroeconomic Shocks Than Others? Hypothesis Tests Based on Panel Data from Peru. *Journal of Development Economics, 56*(1), 181–206. DOI: 10.1016/s0304–3878(98)00058–3

Haughton, J., and Khandker, S.R. (2009). *Handbook on Poverty and Inequality.* Washington, DC: World Bank.

Justino, P., Litchfield, J., and Pham, H.T. (2008). Poverty Dynamics during Trade Reform: Evidence from Rural Vietnam. *Review of Income and Wealth, 54*(2), 166–192. DOI: 10.1111/j.1475–4991.2008.00269.x

Kandil, M. (2009). Determinants of Institutional Quality and Their Impact on Economic Growth in the MENA Region. *International Journal of Development Issues, 8*(2), 34.

Levchenko, A.A. (2004). *Institutional Quality and International Trade.* IMF, Working Paper (No. 04/231), 47.

Nguyen, N.N. (2004). Trends in the Education Sector. In P. Glewwe, N. Agrawal, and D. Dollar (eds) *Economic Growth, Poverty, and Household Welfare in Vietnam* (p. 647). Washington, DC: World Bank.

Niimi, Y., Vasudeva-Dutta, P., and Winters, L.A. (2007). Trade Liberalization and Poverty Dynamics in Vietnam. *Journal of Economic Integration, 22*(4), 819–851.

Perkins, D.H., Radelet, S., and Lindauer, D.L. (2006). *Economics of Development* (6th ed.). New York: W. W. Norton.

Ravallion, M. (1992). *Poverty Comparisons: A Guide to Concepts and Methods.* Living Standards Measurement Study, Working Paper (No. 88), 138.

Ravallion, M. (2013). *The Idea of Antipoverty Policy.* NBER, Working Paper Series (No. 19210).

Rodrik, D. (2002). Trade Policy Reform as Institutional Reform. In B. Hoekman, A. Mattoo, and P. English (eds) *Development, Trade, and the WTO: A Handbook* (pp. 3–10). Washington, DC: World Bank.

Singh, T. (2010). Does International Trade Cause Economic Growth? A Survey. *The World Economy, 33*(11), 1517–1564. DOI: 10.1111/j.1467–9701.2010.01243.x

Tran, T.B., Grafton, R.Q., and Kompas, T. (2008). *Institutions Matter: The Case of Vietnam.* ANU, Working Papers (No. 08–01), 43.

United Nations Development Programme (UNDP) (2005). *What is Poverty? Concepts and Measures.* Poverty in Focus-UNDP International Poverty Centre, 24.

United States Agency for International Development (USAID) and Vietnam Chamber of Commerce and Industry (VCCI) (2006). *The Vietnam Provincial Competitiveness Index 2010.* Hanoi: VCCI.

United States Agency for International Development (USAID) and Vietnam Chamber of Commerce and Industry (VCCI) (2010). *The Vietnam Provincial Competitiveness Index 2010.* Hanoi: VCCI.

World Bank (2012). *Well Begun, Not Yet Done: Vietnam's Remarkable Progress on Poverty Reduction and the Emerging Challenges* (p. 190). Hanoi.

9 Summary, findings, and policy perspective

Developing economies share several common characteristics in terms of the level of economic development, magnitude of unemployment, the severity of poverty, and the degree of openness to the rest of the world. The well-documented gains of 'openness to trade' have motivated many developing countries to undertake economic reforms and to liberalise their trade with the rest of the world. Vietnam initiated its reform process with the adoption of an innovation programme called 'Doi Moi' in 1986, and has since liberalised its trade and obtained membership with the WTO. A number of studies have shown the beneficial effect of trade in terms of the acceleration of economic growth and reduction in poverty (World Bank, 2005, 2006). The major limitations of the studies examining the effects of trade on growth and poverty in Vietnam have been that they appear to provide partial evidence. This study has examined the effects of trade liberalisation on poverty in Vietnam, using all the four channels suggested by Winters (2002) and Winters *et al.* (2004). It has also explained some of the issues relevant to the debate on the relationship between trade liberalisation and poverty. The research questions centre on two general issues. First, the study has sought to answer the question of whether trade liberalisation impacts welfare and poverty in Vietnam. Second, based on the analysis of the relationship between trade and poverty, it has evaluated the effects of trade liberalisation on poverty in terms of the perceptions of farm households who are most poor and most vulnerable to trade liberalisation policies.

The history or context of economic development plays a crucial role in understanding the effects of trade liberalisation on households and poverty. This background has been comprehensively captured by providing an analytical review of Vietnam's economy, the process of trade liberalisation and poverty reduction, and the impacts of trade liberalisation on poverty. The analysis in Chapter 3 has sketched a broad picture of the trade–poverty relationship in Vietnam and has laid the foundations for in-depth investigation in other chapters of the effects of trade liberalisation on economic growth and poverty.

The study thereafter has examined the growth effect of trade liberalisation on poverty as the first channel through which trade liberalisation affects poverty (Chapter 4). For the market effect, the study has undertaken a case study, based on the trade-focused, primary survey of agricultural business on the farm households in the An Giang, Dong Nai, and Daklak provinces in Vietnam, which has provided a better understanding of the marketing system in agricultural production and trade (Chapter 5). The employment effects of trade liberalisation have been analysed by estimating the impacts on rural household welfare and poverty of commune and/or provincial employment in sectors such as manufacturing, exports, and imports (Chapter 6). The relationship between urban poverty and employment has been unveiled by examining the employment effect on urban poverty, thereby completing the picture of the effect of employment on welfare and poverty in Vietnam (Chapter 7). For a more comprehensive picture of the trade–poverty nexus, this study has taken into consideration the institutional effects of trade liberalisation (Chapter 8). This final chapter summarises the key findings of the research and provides the policy implications and perspectives.

9.1   Research findings at a glance

The study has employed various methods, including analytical review and synthesis based on Winters's transmission channels, before–after analysis, partial equilibrium analysis, and a survey-based case study, to take a thorough account of the effects of trade liberalisation on the acceleration of economic growth and reduction in poverty. These complementary methods demystify different angles of the trade–growth–poverty nexus. The findings from the investigation of Winters's channels, through which trade liberalisation affects poverty, are consistent and help to elucidate many aspects of the link. The main findings centre on the trade-related variables in relation to trade-led growth, external trade, local trade, employment, agricultural production, geography, market distribution, and institutions. Trade liberalisation has a positive impact on economic welfare and poverty. The descriptive analytical review of the process of trade liberalisation and poverty reduction demonstrates that trade liberalisation is the main drive for economic growth, employment creation, agricultural exports, and government revenue (Chapter 3). The openness of the economy since the late 1980s led to export boom, accelerated economic growth, halved unemployment and poverty, expanded rice production, and enriched government revenue through export earnings. In terms of the revenue effects of trade liberalisation, no significant links between trade taxes and tax revenue or between tax revenue and social expenditure are identified. This finding supports the hypothesis of the insignificant relationship between government revenue and poverty under the impacts of trade policy reforms. The trade-induced achievements in terms of economic growth and employment also continued throughout the 2000s. The trends identified in this study are consistent with other studies and economic reports on the impacts of trade liberalisation on poverty in Vietnam. The findings from the analysis of the specific channels further support the overall trends.

Economic growth and poverty. Trade liberalisation affects poverty through economic growth. This study has examined both the direct effect of trade on poverty and the indirect effect of trade on poverty through economic growth. First, as described in Chapter 3, the economic growth peaked during the export boom period in the 1990s. The accelerated growth in turn contributed to the reduction in poverty. The overall estimates of the elasticity of poverty with respect to economic growth revealed an approximately one-to-one relationship between growth and poverty reduction (Chapter 4), consistent with other studies of a similar vein. The growth in income also contributed to reducing the incidence, depth, and severity of poverty over the two decades of economic development. Growth, therefore, has been pro-poor in Vietnam. However, the declining impact of growth on poverty over the 2000s indicates an unsustainable development of the economy, as suggested in Chapter 3. The benefits of growth to the poor are likely to be eroded by increasing inflation and economic inequality.

Second, the extended analysis of the elasticity of poverty, with regard to economic growth based on the provincial panel data and poverty regression, provides an even higher impact of growth on poverty. The results also show that rural households benefit more from growth than their urban counterparts do. This suggests that the acceleration of economic growth is crucial to the reduction in poverty. In addition to the growth effect, internal trade is also found to have a pro-poor effect (Chapter 6). The provincial total sales per capita prevented rural households from falling into poverty over the period from 2002 to 2006. Although other studies on the trade–poverty nexus usually refer to the impacts of international trade on poverty, this study indicates that the development of internal trade is important for poverty reduction in rural areas. The study finds that both economic growth and internal trade contribute to the reduction of poverty in Vietnam.

Market distribution and poverty. Agricultural production underpins poverty reduction in Vietnam. The analysis of agricultural trade has revealed several aspects of the effects of trade liberalisation. First, the agriculture-based economy has played a central part in facilitating the smooth transition from the centrally planned economy to a market economy, without much turbulence (Chapter 3). Second, in the aggregate analysis, the agricultural production helps to reduce inequality, but it does not help to alleviate the incidence of poverty (Chapter 4). Third, the decomposition of the impacts of household characteristics on economic welfare shows that the households who are net rice producers had increasing returns over the period from 2002 to 2006 (Chapter 6). Fourth, rice productivity is important for improving rural welfare and helping the poor to escape poverty. It is worthwhile noting that rice productivity probably reflects the level of trade liberalisation in rice exports. Fifth, the analysis of the primary survey results has demonstrated that agricultural production continues to be the main source of income for farm households. The hierarchical marketing distribution of rice and coffee production explains the reason why farm households remain poor, despite the intensive agricultural production and exports (Chapter 5). State food companies may be in implicit collusion with intermediate rice traders to squeeze farmers' profits. The linkage between farm production and exports is disturbed by the chaotic intermediate distribution. Consequently, farm households benefit little from their production. Sixth, the survey results suggest that the farmers who are more receptive to trade policy are better off than those who have less knowledge of trade policy. Their knowledge of trade policy includes prices of input and output, distributional channels, trade opportunities, exports, agricultural supports and services available from the local authorities or agricultural associations, and the cooperation among farmers, enterprises, banks, horticultural scientists, and the government. Better knowledge of networking, marketing, and distributing their products helps them to earn more, and to predict the possible risks relevant to production and distribution. Most of the farm households surveyed had not been provided with enough information, and they had only vague ideas about trade policy. Seventh, crucial to farm households are prices of output and input, as well as of consumer goods and services. The survey results show that sugar prices fluctuated highly in the 2000s, and so too did the price of fertilisers. The protection of the sugar industry is a typical deficiency of the trade policy in Vietnam. Consequently, the sugar industry continues to fall behind that of Thailand, with Vietnamese consumers bearing the high prices of domestically produced sugar. In addition, high and fluctuating prices are a major hindrance to farm households' access to fertilisers. The mismanagement of fertiliser exports and imports is another deficiency of the trade policy. These trade-related inadequacies are all impoverishing farm households.

Employment and poverty. The increase in exports in response to the trade policy reforms has contributed much to the increase in demand for labour. It stimulates high economic growth that helps to boost job creation (Chapter 3). The private sector, predominantly including small and medium enterprises, is crucial to the creation of jobs. This sector would help to sustain employment and reduce poverty in both the short run and long run. This sector, however, is established and developed only under certain conditions, such as an equal playing field and a sound institutional framework. Employment in the trade and manufacturing sectors is found to improve rural welfare and help the poor to escape poverty (Chapter 6). The creation of employment opportunities is important, not only for the reduction in rural poverty, but also for the reduction in urban poverty. The analysis of the effects of employment on urban welfare has shown that both local trade and employment in the import-competing sectors help to improve urban welfare (Chapter 7). These effects on urban welfare are assumed to be transmitted to the urban poor. The results in Chapter 6 and Chapter 7 also indicate that local trade per capita has a consistent impact on welfare and poverty in both rural and urban areas. These results reinforce the important role of internal trade in poverty reduction. In short, the study provides evidence for the effects of employment on poverty reduction. The generation of employment is thus essentially important for the reduction of poverty in Vietnam.

Geography, institutions, and poverty. Weak institutions, accompanied by inadequate trade policies, may drag agricultural production down and impoverish farm households. Vietnam has pursued an export-led growth strategy while maintaining the state-owned enterprise monopolies over some key commodities, such as rice exports (Chapter 3). As a consequence, faster trade reforms have been unable to reconcile state-owned enterprises' interest with other interest groups in the economy. At the microeconomic level, the survey results indicate that the farmers surveyed desire reforms in the functioning of the input market, the technical support system, the rice procurement system, the bank loan system, and the customs procedures. These results suggest that farmers lack essential support from the authorities and agricultural associations. Although the farmers surveyed think highly of logical cooperation amongst enterprises, banks, agricultural scientists, and local authorities, they doubt their role in supporting farmers in reality. These findings underline the need for institutional reforms, especially in agricultural trade and production. This recommendation also draws support from the evidence provided in Chapter 8 that institutional reforms and local trade played an important role in the improvement in rural welfare over the period from 2006 to 2010. These findings further suggest that, although institutional reforms are important for rural poverty, such reforms do not efficiently support farm households.

Geography has emerged in this study as an important determinant of poverty. Although rural households appear to benefit more than their urban counterparts from economic growth, the households in remote or disadvantaged areas are much worse off, compared to those in urban areas. The analysis shows that the new trend of poverty in Vietnam is geographical difference (Chapter 3). The increasing regional disparity with respect to infrastructure, education, and health care contributes to persistent poverty. The results in Chapter 6 indicate that rural households in the north central region of Vietnam are consistently worse off, compared to those in other regions – rural households in the Red River Delta, the central highlands, and the Mekong River Delta are better off and escape poverty faster. In fact, these regions are at the heart of agricultural production and trade activities. This study thus adds further evidence of regional disparity in Vietnam to the literature on poverty.

9.2   Future policy agenda

Many studies have suggested that trade policy reforms should be combined with other reforms. Harrison *et al.* (2003a, 2003b) suggest that trade policy reforms should be in conjunction with the reforms of the labour market, institutions, and enterprise environment. According to Ravallion (2006), trade policy reforms should accompany other effective social protection policies. Trade policy is one of the key macroeconomic policies, and is mutually related to other policies. The promotion of exports requires the support of the foreign exchange policy and the policies on strengthening and boosting the supply side, including the foreign investment sector. Export development helps to improve export earnings and government budget, and to stabilise the balance of payment. The improvement in government revenue increases the government's ability to tackle poverty. The quality of exports is essentially significant, in that the exports with higher value added content increase the national terms of trade. The price of primary exports tends to decline, and therefore it is essential to encourage the export of manufactured products. However, the excessive dependence on the external sector may pose risks for many people in developing countries, especially the poor, who are less capable of coping with economic shocks from the world market. The adverse effects from trade policy reforms, therefore, would need to be offset by other social safety networks and income protection policies.

The empirical findings provide several policy lessons, not only for Vietnam, but also for developing economies in general, and more particularly for transitional economies. First, the finding that economic growth in Vietnam is pro-poor underlines the need to maintain high economic growth to sustain the reduction in poverty. Although increasing inequality, usually along with high growth, can dampen the benefits of growth, the report by the World Bank (2012) suggests that inequality has not yet been a primary concern. The low economic growth may actually frustrate the fulfillment targets of poverty reduction. Another reason for pursuing the high economic growth strategy is that it will help to reduce poverty efficiently, as growth affects rural welfare more than urban welfare, as found in the study.

Second, employment in the import-competing sectors, export sectors, and manufacturing sectors is important for poverty reduction. Chapter 4 finds that the small and medium private enterprises and micro household enterprises are likely to be the crucial sources of employment and the optimal solution for poverty. However, they receive little support from the government. Meanwhile, state-owned enterprises squander enormous resources of the economy, but generate modest outcomes in terms of economic growth and job creation. The efforts to reform the state enterprise sector are daunting because the government continues to maintain the leading role of state-owned enterprises in the economy. The government needs really effective policies to develop private enterprises, so as to sustain employment in the long run.

Third, the development of the agricultural sector is crucial to sustaining the process of economic development. Faster development of the industrial sector, especially the FDI sector, as a consequence of economic reforms and openness, makes Vietnam appear to ignore the role of the agricultural sector. The economy has lost its basic comparative advantage, and has been mired in its longest economic recession since joining the WTO. In reality, agricultural production has been underdeveloped. The chaotic market distribution in agriculture, with numerous private traders, squeezes farmers' profits. They remain poor in one of the leading rice production countries in the world. The analysis also finds an increasing number of landless people in rural areas, resulting in high stakes. The development of the agricultural sector would be the key to sustaining economic development and reduction in poverty.

Fourth, accelerating institutional reforms, especially in rural areas and in agricultural trade, would be by far the most effective way to reduce poverty. In fact, reforms of agricultural trade are institutional reforms. They include the reorganisation of the marketing system, the abolition of the state monopoly on rice, control of the input market, especially fertiliser, and cooperation between farmers, firms, bankers, scientists, and authorities. The key of the reforms is to engage farmers in the reform process, and to make them benefit from it.

9.3   Some future research directions

This study has used the Winters framework and provided evidence of the impacts of trade liberalisation on poverty in Vietnam. The effects of trade liberalisation on poverty are multidimensional and almost indirect. The study has thrown light on many angles of the impacts. Further research is required to address some of the issues that remain unresolved or semiresolved in the study. First, the proxies for the effects of trade liberalisation are still indirect, both because they are outcome-based measures and because data are limited. The study has yet to capture the impacts of the trade policy changes on poverty. Second, the study has confined its attention mainly to the impacts of trade liberalisation, thereby bypassing the detailed analysis of trade reforms. The study, however, has provided an overview of the trade reform process, which is helpful for understanding the impacts of trade liberalisation. Third, the low level of education of farm households surveyed did not allow the survey to capture the more complicated facets of trade policy, such as the difference between farm-gate prices and export prices, the impacts of backward regulations on trade and rice production, and other macroeconomic effects on rice production and exports. Even with these shortcomings, the study indeed provides a better understanding of the trade–poverty link and adds more evidence on the impacts of trade liberalisation on poverty in Vietnam.

The shortcomings of the study suggest some new directions for further investigation of trade liberalisation and its impacts on poverty in Vietnam. First, the study points out that the main deficiency of trade policy has been the marketing system in agriculture. Rice exports rely on the external conditions of the world market that are beyond Vietnam's control. However, Vietnam is more than capable of establishing an effective marketing system for agricultural production and exports that sustains agricultural development and benefits farmers and the poor. Future research could investigate the market distribution channels of the rice and/or coffee market to provide more insight into the inadequate marketing system. Second, Vietnam's trade policy could be best described as protected, but export oriented. In reality, Vietnam has failed to reconcile trade protection with its export-oriented strategy. A study can examine the dilemma of trade policy and how it impacts the economy or poverty. Future research on trade policy and agricultural trade would be able to provide a more comprehensive story of trade policy in Vietnam. More importantly, such research could help to provide better understanding as to why the economy has gone off track.

Overall, the combination of the country-specific approach using Vietnam as a case study and the holistic approach employing Winters's framework is the main contribution of this study to the literature on the trade–poverty nexus and to the argument for the positive impacts of trade liberalisation on poverty in Vietnam. Perhaps the benefits of trade liberalisation to Vietnam's economic development are no longer questionable. Vietnam has been successful in trade liberalisation: the question now is why Vietnam is unable to sustain the benefits of trade liberalisation and, more importantly, make farm households benefit from trade liberalisation. The economy is struggling to stay on track. Not only is Vietnam a country on which trade liberalisation has a strong impact, but the case is also that Vietnam is unable to protract the benefits of trade liberalisation. Analysis of the relationship between trade liberalisation and poverty suggests that the positive effects of trade liberalisation on poverty are unsustainable, primarily because Vietnam has not laid the foundation for taking advantage of the openness. For instance, the inefficient institutional framework and chaotic marketing distribution system drag agricultural production down, and so does the economy. This is also the reason why farm households remain poor in one of the most influential rice export countries in the world. In the future, when the time for low-hanging fruit is over and the competition in rice exports becomes sharper, Vietnam will have difficulty obtaining better economic outcomes. This prediction becomes true for its present economy. The profound reforms of institutions, particularly in agriculture, would be the ultimate in economic reforms for Vietnam to continue to develop and prosper.

References

Harrison, G., Rutherford, T. F., and Tarr, D. G. (2003a). *Quantifying the Impact of Trade Reform on Poverty.* Available at GU Proquest (accessed 23 August 2010).

Harrison, G., Rutherford, T. F., and Tarr, D. G. (2003b). Trade Liberalization, Poverty and Efficient Equity. *Journal of Development Economics, 71*(1), 97–128. DOI: http://dx.doi.org/10.1016/S0304-3878(02)00135-9

Ravallion, M. (2006). Looking Beyond Averages in the Trade and Poverty Debate. *World Development, 34*(8), 1374–1392. DOI: http://dx.doi.org/10.1016/j.worlddev.2005.10.015

Winters, L. A. (2002). Trade Liberalisation and Poverty: What are the Links? *World Economy, 25*(9), 1339–1367. DOI: 10.1111/1467-9701.00495

Winters, L. A., McCulloch, N., and McKay, A. (2004). Trade Liberalization and Poverty: The Evidence So Far. *Journal of Economic Literature, 42*(1), 72–115.

World Bank (2005). Pro-Poor Growth in the 1990s: Lessons and Insights from 14 Countries (p. 116). Washington, DC.

World Bank (2006). *Vietnam Development Report 2006: Vietnam Business.* Washington, DC: World Bank.

World Bank (2012). *Well Begun, Not Yet Done: Vietnam's Remarkable Progress on Poverty Reduction and the Emerging Challenges* (p. 190). Hanoi: World Bank.

Author Index

Subject Index

For Product Safety Concerns and Information please contact our EU
representative GPSR@taylorandfrancis.com
Taylor & Francis Verlag GmbH, Kaufingerstraße 24, 80331 München, Germany